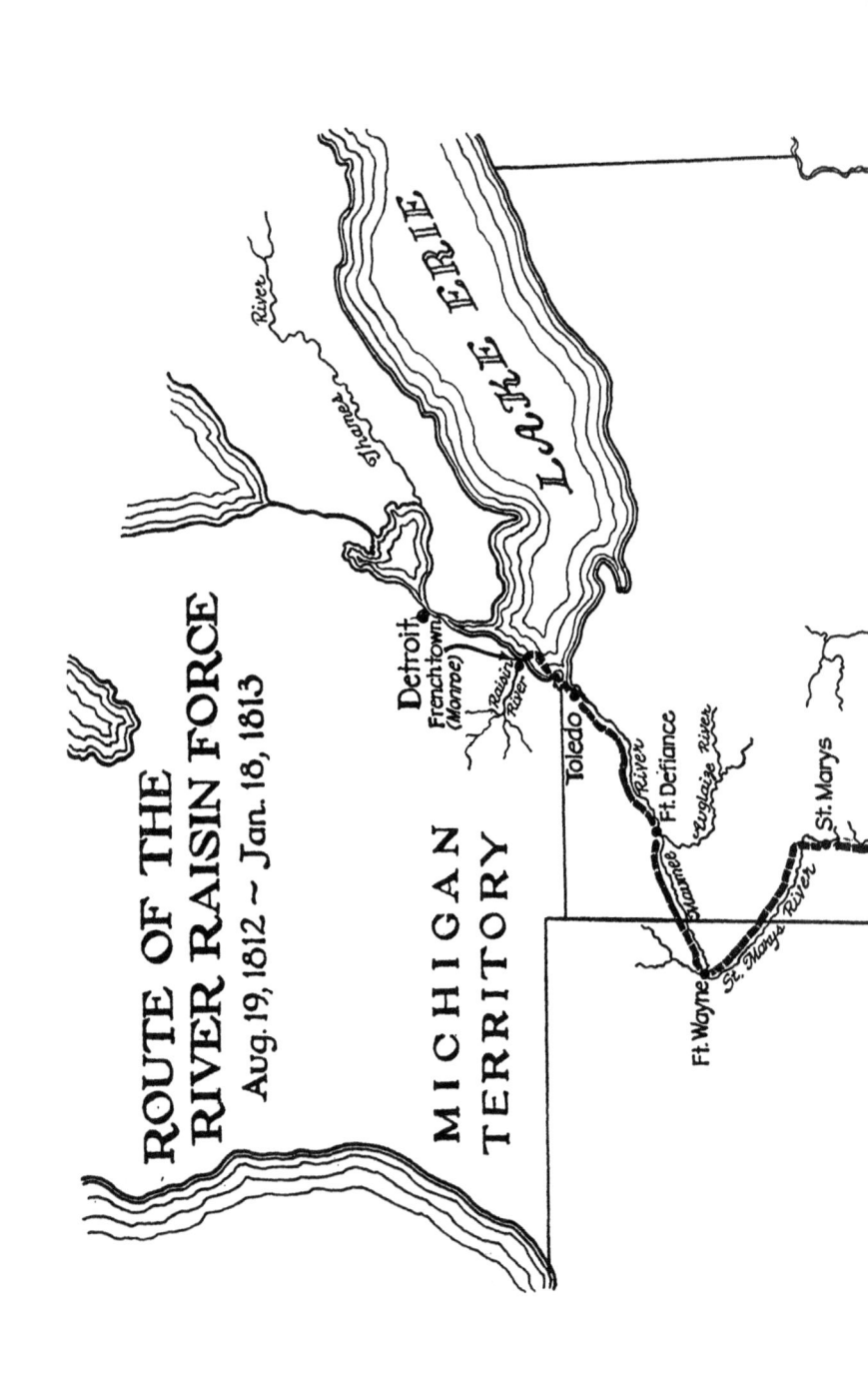

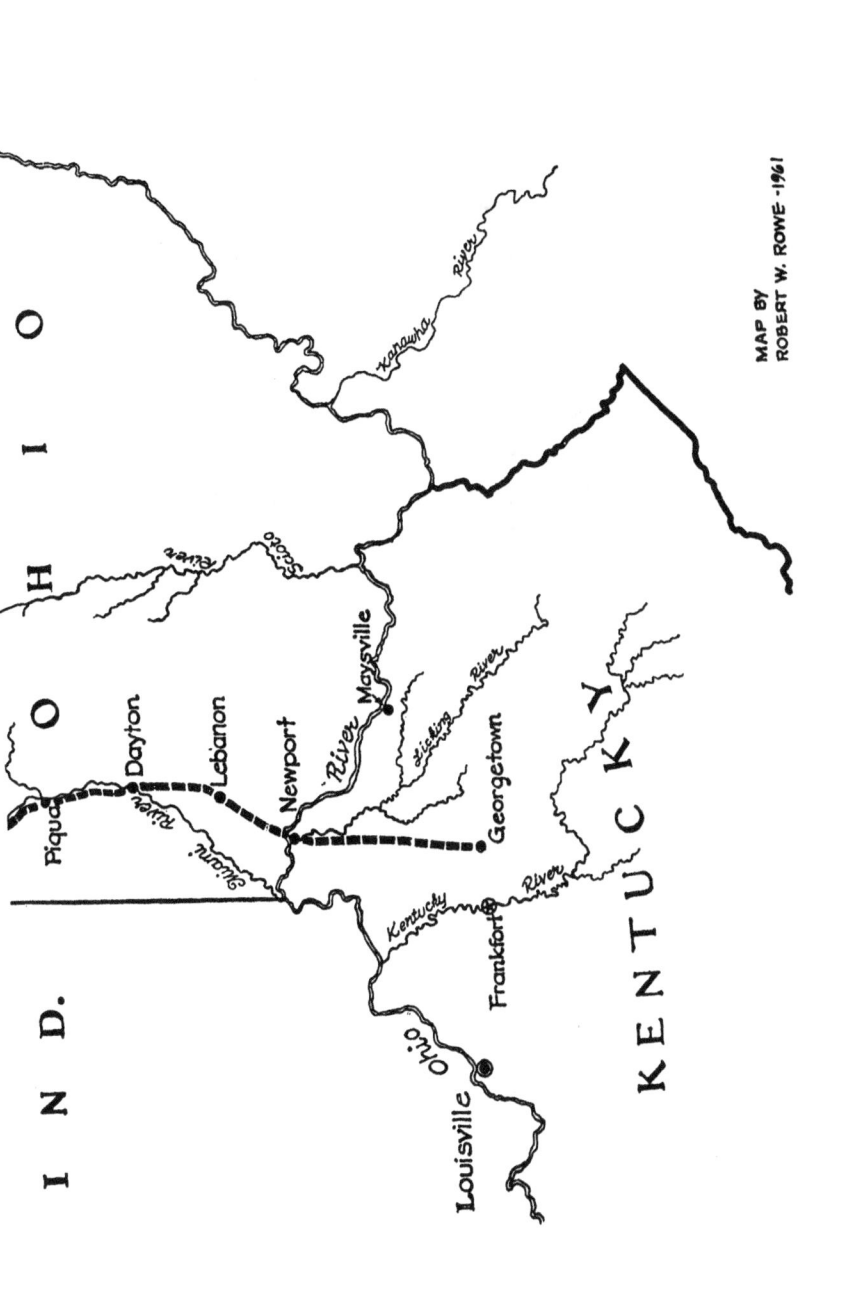

Also by
G. GLENN CLIFT

History of Maysville and Mason County, Kentucky

Kentucky Marriages and Obituaries, 1787-1865

Governors of Kentucky, 1792-1942

A Letter from Salerno

Bibliography of Kentucky Statute Law

"Second Census" of Kentucky — 1800

Guide to the Manuscripts of the Kentucky Historical Society

"Corn Stalk" Militia of Kentucky, 1792-1811

REMEMBER THE RAISIN!
*Kentucky and Kentuckians
in the Battles and Massacre at
Frenchtown, Michigan Territory,
in the War of 1812*

Reprinted With

NOTES ON KENTUCKY VETERANS OF THE WAR OF 1812

G. Glenn Clift

CLEARFIELD

Remember the Raisin! was originally published
by the Kentucky Historical Society, Frankfort, Kentucky
Copyright © 1961. All Rights Reserved.
Reprinted with the permission of the Society.

Notes on Kentucky Veterans of the War of 1812
was originally published in Anchorage, Kentucky, 1964

Reprinted, two volumes in one, for
Clearfield Company, Inc. by
Genealogical Publishing Co., Inc.
Baltimore, Maryland
1995, 1998, 2000, 2002

International Standard Book Number: 0-8063-4520-9

Made in the United States of America

G. GLENN CLIFT

REMEMBER THE RAISIN!

Kentucky and Kentuckians
in the Battles and Massacre at
Frenchtown, Michigan Territory,
in the War of 1812

WITH A PROLOGUE BY E. MERTON COULTER

Kentucky Historical Society
Frankfort, Kentucky
1961

To V. D. G. C.

Contents

	FOREWORD	xi
I	PROLOGUE, BY E. MERTON COULTER	1
II	THE MOBILIZATION	15
III	THE MARCH	22
IV	THE FIRST BATTLE	46
V	THE SECOND BATTLE	62
VI	THE MASSACRE	80
VII	THE LIVING AND DEAD OF RAISIN	92
VIII	BIOGRAPHIES OF THE OFFICERS	107
	APPENDIX: ROSTERS OF TROOPS ENGAGED	173
	BIBLIOGRAPHY	235
	INDEX	247

FOREWORD

THIS STUDY of the two battles and massacre at Frenchtown, present site of Monroe, Michigan, was planned and executed to supply a long needed reference account of an expedition the results of which after almost one hundred and fifty years are still matters of historical speculation and tragic reflection. The Filson Club in Louisville has provided over the years noteworthy discussions of the battles of Tippecanoe, the Thames, and New Orleans — three of the four major engagements of the War of 1812 in which Kentuckians played paramount roles.

Only the march from Georgetown, Kentucky, to the frozen waters of *la Riviere aux Raisins* and the massacre which gave to a young nation the vengeance-fired impetus which ended the second war with Great Britain has been overlooked. The present effort, it is hoped, will round out and complete a tetralogy which in its entirety will record Kentucky's participation in one of the most bitterly contested and brutally waged conflicts engaging American troops to the fighting in Korea.

In every instance possible the story of the march to and engagements at Frenchtown has been told verbatim from the letters, diaries, and statements of the survivors.

The paucity of materials for an authentic day-by-day recounting of the hardships of the Raisin expedition slowed the investigation and made of this a three-year study involving the reading of hundreds of manuscripts, books, and issues of contemporary newspapers. Primary sources, indicated in the notes, are few. The very nature of the campaign precluded strict attention to military records *per se*, and when the final participation was ended by the wholesale slaughter at Frenchtown on January 23, 1813, such manuscript records as might have been kept perished by fire and wanton destruction. Of regularly prescribed unit records only one apparently survived. This is General Winchester's *Orderly Book*, which was left on the battlefield after the massacre. Preserved by an unknown inhabitant of Frenchtown, it was published in *Historical Collections: Collections and Researches made by the Michigan Pioneer and Historical Society* in 1902. Even this document did not completely survive the ravages of time and reached final publication with many pages mutilated and some removed entirely.

Other records had to be discovered by long and tedious processes of patient research. Rosters of those engaged in the campaign were particularly difficult to document. Cooperation of archivists responsible for the United States military records was generously extended but the ultimate conclusion was that lists of troops at Frenchtown, especially those of the United States Army units, were not available. The rosters providing the appendix to this work, therefore, had to be built name by name from many widely separated sources, based on the Kentucky Adjutant General's report of Kentuckians in the War of 1812, published in one slim volume in 1891. The "Remarks" appearing opposite the soldier's name and rank it is believed provide the first attempt to complete these fugitive lists.

Materials for the biographical section likewise were difficult and ofttimes impossible to secure. Of the nine participants in the Raisin campaign for whom Kentucky counties subsequently were named little still is known beyond their record in public life as mirrored in the press and public documents of their day. The same is true of the final disposition of the dead of River Raisin. Kentucky historians interested in this phase of the War of 1812 as it affected Kentuckians have written that these dead now rest in the State lots in the Frankfort Cemetery. These statements have been quoted by latter-day chroniclers and so accepted. In the light of present day research, little has been found to substantiate these statements.

Many thoughtful and helpful people contributed of their interest and time to these pages. Particular thanks are due Mrs. Frank Clifton McClenahan, Toulon, Illinois; Mrs. Katherine W. Ewing, Nashville, Tennessee; Miss Nanon L. Carr, Kansas City, Missouri; Mrs. Jerome A. Esker, Washington, D. C.; Miss Ludie J. Kinkead and Miss Mabel C. Weaks, of the Filson Club, and Colonel Lucien Beckner, of Louisville; Mr. Lewis Beeson, Secretary, Michigan Historical Commission; the late C. Frank Dunn, Miss Julia Patton Hughes Spurr, and Mrs. Horace W. Coleman, Lexington; Mrs. Wade Hampton Whitley, Paris; the archivists of

Foreword xiii

the National Archives and Records Service, Washington, D. C.; and the librarians of many public and special libraries, particularly those of the Reference Department, New York Public Library, and the Frick Art Reference Library, New York.

I am especially indebted to Dr. E. Merton Coulter, historian, Editor of *The Georgia Historical Quarterly,* and friend indeed, for permission to reprint his essay on the causes of the War of 1812, which forms the first chapter of this book.

Mr. Milo M. Quaife writing of the River Raisin massacre in the *Dictionary of American History* noted:

The affair stirred American opinion deeply and "Remember the Raisin" became a rallying-cry throughout the war. A capable British official, castigating Proctor's conduct wrote: *within my hearing protection was promised for those poor people, be assured we have not heard the last of this shameful transaction. I wish to God it could be contradicted!* His words were prophetic; a century and a quarter has not sufficed to erase the blood which stains the fame of General Proctor or to cover with the mantle of forgetfulness the horror he permitted.

If in the pages following is found something of tribute to and permanent record of those Kentuckians of Raisin whose early deaths on a foreign soil contributed much to the eventual greatness of their country, the chronicler will consider his time well spent and his reward generous indeed.

G. Glenn Clift

Frankfort, Kentucky

I
PROLOGUE
By E. Merton Coulter

KENTUCKY was a close and interested observer of the tortuous course of America's relations with the principal European nations. She had noted with growing indignation and exasperation the tyrannical course England had been pursuing. The practice of impressing American seamen was no less resented by Kentucky than by Massachusetts, despite the fact that the former had no shipping interests or seamen to be interfered with. It was enough to know that a foreign nation was offering indignities to the United States of whom Kentucky considered herself an important part. France, whose policy was equally disregardful of American rights, excited little hostility among Kentuckians as she was less able to apply that policy than England, and there still lingered west of the mountains the memories of the ancient friendship between that nation and America.

The prominence given to news of international affairs by the Kentucky newspapers shows the concern with which the people generally followed the events leading up to the second war with Great Britain. The attack of the British man-of-war, *Leopard*, upon the American frigate, *Chesapeake*, in 1807, produced great indignation. Mass-meetings were held in the principal towns of the state where resolutions were passed condemning the piratical acts of England, and pledging the undivided support of Kentucky in whatever course the nation might decide upon.[1] But instead of following the warlike counsel of Kentuckians and others of his countrymen, President Jefferson decided to try a remedy short of war, the embargo. Willing to follow their chosen national leader, Kentuckians acquiesced in this policy and counseled loyal support, regardless of the fact that it at first seemed ruinous to them.[2] But the embargo was after all not a solution to the international difficulties. The pressure for the repeal of this measure soon became so strong that in February, 1809, Jefferson was forced to agree to its abandonment. The non-intercourse act now fol-

[1] See (Lexington) *Kentucky Gazette* and *Palladium* (Frankfort, Ky.) during July, August, and September of 1807.

[2] They, however, soon came to see a good in the embargo after all— it gave perfect protection to their growing and ambitious manufactories.

1

lowed, which opened up commerce to all the nations except France and England, the two great offenders. About this time the British minister to the United States, David Montague Erskine, who was a Whig and well-disposed to America, made an arrangement very favorable to American interests in return for a relaxation of non-intercourse with Great Britain. But no sooner were the terms of this agreement known in London than they were disavowed and Erskine recalled. In his place was sent Francis James Jackson, who was studied in his insults to the United States. His recall was soon demanded. The tangled relations among the United States, England, and France seemed to defy solution. The so-called Macon Bill No. 2 next came as an attempt at settlement by opening up trade to all nations; but with the proviso that if either England or France should cease their violations of American rights, and the other country should not, then non-intercourse should be resumed against the obdurate nation.

But this policy seemed to lead nowhere and Kentuckians were as early in grasping this fact as people were on the seaboard. They had in fact deep in their minds believed when the embargo had been tried, that war was the only solution. Before this policy had been in force a week, the Kentucky House declared, "We cannot repress our indignation when contemplating the acts of perfidy and murder of the British navy, and with one voice express a wish that the general government may adopt prompt and effective measures to support the insulted and degraded majesty of the American nation, and convince her lordly enemies that her rights shall not be invaded, nor her dignity insulted, with impunity." It was quick to add that it not only was willing to express the public sentiment in resolutions but that it also stood ready "to pledge our honor, our blood and treasure in support of such measures as may be adopted by the general government, to secure and protect the peace, dignity and independence of union against foreign invasion, and to chastise and bring to a state of reason our haughty and imperious foes."[3] The war fever was soon running high; it was born, however, not of the desire to embarrass the National Government, but in loyal and loud-spoken support of the Government, tempered with the feeling that the expression of such sentiments might spur the president forward

[3] *Palladium* (Frankfort, Ky.), Jan. 21, 1808, quoted in Robert M. McElroy, *Kentucky in the Nation's History* (New York: Moffat, Yard and Co., 1909), p. 317.

Prologue

to a sterner policy. Richard M. Johnson drew up a set of resolutions at Georgetown, which were unanimously adopted, expressing the united support of Kentucky.[4] But the editor of the *Reporter* was more outspoken in the impatience he felt. He asked if there were any Revolutionary soldiers or their children in Kentucky, "who believed a seven years' war and all its horrors, from '75 to '83, a cheap purchase for liberty and independence, and a freedom of a paltry duty of 4d. per lb. *on foreign tea*—that submit in 1808 to an eternal *British* tax on our cotton, our tobacco, our slaves, our grain, our rice, and every other product of our soil—and more than this, that not a single American vessel shall sail, without being furnished with a British license."[5]

When, in 1808, a call was made upon Kentucky to have in readiness her quota of about 5,000 troops for possible use against hated Britain, Governor Scott called upon the people in a proclamation to come to the support of the National Government and by volunteering help to repel the insults of the insolent enemy.[6] He followed up these sentiments in his message to the Legislature by reminding the people of the dearth of arms and military supplies in the state, and asking them to have in readiness their rifles. He believed that Kentucky should begin the manufacture of military supplies. There was no lack of patriots who would be willing to shoulder the rifles if they were only provided with them.[7] The Legislature soon afterwards, not to be outdone by the governor in the expression of warlike sentiments and support of the Government, resolved, "That the General Assembly of Kentucky would view with the utmost horror a proposition in any shape, to submit to the tributary exactions of great Britain, as attempted to be enforced by her orders of council, or to acquiesce in the violation of neutral rights as menaced by the French decrees; and they pledge themselves to the general government to spend, if necessary, the last shilling, and to exhaust the last drop of blood, in resisting these aggressions."[8]

[4]*Reporter* (Lexington, Ky.), Sept. 26, 1808. Hereinafter cited *Reporter*.
[5]October 24, 1808.
[6]This proclamation was issued November 17, 1808, *Reporter*, Nov. 21, 1808. This call was in compliance with the Act of Congress of March 30.
[7]*Reporter*, Dec. 15, 1808.
[8]*Ibid.*, Dec. 22, 1808; Mann Butler, *A History of the Commonwealth of Kentucky* . . . Second Edition. (Cincinnati: J. A. James, etc., 1836), pp. 328-330; H. Marshall, *History of Kentucky* . . . Two Vols. (Frankfort: Geo. S. Robinson, Printer, 1824), II, 459-460.

The action of Great Britain in repudiating the Erskine agreement was severely condemned in Kentucky. Meetings at Lexington and other towns were called to denounce England for this latest act of perfidy. They called upon the United States to refuse to receive his successor.[9] Shortly afterwards when Jackson had come and was speedily to leave Washington at the insistent demand of the United States, the Kentucky Legislature expressed its high approval and declared "that whatever may be the consequence resulting" from Jackson's recall, "the State of Kentucky will be ready to meet them, and will most cordially co-operate in the support of such measures as may be necessary to secure the interests, and maintain the honor and dignity of the nation."[10] In his message to the Legislature in 1809, Governor Scott was less insistent in his attitude for war. He would be understood as being the last who would bow to a foreign power, but mindful of the rising manufactories in the state, he would not rush into war, and thereby retard this promising development. "We have on the other hand," he said, "to give up only the luxuries of other nations for the sweets of independence and self-government. The people who could not do it with the country and resources we possess, are unworthy of the divine birthright of freedom."[11]

A rather strange and unusual way of showing her extreme antipathy toward Great Britain and all things British was adopted by Kentucky about this time. By a law of the General Assembly it was declared that all reports of cases adjudged in England since July 4, 1776 "shall not be read nor considered as authority in any of the courts of this commonweath, any usage or custom to the contrary notwithstanding." It was only with much difficulty that Henry Clay was able to prevent the law from covering all British reports. The patriotic ardor attached to the date of limitation set may have had some weight. Later in his practice in one of the courts, Clay was forbidden to read from a report coming within the prohibited period a reference to a case adjudged be-

[9]*Reporter*, Aug. 12, 1809. Among the other towns where meetings were held was Springfield in Washington County.

[10]*Acts of the Commonwealth of Kentucky*, 1809, p. 168. This resolution was passed January 22, 1810.

[11]*Reporter*, Dec. 9, 1809.

Prologue 5

fore July 4, 1776.[12] Another example of the thoroughness with which the people were seeking to eradicate all British influence is seen in a procedure taking place directly after war was declared. David Ballengall, an assistant judge of the Nicholas County Circuit Court, was a Scotchman, appointed to his position in 1805, who had neglected to secure American citizenship. On this fact being made known to the Legislature, it resolved that he "being an alien, and subject to the King of Great Britain, is unfit to hold the office aforesaid, and ought to be removed therefrom. . . ."[13]

The irresistible expansive force of the frontier made greater and greater inroads upon the lands yet occupied by the Indians. Directly south of the Ohio the Indians were all but dispossessed; but to the northward they controlled many square miles of fertile prairies and river valleys. Treaties were being constantly made for the relinquishment of these lands, and they were about as often misunderstood and broken. Tecumseh and his brother, Olliwochica, the prophet, saw the utter ruin and destruction of the Indians if the present system continued. They therefore conceived the pregnant idea of binding all the Northwest Indians into a confederacy and allying it with a southern confederacy they would build up. This was the most ambitious scheme yet adopted by the Indians to stop westward migration, and one that had more elements of success. The frontiersmen became alarmed, and with little difficulty they found cause for war. William Henry Harrison, with a regiment of regulars and a number of Kentucky volunteers, in the fall of 1811, set out up the Wabash with the intention of taking possession of certain lands secured by a recent treaty and of punishing, if possible, Indian marauders who had murdered a white man. On November 7th, he came in contact with the redmen in the low bottomland of the upper Wabash, and fought the battle of Tippecanoe. Although heralding it as a great victory, Harrison lost 188 men

---

[12]Lewis N. Dembitz, *Kentucky Jurisprudence* . . . *with an Introduction on the Sources of Kentucky Law* (Louisville: John P. Morton & Co., 1890), p. 7; *Annual Reports of the American Historical Association*, 1896, II, 188; Marshall, *History of Kentucky, op. cit.*, II, 454. This law was strictly enforced for a few years, but by 1821, it had fallen into disuse, and it was finally removed from the statute books in 1852, by omitting it in the revision of that year.

[13]*Acts of the Commonwealth of Kentucky*, 1812, p. 106. No date is given.

killed or wounded, and of these thirty-four were officers.[14] Among those lost in this battle was Joseph Hamilton Daviess, the prosecutor of Aaron Burr and a staunch Federalist.

To Kentuckians this seemed almost their fight alone. A strong wave of patriotic sorrow ensued for the loss of their fellow citizens, and a feeling of gratitude was expressed to those who escaped. The Kentucky House, believing "That it is a country's gratitude that compensates the soldier for his scars, perpetuates grateful recollections of his services, and induces the living to emulate the heroic deeds of the dead—that it is a country's gratitude that softens the rugged pangs of those left to mourn husbands, fathers and friends lost in avenging a country's wrongs," resolved, "That the brave deeds of our officers and soldiers in the late battle on the Wabash, deserves not encomiums only, but unfading fame in the hearts of their countrymen." In memory of the dead the members voted to wear crape on the left arm for thirty days, and as "a further tribute to their memory" to invite John Rowan to deliver a funeral oration "on the death of the late colonels Daviess and Owen, and the other heroes who fell in the battle on the Wabash."[15] A few weeks later Harrison was declared to have "behaved like a hero, a patriot, and a general; and that for his cool, deliberate, skillful and gallant conduct in the battle of Tippecanoe, he well deserves the warmest thanks of his country and the nation."[16]

Indian troubles had long beset the Kentuckians—in fact they had been cradled in savage warfare. They firmly believed that the British were guilty of inciting the Indians against the whites at every time and place possible. They had not forgotten the evidences of English intriguing in the Indian uprisings finally put down by "Mad Anthony" Wayne in 1794; and General Harrison kept the charges of British interference before them by declaring directly after the battle of Tippecanoe that assistance by Great Britain "has been afforded in as ample a manner as it

[14]John B. McMaster, *History of the People of the United States* (New York: D. Appleton & Co., 1883-1913), III, 531-536. For a full account of the expedition with special reference to Kentucky see Alfred Pirtle, *The Battle of Tippecanoe* ("Filson Club Publications," No. 15 [Louisville: John P. Morton & Co., 1900]), 158 pp., and Harrison's report in Marshall, *History of Kentucky, op. cit.*, II, 494-506.

[15]*Niles' Register*, I (Dec. 28, 1811), 297.

[16]*Ibid.*, I (January 25, 1812), 391.

could have been, if war had actually prevailed between us and that power. Within the last three months, the whole of the Indians on this frontier have been completely armed and equipped out of the King's stores at Malden. . . . The Indians, had moreover, had an ample supply of the best British glazed powder —some of their guns had been sent to them so short a time before the action, that they were not divested of the list covering in which they were imported."[17] Harrison also said he was always able to judge the relations between the United States and Great Britain by the behavior of the Indians. The Legislature, in drawing up its bill of indictment against Great Britain, declared that, among other crimes, that country was guilty of "inciting the savages to murder the inhabitants on our defenseless frontiers; furnishing them with arms and ammunition lately, to attack our forces; to the loss of a number of brave men; and by every power of art and intrigue, seeking to dispose of our whole strength and resources, as may suit her unrestrained ambition or interest. . . ."[18] It was in fact not the policy of the British government to incite hostilities—it was rather the opposite; but agents on the frontier were hard to control and they were actually guilty of many of the charges made against the British government and believed to be its settled policy. Moreover the British government actually maintained relations with the Indians within the American jurisdiction, which were not justified under any interpretation of international law or comity among nations. It was a deeply laid feeling among Kentuckians and, indeed, among westerners generally, that war against England was not only desirable, but in fact inevitable. England's guilt did not stop with interfering with the seaboard commerce; it touched the West much more closely. The rivalry in the fur business was also another western factor having its weight.

England was an impossible neighbor. As long as she owned and occupied Canada, the same state of frontier turmoil must continue. Therefore, an additional cause of war was the desire of the West to annex Canada. Henry Clay, in 1810, said in the Senate: "The conquest of Canada is in your power, I trust I shall not be deemed presumptuous when I state that I verily believe that the militia of Kentucky are alone competent to place

[17] Letter to John M. Scott of Frankfort, December 2, 1811, quoted in ibid., I, 311-312.
[18] Ibid., I (January 11, 1812), 337.

Montreal and Upper Canada at your feet."[19] The editor of the *Kentucky Gazette* believed that "Until those *civilized allies of our savage neighbors,* are expelled from our continent, we must expect the frequent recurrence of the late scenes on the Wabash." The signs pointed to a general war with the Indians and England, and to him, "The better the preparation, and the more promptitude and vigor displayed by Congress to meet it, the more will they be entitled to the confidence of the country."[20]

The straining at the leash by the West for war served to nerve the Madison administration for more vigorous action. Another force making for war, which received much of its impetus from the West, was a group of young men who had been elected to Congress which was to meet in 1811. These men knowing little of the horrors of war, but remembering much of British insolence and violence to American rights, stood out boldly for war from the beginning of their power. They came to be known as War Hawks. With such representatives of the group as Clay and Johnson of Kentucky, Porter of New York, Grundy of Tennessee, and Lowndes, Cheves and Calhoun of South Carolina, standing for a bold course of action against England, Madison was soon impelled toward war. In fact it had been charged that a committee of Congress headed by Clay had threatened to prevent his renomination for the presidency unless he should promise to recommend war. His message to Congress in November (1811) was more vigorous. He recounted the outrages suffered at the hands of Great Britain and suggested means of defense. Finally, on June 1 following, he sent a war message to Congress, and on June 18 that body after a sharp debate voted for war in the House 79 to 49 and in the Senate 19 to 13. The stronghold of the opposition to the war was northeast of the Delaware. The West and the South were almost solidly for it.

Whether the effect was great or not, Kentucky abundantly expressed herself for war in the latter days leading up to the actual declaration. In December, 1811, the Legislature, in a set of resolutions claiming the right of that body to express "the sense of the good people of this state, respecting the measures of the National Government," declared that a crisis had arrived

[19] Quoted in Carl R. Fish, *American Diplomacy* (New York: Henry Holt & Co., 1923), p. 174.
[20] (Lexington) *Kentucky Gazette,* Apr. 14, 1812.

in the public affairs of the nation which called upon Kentucky to express her sentiments "respecting the course to be adopted, in order to resist the repeated, long continued and flagrant violations of our rights, as a free and independent nation, by Great Britain and France, and by the former especially—whose pretensions are an insult to our sovereignty, and which, if yielded to, must end in our entire submission to whatever they may think proper to impose." Though Kentuckians were not exposed to the immediate effects of the "piratical depredations" of these nations, they were not less interested in preserving the national honor; for "The state of Kentucky, yielding to none in patriotism; in its deep rooted attachment to the sacred bond of union; in its faithful remembrance of the price of our freedom, and in the heartfelt conviction that our posterity have a sacred claim upon us, to transmit to them unimpaired, this God-like inheritance, cannot fail to be penetrated, with any event which threatens even to impair it; much less than, can she be insensible to those daring wrongs of a foreign power, which lead to its immediate destruction." Kentucky had been willing to depend on the general government to redress these national evils "so intolerable in their progress, and in their consequences so menacing," but it had not been "without a firm and settled purpose, not always to bear the lash, not finally to become beasts of burden." "Forbearance beyond a certain point," it added, "ceases to be moderation, and must end in entire subjection." No arguments were necessary to prove these injuries existed, and as for those who could not feel "wrongs so palpable, no reasoning will convince." Kentuckians would like to be able to say "when Great Britain has ceased to harass and injure us—*when* she has shewn toward us an amicable disposition in the true spirit of justice—*when* she has ceased her efforts to diminish that security and prosperity, which are the eternal barriers of separation from her power, and to impair that liberty and independence forced from her reluctant grasp!" This "unnatural parent" had been guilty of a hundred raids on the peace and security of America, and when her very offers of redress "go only to sanction her wrongs . . . we can be at no loss what course should be pursued." "Should we tamely submit, the world ought to despise us—we should despise ourselves—she herself would despise us. When she shall learn to respect our rights, we shall hasten to forget her injuries." It was, therefore, resolved that "those violations, if not discontinued, and ample compensation made for them, ought to be resisted with the whole power of our country." It was furthermore resolved that since war seemed probable "Kentucky, to the last mite of her strength and resources, will contribute them to maintain the contest and support the right of their country against such lawless violations; and that the citizens of Kentucky are prepared to take the field when called upon." Although Kentucky had full confidence in the national administration, it was believed that the crisis called for "energetic measures; and that a temporizing policy, while it might seem to remove the evil to a greater distance, would serve only to secure its continuance."[21]

These were strong words that bespoke the feelings of an outraged people. It was while the Legislature passing the above resolution was in session that a European traveler visited Frankfort and described the war-like attitude he observed there. He said: "As I passed through Frankfort, on my way from Lexington to Louisville, I was told that the Legislature of Kentucky was just then in session. I resolved to go thither, so that I might compare that body with the sessions of the Territorial Legislature of Louisiana. . . . I had scarcely entered the legislative hall, when I heard a very enthusiastic orator dealing forth a violent diatribe against England, with the following words: 'We must have war with Great Britain—war will ruin her commerce—commerce is the apple in Britain's eye—there we must gouge her!' This flower of oratory was received with great applause; and, it must be confessed, that for such a population as most of the inhabitants of Kentucky formed at that period, it was extremely well timed, and betrayed a certain poetic sweep of thought."[22]

The war fever in the Legislature was truly expressive of conditions outside. Parades and meetings were frequently held over the state to condemn Great Britain and to call for war against her. A parade took place in Lexington a few weeks before war was declared, in which a large number of Kentucky volunteers took part. The editor of the *Kentucky Gazette*, in commenting on it, said: "Thus *Kentucky* will maintain the rank to which she is so justly entitled among her sister states, of being second to none in Patriotism—always on the *right* in the cause of the

[21]*Niles' Register*, I (Jan. 11, 1812), 337-338.
[22]Vincent Nolte, *Fifty Years in Both Hemispheres* . . . (New York: J. S. Redfield, 1854), p. 179.

Prologue

union and republicanism; and may she never be placed on the *left* in her support of the general government."[23]

When the news of the war declaration reached Kentucky, great satisfaction was manifested in many celebrations and mass meetings. According to *Niles' Register,* "The news of war was hailed as a second decree of Independence in Kentucky. The most of the towns were illuminated on the occasion."[24] "Never in any age or country," exclaimed the *Kentucky Gazette,* "has there been more patriotic ardor witnessed than is at this moment to be seen among the citizens of this state. Kentucky seems ready to precipitate itself, *en masse* upon the British and their infernal allies the Indians." He stated that there would soon be 10,000 Kentuckians on the march; and gave this warning: "Let not the tories of New-England, or the secret or avowed enemies of the war, the friends and advocates of British insolence and usurpation, exalt too soon. Their hour is at hand; we are not yet prepared to kiss the hand that wields the tomahawk and scalping knife against the heads of our old men, our women and infants."[25] In Lexington the celebration was accompanied with cannon and musketry firing and was "kept up until late in the evening." The same evidence of enthusiasm was reported in Frankfort.[26] But amidst the apparently universal rejoicing, it was not forgotten that one of the Kentucky senators had voted against the war declaration. The *Reporter* said, "In the moment of joy, when the citizens saw their country, a second time declared independent—it is reported that at Nicholasville and Mount Sterling, Mr. Pope, our senator, who opposed the war was burnt in effigy."[27] Pope had, a few months previously, displeased his constituency by voting for the recharter of the United States Bank, in the very face of numerous instructions to the contrary from many parts of the state. The constant attacks that had been leveled against him for this "disregard of the people's will" had not yet subsided before this fresh cause for censure came. His action was declared to be more reprehensible than that of Humphrey Marshall when

[23] (Lexington) *Kentucky Gazette,* May 26, 1812.
[24] II (July 18, 1812), 335.
[25] September 15, 1812.
[26] *Reporter,* July 1, 1812; (Lexington) *Kentucky Gazette,* June 30, 1812.
[27] *Reporter,* July 1, 1812.

he voted for the Jay Treaty.[28] He was accused of being a Federalist who had forfeited all public respect and support.

Pope had very few followers who agreed with him in his opposition to the war. The federalists, who had never been strong in the state, seemed to be even fewer now, and their voice was all but drowned in the almost universal acclaim for war. There had been an attempt to make political capital out of the death of Daviess at Tippecanoe by asserting that Harrison, a staunch democrat, had mismanaged the expedition and was in fact guilty of the death of the brave federalist.[29]

The state had not only prepared itself for the war in its thoughts and sentiments, but, when it became evident that war was certain, a cry went up for Isaac Shelby for governor. Martin D. Hardin, in April, 1812, wrote Shelby asking him to consent to his name being used for the approaching gubernatorial election. He hoped the venerable old governor would not refuse the people his services, so badly needed in this approaching crisis, "for, with such a head, Kentucky will maintain that preeminence she has taken as the center of the Western part of the Union."[30] Soon a medley of voices was raised, all calling on Shelby to accept the governorship. A writer signing himself "Seventy-six" said: "We are on the eve of a dangerous war, and 'the times that tried men's souls' about to return. The times therefore require a governor of tried integrity and experience—a governor of firmness and decision of character—a governor who can find resources in his own mind to meet with spirit and overcome obstacles and dangers—a governor able to manage our civil concerns or martial our armies in the field of battle—in a word, with the head to plan and the hand to execute such measures as are essential to the public safety.

"Amidst the number which presented themselves to my view, none appeared to have such strong claims on the confidence of

---

[28]See (Lexington) *Kentucky Gazette*, Apr. 9, 1811, etc., and during 1812. Pope had lost one of his arms and was warmly supported by a local Irish politician for the reason, as he gave it, that he had only one arm to thrust into the treasury.

[29]McMaster, *History of the People of the United States, op. cit.*, III, 534-535.

[30]*Durrett MSS.* Letter dated April 10, 1812.

Prologue

his countrymen or so well qualified for the times as Isaac Shelby, the first governor of this state."[31] An "Old Settler" recalled that Shelby had played an important part in winning the battle of King's Mountain in the Revolution and that he had deserved well of his country in many other ways and places. "All agree," he said, "in your capacity to serve as a chief magistrate. From every quarter in the country there is one universal burst of approbation in your favor."[32] Shelby consented to run, and in the following August he was elected with little opposition. He appointed Martin D. Hardin, who had early started the Shelby boom, secretary of state. In November Madison was re-elected President, receiving a solid electoral vote from Kentucky. In some counties of the state the federalists did not poll a single vote. In Fayette the federalist electors received about 90 votes out of about 800.[33]

When the call for troops was issued volunteers came in great numbers, going far beyond the quota fixed for the state. The number apportioned to Kentucky by the law calling for 100,000 was 5,500. A few weeks before war was declared Governor Scott had called for 1,500 volunteers to march to the support of General Hull on the Detroit frontier. But so eager were the volunteers to go that the command was swelled to over 2,000 by those who would not be denied.[34] The Kentucky congressmen were equally enthusiastic. By the beginning of October six had volunteered to leave the legislative halls for the battlefield. Samuel Hopkins became a major-general; Richard M. Johnson, commander of a battalion of mounted infantry; John Simpson, a captain; William P. Duvall, a captain; and Samuel M'Kee and Thomas Montgomery, privates.[35] An account of the day said: "The military spirit beats high in Kentucky. As soon as the requisition of the President was known at *Lexington*, and before the governor's orders reached that place, a company of volunteers of 100 men was formed. They *immediately* equipped themselves, and were

[31] (Lexington) *Kentucky Gazette*, Mar. 12, 1812.

[32] *Ibid.*, May 19, 1812.

[33] *Ibid.*, Nov. 10, 1812.

[34] Nathaniel S. Shaler, *A General Account of the Commonwealth of Kentucky* . . . (Cambridge, Mass.: Press of John Wilson and Son, 1876), p. 158.

[35] *Niles' Register*, III (Oct. 17, 1812), 108.

prepared to march 'to the lakes, to the plains of Abraham, or the consecrated field of Tippecanoe.' It appears that this state will furnish her quota entirely of volunteers."[36]

[36]*Ibid.*, II (June 6, 1812), 239.

[Note: This paper on the causes of the War of 1812 in Kentucky first appeared in Judge Charles Kerr (ed.), *History of Kentucky*. Five Vols. (Chicago and New York: The American Historical Society, 1922,) I, 545-553, and is reprinted here by special permission of the author.]

II

THE MOBILIZATION

ON FRIDAY the first day of May, 1812, Governor Charles Scott received in Frankfort a circular from the War Department calling on the governors of the several states to take measures "to organize, arm and equip, according to law, and hold in readiness to march at a moment's warning, their respective proportion of 100,000 militia. . . ." Governor Scott particularly was requested "to take effectual measures for having his state's quota, 5,500 of the Kentucky militia, detached and duly organized within the shortest period that circumstances would permit."[1]

General orders for the mobilization, dated May 5, were published shortly after throughout the Commonwealth.[2] Response to the call for volunteers was immediate and clamorous. The militia of every county was called to general meetings and enlistments for active service taken. On May 18 the 22nd Regiment assembled on the commons at Frankfort to swell its proportion of the President's call for troops. Martin D. Hardin, himself a volunteer, addressed the citizens' army "recapitulating the embarrassed state of our commerce — the uncertainties of our markets, owing to the crooked and insidious policy of the British Cabinet; the impressment of our seamen; the Henry plot; and the Indian murders daily committed on our defenseless frontiers."[3] Here, as elsewhere over the State, enlistments exceeded the quota required.

Brigadier General James Winchester, who had been appointed to this high rank March 27 with orders to lead the western forces to the relief of Americans in the Northwest, had arrived in Lexington on Sunday, April 26, to make arrangements for immediate recruiting.[4] And by the time Congress had worked its way around to a declaration of war numerous companies had been organized and were drilling daily.

[1] *The Palladium* (Frankfort, Ky.), May 6, 1812. Hereinafter cited *Palladium*.
[2] *Ibid.*, May 13, 1812, *q.v.* for full text.
[3] *Argus of Western America* (Frankfort, Ky.), May 20, 1813. Hereinafter cited *Argus*.
[4] *The Western Citizen* (Paris, Ky.), May 2, 1812, from *Kentucky Gazette*.

15

News of the long awaited declaration of war reached central Kentucky on Friday, June 26, eight days after the formal pronouncement in Washington. In Lexington there was a general celebration with firing of cannon and musketry which was kept up until late in the night. Similar demonstrations took place in Winchester, Richmond, Nicholasville, and other towns. The Lexington press styled it "a moment of joy, when the citizens saw their country a SECOND time declared independent."[5] At Mt. Sterling and Nicholasville Senator John Pope, who had argued against the war, was burned in effigy. The news was announced in Frankfort on Monday, June 29 "by a federal salute, accompanied by every demonstration of pleasure and satisfaction that Congress had, by the energetic act, rescued the country from the foul imputation of weakness and cowardice, and the contempt of all nations. . . ."[6]

Meantime General William Hull, who in the spring of 1812 while on a visit to Washington had been persuaded against his wishes to accept a commission as Brigadier General and the command of the army designed to defend Michigan Territory and attack Upper Canada from Detroit, had been marching with his little army since June first. This force numbered only about 2,000 men and it was expected the Kentuckians would shortly be ordered to march to its relief.

By late July Governor Scott's organization of the State's quota of troops had been completed, in anticipation of this expected demand. In General Orders, dated Frankfort, July 27, 1812, the force destined to meet costly reverses at Frenchtown was set up almost exactly in the order in which it marched a few months later from the Rapids of the Maumee. The First Regiment, to be commanded by Lt. Col. John M. Scott, was given the companies of Captains Collier, Pugh, Morris, West, Redding, Sebree and Glaves; the Fifth Regiment, under the command of Lt. Col. William Lewis, was to be composed of the companies of Captains Hart, Hamilton, Gray, Price, Williams, Martin, Brasfield and Megowan, while the regiment of riflemen [1st Rifle Regiment], commanded by Lt. Col. John Allen, had the companies of Captains Ballard, Hickman, Kerley, Langhorne, Ellis,

[5]*Reporter*, July 1, 1812.
[6]*Argus*, July 1, 1812.

The Mobilization

Edmiston, Simpson, McCracken.[7] To this force would be added only the group of regulars, under the command of Colonel Samuel Wells, itself recruited almost entirely from Kentucky. Captain William Garrard's troop of twelve months Light Dragoons, "The Bourbon Blues," also rendezvoused with the group and remained attached to it during the first three months of the campaign.

Among these short term volunteers, and in the ranks of the regulars, were some of the best and most promising men in the State. High ranking county officers volunteered, when necessary forsaking rank. Of the above named, Captain John Simpson, with Privates Samuel McKee and Thomas Montgomery were members or members-elect of Congress. Colonel John Scott, aged friend and physician of General Harrison, stood high in military as well as medical esteem and Colonel John Allen was head of the Kentucky bar. Major George Madison, long Auditor of Public Accounts and later Governor, was a staff officer. Older men of the earlier Indian campaigns stood beside their younger companions in arms and matched spirits and determination.

The war as it affected this particular group of men came closer Monday, August 3, when Governor Scott received a letter from the Secretary of War requiring him to aid General Winchester in organizing a force of 1,500 infantry to march immediately to the relief of General Hull at Detroit. In pursuance of these orders General Winchester sent an express to Frankfort Monday night requesting the Governor to place 1,100 volunteers in readiness to rendezvous at Newport on or about the 12th of August. Here they would be joined by about 400 regulars under Colonel Wells and ordered to proceed immediately to Detroit.[8]

The urgency of the call was intensified on August 5 when Thomas Davis Carneal, assistant quarter-master to General Hull's army, arrived in Frankfort with a personal request from the General for the needed reinforcements from Kentucky. Carneal had left Hull's headquarters at Sandwich on July 29 and to heighten his appeal brought news that Fort Michilimackinac had been taken by the British, aided by about 1,000 Indians.[9]

[7]These General Orders were published in full in *Western Citizen*, August 1, 1812.

[8]*Reporter*, August 8, 1812; *Palladium*, August 5, 1812.

[9]*Western Citizen*, August 8, 1812.

Marching orders for this group were ready the following day. Addressed to Brigadier General John Payne, of Scott County, who had been named to command, the orders as published on August 6 read:

Brig. Gen. John Payne

Sir — Yourself, with the rifle regiment under the command of Lt. Col. John Allen — The 1st Regiment of Infantry, under the command of Lt. Col. John M. Scott, and the 5th Regiment, under the command of Lt. Col. Wm. Lewis — all of the detachment from the militia of Kentucky, under the Act of Congress of the 10th of April last, will march to join General Hull in Canada — for which purpose, you, with the aid of the said regiments will rendezvous at Georgetown, in Kentucky, on the 15th inst. when and where you will receive further orders.

The men will furnish themselves with provisions and the necessary conveyance to the rendezvous at Georgetown. You will thence be furnished with provisions and the necessary means of conveyance for the residue of the march. Arrangements will be made for the arms, ammunition and camp equipage to be furnished at New-Port, if not sooner.

Should any of the companies reside contiguous to New-Port, so that it would be more convenient for them to make their first rendezvous there, you may at your discretion so order it, but not to be later than the 18th inst. so that they may be ready to join the detachment on their arrival at that place.[10]

Typical of the central Kentucky units raised for the rendezvous was Captain Paschal Hickman's company of Franklin County volunteers, a group of eighty-six of the community's farmers and townsfolk of whom only thirteen are known to have survived the hardships of the Raisin campaign to return to their Franklin homes. Colonel Orlando Brown, whose reminiscenses of early Frankfort and the first seven governors of Kentucky were published in the *Register* of the Kentucky Historical Society in 1951, recalled in that work:[11]

[10]*Reporter*, August 15, 1812.

[11]Orlando Brown, "The Governors of Kentucky," ed. G. Glenn Clift, *Register of the Kentucky Historical Society*, XLIX (1951). Hereinafter cited *Register*.

The Mobilization

The Government did not equip the Kentucky volunteer in the rifle regiment. He furnished his own gun and his own clothes, and was paid eight dollars a month! The equipment of a volunteer in Hickman's company consisted of a hunting-shirt made of linsey, with a slight fringe border, color either blue, such as is obtained from indigo, a pale yellow made from hickory bark, or a dingy brown obtained from the black walnut. His pants were of Kentucky jeans, and he walked in shoes or moccasins, as was his fancy. Around his waist was a leather belt, on one side of which was a leather pocket fastened by leaden tacks, instead of thread, and in this was placed the indispensable tomahawk. Across his shoulder was the strap that held up his powder horn, in which strap was another leather case containing his formidable butcher knife, and another to hold his bullets. A knapsack of home manufacture contained his clothing, and the outside of it was garnished with a glittering tin cup. His well-tried-rifle, faithful and to be trusted in the hour of peril, although it was what is now derisively called the "old flint lock" was his weapon of war; and thus accoutered he went to meet the enemy with a fearless step, and his deeds will well compare with any that have since been performed.

On the day before Captain Hickman led his men to the rendezvous at Georgetown the company paid a hasty visit to Governor Scott's home. Colonel Brown in the memoirs noted above recalled:

Being a patriotic little fellow, we followed, bare headed and bare footed, the soldiers to the Governor's house. We remember the scene as if it were yesterday. The soldiers were drawn up in a line between the front steps and the fence, and servants were busy going from man to man, one bearing a pail full of whiskey and the other a pail of water. The Governor was hobbling along on his crutch with his gray hair streaming in the wind and tears running down his aged cheeks, taking his final leave, and wishing them God speed, and conjuring them to be brave. Some time before this the Governor had fallen on the slick steps of the house, from the effects of which he was ever after lame, and had to use a crutch. By the time he had gone the rounds of the company his emotion had become almost too big for speech, and turning abruptly towards the steps, he wore his crutch out on them, explaining with every blow—"If it hadn't been for you, I could have gone with the boys myself!"

The entire detachment, agreeable to orders, was at the rendezvous at Georgetown on August 15. The camp was on what was then Craig's Hill, just above the Big Spring.[12] Governor Scott was on hand to review the troops early on Sunday, the 16th, when the first parade was held,[13] and more than likely stayed to hear the Reverend James Blythe's sermon and Henry Clay's address when the men were paraded a second time at ten o'clock.[14] Clay, then Speaker of the House, had driven over from Lexington to address the citizen soldiers and advise them that they had "the double character of Americans and Kentuckians to sustain," a phrase later to appear in more than one general order to be issued during the campaign.

Spirits were high as the men drilled, paraded and readied themselves for the first leg of the long march. On the 18th they drew two months' pay in advance, and were immediately given their first insight into military discipline. A general complaint arose among the men respecting sixteen dollars, which was expected to be drawn in lieu of clothing. Major Benjamin Graves paraded his battalion in full regalia and gave the volunteers their choice of going without the sixteen dollars, or of returning home. Of the battalion only six men chose to return and these, "to fix an odium upon them," were drummed out of camp and through Georgetown.[15]

It might be noted that soldier-citizen relations apparently differed little in 1812 from those of more recent conflicts in which the foot soldier has been known to suffer. Shortly after the detachment left Craig's Hill one newspaper editor observed that "very unwarrantable speculations were made on the volunteers at Georgetown, after they had received their pay, by purchasing up the Bank notes at a discount of 20 per cent."[16]

It is to be presumed that those in high command, having studied General Hull's slow progress and generally aware of the

[12]*Commonwealth* (Frankfort, Ky.), May 7, 1833. Hereinafter cited *Commonwealth*; *Register*, XXVI (1928), 320-321.

[13]Elias Darnall (or Darnell), *A Journal, containing an Accurate & Interesting Account of the Hardships, Sufferings, Battles, Defeat and Captivity of those heroic Kentucky Volunteers and Regulars, commanded by General Winchester in the Years 1812-1813* (Paris, Ky.: Printed by Joel R. Lyle, 1813), p. 6. Hereinafter cited Darnall.

[14]*Ibid.*, p. 7.
[15]*Ibid.*
[16]*Reporter*, August 22, 1812.

The Mobilization

difficulties of a winter campaign in a climate far more severe than that known to any of the men, entertained sober reflections as to the days ahead. The geography of the country that lay between them and Detroit should have been familiar to all. The necessity of cutting their own roads through these swamps and Indian infested reaches, of carrying their own supplies and munitions of war and of extending their lines beyond the immediate reach of a supply train, all was probably apparent to some. The high spirits of the men, however, were everywhere evident as they paraded and listened to Mr. Clay — unknowingly on the same day that General Hull was surrendering his little army to the British at Detroit. If any cloud darkened the near horizon of any particular man, it assumed the general outline of General James Winchester. The volunteers were openly desirous of being commanded by General William Henry Harrison, the trusted stalwart of Tippecanoe, and even this, if they could believe the counsel of such leaders as Colonel Richard M. Johnson and Mr. Clay, would be granted them very shortly.

As the troops prepared to move out of Georgetown, another representative citizen soldier of the Northwest Army made ready for his own solitary expedition "above and beyond the call of duty." Behind the overt hustle and pageantry of troop concentration and lost to the patriotic aspects of the mobilization, Nathaniel Hart, Sr., of Woodford County, was handed the responsibility of procuring money for the campaign. Thirty-two years later when a newspaper chronicled his death at *Spring Hill* the deed was recalled:

> In the autumn and winter of 1812, at the instance of the Federal Government, and as Agent of the Bank of Kentucky, Mr. Hart made two trips, in quick succession, on horseback, to Philadelphia, for the purpose of transporting, as he did, over the mountains and through the wilderness of Ohio, in a private carriage without a guard, large amounts of money in gold to the Capitol of Kentucky, where it was needed by the Government to procure the sinews of war to sustain the Northwest army, which was mainly dependent upon this State for its supply of troops and provisions.[17]

[17]Nathaniel Hart, Sr., early settler of Kentucky and authority on its history, was born in Caswell County, N. C., and died at his home, *Spring Hill,* Woodford County, Ky., February 7, 1844, in his 74th year. *Commonwealth,* April 2, 1844.

III
THE MARCH

The Army of Canada struck its tents at Georgetown at twelve o'clock noon on Wednesday, August 19, and proceeded on the march to Detroit,[1] each regiment for speed and convenience marching separately to Newport, first objective of the long walk. Most of the eighty miles was made through rain, introducing the citizen's army to an early acquaintance with weariness and the discomfort of water-soaked camps. "These hardships tended a little to quench the excessive patriotic flame that had blazed so conspicuously at the different musters and barbecues."[2]

Newport was reached six days later and here the men were advised of General Hull's August 16 surrender of Detroit and Michigan Territory to General Brock. "This we could not believe until confirmed by handbills and good authority," wrote Elias Darnell. "When thus confirmed, it appeared to make serious impressions on the minds of officers and privates. Those high expectations of participating with General Hull in the laurels to be acquired by the conquest of Malden and Upper Canada, were entirely abandoned."[3]

Meantime, while the sobered detachment waited at the Ohio for arms and a settlement of differences arising as to leadership of the campaign, retiring Governor Charles Scott had reached a decision as to the leadership he desired. Obstacles in the way of appointment of Governor William Henry Harrison to command confronted the old soldier-governor at every hand. Harrison was not a citizen of Kentucky, and the laws of the Commonwealth would not sanction appointment of any other to an office in the State militia. Again, a major general had been appointed for the detached militia, and only one was authorized.

The venerable Scott had other troubles. His term of office was drawing to a close and if he would cause honor to be done to a compatriot of other war days, he would have to act quickly or not at all. At last, to guard his own sentiments from public censure, he called a caucas of such leaders as were readily avail-

[1]*Reporter*, August 22, 1812.
[2]Darnall, *op. cit.*, p. 7.
[3]*Ibid.*, p. 8.

The March

able, and placed the final vote in the hands of members Henry Clay, then Speaker of the House, Thomas Todd, governor-elect Isaac Shelby, former governor Christopher Greenup, Major General Samuel Hopkins and Richard M. Johnson. At this meeting of August 24 it was unanimously resolved to recommend to the Governor that he give Harrison a brevet commission of Major General in the Kentucky Militia and authorize him to take command of the detachment then on its march to Detroit. The Governor, on August 25, acted accordingly and to the evident satisfaction of all Kentuckians.[4]

Harrison, who had arrived from Lexington on Monday, August 24, set out the following Saturday morning to relieve General Payne and take the authorized command.[5] Learning enroute to Cincinnati of Hull's surrender he at once realized that Fort Wayne, key to the Wabash Valley, would be the next British objective, and that if this fort were to be saved, prompt action was demanded. He accordingly decided on a swift march, using his own authority to so order it.

By Thursday, August 27, arms and supplies in quantities sufficient for the march had been received and the Ohio was crossed. Colonel Wells with his 400 regulars had effected the river crossing the day before. "The whole were in high spirits and are some of the best stuff in Kentucky," wrote one Cincinnati editor. "They seemed indignant at the late news and are anxious to wipe off the stain from the American name; and all of them were eager and determined to march under the banner of Harrison, who has taken command of the North Western Army."[6]

General Harrison overtook the troops on the last day of August as they moved from Lebanon toward Dayton. Colonel John M. Scott wrote from camp ten miles from the latter place on September 1: "Governor [William H.] Harrison yesterday

[4]Robert B. McAfee, *History of the Late War in the Western Country* . . . (Lexington, Ky.: Worsley & Smith, 1816), pp. 107-08. Hereinafter cited McAfee; Freeman Cleaves, *Old Tippecanoe: William Henry Harrison and his Time* (New York: Charles Scribner's Sons, 1939), p. 116. Hereinafter cited Cleaves.

[5]*Reporter*, August 29, 1812.

[6]*Western Spy* (Cincinnati, Ohio), as reported in *Western Citizen*, September 12, 1812.

joined us. He was received with loud acclamations of joy. They [the army] have such complete and entire confidence in him that they will support him in all his measures."[7]

As the Kentuckians moved northward, precise descriptions of the march were sent home by the men. One volunteer wrote:

The army arrived at Dayton early on Tuesday September 1 and encamped on Mud [i.e., Mad] River. We found the people here in a state of ferment and commotion. I have conversed with several of the Ohio Militia, who were at the surrender of Detroit — the disgrace of the transaction appears to be divided between the stupidity and treachery of Hull. Gen. Brock treated the volunteers with great civility and politeness — it is said they are not even bound to remain neutral during the war. Many of the officers and men *assured* the British general that they would again return to the field.

A number of men have left this place for the relief of Fort Wayne, which is certainly threatened with a siege. Several companies of drafted militia are at this moment starting to Grenville, to build a garrison, etc. It is situated about 160 [miles] W. of N. near the frontier line.

General Harrison passed through this place to-day for Piqua (20 miles from this place) where the Indians are said to be in great number, and the great council is sitting. He is highly esteemed by every officer and soldier in the army. The Indians at Piqua are panic struck at our coming. I am informed they will be off as soon as possible. The lesson taught them by WAYNE is not forgotten. Capt. Garrard's Paris troop of horse is composed of choice spirits — when they found that neither horsemen's armour nor weapons could be obtained at the arsenal at New Port, they willingly received muskets and bayonets. The regulars generally encamped a few miles ahead of our brigade. Probably the officers do not wish them to mix with the militia. The illegal practice of *paddling* these poor fellows is still continued.[8]

On the first day of September, while the army was on the march from Dayton to Piqua an express was received from Harrison ordering Colonel Allen's Rifle Regiment, reinforced, to proceed directly to Fort Wayne to secure that stronghold before the Indians could entrench there. "I was ordered with my regi-

[7]*Reporter*, September 12, 1812.
[8]*Western Citizen*, September 12, 1812.

The March

ment to leave our heavy Baggage — draw ammunition & proceed to Ft. Wayne under which order I left the army and marched with my regt. to Picqua where I recd. a second order to stop until I recd. three companies detached from Scott's and Lewis's regmts to be joined with mine," Colonel Allen wrote a few days later.[9] The First Rifle Regiment, accordingly, was reinforced with the companies of Captain Coleman Collier, from Scott's Regiment, and Captains James C. Price and Wiley R. Brasfield, from Lewis's Regiment, and marched from Piqua September 3.[10] Colonel Allen was again proceeding in haste when he received a further order from Harrison that in consequence of information of a force sent from British held Malden to Fort Wayne the enemy would in all probability be too strong for his numbers. Colonel Allen was directed instead to proceed to St. Mary's and there await the whole army which Harrison was bringing up.[11]

Advanced elements of the army, meantime, had arrived at Piqua on September 3 without incident. One local event of the march to Piqua was related years afterward by Colonel A. H. Rennick, of Frankfort, one of the survivors of the campaign.

It seems that during Wayne's campaign in '94, Captain Paschal Hickman had served as a spy or scout. Dressed and painted in regular Indian style, he scoured the woods in search of information essential to the commanding General in his plans of offense and defense. While riding through the forest one day, engaged in his dangerous work, he discovered some distance in his front a solitary Indian, riding in the same direction. Hickman resolved on his capture. Urging his horse at a slightly increased pace, he managed to overtake the Indian in a mile or two. The latter, having noticed what he supposed to be a comrade in his rear, from his paint and attire, leisurely jogged along, without taking alarm. Riding up beside the savage, Hickman suddenly clasped him in his arms and by main strength made him a captive. The prisoner was taken to Wayne's headquarters, who, anxious for peace, sent him to his tribe with propositions of that nature. The Indian took care not to return. It was now eighteen years after that event, and Hickman, grown from a moderate sized man of

---

[9]Colonel John Allen to Judge William Logan, Camp at Defiance, October 2, 1812, *Ohio Archaeological and Historical Publications*, XXXVI (1927), 334-339.

[10]*Reporter*, September 12, 1812.

[11]Colonel John Allen to Judge William Logan, October 2, 1812, *op. cit.*

160 pounds to a corpulency of 220, and otherwise changed, was marching along at the head of his company, when he noticed an Indian sitting on the stump of a fallen tree. Going up to him, and slapping him familiarly on the back, Hickman extended his hand, which was eagerly seized by the other with a 'How de do? How de do?' falling from his lips.

'Do you know me?' asked Hickman.

'Yes . . .' responded the savage, and indeed it was the very same Indian that Hickman had captured while a spy under Wayne in '94. Hickman himself had probably recognized the former prisoner by his having a double lip, a phenomenon unusual among his race.[12]

"We are to march tomorrow for Fort Wayne, to open communications between that place and St. Mary's," Brigade Inspector James Garrard wrote his father Colonel James Garrard from Piqua. He added:

There will be about 30 pack-horses with provisions, accompanying the detachment. There are at St. Mary's . . . 300 Ohio militia who are afraid to venture on to Fort Wayne without a reinforcement. There were Spies sent out to Fort Wayne who have been driven back. It is probable the detachment will have a brush with the Indians. The men appear extremely anxious to have an engagement with them. We shall stay here two or three days to make preparations for our march to St. Mary's. The waggons will have to be sent back for forage before we can march, which will probably detain us three days.[13]

Two days later General Harrison paraded the remaining part of the army in a circle in close order and briefed them as to the situation, in familiar procedure taking time to read some of the articles of war. He closed his remarks with a warning that any who were not willing to submit to and abide by the strict regulations and restrictions might as well return home at once. Only one man chose to return and he was ridden on a rail to a

---

[12]*Commonwealth*, May 26, 1871.

[13]Letter dated Head Quarters, Piqua, September 3, 1812, in *Western Citizen*, September 12, 1812.

nearby river, where his friends "ducked him several times in the water, and washed away all his patriotism."[14]

The volunteers marched from Piqua at 12 o'clock noon on the sixth, leaving all sick and parts of the clothing and baggage at Piqua for the forced march. St. Mary's was a hike of thirty miles, through some first-rate woodland and prairie land. Prior to taking up the line of march General Harrison placed the force on half rations of flour, but promised that the men could draw a ration and a half of beer. All who felt they could not proceed on this ration were granted permission to remain behind, where they might have plenty. This time none hesitated.

During the hot day of the ninth the army had to depend on water in the wagon-ruts for drinking purposes, and found precious little of that. A point near the river St. Mary's was reached on September 9 and from that camp the force proceeded in battle formation. The first and fifth regiments formed one line in single file on the left, two hundred yards from the road; the 17th United States Infantry and rifle regiment on the right, in the same formation. Baggage followed in the road. Ohio volunteers were half a mile in the lead and on the right flank, with the Kentucky mounted riflemen on the left flank and Captain Garrard's troop forming the rear guard.[15]

After six days of forced marches, on reduced rations and harassed by the expected alarms and accidents of the movement, the army reached Fort Wayne. Captain Maurice Langhorne wrote to his brother at Paris:

> We arrived here on Saturday last [September 12] after a very fatiguing march from Piqua, having but half allowance of provisions, and no water except such as we found in ponds, and that so rare, that the day before we got here, we marched 25 miles without seeing a drop. We however have the satisfaction of having, by thus marching, saved the fort, which had been for three weeks assailed by a considerable number of Indians, principally Potawatamies. They had burned most of the houses around the fort, and destroyed everything

---

[14]Darnall, *op. cit.*, p. 11; see also William H. Richardson to Mrs. Judith L. Richardson, Georgetown, Ky., dated Piqua, Surgeon's Tent, September 6, 1812. MSS in Shane Collection, Presbyterian Society.

[15]Darnall, *op. cit.*, p. 14.

they could get hold of, and would probably have succeeded in burning the fort in a day or two if we had not arrived.[16]

Another volunteer wrote:

The Indians committed all possible depredations about the Fort. A week ago they killed two of the Regular soldiers a few yards from the garrison gate, Johnson and the Indian agent were killed a few days ago at this place. 'Tis almost impossible to travel through the woods in the vicinity of Fort Wayne, the stench arising from the Hogs and Cattle, destroyed by the Indians, being so *great*. The Indians were busy firing on the Fort for two days previous to our arrival, when we arrived they were on the opposite side of the River. They were pursued but not overtaken. Johnson's Mounted Riflemen have killed one Indian. We have no prospect of a general engagement — the Indians say KENTUCKY. TOO MUCH! We are reduced to 9 oz. flour per day. This we can live on, and fight on. We shall have plenty of Indian-Corn in a few hours. No officer can possibly be more beloved and confided in than Gen. Harrison.[17]

Captain Langhorne observed:

Fort Wayne is one of the most elegant situations I ever saw and must be a most important place to the United States. Three weeks ago the neighborhood around the Fort exhibited a spectacle highly pleasing to the eye, that had seen nothing but a wilderness of 100 miles. A number of well cultivated farms with neat houses in view of the Fort exhibited a scene of pleasure and comfort. I suppose there were 4 or 500 acres of land in cultivation. But the savages have burned every house, all the small grain and hay, destroyed as much of the corn as they could, and have killed and destroyed every species of stock, which I am told was very considerable. The army generally have been in much better health that I expected. My Company particularly are all well, except James Sapp, who has been very sick; but I am in hopes he is on the recovery. *Thomas Parmer* deserted from us at Dayton. He then complained of being sick, and I gave him a furlow for a week, on his promising to overtake us. But I am now

---

[16]Captain M. Langhorne to his brother, dated Fort Wayne, September 18, 1812, in *Western Citizen*, September 26, 1812.

[17]Letter from a volunteer in the Bourbon Troop, dated Fort Wayne, September 13, 1812, in *ibid.*, September 26, 1812.

The March

convinced that he was not at that time half as sick as a number of others in the company, and that he never intended coming on. You will be good enough to have at least so much of this, as relates to him, published in order that his fellow citizens may know how to estimate him.[18]

The high command, having faced the probability of a winter in the field, now at least had secured one of the line of defense posts which it was planned would extend to the foot of Maumee Rapids, inclusive.

But trouble from an unforeseen source loomed before the Kentuckians. Rumor that Winchester would replace Harrison produced anger and discouragement. Thomas Smith, a secretary on Harrison's staff, was forthright with his brother-in-law and later fellow editor, W. W. Worsley.

I have just heard that Harrison will leave the army and return to his territory — and that Winchester will command us. This will produce great discontent and murmuring, if not absolute rebellion. I fear this large army has been embodied to effect *nothing*. The people will be saddled with an enormous expense — you have no idea of the amount. I very much suspect *energy* and *arrangement* is every where lacking. At the prospect before us, Winchester's commanding, &c., I am really disheartened — quite low spirited and out of temper. You know the extent of this man's talents, and you know by whom he will be governed.[19]

Forces in the field, however, continued despite the grumbling to carry out orders — even though they were often difficult to understand and seemingly remote to accomplishment. Colonel

[18]Captain M. Langhorne to his brother, dated Fort Wayne, September 18, 1812, *op. cit.*

[19]Thomas Smith to W. W. Worsley, dated Fort Wayne, September 17, 1812, State Historical Society of Wisconsin Library, Draper MSS, Kentucky Papers 5CC45. Thomas Smith bought the Lexington, Kentucky, *Kentucky Gazette* in September, 1809, and remained as proprietor and editor except for the period of his service as a volunteer in the War of 1812, when W. W. Worsley acted as manager, until September, 1813. Aside from his duties as secretary, Smith managed to serve as war correspondent for the *Gazette*, sending back to Worsley all that he considered newsworthy. On October 5, 1812, Smith was appointed General Payne's aide-de-camp. See Winchester's "Orderly Book," this date.

Allen's account of troop movements during these critical mid-September days reflects this general sense of movement without great purpose and fatigue with undue results.

> Genl. Harrison [after reaching Fort Wayne] detached Colo. Wells with the regulars & Colo. Scotts regt. to Destroy the Pottowattomy Town on the Elkhart river waters of lake Michigan about 60 miles from Ft. Wayne & the Turtles Town about 15 miles from Ft. Wayne also detached Genl. Payne with Colo. Lewis's and my Regts to destroy the Towns about the Forks of the Wabash. We did our work and returned a good deal fatigued. The thickets thro which we had to force our way nearly wore out our cloaths and the swamps & thickets very much jaded our horses — for besides the minor swampings they were occasionally so deep that we had to throw ourselves off and let them scuffle out. On our arrival at Ft. Wayne on our return we found Colo. Simrall with his regmt. of horse — afterward Colo. Wells returned having destroyed the Town on Elkhart but for the want of provisions had not delayed to destroy the Turtles town. Colo. Simrall & his horse were then sent off, who destroyed that town and returned. Genl. Harrison then gave up to Genl. Winchester the troops then at Ft. Wayne (except Simrall's horse). This had nearly produced a revolt but by the exertion of the officers all was got smoothe again.[20]

This revolt was deep rooted and extended to high as well as the lower ranks. Major Richard M. Johnson was unrestrained in his remarks to President Madison:

> Let me inform you that no event is now so important to the cause . . . as the giving Govr Harrison command of the forces from Kentucky . . . He has the confidence of the forces without a parrallel in our History except in the case of Genl. Washington in the revolution . . . The united exertions of us all cannot reconcile them to the transfer of the command. I speak what I know.[21]

The venerable Isaac Shelby, who had succeeded Charles Scott as governor late in August, spoke his fears to Secretary of War

---

[20] Colonel John Allen to Judge William Logan, Camp at Defiance, October 2, 1812, *op. cit.*

[21] Quoted in Cleaves, *op. cit.*, p. 120, *q. v.*, for a full discussion of the tardy appointment of Harrison to full command.

The March

Monroe: "... I have received a dispatch from governor Harrison, dated at Piqua, of the second instant, in which he informs me that General Winchester is ordered on to take command of the detachment sent from this state for the relief of General Hull. This arrangement at once divides the army under governor Harrison, and renders either part unequal to any object of importance, and ruins the fairest prospects of the expedition."[22]

The volunteers, to the man, refused to be commanded by a "Regular" officer, and all but resolved to return home in a body. Private William B. Northcutt, of Captain Garrard's troop of horse, later wrote in his diary account of the campaign:

> I always had some misgiveings about Winchester's Success with his Army, Knowing that he was not loved by his men, for they all despised him, and were continually playing some of their tricks of[f] on him. At one Encampment, they killed a porcupine and skined it and stretched the Skin over a pole that he used for a particular purpose in the night, and he went and sat down on it, and it like to have ruined him. At another Encampment they sawed his pole that he had for the same purpose nearly in two, so that when he went to use it in the night it broke intoo and let his Generalship, Uniform and all fall Backwards in no very decent place, for I seen his Rigementals hanging high upon a pole the next day taking the fresh air.[23]

General Winchester had arrived at Fort Wayne on September 18 and on the following day Harrison had formally resigned all command into his hands. Popular as he was with the troops and eager as they were to do his bidding, it required all of Harrison's eloquence to quell the feeling toward Winchester and extract assurances that the troops would carry on the expedition. A final uneasy quiet was effected when the men were permitted to believe that Harrison might soon be restored to the command.

Actually War Department orders assigning Harrison to full command had been penned and dated September 17, and included his orders for the northwestern army's campaign: "Having

---

[22] Shelby to Monroe, September 5, 1812, in Logan Esarey (ed.), *Messages and Letters of William Henry Harrison* (Indianapolis: Indiana Historical Commission, 1922), II, 111. Hereinafter cited Esarey (ed.).

[23] William B. Northcutt, "Diary." MSS, Kentucky Historical Society, p. 35.

provided for the protection of the Western frontier, you will retake Detroit; and with a view to the Conquest of Upper Canada, you will penetrate that country as far as the force under your Command will in your judgment justify."[24]

This order, however, did not reach Harrison until September 24, at Piqua, where he had gone to plan a move to attack Detroit along the line of a path "which has sometimes been used by the Indians, leading up the St. Joseph's and from thence, by the head waters of the River Raisin to Detroit."[25] The next day he addressed a letter to Winchester advising him of the change in command. ". . . the express brought me another letter from the war department, announcing my appointment to the command of the north-western army. Need I add, that it would give me the most heartfelt pleasure if you could determine to remain with us. . . . I have written general Payne, but have said nothing about my resuming the command, choosing that you should announce it in the manner you thought best."[26]

Colonel John Allen's report noted that

During all this we heard nothing further from the British detachment from Malden, which we had heard was Mjr. Chambers with 200 to 300 British & some pieces of artillery & Tecomsah (who they had made a Brigadier Genl.) with from 600 to 900 Indians — Genl. Harrison set out to return to St. Marys to forward on Colo. Jennyngs (William Jennings) with provisions for us to the mouth of The Auglase where Fort Defiance had stood — (say 60 miles from St. Marys) — Genl. Winchester with Colo. Wells', Colo. Scott's — Colo. Lewis's & The rifle regt. under my command & Capt. Garrard's troop of horse set out for Defiance say 47 or 50 miles from Ft. Wayne — Capt. B. W. Ballard, Lieut. Harrison Monday of Capt. Kerley's Company of my regt. Ensign James Liggett of Colo. Wells regt. & 60 men chiefly from my regt. were organized into a Spy Company & detached on that service. — We proceeded slowly having the road to cut — On the Evening of the 25th Ulto. [25 September] Capt. Ballard came to camp

[24]Secretary of War to Harrison, September 17, 1812, Esarey (ed.), *op. cit.*, II, 136-137.

[25]Harrison to Shelby, St. Mary's, September 22, 1812. MSS in Mitten Collection, Indiana Historical Society.

[26]Harrison to Winchester, September 25, 1812, Esarey (ed.), *op. cit.*, II, 152. The appointment was confirmed by the Senate December 2, 1812.

The March

to draw provisions, to report & to receive orders if any further were to be given — also informed me that Ensign Liggett with four others had left them to proceed to Defiance which gave us both unasiness — On the next day several alarms had delayed us much — Capt. Ballard returned with the spies with him & informed that Ligget & the four men with him had been killed and scalped, that the Indians were about them so strong that he was unwilling to give them battle and therefore had returned & was closely pursued — From what afterwards appeared he made a very masterly retreat or he would have been cut off for they were not only beyond him in numbers but Many of them mounted — he also reported that many of them were dressed in blue. The same Evening Lieutenant Monday [Harrison Munday, of Kerley's Company] with part of the Spies with him had fallen in with another party of Indians apparently too strong for him but being evidently near a larger party & he in a situation not likely to escape if then seen — Made a bold and desperate charge which made the Indians run which gave him an opportunity to gain advantageous ground & run & so he & his party escaped with a very hard race

Next morning Capt. Ballard with 45 men & Capt. Garrards horse were sent out to bury the dead, to spy & report &c — The horse were directed to Keep behind the Spies about 200 yards so as to be in supporting distance & at the same time not be so near as by their noise to interrupt his hearing &c They had a deep difficult creek to pass — which retarded the horses so as to throw them nearly a quarter of a Mile behind — at this difficult place the Indians attempted an attack on Ballard but he having crossed at a place not exactly suiting their ambuscade they were obliged to show themselves in part — both parties Run to gain the highest ground — The Indians gained it & the Battle Began one of our men of Capt. Edmonstons Company of my Regmt was wounded in the ancle which was all the injury we then sustained the fire of our men were so well directed that I believe nearly Every Shot hit two or three were seen to fall — The Charge made by Ballard & his company & the noise of the horse coming to his support made the Indians give way — They were persued and driven across the Miami [Maumee] River — From the best account I can get of those in different places in & near the action there were about 100 Indians — The dead who had been previously killed were buried — The next morning a firing by the Spies in front of the March This with the large trales & indian signs induced a suspicion that they intended to fight us — none of our spies were hurt but they found Indian blood — we were then in an old trace & had the Maimi to Cross & from appearances & council held it was supposed they were ready for us at the fording & would attack us in the river which was deep — This caused us to wheel off & cross the river at a different place higher up — Immediately on gaining the Bank we discovered a large trale & marks of waggon wheels which at first was supposed to be Colo. Jennyngs Regt with our provisions which had gone down altho a little out of its way — But the Mistake was soon discovered They turned out to be a large party of British & Indians going with artillery towards Ft. Wayne But about opposite the place where Ballard had departed the party they had turned round & gone Back had escaped in an advantageous place below the fording & waited for us but on being defeated in their intention at the river they had decamped put their artillery in some kind of craft & had hurried off — At that time we were out of flour & nearly out of beef so that we could not pursue I have not tasted bread since our last Beef has been killed & we are on the Brink of being out of provisions. Something had delayed Colo Jennyngs & in addition to this his spies having discovered so much appearances of Indians where we are now that he stopped to build a Blockhouse — we sent an Escort & this Evening (a few minutes ago) some flour arrived — Thus we a second time have saved Ft. Wayne for there is now no doubt with us it was the party of British & Indians we had heard of with Chambers & Tecomsah who were thus on their way to take Ft. Wayne. It so turned round by us Their spies had killed our friend Ligget & the four others with him who were fine young men of Capt McCrackens Company of my regt. (My feelings are much hurt & aroused by the incident.)[27]

The overall plan was to unite General Harrison's scattered army at the Maumee Rapids, near the present city of Toledo. General Winchester's instructions were to facilitate transportation of supplies to Fort Defiance and then move as soon as expedient on to the Rapids. Travelling on the northwest side of the Maumee River, the left wing reached a point about one and a half miles above Fort Defiance, on a bluff at the confluence of the Auglaize and Maumee Rivers, on the last day of September. Tents were pitched near the crumbled fort and strong breastworks thrown up around the camp. Here, and at camps nearby, the Raisin Force was destined to remain until December 30 when the detachment jumped off for the River Raisin.

[27]Colonel John Allen to Judge William Logan, Camp at Defiance, October 2, 1812, op. cit.

The March

The brush had grown to such an extent since General Wayne's clearing of eighteen years previous that details were formed to clear the ground across the Auglaize and to the fort proper. General Orders for the detail were:

A fatigue party shall be detached to consist of 1 Lt. Col. 2 Majors 8 Captains 8 Lieutenants — 8 Ensigns — 32 sergeants 32 corporals 2 musicians and 508 privates to be employed in erecting four Block houses at the point, the logs to be cut 20 feet long for the lower story and 22 [later changed to read 24] for the upper story; to be raised about 15 or 16 feet high; a store house and hospital each 18 by 24 feet; the former about 10 feet high, the latter eight; all of rough logs; with cabbin roofs; also to picket the lines between the bastains and build a watch house over the gate; and remove the brush in the vicinity of the site. A sergeant from each regiment, and a private from each company, shall be turned out, for soap and candle makers. . . .[28]

Here, three days after arrival, the scarcity of provisions and clothing gave rise to "great murmuring in camp, which threatened a dissolution of the army."[29] General Harrison had been apprised of the threatened mutiny the evening before when he had arrived unannounced in camp. Declining immediate action, he sent an aide to advise Winchester that on the following morning he would order a beating of the alarm rather than reveille.

When the men crawled from their tents, cold and hungry and expecting the enemy, they found instead their familiar leader and new cheer was immediate. Harrison's speech to the men brought somewhat of order. He was followed by Colonel Allen whose years of persuasive speech-making determined the day and soothed the men to accepted order.[30] Too, a good breakfast fur-

[28] "Papers and Orderly Book of Brigadier General James Winchester," *Historical Collections, Collections and Researches made by the Michigan Pioneer and Historical Society*, XXXI (1902), p. 258.
[29] Darnall, *op. cit.*, p. 26.
[30] In the first edition of his *History of the Commonwealth of Kentucky* Mann Butler wrote that the main revolt took place in Colonel John Allen's regiment. Survivors of Captain Paschal Hickman's company took the following public exception to the statement:
We belong to the second Battalion, under the command of Madison and Hickman, who will ever be remembered by their country; and we know there was no revolt in Hickman's company, nor do we believe that there was any in Madison's command. The revolt, if any, was in Major M. D. Hardin's

nished from provisions brought by Harrison's troops and Winchester's sudden announcement of the switch in command changed many a man's mind about returning home.

This announcement of Harrison's reappointment to the command, read to the men at this time, came in the form of the following General Order:

>Camp at Defiance 3rd October–1812
>General Orders
>
>I have the honor of announcing to this army the arrival of General Harrison, who is duly authorized by the executive of the federal government, to take command of the N. W. Army. This officer enjoying the implicite confidence of the States from whose citizens, this army is & will be collected, and possessing himself great military skill and reputation, The Genl. is confident in the belief that his presence, in this army in the character of its chief will be hailed with universal approbation
>
>J Winchester B Genl.[31]
>U. S. Army

It might be noted that Harrison's consideration of the demoted Winchester was in good tradition. The latter was assigned at once to the command of the left wing of the army and shortly after when the fort was completed it was rechristened Fort Winchester. (By General Orders of the same day Winchester published the news that he was still in command, by direction of the general commanding the Northwestern force, of the left wing and that it was to be composed of the detachment of the 17th U. S. regiment under Colonel Samuel Wells, a detachment of the 19th U. S. regiment, and the regiments of Kentucky troops com-

---

command, and did not include more than from four to six persons. The historian is in error as to the time of the arrival of General Harrison. He arrived some time before sundown, bringing with him a number of packhorses loaded with flour, which were truly joyously welcomed, for there was only one small bullock left to feed two thousand men. We (Allen's Regiment) gave him three cheers, as we expected to have starved without some such seasonable supply." *Commonwealth* (Frankfort, Ky.), July 15, 1834.

[31]"Papers and Orderly Book of Brigadier General James Winchester," *op. cit.*, p. 261.

The March

manded by Colonels Scott, Jennings, Pogue, Lewis, Barbee and Allen.)[32]

In early October, however, the old fort was in ruins and the fatigue party mentioned above — thinly clad and working on reduced rations in extremely inclement weather — struggled valiantly to complete the post in the record time of fourteen days. Dr. Charles F. Slocum, authority on the completed fort, notes that it was built along the higher and precipitous west bank of the Auglaize River, a line of apple trees, planted by the early French settlers, alone intervening. Beginning about 80 rods south of the ruins of Fort Defiance, near the present First Street of the city of Defiance, Ohio, the fort extended southward to, or south of, Third Street, a distance of something over six hundred feet, and including the highest ground. Its east line was about Washington Street. It was in the form of a parallelogram, and extended in width to about Jefferson Street. Its walls enclosed three acres or more of land. There was a strong two-story blockhouse at each of its four corners, a large gate midway of each side and end with a sentinel house above each one, and all were connected by a strong stockade of timbers set on end deep into the ground snug together, and extending twelve to fifteen feet above ground, all pointed at the upper ends. A cellar was excavated under the blockhouse at the northeast corner, and from it a passage way under ground was made to the rock-bed of the river and was there protected by timbers so that abundance of water could be obtained from the river under cover.[33]

Immediately the fort was finished, and rechristened Fort Winchester, General Winchester reported that the job had been completed, that pirogues were ready for transportation to the Rapids but that supplies were sorely needed.

The men were ready to move forward. They were hungry and poorly clothed and Major Garrard, sent on reconnaissance to the Rapids, added increased incentive by reporting that his men had discovered there large quantities of corn, some hogs and cattle. However, in its weakened condition the detachment could not move. The horses even were so weak as to be almost incapable

[32]*Ibid.*

[33]Charles E. Slocum, "The Origin, Description and Service of Fort Winchester . . .," *Ohio Archaeological and Historical Society Publications,* IX (1900-1901), 253-277. Hereinafter cited Slocum.

of pulling empty baggage wagons.³⁴ Until supplies of clothing and food could be provided, therefore, it was decided that the Raisin Force would remain at Fort Winchester.

It is possible that this winter halt provided for Winchester's little army as much suffering as any unit was ever called upon to endure.

Unseasonably cold rains began October 11 and fever hit the camp in early November. With the continued short rations and delay in receipt of winter clothing, spirits sank and resistance to sickness lessened rapidly. Nearly every day one or more soldiers were buried. To combat unhealthy aspects of the Fort, Winchester on November 2 moved the field soldiers across the Maumee, opposite the point, to high and very level terrain where it was hoped firewood would be easier to get. When this camp proved equally wet, the General ordered another move, this time further down the river. It was a cold, wet and heartbreaking move. There were only a few wagons and one regiment moved at a time. This site was marshy but generally better than the former. Thomas Smith on November 7 wrote his editor:

> The left wing of the North Western army has removed from its encampment at the Point, about one mile below, on the opposite side of the river, for the convenience of procuring fuel. Detached fatigue parties have been engaged latterly in erecting additional buildings at the Fort, to be used as Barracks, others are employed in making more Pirogues. The health of the army is not unfavourable. The Typhus fever has carried off several (eight died on the march from Fort Wayne and were buried at the Garrison with the honors of war)—a few doubtful cases still exist. General Winchester is a fine generous hearted old fellow and his family is an agreeable one, viz: Dr. Irvin, Dr. McIlvain and Dr. Feris (Medical Aids), J. Woolfolk, the General's aide, and the General's son Marcus, a sprightly boy of eighteen or nineteen, who assists in writing.³⁵

The health of the army did not improve greatly and on November 10 a third change of camps was ordered, this time six

---

³⁴John H. DeWitt, "General James Winchester, 1752-1826," *Tennessee Historical Magazine*, I (1915), 93.

³⁵Thomas Smith to W. W. Worsley, Camp near Fort Winchester, November 7, 1812, State Historical Society of Wisconsin Library, Draper MSS, Kentucky Papers, 5CC69.

The March

miles down the river to a bivouac where the ground was reasonably dry, firewood was plentiful and the prospect so improved that the encampment here was maintained for eight weeks.[36]

Military funerals, however, were still the rule rather than the exception. During the day following the move to Camp No. 3 four more of the Kentucky men were buried, to add to the one hundred lives already lost due to inadequate food and clothing and hospital facilities. As many as three hundred sick at a time were exposed to the cold, wet ground and lack of proper nourishment. Discipline became increasingly difficult to maintain. Impelled by hunger the men wandered from camp, against orders, in search of game, wild fruit and fish from the Maumee. Some, in their weakened state and without shoes, were drummed out of camp for attempted desertion and sentenced to ride the wooden horse before the whole army for lesser misdemeanors. Courts martial were held frequently, involving many officers as well as men. Captains Collier and Kerley and Dr. Gustavus Bower, Surgeon's Mate of Lewis's regiment, were a few tried in the tents of the senior officers and later restored to good standing. Others not so fortunate were sentenced to death by the firing squad for sleeping at their posts.[37] Often for days at a stretch the day's ration was beef without salt, hickory nuts and wild fruits, the beef being of such poor quality due to lack of forage that it was nearly worse than none.[38]

During the first days of December all troops began to build huts, far preferable to the tents, and to fashion moccasins out of green hides. At this time there were many without shoes and clothing sufficient to keep them from freezing had they been ordered to move from the bivouac. Letters sent home by the volunteers descriptive of their sufferings from cold, hunger and nakedness produced creditable results in all Kentucky communities, but the promised clothing continued to linger along the long supply route. As in other wars, the home front was at a loss to understand this delay. Over the Commonwealth the ladies had united for the

[36] Darnall, op. cit., pp. 31-33.

[37] "Papers and Orderly Book of Brigadier General James Winchester," op. cit., dated October 10, 13, December 29, 1812.

[38] William Atherton, Narrative of the Suffering & Defeat of the North-Western Army, under General Winchester: Massacre of the Prisoners . . . (Frankfort, Ky.: A. G. Hodges, 1842), pp. 18-19. Hereinafter cited Atherton.

purpose of making and sending this clothing to their men. They had formed sewing societies, made hunting shirts, knit socks, purchased blankets and fitted all kinds of garments. The ladies of Franklin County alone sent two wagon loads of clothing northward, and received weekly letters telling of the complete lack of clothes at the front.

As early as November 1 General Winchester had announced the prospect of an early supply of winter clothing, an announcement prompted by promises from Kentucky that large quantities would shortly be with the soldiers. Few at home, however, could envision the difficulties of transportation through the "Black Swamp" region. Throughout the period of the build-up at Fort Winchester the weather was such that it was next to impossible to move even an unloaded wagon through the mud. Pack horses brought into service proved of little more use, due to their weakened condition, the wet weather and depth of the mud. The few provisions brought into camp in this manner were often as not spoiled beyond use of any but starving men.

Robert McAfee in his *History of the Late War in the Western Country* wrote from first-hand observation of these supply difficulties.

About the first of December Major Bodley, an enterprising officer, who was quartermaster of the Kentucky troops, made an attempt to send near 200 barrels of flour down the St. Mary in piroques to the left wing below Defiance. Previous to this time the water had rarely been high enough to venture on a voyage in those small streams. The flour was now shipped in fifteen or twenty piroques and canoes, and placed under the command of Captain Jordan and Lieutenant Cardwell, with upwards of twenty men. They descended the river and arrived about a week afterward at Shane's Crossing, upwards of 100 miles by water, but only twenty by land from the place where they started. The river was so narrow, crooked, full of logs, and trees overhanging the banks, that it was with great difficulty they could make any progress. And now in one freezing night they were completely ice-bound. Lieutenant Cardwell waded back through ice and swamps to Fort Barbee with intelligence of their situation. Major Bodley returned with him to the flour, and offered the men extra wages to cut through the ice and push forward; but having gained only one mile by two days' labor, the project was abandoned, and a guard left with the flour. A few days before Christmas a temporary thaw took place which enabled them with much difficulty and suffering to reach within a few miles of Fort Wayne, where they were again frozen up. They now abandoned the voyage and made sleds on which the men hauled the flour to Fort Wayne and left it there.[39]

On December 14 an express reached the camp below Fort Winchester certifying that Major Bodley's boats which had started from St. Mary's ten days before were frozen in the St. Mary's river. Captain Paschal Hickman, on the morning after, left Camp No. 3 with pack horses to bring forward at least a part of the needed supplies.[40] The detachment had drawn no flour since the 10th of December and on the 16th a general movement was born after certain of the volunteers handed to General Winchester a letter stating that unless flour was forthcoming within two days, they would start and go to the supplies. When this threatened mutiny was quieted, the last of the beef and pork was issued to the troops in the evening of the same day. The next ration was dependent on a drove of hogs which had been expected several days. Fortunately on December 17 three hundred head of hogs reached the camp.[41] Then on Christmas Eve, just after dark, Captain Hickman's detail arrived with a supply of flour, producing a joyous (and unmilitary) celebration. Two days later a part of the clothing from Kentucky was brought into camp and carefully apportioned.

Having determined to take advantage of the frozen country to attempt a February march first against Malden, then on to Detroit, Harrison sent his orders to Winchester, by Charles S. Todd, division Judge Advocate of the Kentucky troops. These orders provided that as soon as Winchester

had accumulated provisions for 20 days, he was authorized to advance to the Rapids, where he was to commence the building of huts, to induce the enemy to believe that he was going into winter quarters—that he was to construct sleds for the main expedition against Malden, but to impress it on the minds of his men that they were for transporting provisions from the interior—that the different lines of the army would be concentrated at this place, and a choice detachment from the whole would then be marching rapidly on Malden—that in

[39]McAfee, *op. cit.*, p. 185.
[40]Darnall, *op. cit.*, p. 38.
[41]*Ibid.*, pp. 38-39.

the meantime he was to occupy the Rapids, for the purpose of securing the provisions and stores forwarded from the other wings of the army.[42]

By another chance of misfortune, which had attended the Raisin Force so long, Todd met and passed somewhere in the cold reaches of the "Black Swamp" two lonely volunteers sent by Winchester to advise Harrison of his move to the Rapids. On December 30, the day which saw the beginning of the march to the Rapids, General Winchester had dispatched Leslie Combs, with a single guide, to find General Harrison and inform him of the move to the Rapids in order that food and provisions might be sent forward as soon as possible. Despite their heroic penetration of some eighty miles to Fort McArthur, on Hull's Road, the message did not reach Harrison until January 11, at Upper Sandusky.

Certainly Combs did his best. "What he suffered on this tramp may be imagined, but cannot well be described. He had been accustomed only to wear his sword, after sending his horse to the interior, and their daily marching had ceased for some two months. He was on this occasion loaded with a heavy musket and accoutrements, in addition to a blanket and four day's provisions on his back." The snow commenced falling on the morning of the 31st of December, and continued without intermission for two days and nights, so that on the third day of their journey, young Combs and his companion (A. Riddle) found it over two feet deep. They were in a dense forest, without path or compass, and guided only by the unerring skill of his companion, who had been some fifteen years in early life, a captive among the Indians in this region, and was well skilled in all their ways and customs. Several nights they encamped in the black swamp, and could not find a place to lie down and rest, even on the snow, but were compelled to sit up all night with a small fire at their feet, made of such old brush as they could collect, and wrapping themselves in their blankets, shivering through the long hours till daylight enabled them again to resume their tiresome march. On the sixth day, their four days' provisions were entirely exhausted, and they had early put themselves on short allowance. Young Combs was extremely ill nearly all night, so much so, that it was concluded that Riddle must leave him in the morning to his fate, and for

---

[42] McAfee, *op. cit.*, p. 200.

The March

himself to make the best of his way to the nearest fort or settlement, and endeavor to save Combs, if he should survive till his return. Fortunately Combs managed to push on and kept moving for three days and nights longer, without a mouthful of food for either himself or his companion, except slippery elm bark. On the ninth evening, after dark, they reached Fort McArthur. Here Combs gave way to sickness and exhaustion and his message was sent forward to Harrison at Upper Sandusky, reaching that General as noted above on January 11, one day after Winchester had reached Hull's Road at the Rapids.[43]

While Combs and his guide were crossing the "Black Swamp," the men at Camp No. 3, renamed by the men Fort Starvation, were preparing to move out. Due to the frozen condition of the river, the plan to move to the Rapids via water had been completely frustrated. About sixty pirogues had been built for the contemplated movement and now had to be considered excess and to be left behind. On December 21 Winchester issued orders for each company to be provided with sleds in sufficient number to convey their baggage to the Rapids. Even as the men built these crude vehicles they realized that there was not in the whole camp a horse capable of pulling even an empty sled, and that the men themselves would have to serve in that capacity.

Diarist Elias Darnell wrote on December 29:

We are now about commencing one of the most serious marches ever performed by the Americans. Destitute, in a measure, of clothes, shoes and provisions, the most essential articles necessary for the existence and preservation of the human species in this world, and more particularly in this cold climate. Three sleds are prepared for each company, each to be pulled by a packhorse, which has been without food for two weeks, except brush, and will not be better fed while in our service; probably the most of these horses never had harness on, but the presumption is that they will be too tame; we have prepared harness out of green hides.[44]

So it was that after a succession of confused orders and counterorders, of forced marches under extremely difficult conditions,

[43]*Narrative of the Life of General Leslie Combs: Embracing Incidents in the Early History of the Northwestern Territory* (Washington: J. T. and Lem. Towers, 1855), pp. 6-7.
[44]Darnall, *op. cit.*, p. 41.

most of the time on half rations and often as not on none, the left wing of Harrison's force was ready to lead off on the long awaited chance to strike at Detroit. It was a "now or never" situation for General Winchester. His men had suffered all that soldiers could be called upon to suffer. Their terms of enlistment had been extended from the original two to six months, but would nonetheless expire in February and if anything was to be accomplished it had to be soon.

The sick were provided for at Camp No. 3 and guards left with them. And on December 30 the detachment moved out, preceded on the 29th by Colonel Wells's regiment. "We commenced our march in great splendor; our elegant equipage cast a brilliant lustre on the surrounding objects as it passed! our clothes and blankets looked as if they had never been acquainted with water, but intimately with dirt, smoke, and soot; in fact, we have become acquainted with one much despised in Kentucky, under whose government we are obliged to live, whose name is 'Poverty.'"[45]

The first day's march covered only six miles, moving up to Colonel Wells's encampment. The second day out brought a sudden melt which limited progress to two miles, and further taxed the weakened horses. Then on January 2 the snow began to fall again and continued for two days and nights. When the last flakes had settled on the huddled volunteers the snow had reached a depth of twenty-four inches. Temporarily halted by the snow, the march was resumed January 3 and progressed slowly until mid-afternoon when the small army had to begin scraping snow for its tents and hunting for bark or bushes to lie on.

The deep snow proved too much for the horses and one by one they gave out. "I have seen six Kentuckians substituted instead of a horse, pulling their plunder, drudging along through the snow, and keeping pace with the foremost," observed Darnell.[46]

Passing through Wolftown the detachment reached Roche De Baut, four miles above Hull's Road, on January 9. It was while on the second day of the march that Winchester received a dispatch from Harrison in which the latter recommended that Winchester abandon his march to the Rapids and fall back with the greater part of his force to Fort Jennings, a recommendation prompted by intelligence that Harrison had received of a formid-

[45]Ibid.
[46]Ibid., p. 43; Niles, *The Weekly Register*, IV (March 6, 1813), p. 12.

The March

able Indian force, under Tecumseh, on the Wabash. This advice Winchester declined following and pressing forward on January 10, 1813, he reached the designated rendezvous a little above Wayne's battle ground of 1794, on an eminence known as Presque Isle Hill.[47]

Early in the morning of the day of arrival at the Rapids, a strong detachment of 675 men under Colonel Payne was sent to investigate the reported Indian force. After one night in the field and no signs of the enemy force, this detachment dined on "an elegant supper of parched corn," and returned to camp in the morning.[48]

This easy occupation of the first objective brought to the men their first sense of accomplishment. The left wing, made up almost exclusively of Kentuckians, was now one hundred and forty-five days from home. Countless friends, and kinsmen, had been buried along the way or left to make their painful way alone back to Kentucky. Those left now at the Rapids were sorely in need of this morale boost. This latest move had carried them deep into enemy territory and far ahead of supply lines. Now in addition to the constantly worsening weather, they had to fight anew the lack of arms and munitions, of clothing and adequate provisions. And General Winchester, relying considerably on action to keep his little force together and unified, looked ahead for the opportunity and the moment when further, sorely needed action might be forthcoming.

[47]McAfee, *op. cit.*, pp. 201-202; Benson J. Lossing, *The Pictorial Field-Book of the War of 1812* . . . (New York: Harper & Brothers, 1869), p. 350. Hereinafter cited Lossing; Darnall, *op. cit.*, pp. 42-43. See John Armstrong, *Notices of the War of 1812* (New York: Wiley & Putnam, 1840), I, 197, for Winchester's reasons for declining Harrison's recommendations that he turn back.

[48]Darnall, *op. cit.*, p. 44; McAfee, *op. cit.*, p. 202.

IV

THE FIRST BATTLE

AT THE Rapids the detachment fed on corn and found new life. A large, strong house was constructed to serve the dual purpose of housing supplies and as a place of defense against attack.[1] Indian attacks and rumors of attacks kept the force on guard, and as Winchester had hoped, occupied.

The matter of morale at this time was a real problem to the old general. He had been requested by Harrison to endeavor to raise a new regiment among the volunteers, whose enlistments would expire in February, to serve six months longer. Inaction and suffering, however, had led to insubordination and laxity to such an extent that Winchester had little confidence in their strength.[2] Meantime, he endeavored to keep the detachment busy with building, scouting and building of apparatus for pounding and sifting the corn for bread.

Under date of January 11, Winchester had advised Harrison of his arrival and situation at the Rapids. This dispatch, however, was sent by a circuitous route, in the hands of persons taking the worn out and starved packhorses by Fort McArthur. "Of our arrival and situation the General was informed, by the best means I had—a party returning to McArthur's blockhouse; by whom I also requested a fulfilment of his promise of a speedy reinforcement," stated General Winchester on his return from captivity.[3] The message, at any rate, did not reach Harrison until almost daylight of January 19, one day after the first battle had been fought at Frenchtown.

The enemy was alerted as early as January 11, one day after the arrival at the Rapids. Signs of enemy occupation and movement near the camp on this day caused the command to send out a detachment of twenty-four men under Captain [Samuel?] Williams. The patrol contacted the Indians and spirited firing on both sides ensued before the Indians turned and gave up the

---

[1]Winchester to Secretary of War, quoted in Armstrong, *op. cit.*, I, 196-201.

[2]Lossing, *op. cit.*, p. 351.

[3]Armstrong, *op. cit.*, I, 198.

fight.⁴ This small group of the enemy carried intelligence of the occupation at the Rapids to the British command at Frenchtown, and inadvertently two days later gave General Winchester the immediate plan he had been seeking.

On January 13 two Frenchmen arrived in camp from the Raisin with alarming news. The Indians routed by Captain Williams, they reported, had passed through Frenchtown and on to Malden with their news of Winchester's presence at the Rapids. In passing through they had threatened to burn the homes of the French and make other reprisals as necessary to forestall aid and assistance to the Americans. Two days later, on January 15, another Frenchman came into camp with intelligence confirming that of his companions. He as well implored protection of his people and their property. A third messenger arrived on January 17, bringing news that two companies of British had just arrived from Canada and that Indians were collecting and intended to burn Frenchtown shortly.⁵

Sensing an ideal opportunity for needed action, General Winchester during the night of January 16 called a council of his officers and placed before them the choice of voting for or vetoing the solicitations of the French. Historians generally agree that the officers at once agreed on the march to Frenchtown. "To the best of my recollections," Major George Madison later stated, "they [the officers] were unanimously of opinion, that a detachment ought to be sent to the relief of the inhabitants at Raisin, as soon as practicable."⁶

The following day Winchester wrote Harrison informing him of the entreaties of the inhabitants of Frenchtown and of the enemy's movements.

They all agree in stating that the enemy is searching for, and taking all suspected persons whom they can lay hold of and confining them in Malden prison. . . . I am also informed that the enemy is engaging all the sleighs he can procure, for the purpose [of] carrying off the flour and grain. In this latter purpose, I have determined to disappoint him, or oblige him to pay a dear price for it; for which purpose, I have this morning detached Colonel Lewis and Allen with

⁴Darnall, *op. cit.*, p. 44.
⁵*Ibid.*, pp. 46-7.
⁶Armstrong, *op. cit.*, I, 205.

a command suitable to effect the object intended. I am informed that they will have to contend with two companies of Canadians and about two hundred Indians. If we get possession, it is my intention to retain it; therefore a cooperating force from the right wing may be acceptable. Nothing will reconcile an extension of the period of service of the volunteers, but progressive operations; indeed some have calculated on being discharged within their own state on, or before the expiration of their term of service.[7]

The volunteers indeed were mentally more nearly ready for action than at any time in recent months. Clothing from Kentucky had arrived in camp on January 15, eliciting from Elias Darnell: "The ladies who sent this clothing deserve the highest encomiums. If it had not been for their unexampled exertions, we must have suffered beyond conception. May they long live under the auspicious protection of a free government, and may kind heaven reward their unparalleled benevolence."[8] Warmed by the fresh clothing, the men gradually were reviving from the hard march to the Rapids and although they never had flour while in the camp, they were in possession of some three hundred acres of corn and other provisions which rendered their supplies as good or better than at any time in their service.

According to agreements reached after darkness on January 16 by the council of officers, Colonel William Lewis was to march with a selected detachment of some 550 early on January 17, under the command of Colonel Lewis, Majors George Madison and Benjamin Graves. As events progressed, however, shortly after Colonel Lewis's group left the camp at the Rapids, General Winchester determined, from further information received, to send an additional two companies of men, numbering 110 effectives, under the command of Colonel John Allen.[9] This latter

[7]Winchester to Harrison, January 17, 1813, Esarey (ed.), *op. cit.*, II, 314.

[8]Darnall, *op. cit.*, p. 45.

[9]Contemporary sources, including Brigade Inspector James Garrard's report of the killed, wounded, and missing of January 22-23, tend to indicate a force of approximately 650. Garrard's report shows 934 killed, missing, and captured on January 22. This number plus the twenty-five or thirty privates and three officers known to have escaped, placed the January 22 force at approximately 965. This total minus the almost 300 under Colonel Wells, not in the battle of January 18, would support the contemporary figure of about 600 in action on the latter date.

detachment, subsequently commanded by Captain Paschal Hickman as a part of the advance wing, was made up from the companies of Captains Hickman and Virgil McCracken. Joseph Clark, of Frankfort, who served in Hickman's company and escaped the six days at Raisin, recalled fifty-eight years later:

As there were in the first detachment a part of the men of Captain Hickman's company, it was proposed and agreed that an exchange of these men should occur, so as to get all officers' men in his own command. This arrangement was effected as to all except Clark and Frank Mayhall, who were respectively in commands other than their own. Not desiring to be separated from his comrads, Clark proposed to Captain Hickman that Mayhall and himself should also exchange, and after some parley this was effected. It proved for Clark a most fortunate and providential arrangement, for all of Captain McCracken's company, including Mayhall, were massacred in the retreat from the River Raisin.[10]

Agreeable to orders Colonel Lewis's detachment marched early on January 17, with three days' provisions—and little else in the way of munitions and supplies of war. Left behind in camp were many of the field officers from whose companies the Raisin Force had been formed. Of these were Captains Patrick Gray, Thomas Morris, George Pugh and Joseph Redding.[11]

The first day's march carried eighteen miles to Presque Isle (Presquille), about half way to Frenchtown. Here Colonel Lewis halted and was joined at 7 p.m. by the 110 men under Colonel Allen. "The sight of this village filled each heart with emotion of cheerfulness and joy," Darnell noted in his diary, "for we had been nearly five months in the wilderness, exposed to every inconvenience, and excluded from every thing that had the appearance of a civilized country. When the inhabitants of the village discovered us, they met us with a white flag, and expressed particular friendship for us."[12]

British forces, in the meantime, were building up at Frenchtown. Major Ebenezer Reynolds, commander of the Essex Militia,

[10]*Commonwealth*, June 9, 1871.

[11]Charles S. Todd and Benjamin Drake, *Sketches of the Civil and Military Services of William Henry Harrison*, rev. and enlarged by James H. Perkins (Cincinnati: J. A. and U. P. James, 1847), p. 61.

[12]Darnall, *op. cit.*, p. 46.

had been ordered to occupy Frenchtown to keep an eye on the movements of Winchester at the Rapids. This British garrison force consisted of two companies of militia, mostly French Canadians of the Cote, a force of Indians and one three-pounder. British authorities disagree as to the number of Indians under Reynolds. "He was backed by some Indians—how many can hardly be said, they were so uncertain,—one day, 20; the next, 100; the next, 50; the next, none at all."[13] Richardson[14] concludes there were only 200 Indians in the town at the time of the attack.

Colonel Lewis remained all night at Presque Isle. The weather was intensely cold. Strong ice covered Maumee Bay and the shore of Lake Erie. During the night of January 17 he received information from Frenchtown that 400 British Indians were in the town and that Colonel Elliott was expected from Malden, only eighteen miles away, to attack Winchester's army at the Rapids. This intelligence was sent immediately to Winchester, and caught the General's courier just about to leave for Harrison's headquarters with news of the advance toward Frenchtown.[15]

Armed with this new information, it became the duty of Colonel Lewis to anticipate the juncture of Elliott and Reynolds. Before dawn of January 18, therefore, he called together his officers and decided the line of attack. At the same time he had prepared three copies of his orders of the day and placed them in the hands of his battalion commanders, Allen, Madison, and Graves. These orders, Lewis specified, were not to be read until the men were actually going into battle.[16]

The cold, illy clad and poorly equipped army was routed early on the morning of January 18 and formed in marching order. Moving out across the ice of the lake, the force rapidly narrowed

[13] William F. Coffin, *1812: The War, and its Moral: A Canadian Chronicle* (Montreal: John Lovell . . . 1864), p. 208. Hereinafter cited Coffin.

[14] John Richardson, *Richardson's War of 1812: With Notes and a Life of the Author,* by Alexander Clark Casselman (Toronto: Historical Publishing Co., 1902), p. 132. Hereinafter cited Richardson.

[15] Lossing, *op. cit.,* p. 351; *Commonwealth,* May 7, 1833.

[16] B., "Recollections of the late War, the River Raisin Battle," *Commonwealth,* May 7, 1833. Part two of these reminiscences appeared in *ibid.,* May 28, 1833.

The First Battle

the distance between it and Frenchtown. Between twelve and one o'clock, nearing the Raisin River, a halt was made while the men threw their blankets on the deep snow and ate a hurried, cold lunch. They were now meeting natives of Frenchtown fleeing the expected engagement and Indian threats. One of the Kentuckians inquired as to the enemy's artillery and was told the British had two pieces "about large enough to kill a mouse."[17]

The advance had carried to within three miles of the town before the Americans were discovered by the enemy. Colonel Lewis immediately formed his force in the following combat order: The right wing, composed of the companies commanded by Captain Virgil McCracken, subaltern Lieutenant William and Ensign George M. McClary; Captain Richard Bledsoe, subalterns Ensign Morrison (acting as Lieutenant) and Ensign Thomas Chinn; Captain Richard Matson, subalterns Ensign William Nash (acting as Lieutenant) and Ensign Caldwell, the wing commanded by Colonel John Allen. The left wing, composed of the companies commanded by Captain John Hamilton, subalterns Lieutenant William H. Moore and Ensign James Heron; Captain Samuel L. Williams, subalterns Lieutenant John Higgins and Ensign Joseph Harrow; Captain Joseph Kelly, subalterns Lieutenant William McGuire and Ensign John W. Nash, the left wing commanded by Major Benjamin Graves. The center column, composed of the companies commanded by Captain Richard Hightower, of the 17th U.S. Infantry, subalterns Lieutenant Caleb H. Holder and Ensign William O. Butler (on detached service); Captain Coleman Collier, subalterns Lieutenant Story[18] and Ensign William Fleet; Captain Uriel Sebree, subalterns Lieutenant Bryan Rule and Ensign Bowles,[19] the center column under the command of Major George Madison. In the advance, commanded by Captain Bland W. Ballard, acting as Major, was placed the force made up of the companies of Captain Paschal Hickman, with subaltern Lieutenant John T. Chinn; Captain Michael Glaves,

---

[17]Thomas P. Dudley, "Battles and Massacre at Frenchtown, Michigan, January, 1813," *Western Reserve Historical Society, Historical and Archaeological Tracts, No. 1* [reprinted in *Michigan Pioneer and Historical Collections*, XXII (1893).] Hereinafter cited Dudley.

[18]Probably Thomas Story of Captain Lynn West's company.

[19]Probably Joseph Bowles of Captain Thomas Morris's company.

subaltern Lieutenant Comstock,[20] and Captain Henry James, of the 2nd Regiment, with his spies.[21]

The line of battle formed, the battalion commanders then read Colonel Lewis's orders of the day, while the men stood in the deep snow:

SOLDIERS!
Your ancient enemy is before you. The wrongs that he has inflicted upon your country are fresh in your memory. That country calls upon you this day to vindicate her honor and her interests by inflicting upon him condign punishment. In the hour of battle remember what the Patriot Orator said to you at Georgetown, "You have the double character of Americans and Kentuckians to sustain." Do so, as I feel assured you will, and all will be well.

Wm. Lewis[22]

In battle order the columns moved to within a quarter of a mile of Frenchtown before receiving enemy fire from a howitzer.[23] This first fire passed some twenty feet over the heads of the men yet produced some alarm and tension in the ranks. A second shot moved nearer, and brought from a man by the name of Strode[24] a shout of derision in the form of a cock's crowing[25] and shouts from the men, others crowing like chicken cocks, some barking like dogs and many calling out "fire away with your mouse cannon again."[26]

The whole detachment was ordered by Colonel Lewis to move forward in the direction of the enemy. This was about three o'clock in the afternoon.

[20]Probably Lyndon Comstock of Captain Nathaniel Hart's company.

[21]Colonel Lewis's official report, dated Camp at French-town, January 20, 1813, On the River-Raisin, from which account of action on this date mainly was taken. *Niles' Weekly Register*, IV (March 20, 1813), 49; Esarey (ed.), *op. cit.*, II, 319-321.

[22]B., "Recollections of the late War, the River Raisin Battle," *op. cit.*, May 7, 1833.

[23]Colonel Lewis's official report, dated Camp at French-town, January 20, 1813, *op. cit.*

[24]More than likely Stephen Strode, of Captain John Martin's company, who survived the action of January 18 but was captured January 22.

[25]B., "Recollections of the late War, the River Raisin Battle," May 7, 1833, *op. cit.*

[26]Dudley, *op. cit.*

The First Battle

Captain Bland W. Ballard, in the advance, carried the attack across the frozen but slippery River Raisin while the long roll was beat as signal for a general charge. Majors Benjamin Graves and George Madison were ordered with their battalions to possess themselves of the houses and picketing about which the enemy had collected and where they had placed their artillery.[27]

The advance wing continued across the river into the face of the British and Indians, now considered to be in strength about 500. The bank nearest the village was covered with a dense growth of cane, somewhat boggy. Captain Hickman, with the advance, had become lame during the march and was riding on horseback before his men. His horse broke through the bog frequently, floundering with its rider to the ice and bank of the river. His men replaced him each time in his seat and continued to advance. Captain Hickman was the only man hit as the Kentuckians charged up the enemy bank toward the village. He received a shot in the leg, breaking the bone, and completely disabling him.[28]

The charge carried quickly into Frenchtown, neither the incessant shower of bullets nor the picketing and fencing slowing the Americans until they had gained their objective, completely dislodging the enemy from that quarter.[29]

Colonel Lewis was at the point of congratulating his successful battalions when sudden firing about half a mile to the right brought all to the alert. Investigation revealed that Colonel John Allen, with no more than 100 men, had fallen in with the retreating enemy force after pursuing it a distance of more than half a mile. Actually the enemy had made a stand with their howitzer and small arms, covered by a chain of enclosed lots and a group of buildings.[30]

Brigade Major James Garrard, one of Lewis's aides, was immediately instructed to send Majors Graves and Madison to the enemy's rear, which offered cover in the form of a thick, bushy

[27]Colonel Lewis's official report, dated Camp at French-town, January 20, 1813, *op. cit.*
[28]*Commonwealth*, June 9, 1871.
[29]Colonel Lewis's official report, dated Camp at French-town, January 20, 1813, *op. cit.*
[30]*Ibid.*

wood of fallen timber. This force moved out at once, on the left, and diverting the enemy's attention from Colonel Allen's group, moved into positions and drew distracting fire away from Colonel Allen's men who regrouped and advanced accordingly. The British and Indians were soon driven from behind the fences and buildings and began a delaying action as they moved deeper into the woods behind them.

The fire now became intense on the right wing as the fighting became close. As leaders were wounded, the Kentuckians reverted to Indian-fighting tactics, every man for himself. After Captain Hickman had been taken to one of the houses in Frenchtown to have his wound dressed, the men under him were commanded by Lieutenant Francis Chinn. He, too, was wounded and after that the men fought pretty much on their own.[31]

The undernourished Kentuckians soon tired. They were above reproach in effort, however, and were able to keep the enemy moving in retreat a distance of not less than two miles, every foot of the way under a continual charge. The battle in the woods continued until late at night, the Americans returning the enemy's fire by directing their shots at the flashes made by the British and Indian guns.[32]

As pointed out by Colonel Lewis in his official report of the action, "It would be an almost endless task to particularize all who distinguished themselves; for as all had an opportunity to do so, there was none but what accepted it." [33]

One example could be recounted. After the enemy had been driven from the village and halted for a stand at the wood, it was found that a close fence crossed intervening ground about two hundred yards short of the wood, and that is was necessary to secure it in order to cover the advance of the column. In this column was Ensign William O. Butler, who with others saw that the Indians were bent on securing this vital defense position. Taking ten or fifteen men, Butler led them on a dash for the fence. Both Indians and Kentuckians were running directly toward each other, each group hoping to be first at the fence and thus in command of the action. Butler's unit fortunately reached it

[31]*Commonwealth*, June 9, 1871.
[32]*Ibid.*
[33]Colonel Lewis's official report, dated Camp at French-town, January 20, 1813, *op. cit.*

The First Battle

first and without adequate cover the Indians were forced to retreat, leaving the Americans free to advance and carry the attack on their own terms.[34]

The detachment was drawn off in good order and moved back to Frenchtown where it encamped in quarters lately occupied by the enemy. After roll call it was found that the American loss had been twelve killed and fifty-five wounded, one of whom had died by the time Colonel Lewis wrote his official report on January 20. The dead, because of darkness, had been left on the field. The wounded were placed in the houses within the village.

The day had been carried with great success. The American flag had been raised on the soil which twenty-four years later, to the month, was to be the great state of Michigan. British losses were determined as approximately 30 killed, 50 wounded, and three taken prisoner.[35] The latter were two Canadian militiamen and one Potawatomi Indian.[36] Captured as well were about thirty barrels of His Majesty's flour, 2,000 pounds of beef and a considerable quantity of wheat.[37]

The day had been planned otherwise by the British at Frenchtown. January 18 was the anniversary of the birth of "old Queen Charlotte" and arrangements had been made for a grand ball in the village. Abundant food had been prepared and the ladies of Frenchtown had been invited.[38] British accounts of the day, however, corroborated Colonel Lewis's report.

... the [Americans] are in Possession of Frenchtown, on the River Raisin, 26 miles from Detroit, after experiencing every resistance that Major Reynolds of the Essex Militia had it in his power to make, with a three Pounder well served and directed by Bombadier Kitson of

[34]*Kentucky Yeoman Extra*, n. d. "The Democratic Candidate for Governor and Lieutenant Governor of Kentucky [Colonel William O. Butler and William S. Pilcher]."

[35]*Niles' Weekly Register*, X (May 4, 1816), 154-155.

[36]Martin D. Hardin to Shelby, Camp at Hull's Crossing of the Rapids, January 21, 1813, *Reporter*, Feb. 13, 1813.

[37]*Ibid.*

[38]Thomas Smith to W. W. Worsley, Camp Frenchtown, River Raisin, 18 miles from His Majesty's Fort, January 21, 1813. Draper MSS, Kentucky Papers, 5CC28.

the Royal Artillery, and the Militia men, whom he had well trained to the use of it. The Retreat of the Gun was covered by a brave band of Indians who made the enemy pay dearly for what he obtained.[39]

Colonel Lewis was extravagant in praise for his troops, pointing out to General Winchester that they had indeed supported the double character of Americans and Kentuckians and that "so steady and composed were our men in this assault that while the Enemy were killed or drove from the houses not a woman or child was hurt."[40]

The wearied detachment, bearing its wounded, moved back into Frenchtown under cover of darkness to prepare camp. Colonel Lewis encamped his men on the night of the battle in the most thickly settled part of the village, in the shape of a half-moon, the extremity of either end of which line rested on the river bank. This bank being very high it was determined that there existed no necessity for soldiers along the line. The camp was fortified as well as garden pickets and fence rails could make it.[41]

This night, after immediately sending an express, with the captured Potawatomi, to General Winchester at the Rapids, Colonel Lewis permitted his men the rewards of a successful and hard won engagement. The British stores were set upon and the men enjoyed rations more extravagant than any tasted since leaving home. All was "joy and gladness with both Officers and Soldiers. There were all the conveniencies and luxuries of an old settlement, cider and Apples in abundance and to a soldier, who has been out four or five months, in an Indian campaign, the sight of a woman is not the most uncomely object that can be conceived of." [42]

The next day, January 19, a detail of one hundred men was sent out to search the battlefield and bring in the dead. One of this detail was Joseph Clark, of Frankfort, who recalled in 1871:

[39]Colonel Henry Proctor to Major General Sheaffe, Sandwich, January 25, 1813, *Michigan Pioneer and Historical Collections*, XV (1889), 227.

[40]Colonel Lewis's official report, dated Camp at French-town, January 20, 1813, *op. cit.*

[41]*Commonwealth*, May 28, 1833.

[42]E. Whittlesey to his wife, River at the Crossings of Hull's Road, January 25, 1813, *Western Reserve Historical Society . . . Tracts, No. 92*, pp. 100-101; Darnall, *op. cit.*, pp. 49-50.

The First Battle

"All the men found—thirteen in number—were scalped and stripped of their clothing, their bodies frozen stiff, and presenting a horrible and sad sight. One of the dead only—a young Simpson or Shelby—escaped the scalping and stripping. Another had evidently been tomahawked and scalped while alive, as one of his fingers was cut off while he was protecting his head from the impending blow. The dead were brought to the village and decently buried." [43] All were buried, without coffins, in a common grave.[44]

General Winchester, meantime, having received news from Colonel Lewis's express of the successful action on the 18th, at once sent Harrison intelligence of the victory.[45] This news Harrison received late on the same day and the following day promptly advised the Secretary of War of the successful action, noting that "Genl. Winchester very properly marched yesterday with two hundred and fifty men to reinforce him [Colonel Lewis] and take the command. . . . It is absolutely necessary to maintain the position at the River Raisin and I am assembling Troops as fast as possible for the purpose." Harrison added, however, that he feared "nothing but that the enemy may overpower Genl. Winchester" before he could send him a sufficient reinforcement.[46]

General Winchester reached Frenchtown on the morning of January 20. "The town, lying on the north side of the river, was picketed on three sides—the longest, facing the north and making a front," he recalled after returning from his subsequent captivity. "Within these pickets, Colonel Lewis's corps was found. Not thinking the position elegible, nor the pickets sufficient defense against artillery, I would have retreated, but for the wounded, of whom there were fifty-five." [47]

Colonel Wells at the head of his 250 regulars arrived about three o'clock of the same afternoon,[48] and was directed to encamp

[43]*Commonwealth*, June 9, 1871.
[44]*Ibid.*, May 28, 1833.
[45]Winchester to Harrison, Camp Miami Rapids, January 19, 1813, Esarey (ed.), *op. cit.*, II, 315-316.
[46]Harrison to Secretary of War, Head Quarters N. W. Army, Miami Rapids, January 20, 1813, *ibid.*, II, 316-317.
[47]Winchester, quoted in Armstrong, *op. cit.*, I, 199; McAfee, *op. cit.*, p. 228.
[48]Lossing, *op. cit.*, p. 353; Atherton, *op. cit.*, p. 41; *Commonwealth*, May 28, 1833.

on the right of Colonel Lewis, in an open field, immediately without the picketing—the traditional position dictated by military rule. "The officers having viewed and laid off a piece of ground for a camp and breastworks, resolved it was too late to remove and erect fortifications that evening," reported Elias Darnell.[49]

Meanwhile at his home in Frenchtown, Jacques Lascelle was dictating a letter to his well educated daughter, Nannette. The note outlined precisely the situation of the Americans, Colonel Lewis with 500 men at one point, and 300 at another; it suggested that by getting a striking force between the Americans the latter "could be defeated in detail." George Blue Jacket, Lascelle's brother-in-law, bore the letter to General Proctor at Malden, the fate of Winchester's little army moving with him through the night.[50]

The night of January 20 was one of long-awaited joy and relaxation for the men, of considerable anxiety for Colonel Lewis and his officers. General Harrison, they knew, was rushing reinforcements but the advance had carried ever deeper into enemy territory and they realized that an attack was almost a certainty. Too, as Winchester properly observed to Harrison, the ground held was anything but favorable for defense. The Kentuckians were on level land close to Hull's Road, along which the enemy might advance easily with artillery. The frozen Raisin River with its protective bank lay behind them, and worse, Colonel Wells's detachment had done little if anything to strengthen its position in the open field beyond the picketing. General Winchester, with his young son, had recrossed the river and taken up headquarters at the house of Colonel Francis Navarre, nearly half a mile from any part of the encampment.

By January 21 a reinforcement of some 200 under Major W. W. Cotgreave and a second group of 350 under Colonel John Andrews were making their slow and painful way across the ice toward Frenchtown to strengthen General Winchester's position.

To determine Winchester's immediate plans and opinions of the situation, Harrison sent his courier, Captain Nathaniel Hart, brother-in-law of Henry Clay and captain of the Lexington Light Infantry Company, then mostly at Frenchtown, forward to the

[49]Darnall, *op. cit.*, p. 50.
[50]Lyman C. Draper, "Biographical Field Notes," *Quarterly Bulletin of The Historical Society of Northwestern Ohio*, V (Oct., 1933), [84].

The First Battle

Raisin with a request for this information. At the same time he sent a note to Winchester containing the advice "to hold the ground we had got at any rate."[51]

Prior to Hart's arrival, however, two or three Frenchmen from the north brought word to Winchester that the enemy in strength was pressing toward Frenchtown and that an attack surely would be forthcoming. ". . . knowing nothing of the kind or extent of the preparation made or making, what he [the Frenchman] brought was thought to be only conjecture, and such as led to a belief, that it would be some days before Proctor would be ready to do anything," was Winchester's reaction to this news.[52]

The arrival of Captain Hart, in company with Major McClanahan and Surgeons Irvine and Montgomery, accordingly found the officers behind the pickets in a state of extreme anxiety. Sensing at once the alarm of the Kentuckians, obviously ill prepared for an attack by possibly superior numbers and separated by half a mile from active command, Hart decided upon a hurried message to General Harrison warning him of the situation and the possible outcome both for the troops and the French who had aided in the taking of Frenchtown.[53]

His courier was Colonel Samuel Wells, commander of the 17th U.S. Infantry, still encamped in the open fields.

Various contemporary writers are bitter in their accounts of how and why Colonel Wells left the camp at Frenchtown this fatal sundown of January 21. The Reverend Thomas Parker Dudley in his account of the massacre of the 22nd later wrote:

On the 21st morning Wells asked leave to return to the camp, which he had recently left, for his baggage. General Winchester declined giving leave, informing Wells that we would certainly and very soon be attacked. In the afternoon Wells again applied for leave to return for his baggage. General Winchester again replied, 'The spies bring intelligence that the enemy have reached Stony Creek, five miles from here. If you are disposed to leave your command in the immediate vicinity of the enemy, when a battle is certain, you can go.' Wells left and went back.[54]

[51]Cleaves, *op. cit.*, p. 141; Armstrong, *op. cit.*, I, 200.
[52]Armstrong, *op. cit.*, I., 199-200.
[53]Cleaves, *op. cit.*, pp. 140-141.
[54]Dudley, *op. cit., Michigan Pioneer and Historical Collections*, XXII (1893), 437-438.

Other accounts were quite different, however, and inasmuch as Wells was selected by Captain Hart to bear his message to Harrison, his departure on the eve of battle would have been in order.

Colonel Wells, on the evening before the battle [of January 22], learned from some of the French inhabitants that the enemy would attack that night. He immediately communicated this information to General Winchester, and begged him to order the cartridges to be distributed among the men,[55] the encampment to be formed in line of battle, and every preparation immediately taken to fortify it; but unfortunately the General could not admit the necessity of these measures, and spoke contemptuously of an attack from the Indians, who had been routed only a few days before. At this time the General was quartered three fourths of a mile from the camp, and most of the other officers at other houses along the river. Colonel Wells could not prevail upon his excellency to take any of these precautionary measures, and being alarmed for the exposed situation of the camp, immediately returned with all possible speed, accompanied by Capt. Langham,[56] to the Rapids, for a reinforcement, and meeting a detachment previously dispatched by Gen. Harrison, had returned to within a few miles of the River Raisin when news of the defeat reached them.[57]

At any rate it was Colonel Wells who left the camp at Raisin, about sundown, with Captain Hart's message to Harrison. There is no evidence to indicate, however, that the Colonel, before leaving, communicated to his men the same arguments for strengthening their position in the open field. The message read:

My dear Sir: Colonel Wells will give you the news we have received. The importance of holding this post I know you have fully weighed. In the event of its loss, the people having taken an active part against the British, will be subject to utter ruin—perhaps scalped.

The officers here are truly desirous of seeing you here, if it were

[55]It is possible that the men at this time had only ten cartridges each. See General Winchester's "Orderly Book," date of Camp No. 3, Miami, 17th Novm. 1812.

[56]Probably Captain Angus Lewis Langham of the 19th U. S. Infantry.

[57]Letter to the Editor of *Niles'*, dated Chillicothe, February 3, 1813, *Niles' Weekly Register*, III (Feb. 13, 1813), p. 382.

even for a day. Many things ought to be done, which you only know how to do properly. Such, however, is the opinion they entertain of you.

With great respect, yours,
Nathaniel G. S. Hart[58]

As the cold January sun went down the men settled into a night of dread and wakefulness. Guards, as usual, were placed "but as it was extremely cold, no picket guard was placed upon the road by which the enemy was expected to advance."[59]

The night, however, passed without alarm. Commanding within the pickets with a force of some 600 men, were Colonels Lewis and Allen, Major Madison, James Garrard, the Brigade Inspector, John McCalla, acting adjutant of the detachment, Pollard Keene, Quarter Master, Surgeon John Todd, and Captains Coleman A. Collier, Uriel Sebree, Samuel Williams, Joseph Kelly, Richard Bledsoe, Richard Hightower, James C. Price, John H. Woolfolk, Nathaniel G. S. Hart, Virgil McCracken, John Simpson, and Major Benjamin Graves. Command of the regulars of the 17th U.S. Infantry, encamped on the right of the picketing, had devolved upon Major Elijah McClanahan. With him were Captains James Meade, Robert Edwards and his Surgeon, Alexander Montgomery.[60]

As the night deepened those who could slept. The surgeons moved through the houses of Frenchtown tending fires, administering to the wounded. And in his quarters Colonel John Allen penned his last letter, concluding with the observation: "We meet the enemy tomorrow. I trust that we will render a good account of ourselves, or that I will never live to tell the tale of our disgrace."[61]

[58]Moses Dawson, *A Historical Narrative of the Civil and Military Services of Major-General William H. Harrison* (Cincinnati, 1824), p. 456.

[59]Atherton, *op. cit.*, p. 42; "Neither night-patrole, nor night-pickets were ordered by me, from a belief, that both were matters of routine and in constant use," Winchester quoted in Armstrong, *op. cit.*, I, 200.

[60]*Niles' Weekly Register*, V (Oct. 23, 1813), 125; IV (Apr. 3, 1813), 83; *Reporter*, May 4, 1813.

[61]Thomas Marshall Green in his *Historic Families of Kentucky* . . . (Cincinnati: Robert Clarke & Co., 1889), p. 246, states that this letter was written to Allen's old preceptor and friend, Judge Archibald Stuart, and that it was then in the possession of the Judge's son, the Honorable A. H. H. Stuart, of Staunton. Investigation among the papers of the latter, however, failed to produce the complete text of the letter.

V

THE SECOND BATTLE

NEWS OF Colonel Lewis's victory of January 18 reached British Amherstburg or Fort Malden almost immediately and during the course of the same night Colonel Henry A. Proctor made plans for an instant advance upon the captured positions before the Americans would have had time to fortify them.

Squire Reynolds, of Amherstburg, whose reminiscences later furnished historians much material for their studies of the war in Canada, recalled of that night:

> On the 18th Jan., 1813, being the anniversary of old Queen Charlotte's birthday, all the young fellows on the coast side—les jeunes gens de la cote—combined with the military to give a ball. We had assembled at Mrs. Drapers' Tavern, here in Amherstburg, and the lads and lasses were full of dance and fun, when in walked Colonel St. George equipped for the field.
>
> 'My boys,' said he, in a loud voice, 'you must prepare to dance to a different tune; the enemy is upon us, and we are going to surprise them. We shall take the route about four in the morning, so get ready at once.'
>
> Of course there was some confusion and surprise, but I believe the fellows liked the fighting as much as the dancing. The ball broke up at once, and every man was at his appointed post at the proper time. It had been very cold, but no snow had fallen. The river had taken across (?), and we started for Brownstown, four miles distant, on the ice. It was not considered strong enough to bear more than the small 4-pounders. The men marched in extended order.
>
> It appears that the General had got intelligence that General Winchester was advancing rapidly to attack Fort Malden or Detroit, and had resolved to anticipate him. The American Generals, Winchester and Harrison, were at loggerheads. Winchester, an old revolutionary officer, did not like to be superseded by Harrison, and aimed at a great blow, on his own account, before the other could come up to share the glory.[1]

The whole disposable force of the British garrison was ordered upon this march, leaving only a handful of men to occupy the Fort. Early on the morning of January 19 the British crossed

---
[1]Coffin, *op. cit.*, p. 203.

The Second Battle 63

the Detroit River opposite Amherstburg, with a body of 500 troops and militia, 800 Indians under Chief Roundhead and three 3-pounders. From vessels laid up for the season, parts of crews were brought in to serve with the artillery. There were also attached to the brigade two companies of the Newfoundland Fencibles.²

The enemy force marched throughout the days of January 19-21, and on the night of the 21st halted and bivouacked in the open air, about five miles from the American positions.

In Frenchtown all was still by this cold morning light of January 22. On the exposed right flank the regulars were burrowed deep in their blankets against the penetrating cold; behind the pickets the defenders found some measure of protection as the mist started to rise. And at least one advanced sentry turned gratefully as the beating of reveille was begun inside the garrison. It was approximately six o'clock in the morning.

The British and Indians were advancing in attack formation as the rattling of drums called the Americans to wakefulness. And listening to the drums, alone in the mist, the American sentry did not hear the enemy until reveille had finished and the rumble of enemy gun-carriages loomed before him, within musket shot.³

Even so the Kentuckians drew the first blood. The sentry "turned and fired, and hit Gates, the leading grenadier of the 41st, right through the head," recalled Squire Reynolds. "The ball went in at one ear and out of the other."⁴

The British immediately deployed to the right and left, in the open, and laid down a withering fire supported by their artillery. The Americans were ready almost as soon as the first shot had been fired, the picketed defenders gaining the most advantage inasmuch as the initial attack had been directed against

²Richardson, *op. cit.*, pp. 133-134. "At the *River au Raisin* the Potewatemys composed the Right Wing of the Army under the command of Genl. Proctor and when 300 of the Enemy under Genl. Winchester made an attempt to out flank our English Father the Potewatemys rushed upon them and cut those 300 into pieces in consequence of which our English Father gained a signal victory for the remainder of the Enemy's Army surrendered." Speech of Waindawgay at a council held at Michilimackinac October 28, 1814, between Waindawgay and Mishpawkissh Potewatemys . . . and Lieutenant Colonel McDonall commanding Michigan, in *Michigan Pioneer and Historical Collections*, XXIII (1893), 453-455.

³Coffin, *op. cit.*, p. 204.
⁴*Ibid.*

the unprepared regulars on the exposed right flank. The concentrated fire of the British artillery, using grape shot and bombs, soon took heavy toll among the regulars, who nonetheless contained the assault for about twenty minutes.[5] This same artillery, however, fortunately was disposed in a manner momentarily favorable to the Americans. "Proctor made a strange disposition of his line," wrote Squire Reynolds. "He put a gun on each flank, and advanced one gun in front of the centre, so that every ball of the enemy, which missed the gun, struck the men in the rear, and some of our own musketry hit the gunners."[6]

Forces behind the garden pickets more than held their own and it was not until after the action was fifteen or twenty minutes old that they were aware that the regulars were falling back toward the river, ostensibly to regroup under cover of the river banks. General Winchester, aroused by friendly French natives of the town, arrived on the scene of action about this time and had his attention drawn immediately to that portion of his force which had left its lines.[7] At about the same time Colonels John Allen and William Lewis, with approximately fifty men each, made a dash from behind the pickets to reinforce the regulars under Major Elijah McClanahan and attempt to stabilize their lines.[8]

[5] Captain Richard Matson in *Western Citizen*, February 13, 1813.
[6] Coffin, *op. cit.*, p. 204.
[7] Statement of captured officers in (Lexington) *Kentucky Reporter*, March 13, 1813: "The report that General Winchester, with his officers, had, the evening previous to the attack, retired after a frolic, and under the influence of liquor, and thereby incapacitated for duty, is without foundation; for my informant Robert Navarre, now living, then a young man in his twenty-first year, was aroused at midnight by his father, Colonel Francis Navarre, and remembers distinctly his father's going upstairs and arousing the General and his officers. They were somewhat bewildered, as they could distinctly hear from the battlefield the sharp crack of the rifle, reports of musketry, and the booming of cannon. The General, in haste, repaired to the barn, leaving his uniform coat behind him in the house, mounted his horse, and the two officers, by direction of Colonel Navarre, mounted the Colonel's horses and rode to the scene of battle," from Talcott E. Wing, "History of Monroe County, Michigan," in *Michigan Historical and Pioneer Collections*, IV (1881), 320-321.
[8] This force very likely was drawn from the companies of Captain Virgil McCracken and Captain Michael Glaves, and in the retreat of which, in the center, Colonel Allen was killed. See Major Elijah McClanahan's statement in *Reporter*, May 4, 1813, in which he states that Colonel Allen did not assist in rallying the right wing but conducted the retreat of the center, composed of the above named companies.

The Second Battle

The first serious American losses came with this attempted reinforcement and retreat of the regulars. Lost at the beginning of the retreat and shortly afterwards were Colonel Allen, Captains John Simpson and John M. Edmiston of the volunteers, Captains James Meade, Robert Edwards, Lieutenants Thomas C. Graves, Thomas J. Overton, of the regulars, and Doctors Alexander Montgomery and Thomas McIlvain.[9]

During the retreat of the right flank, General Winchester ordered Captain James C. Price, leader of the "Jessamine County Blues," with fifty men of his company, to bring in all the wounded and carry them beyond the reach of the Indians. This group was the first to discover that the Indians, before or during the frontal assault, had encircled the town and formed on three sides, offering as the only avenue of retreat a small lane from either side of which they could fire at will. In this trap the Jessamine county men were surrounded and cut to pieces before they could flounder through the deep snow and get away from the river. Captain Price was hit in the right shoulder by a musket ball, disabling his right arm. Almost at the same time he was attacked by three Indians. He managed to run his sword through one but was soon overpowered, killed and scalped. Eight of the company, in addition to their captain, were massacred in the lane. More than thirty escaped. William Caldwell, second in command of the Blues and later acting captain, escaped with five bullet holes in his hat and clothing, only to be captured later in the morning.[10]

Major McClanahan aided in the retreat of Captain Price and his men. "I assisted Captain Price, Captain (Michael) Glaves and others in the retreat," he stated in May, 1813. "Captain Glaves was wounded, but I succeeded in getting him off, and should have saved Captain Price also, but for the weakness of my horse."[11] The Major, Captains Glaves and Richard Matson and twenty-five to thirty privates were the only ones to escape the battle of this day.

[9]Dudley, *op. cit.*, p. 438.

[10]William Caldwell to Mrs. Mary Price, In Camp, Near Newport, Ky., February 20, 1813, in Bennett H. Young, *History of Jessamine County, Kentucky* (Louisville: Courier-Journal Job Printing Co., 1898), pp. 132-135.

[11]Major Elijah McClanahan, in *Reporter*, May 4, 1813.

Colonel John Allen, wounded in the thigh, tried unsuccessfully to halt the troops and make a stand. He had escaped about two miles when exhausted and suffering from his wound, he sat down on a log—undoubtedly preferring, as he had written, to perish rather than live to tell of the defeat. Captain Richard Bledsoe, six months after the battle, gave to the Frankfort press the most acceptable account of the manner in which Colonel Allen lost his life. While a prisoner of war at Malden and Sandwich, Captain Bledsoe became acquainted with a Huron Indian, whom he thought to be a chief, and who spoke very good English. One day the Kentuckian asked the Huron if he could tell him anything of Colonel Allen.

"Yes," the Indian answered. "He is killed. Yonder is his sword." The chief pointed to another Indian some distance off.

At the request of Captain Bledsoe the other called the Indian to them. Captain Bledsoe knew the sword well.

The chief stated that he had noticed Colonel Allen in the retreat, and seeing he was a brave man, determined to save him. He ordered his men to take the Colonel and the latter was immediately surrounded. The chief said he threw his gun across his lap and told Allen if he would surrender he should be safe. But at that instant one of the Indians, unordered, advanced on the Kentuckian, for what purpose the chief knew not. Colonel Allen faced the advancing Indian and with one stroke of his sword killed him instantly. Another Indian immediately and without orders then shot Colonel Allen. The chief attributed his death to the conduct of the warrior who advanced upon him, and spoke of the incident with regret.[12]

Lieutenant Ashton Garrett, of the 17th U. S. Infantry, with Lieutenant Francis Chinn, formed between fifteen and twenty of the retreating men and endeavored to lead them to safety. About sixty Indians soon surrounded them and Lieutenant Garrett ordered the group to ground arms. The Indians then came forward, secured the arms of the men, and at once shot them, including Lieutenant Chinn, Garrett only escaping the mas-

[12]Reported, with Frankfort, Ky., May 10, 1813, dateline in *Niles' Weekly Register*, IV (June 5, 1813), 223.

The Second Battle 67

sacre.[13] Another body of about thirty retreated safely nearly three miles when they were overtaken by the Indians and about half of them shot and tomahawked.[14]

The wounded in the houses of Frenchtown had watched from the doors and windows as their comrades had fallen back. Captain Richard Matson, who had been wounded in the first battle of January 18, did not hesitate. Leaving the hospital, some distance from the troops, he joined in the retreat. General Winchester ordered the force to recross the river, hoping there to reform and make a stand. Because of houses between them and the enemy, however, this proved impossible and the retreat was carried through the lane for about one hundred yards. On each side of the lane the Indians were continuing to take terrific toll of the running, stumbling Kentuckians. After safely negotiating some three miles of the gauntlet, the men came to a field through which those on foot passed, and those on horseback were obliged to ride around. Here Captain Matson saw General Winchester, Colonel Lewis, Dr. John Irvine, and Dr. Patrick going on, their horses greatly fatigued, and a number of Indians in close pursuit. Matson, finding Indians closing in at a distance of one hundred yards, slipped through a fence, pulled off his shoes, and running Indian fashion along the fence escaped to return to the Rapids.[15]

In another of the houses containing the wounded, a Nuvel (probably Hugh Newell of Captain Price's Company) took the gun of a wounded companion, Edward McConnell, and moved toward the enemy. Dr. Thomas C. Davis, of Frankfort, halted him, took the gun himself and went into action. This was the last time Dr. Davis was seen alive. Nuvel (or Newell) stayed

[13] In his report Garrett names him only as Lieut. Chinn. However, Lieutenant Francis Chinn, promoted from Ensign December 15, 1812, fell at Frenchtown and this unquestionably is how and where he died. Lieutenant Garrett's account of his escape and of Chinn's death was sworn to before J. H. Morton, Justice of the Peace, at Lexington, Ky., April 13, 1813, and published in *American State Papers: Documents, Legislative and Executive . . . Class V, Military Affairs*, I, 375.

[14] McAfee, *op. cit.*, p. 214.

[15] Captain Richard Matson's account was published in *The Western Citizen*, February 13, 1813. Previous accounts of the battle of January 22 note that only two officers, Major McClanahan and Captain Michael Glaves, escaped.

in the houses until the fire became too near, then he too joined the retreat and escaped.[16]

Leslie Combs, back with the army after his heroic trip through the "Black Swamp" and now in command of a small party of Videttes, moved through the frozen countryside aiding the escaped wounded and others to reach the safety of the Rapids.[17]

Probably among those helped by Combs was Private John J. Brice, of Captain Price's ill-fated company, who also made his escape by pulling off his shoes and running through the snow in his stockinged feet so as to leave tracks resembling those of an Indian's "and was the first to report the defeat and surrender to General Harrison's headquarters."[18]

After clearing the open field, General Winchester with Colonel Lewis and those on their horses were captured by the Indians.

Although the capture of General Winchester generally is attributed to Roundhead, a Wyandot chief who was leader of the Indian forces on January 22, Squire Reynolds maintained the capture was made by a drunken Indian known by the soubriquet of Brandy Jack. The General's captor took Winchester's cocked hat, coat and epaulets and donned this insignia of rank and thereafter cut a pretty figure among his friends. Brandy Jack described how the General had fired his small gun (pistol) at him while the former grunted "no good."[19] With General Winchester and Colonel Lewis was the General's son, Major James Overton, his aide, and others. All were immediately conducted to the rear and presented to Proctor.

Meantime, throughout the falling back of the right wing, which retreat carried with it the one hundred men from the pickets under Colonels Allen and Lewis, the force within the garden picket had been fighting gallantly and effectually despite the extra hazard of the Indian force which had gotten around in the rear of the position, under the bank and on the

[16]*Ibid.*
[17]*Commonwealth*, February 25, 1834.
[18]*History of Pike County, Missouri* . . . (Des Moines, Iowa: Mills and Co., 1883), pp. 226-227.
[19]Coffin, *op. cit.*, p. 204; Lyman C. Draper, "Biographical Field Notes," *Historical Society of Northwestern Ohio Quarterly Bulletin*, V (October, 1933), Note 134.

The Second Battle

same side of the river, and was picking off some of the picket defenders. Three different charges were made by the enemy against the pickets, and each shock was received with distinguished coolness and driven back.[20]

Individual heroism was attained practically by every man defending within the pickets as the battle wore on from daybreak until well into the morning. And again it was Ensign William O. Butler who drew cheers from his companions for one singular act of bravery. During the height of the battle it was discovered that the British and Indians were about to take possession of a large double barn, about one hundred and fifty yards in front of the American lines, from which vantage point they could direct fire into the pickets. When Major George Madison, senior officer left on the line, called for a volunteer to destroy the barn, young Butler secured a fire brand and in the face of enemy fire raced to the barn, reaching it safely just as some of the enemy were entering it from the rear. Finding some straw, he set it afire and retreated again into the hail of bullets directed at him. On the way back to his own lines he stopped to survey the fire, and finding it burning too slowly, returned and added fuel to the already blazing straw. When he again reached the pickets his clothes had been riddled with balls from head to foot. (After this close call from death or wounds, Butler shortly after was struck and suffered many weeks from one sharpshooter's bullet.)[21]

Behind the pickets only five had been killed and about forty wounded, compared with the heavy losses of the British and Indians who had stormed the puny defense. About eleven o'clock enemy fire slackened and shortly afterward ceased except for stray shots from Indian scouts.[22]

[20]Statements of prisoners of war on their return to Pittsburgh, reported in *Niles' Weekly Register*, IV (March 6, 1813), 10-13.

[21]*Kentucky Yeoman Extra*, n.d., p. 3. When the Montgomery County volunteers, commanded by Captain Samuel L. Williams, returned to Kentucky after captivity they were given a large public dinner at Mt. Sterling. One of the toasts of the occasion was "To James Higgins, our countryman, who volunteered under Captain Hart, who, in the action of the 22nd, undauntedly put fire to a barn, under a heavy shower of shot from the enemy, under cover of the barn—may his country reward his services," *Reporter*, April 10, 1813.

[22]Statements of prisoners of war on their return to Pittsburgh, reported in *Niles' Weekly Register*, IV (Mar. 6, 1813), 10-13, *op. cit.*

The men facing the enemy from the garden, wondering at the sudden quiet peered through holes in the fence and speculated as to the fortunes of battle. Many ate their light breakfasts, secure in the belief that they had again bested the enemy; and not knowing the fate of the right flank, were satisfied.

British historians generally agree that the picket force was right. Richardson summed up:

> The conduct of Colonel Proctor on this occasion has ever been a matter of astonishment to me, and on no one principle that I am aware of, can it be satisfactorily accounted for. The Americans were lying in their beds, undressed and unarmed, and a prompt and forward movement of the line, either would have enabled us to have taken them with the bayonet at advantage, or to have seized the intermediate close fence, forming a parapet from which they shortly afterwards so severely annoyed us. Instead of this, he commenced firing his three-pounders in answer to the alarm of the sentinels who, at length perceiving us, had rapidly discharged their muskets—thus affording them time and facility for arming and occupying the only position from which they could seriously check our advance. Resting their rifles on the breastwork by which they were covered, the Americans fought under every advantage, the dark line of troops before them serving as a point of direction, which could not fail to be perceived along the field of snow by which they were surrounded. Much execution was done among the artillery and seamen. Placed in front of the line, and singled out by (American) marksmen, the officers and men of those departments were particularly exposed, and many of the guns were abandoned from want of hands to work them. The fire of the enemy was not less galling to the troops, yet although falling at every step, they continued to advance with the utmost resolution and gallantry.... In this affair, which, if properly conducted, would have been attended by little loss to the assailants, we had 24 rank and file killed and 11 officers and 158 rank and file wounded, exclusive of sergeants whose number is not recorded.[23]

Dr. Robert Richardson, writing from Amherstburg February 7, offered about the same sentiment:

[23]Richardson, *op. cit.*, pp. 134-136; Richardson's estimate of British losses must have been taken from Proctor's official return, which lists total in action [less Indians], 597; total killed, 24; total wounded, 161. See *Michigan Historical and Pioneer Collections*, XV (1890), 237.

The Second Battle

The loss (on the British side) has been very severe, indeed ten times more than was necessary. We succeeded tis true but we have to thank the fears and want of Conduct in the Enemy, and a kind of protecting providence, much more than our own good conduct. If the Americans had been soldiers, they would have come out when our men were completely broke and nearly half of them killed and wounded, and would have taken or killed every man. I am sure two hundred men could not then have been got together, and the Americans had 450 all together.[24]

The Kentuckians in the gardens of Frenchtown knew nothing of this confusion and indecision in the enemy's lines. They only heard the quiet, always ominous after battle, and waited in what readiness they could for the next attack. Ammunition was woefully scarce and it was doubtful if there was sufficient to meet another enemy charge. The assault when it came, however, was surprisingly of a different nature.

A flag was shortly seen emerging from the enemy's lines. The men behind the pickets were enthusiastic as it neared the garden fence. The enemy was weary of the fight, and was sending a truce: they wanted permission to bury their dead and gather in their wounded. It was not until the men saw that it was their own Major James Overton who was bearing the colors did doubt enter into their calculations.

Major John McCalla, as adjutant of the picket force, bore the flag of truce out to meet Major Overton. With him was Major George Madison.[25] When the latter approached the flag he was met by Proctor who immediately demanded surrender of the picket force. Threats to burn the village and release the Indians to plunder of war followed the surrender demand. When word of this, along with news that General Winchester had

[24]R. Richardson to John Askin, Amherstburg, February 7, 1813, in *Burton Historical Records*, II, *The John Askin Papers, II, 1796-1820*, Milo M. Quaife (ed.) (Detroit: Detroit Library Commission, 1931) pp. 749-750.

[25]Statement of General McCalla at the National Convention, Soldiers of the War of 1812, Hall of Independence, Philadelphia, January 9, 1854, in *Proceedings* of the meeting, p. 19.

been captured and was ordering the surrender,²⁶ reached the men watching from the garden "it was like a shock of lightning from one end of the line to the other. A number declared that they would never submit, let the consequences be what they might."²⁷

A French inhabitant of the town, Medard Labadie, who had been captured by two Wyandot Indians and held near the scene of action later testified: "The battle terminated after the sun was some hours high, not far from 11 o'clock A.M. by the surrender of the American forces that then remained on the ground." He saw the flag hoisted by the British sent to the American force and saw it pass three times to the men behind the pickets before the surrender.²⁸

The flag evidently was returned to the pickets that the men might hear the terms of capitulation. At least once Madison went back to the houses to ask the opinions of Major Graves and several other wounded officers who were watching the tense proceedings. Major Madison had at first observed that "it has been customary for the Indians to massacre the wounded prisoners and that he could not agree to any capitulation which General Winchester might direct, unless the safety and protection of his men were secured."²⁹

Colonel Proctor received this with haughtiness. "Sir, do you mean to dictate for me?"

---

[26] "I understood that our troops were defending themselves in a state of desperation, and was informed by the commanding officer of the enemy, that he would afford them an opportunity of surrendering themselves prisoners of war; to which I acceded. I was the more ready to make the surrender from being assured, that unless done quickly, the buildings adjacent would be immediately set on fire, and that no responsibility would be taken for the conduct of the savages, who were then assembled in great numbers," General Winchester to Secretary of War, dated Malden, January 23, 1813, in *Niles' Weekly Register*, IV (March 6, 1813), 9-10.

[27] Atherton, *op. cit.*, p. 52.

[28] Statement of Medard Labadie, sworn to before C. S. Todd, February 11, 1813, at the Camp at the Foot of the Rapids, in *American State Papers*, XII, *Military Affairs*, I, 371; also in *Niles' Weekly Register*, V (Oct. 23, 1813), 125.

[29] Atherton, *op. cit.*, p. 53.

The Second Battle

"No," replied Madison, "I mean to dictate for myself—and we prefer to sell our lives as dearly as possible, rather than be massacred in cold blood."[30]

Major Madison, however, was left little choice. Ammunition was nearly exhausted, the enemy was concentrating his light forces on the right and left, determined to fire on the village with his artillery and, more importantly, assurances were given that if driven to that extremity no responsibility could be assumed for the conduct of the Indians who then surrounded the Kentuckians in great numbers. A retreat on the part of the latter was impossible and no alternative remained but to surrender or to suffer the wounded to be fired on and possibly massacred.[31]

Surrender terms, after Madison's stand, were honorable as stated and agreed upon both by Madison and the British. All private property should be respected; sleds would be sent the following morning to transport the American wounded to Amherstburg—and that in the meantime the wounded would be protected by guards. Side arms of the officers, it was promised, would be restored to those officers at Malden.[32]

Proctor's promises were questioned immediately afterward when the Indians, in prompt violation of the articles of capitulation, crowded around the Kentuckians and began plundering their property. Madison at once appealed to Colonel Proctor to keep the savages off.

"The Indians are fierce and unmanageable," the British officer answered, "*it cannot be done.*"

"If you cannot disperse them, I will," Madison replied, and ordered his men to shoulder arms. Proctor, fearing the order to 'charge bayonet' would follow, waved his sword and the Indians instantly withdrew.[33]

The surrender was concluded quickly to the accompaniment of constant urging for speed on the part of the British. "Three hundred and eighty-four of our men who remained behind the

[30]*Ibid.*

[31]Statement of captured officers, in *Reporter*, March 13, 1813.

[32]Atherton, *op. cit.*, pp. 53-54.

[33]Reported in *Kentucky Gazette*, reprinted in *Niles' Weekly Register*, IV (April 10, 1813), 98.

garden fence, exclusive of non-commissioned officers and those bearing commissions, were surrendered as prisoners of war."[34]

The men marched out of the pickets "in heat and bitterness of spirit," and grounded their arms. Those of the wounded who could walk were ordered into line with the picket force. Dr. John Todd and his mate, Dr. Gustavus M. Bower, the two surviving surgeons, were ordered to remain in charge of the non-movable wounded in the houses at Frenchtown.[35] Captain William Elliott, in charge of the British Indians, was left with three interpreters to guard the wounded until sleds came for them on the morning following.[36]

The anxiety of the British to quit the scene and be off to their own lines was evidenced at every turn, and of concern even to the British soldiers. Apparently Proctor had received intelligence of Harrison's nearness with reinforcements. "Proctor got alarmed," according to Squire Reynolds, "and ordered a retreat. This was all right, but there was no need to hurry about it. . . . Proctor was greatly blamed by us [for leaving the American wounded with insufficient guard] though he was made Major-General, and got the thanks of the Lower Canadian Parliament. He need not have retired so precipitately. Why, he left his own dead and wounded, including Colonel St. George, hit in three places."[37]

At any rate the American prisoners of war, the hale as well as the walking wounded, were hurried northward as soon as lines could be formed. They were not a pretty sight. One British observer later wrote:

> The appearances of the American prisoners captured at Frenchtown were miserable to the last degree. They had the air of men to whom cleanliness was a virtue unknown, and their squalid bodies were covered by habiliments that had evidently undergone every change of season, and were arrived at the last stage of repair. It has already been remarked that it was in the depth of winter; but scarcely an individual was in possession of a great coat or cloak, and few of them wore garments of wool of any description. They still retained

[34]Statement of captured officers, *Reporter*, March 13, 1813.
[35]Darnall, *op. cit.*, p. 56.
[36]Dudley, *op. cit.*, p. 439; Atherton, *op. cit.*, p. 58.
[37]Coffin, *op. cit.*, pp. 205-206.

The Second Battle 75

their summer dress, consisting of cotton stuff of various colors, shaped into frocks, and descending to the knee; their trousers were of the same material. They were covered with slouched hats, worn bare by constant use, beneath which their long hair fell matted and uncombed over their cheeks; and these, together with the dirty blankets wrapped around their loins to protect them against the inclemency of the season, and fastened by broad leathern belts, into which were thrust axes and knives of an enormous length, gave them an air of wildness and savageness. . . . The only distinction between the garb of the officers and that of the soldier was, that the one, in addition to his sword, carried a short rifle instead of a long one, while a dagger, often curiously worked and of some value, supplied the place of the knife."[38]

Those of the wounded who could move to the doors and windows watched their companions marched off. "They braved it off as well as might have been expected," wrote wounded William Atherton. "Some looked a little dejected—others joked and laughed. One, who had not yet fallen into the ranks, was standing upon a stile-block, and said to the English: 'Well, you have taken the greatest set of game cocks that ever came from Kentucky.' "[39]

It was a solemn and to many a farewell parting. The men of wounded Captains Paschal Hickman's and Nathaniel Hart's companies hailed their officers as they were herded off. Brothers and in some instances fathers and sons were parted, the one going to the comparative safety of British prisoner of war camps, the other left to the doubtful state of security in Frenchtown.

After the conquerors and the conquered had departed all was suddenly and ominously quiet at Frenchtown. An occassional Indian prowled through the houses seeking plunder, yet manifesting no hostility.

As the afternoon waned into early winter twilight the uneasiness of the wounded and their caretakers began to increase. General Harrison, they felt, should be well on his way to the Raisin by this time, but his arrival was nowhere evident or truthfully expected. Captain Elliott with his three interpreters formed the only guard and it must have been apparent to all that the

[38]Richardson, *op. cit.*, p. 140.
[39]Atherton, *op. cit.*, p. 54.

wounded were eagerly looking for the first hint of Harrison's entry into Frenchtown. And when night fell Elliott, after assuring his former room-mate and friend, Captain Hart, that all would be well when the sleds arrived in the morning, quietly slipped away and was seen no more by the Kentuckians. He even took wounded Major Graves's horse for a more speedy getaway.

This night following the battle of January 22 was a fearful one both for the Kentucky wounded and the inhabitants of Frenchtown. It was known that Proctor had promised his Indian allies a victory "frolic" at Stony Creek, only six miles distant from the Raisin River. That these Indians, after hours of drunken celebration, might think of the wounded prisoners at Frenchtown and decide to return was a thought uppermost in every man's mind.

Sleep virtually was impossible for those not actually suffering from wounds. Captain Hickman and others not capable of attending themselves talked quietly with Doctors Todd and Bower, trying to encourage each other that the morning indeed would bring sleds and safe transportation to the British camps and out of reach of the Indians.

And in one of the houses shielding the wounded from the raw winter night young William Orlando Butler sought to put on paper his confused and anguished thoughts:

A NIGHT VIEW OF THE BATTLE OF RAISIN,
JANY. 22nd, 1813

Written on the field by Ensign William O. Butler

The Battle's o'er, the din is past!
Night's mantle on the field is cast
The moon with Sad and pensive beam
Hangs sorrowing o'er the bloody Stream
The Indian yell is heard no more
And Silence broods on Erie's shore
O! What an hour is this to tread,
The field on which our warriors bled.
To raise the wounded chieftan's crest
Or warm with Tears his icy breast
To treasure up his last command

The Second Battle

And bear it to his native land
It may one ray of Joy impart,
To the fond Mother's bleeding heart
Or for a moment, it may dry
The tear drop in the widow's eye!
Vain hope away! the widow ne'er
Her Warrior's dying wish shall hear
The zephyr bears no feeble sigh
No stragling chieftan meets the eye
Sound is his Sleep on Erie's wave
Or Raisin's waters are his grave.
Then muffle the cold funeral string
And give the Harp to sorrow's hand
For sad's the dirge the muse must sing
Fallen are the Flowers of the land
How many Hopes lie buried here?
The Father's joy, the Mother's pride
The Country's boast, the Foeman's fear
In wildered havoc side by side
Of all the young and blooming train
Who to the combat rushed amain
How few shall mix in fight again?
How many strew the fatal plain?
O! gentle moon one ray of light
Throw on the dusky face of Night!
And give to view each gallant form
That sunk beneath the morning storm
The murky cloud has passed away!
The moon beams on the waters play:
Upon their brink a soldier lay
His eye was dim, his visage pale
And like a stranded vessel's sail
His red locks wanton'd in the gale.
It was the gay, the gallant Mead!
In peace, mild as the setting beam
That guides at Eve the wilder'd stream
In war the fiery battle Steed.
The foe no more shall shun his arm
His mirth no more the ear shall charm
Yet o'er his low and silent grave
The Laurel fresh and green shall wave.

*And who is that so pale and low
Stretched on his Bier of Bloody snow
Beside the waters silent flow?
The fire of his eye is gone
The ruddy glow of his cheeks has flown
Yet sweet in death his corpse appears
Smooth is his brow and few his years.
For the sweet youth the sigh shall start
From a fond Mother's anxious heart
For thee some Virgin's cheek shall feel
At mid-night hour the tear drop steal
And playmates of your childhood hour
Pour o'er your grave youth's generous shower.
O! could modest merit save
Its dear possessor from the grave
Thy corpse Montgomery ne'er had lain
Upon this wild unhaloed plain
But what were modest merit here
Or what were Friendship's pleading tear
The fiend that laid that flower low
Smiled as he hurl'd the fatal dart
And saw with pride the life blood flow
That warmed a young and generous heart
Here sleep sweet youth! tho far away
From home, and friends, thy relicks lay
Yet oft on Fancy's pinions borne
Friendship shall seek thy lowly urn
Spring shall thine icy Sheet untwine
And shroud thee with the roseate vine:
Here shall the streamlet gently flow
Here shall the zephyrs softly blow
Here shall the wild Flower love to bloom
And shed its fragrance round thy tomb
Here shall the wearied wild bird rest
Here shall the ring-Dove build her nest;
And win from every passer by
With notes of saddest melody
A Tear for young Montgomery.
Close by his side young McIlvain
Lay stretched along the bloody plain
Upon his visage smoothe and mild*

The Second Battle

Death calmly sat and sweetly smiled:
Tis thus an Infant sinks to rest
In quiet on its mother's breast
When no rude thoughts its mind employs
To damp its present or its future Joy:
Yet seem'd his eye of tender blue
Still wet with pity's pearly due!
Yes Pity was his better part
Pity and Friendship form'd his heart
And ne'er was heart so good and kind
Accompanied by such noble mind;
No more the sentry from his post
While all the camp in sleep is lost
Shall see him by the sick man's side
Nursing life's feebly ebbing tide
No more the soldier's latest breath
Shall bless him on his bed of death
Yet shall his cold and timeless Bier
Be mourn'd by many a veteran's tear
Oh! Pitying Moon! Withdraw thy light
And leave the world in murkiest night!
For I have seen too much of Death,
Too much of this dark fatal heath
Here Graves and Allen meet the eye
And Simpson's giant form is nigh
And Edmiston a Warrior old
And Hart the boldest of the bold.
These and their brave compatriot band
Ask the sedate Historian's hand.
Mine, only strews the fading Flower
That Mem'ry culls from Friendship's bower
But His, shall twine the Deathless Bays
That fairer grows through future days.
                                Orlando

(From original manuscript copy, Kentucky Historical Society)

VI

THE MASSACRE

AFTER LONG, uncertain hours of waiting the wounded in the houses of Frenchtown at length saw an overcast dawn begin to light the windows. Elias Darnell, Thomas Pollard and others who though not wounded in either battle had remained with the helpless, began at first light to prepare their companions for the promised sleds which would transport them to Malden and away from the constant dread of the Indians.

Dr. John Todd had been up nearly all night attending the men. About an hour after daylight he saw the interpreters suddenly leave camp. About the same time the first groups of Indians appeared in the town.[1]

The savages might have had some whiskey before coming to Frenchtown yet throughout this morning of January 23, 1813, they exhibited no manifestations of drunkenness. Dr. Todd, in dire need of spirits for the gravely wounded, had exhausted every possible source hours before. "Whiskey," stated Dr. Todd, "was not the cause of the massacre. Their deliberate pilfering, and their orderly conduct throughout was not such as would be expected from drunken Indians.[2]

---

[1]Statement of John Todd, M.D., dated Lexington, Ky., May 2, 1813, in *American State Papers, Military Affairs*, I, 372-373.
Canadians of Frenchtown agreed that the Indians had access to whiskey either before or during the massacre. An "old log building . . . was occupied by Colonel John Anderson as a fur and Indian trading post, liberally supplied with goods adapted to the wants of Indians, together with an abundant supply of 'fire water.' When the news reached him of the capture of General Winchester and his forces, knowing full well the barbarous habits and customs of the savages, especially when under the influence of liquor, he hurried to the cellar of his store, where his liquors were stored, and knocked in the heads of his whiskey barrels, and then concealed himself under the plates of a neighboring barn for nearly two days. The Indians burst in the door, ransacked his store, then prostrated themselves on their breasts in the cellar, and filled themselves with whiskey. When besotted, drunk, and wild, they repaired to the residence of Colonel Anderson, and, with the most unearthly yells and whoops, emptied the scalps they had gathered in bags on the parlor floor, and, dancing around the room, slapped the bleeding scalps against and bespattering and disfiguring the walls and ceiling." *Michigan Historical and Pioneer Collections*, IV (1881), 322.
[2]*Ibid.*

The Massacre

It is more probable that the British assertion of retaliation cannot be discarded entirely. One contemporary English writer cited the killing of an Indian by the Americans during the battle of January 18 when the latter "tore him literally to pieces, so exasperating the Indians that they refused burial of the Americans killed on the 22nd."[3] And Thomas Monks, a private in Captain Hart's company, told in 1844 how he had cut a "razor strop" from the back of an Indian when escaping the battle of the 22nd of January.[4]

At any rate their sudden appearance in Frenchtown this early January morning foretold nothing but evil for the Americans.

Between the hours of nine and ten o'clock in the morning, after approximately one to two hundred Indians had entered the town,[5] they headed for the houses from which the wounded were watching their every move.

Inasmuch as many of the survivors of this massacre were shortly after caused to prepare or to dictate affidavits relative to the affair, eyewitness accounts of the wholesale slaughter have been preserved. These accounts by those present in Frenchtown on that day narrate far better than could the present investigator the events that transpired between sunup and mid-afternoon of January 23, 1813.

Thomas Parker Dudley occupied with Major Benjamin Graves, Captains Nathaniel Hart, Paschal Hickman and others a house which had been used as a tavern. Many years later he wrote:

> Pretty soon they came crowding into the room where we were in which there was a bureau, two beds, a chair or two and perhaps a small table. They forced the drawers of the bureau, which were filled with towels, table cloths, shirts, pillow slips, &c. About this time Major Graves and Captain Hart left the room. The Indians took the bed clothing, ripped open the bed tick, threw out the feathers, and apportioned the ticks to themselves. They took the overcoat, close-bodied coat, hat and shoes from the writer.

[3]John Strachan, D.D., to Thomas Jefferson, York, January 30, 1815, in Coffin, *op. cit.*, p. 283.
[4]C. Frank Dunn Collection, "Book 111-33," MSS at Kentucky Historical Society.
[5]Statement of Joseph Robert, February 4, 1813, in *American State Papers, Military Affairs,* I, 368.

When they turned to leave the room, just as he turned, the Indians tomahawked Captain Hickman in less than six feet from me. I went out on a porch, next the street, when I heard voices in a room at a short distance, went into the room where Captain Hart was engaged in conversation with the interpreter.

He asked: 'What do the Indians intend to do with us.'

The reply was: 'They intend to kill you.'

Hart rejoined: 'Ask liberty of them for me to make a speech to them before they kill us.'

The interpreter replied: 'They can't understand.'

'But,' said Hart, 'You can interpret for me.'

The interpreter replied: 'If we undertook to interpret for you, they will as soon kill us as you.'

A few minutes after leaving the room, where I had met Hart and the interpreter, and while standing in the snow eighteen inches deep, the Indians brought Captain Hickman out on the porch, stripped of clothing except a flannel shirt, and tossed him out on to the snow within a few feet of us, after which he breathed once or twice and expired. While standing in the yard, without coat, hat or shoes, Major Graves approached me in charge of an Indian, and asked if I had been taken. I answered no. He proposed that I should go along with the Indian who had taken him. I replied 'No, if you are safe I am satisfied.' He passed on and I never saw him afterwards.

While standing in the snow two or three Indians approached me at different times, and I made signs that the ball I received was still in my shoulder. They shook their heads, leaving the impression that they designed a more horrid death for me. I felt that it would be a mercy to me if they would shoot me down at once, and put me out of my misery. About this time I placed my hand under my vest, and over the severe wound I had received, induced thereto by the cold, which increased my suffering.[6]

Dr. Todd, along with the wounded in the room he had occupied, had been stripped as the Indians systematically moved from man to man. He said five months later:

The room was so crowded with Indians and Captain Hart's wound, already painful, being injured by the Indians, I conveyed him to an adjoining house which had been plundered and was empty,

[6]Dudley, *op. cit.*, p. 441.

The Massacre

where I met the Indian who on the previous day had requested that the interpreters should be left, and he knew my rank. He inquired why the surgeons were left, and why the wounded were left? I replied, it was the wish of Colonel Proctor we should remain until the morning. He shook his head significantly, and replied they were damned rascals, or we would have been taken off the preceding day. The Indian informed me every individual would be killed, and requested me to be quiet, for the chiefs were then in council, and 'may be' only the wounded would be killed.

Captain Hart offered him $100 to take him to Malden. He replied, 'you are too badly wounded.'

While we were conversing, one of the wounded was tomahawked at our feet. Shortly after, the Indian returned and told me I was a prisoner, and must go. I was taken by the Indian to the house I had left, and there discovered that Captain Hickman and two others had, in my absence, been tomahawked, scalped and stripped.[7]

Captain John H. Woolfolk, General Winchester's secretary, had been in the house reserved for the officers and after being claimed as prisoner by an Indian was placed on a horse just beyond the house. "Seven or eight Indians were near the house, one of whom shot him in the head with a rifle. He did not fall off his horse until another Indian, drawing a sabre, struck him on the head several times, and then he fell to the ground, was scalped and stript of his clothes, and left on the road. The body remained two days on the roadway, before the door of Antoine Boulard, and was part eat up by the hogs. On the evening of the second day four Frenchmen took up the body, carried it to the skirts of the woods, and covered it with a few branches, where the hogs did not go. They dared not bury it, for fear of being surprised by the Indians.[8]

In the buildings housing the wounded of the rank and file things were faring little better. Albert Ammerman, a private of Captain Michael Glaves's company, had been wounded since the battle of January 18.

[7]Statement of John Todd, M. D., dated Lexington, Ky., May 2, 1813, *op. cit.*

[8]Statements of Antoine Boulard and Louis Bernard, February 5, 1813, in *American State Papers, Military Affairs,* I, 369.

The first Indian that came to the room I was lodged in, could speak the English language. He was asked by one of the wounded what was to be done with the wounded. He replied that all were to be killed that could not walk and shortly after a general massacre commenced. I instantly put on my knapsack and went out of the house; my knapsack was demanded by an Indian at the door, to whom I gave it. He conducted me to a log some distance from the house, on which I sat down, where I witnessed the butchery of many of my fellow citizens, sufferers by the tomahawk and scalping knife.[9]

Charles Bradford, private in Captain Hart's company, escaped the methodical killings in his quarters and joined a number of his fellow prisoners in the snow outside of the house. He was there claimed as a prisoner by one of the Indians, who gave him some articles to hold while he plundered more. At this time Bradford was standing with Dr. Bower and James E. Blythe, son of the president of Transylvania University, when an Indian without warning tomahawked young Blythe and scalped him.[10]

By mid-morning actual destruction or capture of all Americans in the village had been completed with the exception of some of the badly wounded still in the houses. The work was completed when the Indians set fire to these dwellings. "The Indians burnt first the house of Jean Baptiste Jereaume, and afterwards that of Gabriel Godfroy, Jr. There were about forty-eight or forty-nine prisoners in the two houses."[11] Those who could by superhuman effort drag themselves to the doors were tomahawked as they struggled to escape the flames. Others unable to leave their beds were burned as they lay helpless.

After the houses were nearly consumed, the men received marching orders, stated Dr. Bower in April following,

and after arriving at Sandy Creek, the Indians called a halt, and commenced cooking; after preparing and eating a little sweatened gruel, Messrs. [Charles] Bradford, [Charles] Searles, and [Julius] Turner, and myself received some, and were eating when an Indian came

[9]Statement of Albert Ammerman, at Falmouth, Ky., April 21, 1813, in *ibid.*, I, 374.
[10]Statement of Charles Bradford, at Lexington, Ky., April 29, 1813, in *ibid.*, I, 375.
[11]Statement of Joseph Robert, February 4, 1813, in *ibid.*, I, 368.

up and proposed exchanging his moccasins for Mr. Searles's shoes, which he readily complied with. They then exchanged hats, after which the Indian inquired how many men Harrison had with him, and, at the same time calling Searles a Washington or Madison, then raised his tomahawk and struck him on the shoulder, which cut into the cavity of the body. Searles then caught hold of the tomahawk and appeared to resist, and upon my telling him that his fate was inevitable, he closed his eyes and received the savage blow which terminated his existence. I was near enough to him to receive the brains and blood, after the fatal blow, on my blanket. A short time after the death of Searles, I saw three others share a similar fate.[12]

Others were marched toward Brownstown. "A number were taken toward Malden, but being unable to march with speed, were inhumanely massacred," recalled Elias Darnell.[13]

The road was, for miles, strewed with the mangled bodies, and all of them were left like those slain in battle, on the 22d, for birds and beasts to tear in pieces and devour. In traveling about one quarter of a mile, two of the wounded lagged behind about twenty yards. The Indians, turning round, shot one and scalped him. They shot the other and missed him; he, running up to them, begged they would not shoot him. He said he would keep up, and give them money. But these murderers were not moved with his doleful cries. They shot him down; and, rushing on him in a crowd, scalped him. In like manner my brother Allen[14] perished.

As the wounded struggled to keep pace with the Indians, William Atherton, safely a prisoner of an Indian who evidenced intentions of protecting him, remained captive beside the road and watched his companions march. "Here," he told in his book,[15] "I saw a striking example of the estimate a man places on life. I saw some of our own company—old acquaintances who were so badly wounded that they could scarcely be moved in their beds, understanding that those who could not travel on foot to Malden were

[12]Statement of Dr. Gustavus M. Bower, in Jessamine County, Ky., April 24, 1813, in *ibid.*, I, 372.
[13]Darnall, *op. cit.*, pp. 61-62.
[14]Allen Darnell, with his brother Elias, were Privates in Captain Samuel L. Williams' Company.
[15]Atherton, *op. cit.*, pp. 65-66.

all to be tomahawked, pass on their way to Malden, hobbling along on sticks. Poor fellows, they were soon overtaken by their merciless enemies and inhumanely butchered."

Captain Nathaniel Hart, although severely wounded, had hopes that his life would be spared. His captor after having accepted Hart's promise of a monetary reward, had placed the Kentuckian on his own horse and made signs for him to follow up the River Raisin, to get out of the way of other Indians. On their way up the river, about 100 rods west of the battle-ground, the Indian stopped with others at the house of a Frenchman and made signs for Hart to proceed on. This the captain did and shortly arrived in front of the home of Francois Lasselle, whom he asked for help. This, for fear of reprisals, Mr. Lasselle was unable to do but he did entreat Hart's captor to take good care of the Kentuckian.

Captain Hart, in despair and severely wounded, followed his Indian master. Unfortunately in the house they next came to and in front of it were a number of Delaware Indians who had entered the dwelling for plunder and had found some whiskey. The Indians within the house called for Hart's Indian to join them, which he did after tying the halter of Hart's horse to the gate post.[16]

Albert Ammerman, who had been carried off in the same direction, was at Sandy Creek

when we were overtaken by two Indians who had Captain Hart in custody, mounted on a horse. As they approached nearly to us, I noticed they were speaking loud and animated as if in a quarrel, but not understanding their language, did not understand what passed between them, but think it is probable that the quarrel was occasioned respecting one hundred dollars which I understood Captain Hart had given to one of the Indians, to convey him to Malden. The quarrel appeared to grow very warm, so much so that the Indians took aim at each other with their guns; and, as if to settle the dispute, it appeared to me as if they had mutually agreed to kill Captain Hart, and plunder him of the rest of his money and effects, which they did, by taking him off his horse, then knocked him down with a war club, scalped and tomahawked him, and stripped him naked, leaving his

[16]Judge L. Durocher's narrative of Captain Hart's massacre, affidavit dated Monroe, March 29, 1858, in *Michigan Historical and Pioneer Collections*, VIII (1885), 644-646.

The Massacre

body on the ground. I was gratified in observing that during this scene of trial, Captain Hart refrained from supplication or entreaty, but appeared perfectly calm and collected. He met his fate with that firmness which was his particular characteristic. No other prisoner of our army of the United States was present to witness this melancholy scene, the death of Captain Hart.[17]

The massacre of the prisoners and capture of those able to keep up with the retreating Indians was completed by mid-afternoon, leaving Frenchtown void of all life save for the smouldering ruins of the houses. The scalped, stripped and burned Kentuckians lay where they had fallen, many decapitated, and all consigned to the hogs and other beasts of prey.

How many, in addition to those named herein, were slain is not positively known. Ensign Baker ascertained about sixty were massacred, with thirty to forty prisoners still alive after the massacre. An eye witness stated for *Niles' Weekly Register* of March 6, 1813, that "The wounded, amounting to 64, were left on the ground [in Frenchtown], under the care of Drs. Todd and Bowers, the two surviving surgeons." These estimates support an approximation of between sixty and sixty-five massacred January 23 and subsequently. All authorities agree that Governor Shelby's victorious army reinterred sixty-five on its return from the battle of the Thames. The list at any rate is long and includes the most respected names of the day. In honor of the leaders at Raisin the Commonwealth of Kentucky eventually assigned to nine counties formed after the battles and massacre the names of Allen, Ballard, Edmonson, Graves, Hart, Hickman, McCracken, Meade, and Simpson.[18]

Americans were shocked when news of the disaster filtered to the south and east. The press of the nation called for an early revenge and Congress immediately employed the massacre of the wounded to fan enthusiasm for a renewed war effort. Letters from Americans close to the scene fanned the already crest-high anger of those at home. Two days after the massacre Richard M. Gano wrote to his brother, General John Stites Gano, from Camp Carron River:

[17]Statement of Albert Ammerman, at Falmouth, Ky., April 21, 1813, *op. cit.*
[18]See biographies of these men in Chapter VIII for dates of formation of these counties.

What shall I say or how begin. My God, my God, my God! hast thou forsaken us. General Winchester at the River Raisin . . . was totally defeated—did I say totally—yes, out of 1050 Officers and men not more than 30 have escaped the infernal British and savages and oh, to call to mind the situation of our best Kentucky blood, to see officers and men sinking under the tomahawk without resistance—saying 'Damn you—tomahawk me, it is all you can do.' Out of three Kentucky Regts. not a Battalion remains. But two officers in the engagement have got in, viz: Major McClenahan and Capt. Glaves of our Regt.—the latter wounded in two places but trifling.[19]

The editor of Niles' Weekly Register added fuel to the surge of hatred toward the British:

As the man who sees the serpent in his way, is startled and surprised; so shall the future historian regard the body of evidence and of facts it is our melancholy duty this week to **Register**. We have confirmation strong—'almost as strong as proofs from holy writ,' of the most horrid assassination and cold-blooded butchery ever committed, or suffered to be done, by **civilized** men. The high professions of the British in **religion**; their boasted **magnanimity**; their advancement in the arts, sciences and literature; and their much extolled love of **liberty**, with the excellency of their general policy, instead of washing out this 'damned spot' will tint it with the deeper crimson; and faithful history shall record these **murders of the wounded**, without the plea of necessity; the day after the battle, when the heat of the contest had cooled. As was eloquently observed by a writer on this subject, 'we cling to the hope of an hereafter as the only adequate means of punishing the wretches.'[20]

---

[19]Richard M. Gano to General Stites Gano, Camp Carron River, January 25, 1813, in *Ohio Historical and Philosophical Quarterly*, XVI (1921), 34-37; Richard M. Gano was born July 7,1775, in New York, a son of the Reverend John Gano. Settling early in Georgetown, Ky., he was a merchant there early in 1800. He entered the war as a Major in Colonel Scott's regiment, and succeeded him as Colonel of that unit when Scott had to retire because of ill health late in 1812. He commanded the regiment at the battle of the Thames and at the close of the war was made Brigadier General for gallant services during the war. He died October 22, 1815, aged but forty-one years. See *Kentucky Gazette* for extended sketch, issue of October 30, 1815.

[20]*Niles' Weekly Register*, IV (April 10, 1813), 97.

British subjects were no less disturbed. Dr. Robert Richardson writing from Amherstburg February 7, 1813, observed:

> I suppose it would be considered high treason to speak out this way. There is another circumstance which has hurt me more than I can express. That is with respect to some wounded men belonging to the Americans who were left without proper protection and some of whom I have been informed were the same evening murdered by the Indians. Had I been commanding officer I should have considered myself responsible for the lives of every one of them, and within my hearing protection was promised for those poor people. Be assured we have not heard the last of this shameful transaction. I wish to God it could be contradicted.[21]

The writings of Squire Reynolds echo the same sentiment.

> The prisoners and many of the wounded were removed safely; but some of the wounded, too much hurt to be moved, were left in the stockaded house, where there was also a store of liquors. The Indians—not Tecumseh's people, but Indians of the Lake, under Dickson—prowlers and plunderers, who, it is believed, did not fight at all, got at the liquor, and, when mad with drink, assailed the prisoners. The guard was insufficient. It is feared that some of the wounded were murdered, too. It was a sad affair, and caused intense feeling in our camp.[22]

Regardless of where the war guilt might be placed, the fatal blow suffered by General Winchester's little band brought an abrupt halt to the American effort in the Northwest, an effort as it turned out, however, which was only strengthened in spirit and determination because of the reverses at Frenchtown. At the moment there was nothing for Harrison to do but pull back and regroup his forces for another assault northward in the spring.

Colonel Samuel Wells was sent back to Governor Shelby with official news of the overwhelming defeat. "I send Colonel Wells to you," wrote Harrison two days after the massacre, "to communicate the particulars (as far as we are acquainted with them) of

---

[21]Dr. Robert Richardson to John Askin, in *Burton Historical Records*, II: *The John Askin Papers, II, 1796-1820*, by Milo M. Quaife (ed.), *op cit.*, 749-750.

[22]Coffin, *op. cit.*, pp. 205-206.

an event that will overwhelm your mind with grief, and fill your whole State with mourning."[23]

When the news reached Frankfort on the evening of February 2, almost the whole town was at the theatre, Governor Shelby among the rest. He was called out and given the news. It spread through the house immediately and by the conclusion of the third act of the drama being offered the whole audience had retired. In the town, noted one writer, "you see fathers going about half distracted, while mothers, wives and sisters are weeping at home. The voice of lamentation is loud; the distress is deep; yet neither public nor private distress can damp the ardor of the people. Already they propose raising a new army to revenge the loss of their brave countrymen. It is confidently expected our town will raise a company in a few days. You witnessed the emotion of all ranks of people after the shameful surrender of Hull. I need only say, the same spirit prevails at present."[24]

"The melancholy event has filled the state with mourning, and every heart bleeds with anguish," Governor Shelby wrote Harrison. "The Legislature of this State was on the point of rising at the moment when Col. Wells arrived but continued their session during the whole of the 3rd inst., in consequence of the intelligence contained in your dispatches by him and passed an act, authorizing the organization of three thousand militia for any term not exceeding six months and for any service of the United States...."[25]

This was the army which Shelby himself led into the north and which under General Harrison at the Thames, on October 5, 1813, restored in the Northwest the American dominance which Hull had lost in August, 1812.

When the final charge was made against General Henry A. Proctor across the swampland adjoining the Thames the tense stillness of impending combat was upon the Americans. But when the 'Forward, Charge!' order echoed through the ranks

[23]Harrison to Shelby, Camp on Carrying Back, 15 Miles from the Rapids, January 24, 1813, in Richardson, *op. cit.*, pp. 146-147.

[24]*Niles' Weekly Register*, III (February 20, 1813), 397.

[25]Shelby to Harrison, February 9, 1813, in "Letter Book A," No. 41, MSS at Kentucky Historical Society.

The Massacre

another cry, terrible in its intensity and with foreboding wrath in its tones, filled the space overshadowed by the mighty monarchs of the forest. From the stalwart throats of nearly six hundred Kentuckians there arose the cry, 'Remember the Raisin!' As they lifted this mighty cry to Heaven they saw about them the forms of their murdered comrades and friends and relatives. They beheld the bedizened, painted savages, with barbarous cruelty, strike their wounded foes and casting their bodies, when dead or writhing, into the flames to be consumed. . . . As the cry of these Kentuckians resounded through the forests, it fell upon the ears of British regulars, who themselves had been at the battle of the Raisin, and whose officers had connived at, or at least permitted, the slaughter of Allen, Graves, Hickman, Woolfolk, Simpson and their noble commands. In the fierce charge there was but one cry, oft repeated, but rising each time in sharper and sterner tones, 'Remember the Raisin!' 'Remember the Raisin!'[26]

[26]Bennett H. Young in his *The Battle of the Thames* ("Filson Club Publications," No. 18) [Louisville, Ky.: John P. Morton and Co., 1903], pp. 76-78.

VII

THE LIVING AND THE DEAD OF RAISIN

THE MAIN body of the prisoners, surrendered from the pickets, captured during the retreat back across the Raisin, and taken from among the wounded in the houses, was marched directly to Malden where Proctor's forces had bivouacked the night of the battle. The prisoners now numbered between 500 and 512 officers and men.

Oliver Bellair, a boy living with his parents at Malden at the time, later described the entry of the prisoners and their brief stay in the fort.[1] The men, he stated, were pictures of misery as they arrived at Malden. The long, cold march from the States in mid-winter, camping and fighting in the deep snow and subsequent robbery of all of their effects, had left them destitute of any comforts. Many also were wounded. The blood, dust and smoke of battle were yet upon them. In the Fort they were driven into an open woodyard and thinly clad, without tents or covering of any nature, had to endure the long January night. They were surrounded by a strong chain of sentinels to prevent their escape and to keep off the Indians who constantly pressed hard to enter the enclosure.

The inhabitants of Malden in large numbers crowded around the yard at night and thus favored the escape of a few of the prisoners. One, slightly wounded, passed out unseen by the guard and mingled with the mass of townsfolk, walked quietly off to the outskirts of the village and boldly entered the home of Mr. Bellair. This gentleman later helped the Kentuckian effect his escape. All evidence tends to indicate that the French of Malden were kind to the prisoners.

The Fort at this time, recalled Mr. Bellair, presented a horrible spectacle. The Indians had cut off the heads of some of those who had fallen in the battle of the 22nd and in the massacre of January 23rd

---

[1] B. F. H. Witherell, "Reminiscences of the North-West," *Third Annual Report and Collections of the State Historical Society of Wisconisn for the Year 1856* (Madison, Wisc.: Calkins & Webb, 1857), III, 306-308.

to a number of a hundred or more, brought them to Malden and stuck them up in rows on the top of a high, sharp-pointed picket fence. And there, for all as well as the Kentuckians to see, they hung, their matted locks deeply stained with their own gore—their eyes wide open, staring out upon the multitude, exhibiting all variety of feature; some with a pleasant smile; others, who had probably lingered long in mortal agony, had a scowl of defiance, despair or revenge; and others wore the appearance of deep distress and sorrow,—they may have died thinking of their far-off wives and children, and friends, and pleasant homes which they should visit no more; the winter's frost had fixed their features as they had died, and they changed not.[2]

The Indians had also brought back many scalps, which they strung up some twenty on a pole, and carried about the town to the music of the war-whoop and the scalp yell. The British did not attempt to restrain their allies, answering criticisms with "The Indians are necessary to his Majesty's service, and must be indulged."[3]

On January 29 Ensign Isaac L. Baker, of the 2nd Regiment, U. S. Infantry, who had served at Raisin and had been captured, was ordered by General Winchester to take charge of other prisoners at Sandwich. His work with these men, wounded and not, and his reports published throughout the country were generally praised. In his charge were fifty-five American prisoners, some of whom were sent to Detroit and others, under the care of Dr. Bower, went directly to British Niagara and eventually were paroled.[4] A number of prisoners in the hands of the Indians did not make their escapes and find their various ways back to Kentucky for many months.

General Harrison on January 30 sent Dr. Samuel McKeehan, surgeon of the Ohio volunteer militia, to Frenchtown under flag of truce to care for the wounded, and to go on to Malden to attend them if necessary. He was wounded and captured by the Indians, however, and his flag of truce ignored.

[2]*Ibid.*
[3]*Ibid.*
[4]Ensign Baker's statement, published widely. See *Niles' Weekly Register*, IV (Mar. 27, 1813), 66-68; IV (Apr. 10, 1813), 97-98.

The main body of the prisoners remained at Malden until January 26, when by prisoner of war agreements they were divided into two divisions and began their long march to liberation by way of parole.

On this date the first division marched seventeen miles to Sandwich where the men were bivouacked in houses and for the first time since leaving Frenchtown saw and felt fire. The following day, January 27, after drawing a ration of bread and fresh beef (which they could not cook), the division commenced the march at one o'clock and carried ten miles toward Lake St. Clair. That night the men were placed in cold barns and held without fire until the cold, miserable trek was continued early the next day. Moving on past Lake St. Clair to the Thames the columns continued up that river some five miles in sub-zero weather. The prisoners had to run to keep from freezing and having drawn no rations since leaving Sandwich, were compelled to pick up apple peelings and frozen potatoes from the yards of homes along the way. On January 31 snow fell the entire day, adding almost unbearable fatigue to the cold. Feet were frostbitten and on this night in an unheated barn some slept with their shoes under their heads to keep them from freezing. By February 4 the group had reached the headwaters of the Thames, having plodded through snow twenty-four inches deep and going two entire days without provisions. The 284-mile march was concluded February 10 when the division reached the Niagara River where it empties into Lake Ontario, after averaging nineteen miles per marching day on inadequate rations and in exceedingly inclement weather. The second division, which had been held up one day to lessen the task of providing provisions along the route of march, arrived the day following. Here the groups were detained only long enough to arrange passage across the river into New York State. British officials took the name, company and regiment of each man and shortly after hoisted a flag and saw the men landed on American soil. The number taken across was 512.[5]

The Americans were paroled on condition that they not serve again during the war against Great Britain, or her allies, unless regularly exchanged. When offered the parole papers for his signature, one Kentuckian demanded to know 'who were

[5]Darnall, *op. cit.*, pp. 68-75.

his Majesty's allies.' The British official deterred from naming the Indians, replying only that 'his Majesty's allies are known!'[6]

After eating and drinking their fill of the plenty offered them by the inhabitants of New York, the liberated men turned their faces homeward. Proceeding up the Niagara River they passed Niagara Falls, reached Buffalo, and marching on through Erie, Pennsylvania, passed on by way of Waterford and Meadville to Pittsburgh. Here they managed to find passage down the Ohio to Maysville and other points nearest their Kentucky homes.[7]

Two other prisoners of the Indians when last heard from, in April, 1813, were acting as valets to the Indian chiefs. These were Solomon, Colonel John Allen's servant, and that of Colonel William Lewis. Captain Hart's servant at the same time was reported alive but his whereabouts uncertain.

Prisoners continued to arrive home, alone and in companies of two and three, throughout the summer, while others unable to escape their Indian captors and the British prisoner of war camps did not reach Kentucky until the year following. In Franklin County, which had lost all of its company of eighty-eight men but twelve or thirteen, a cannon was fired each time a survivor reached home, and all within sound of the shot would hasten to Frankfort to greet the returned soldier or to enquire about the lost ones.[8]

Major George Madison and Colonel William Lewis were among the last to be released from imprisonment. The former arrived in Frankfort Thursday night, May 5, 1814, after nearly two years away from his home and family, and was accorded a warm welcome by his fellow townsmen. The editor of the *Argus* in noting the Major's homecoming appended the following lines, inspired by the return of this popular Virginian who two years later was elevated to the governorship of the Commonwealth:

[6]*Niles' Weekly Register*, IV (Mar. 6, 1813), 12.

[7]Darnall, *op. cit.*, pp. 78-79.

[8]L. F. Johnson, *The History of Franklin County, Kentucky* (Frankfort: Roberts Printing Co., 1912), p. 57. Hereinafter cited Johnson.

FRIDAY MORNING

*Now pleasure thrills thro' every vein,
All hearts now beat in unison,
To find his country once again,
Has bless'd the sight of MADISON.*

*Last night, at ten, the cannon's roar,
The shrill ton'd fife and hollow drum,
Announced he had returned once more
To greet those of his native land.*

*Then soon were lin'd the crowded streets,
The young, the old, all sally forth,
And each "a welcome home" repeats
To this brave, modest man of worth.*

*Huzzas, thrice six, were loudly giv'n,
And joyous sparkled ev'ry eye,
Whilst some, in whispers, asked of Heav'n,
That Liberty might never die.*[9]

    Major Madison arrived home in time to find several of his enemies of the year before in much the same predicament he had endured since his captivity in 1813.

    In November of that year the Secretary of State had written Governor Shelby of incidents leading up to the transfer of certain British prisoners of war to the State Penitentiary at Frankfort. These events briefly were: Earlier in 1813 the British commander at Quebec had seized and sent to England twenty-three American prisoners of war, to be tried for treason on the grounds that they were British subjects. The President of the United States immediately ordered confined an equal number of British prisoners, with the expectation that the British government would relax its policy concerning the twenty-three soldiers. Instead the Prince Regent ordered into close confinement forty-six officers of the United States in retaliation. President James Madison met this measure by ordering confined an equal number of British officers. This group was ordered to to be conveyed to Frankfort and to be confined there in the

[9] *The Argus*, May 7, 1814.

State Penitentiary, which was represented to him "to be a building affording the two-fold advantages of good and safe accommodations."[10]

Governor Shelby accordingly advised Major Anderson Miller, Keeper of the Penitentiary, of the planned confinement of the British officers:

> You will forthwith have put in readiness and appropriated for that purpose the rooms which were designated in a verbal communication with you, and permit the Marshal of the United States of this district who will have them in custody to have the entire control and management of those apartments. As these buildings have been selected because they afforded more secure and better rooms than any other prison in the Western Country—and not out of any disrespect to, nor with any intention of wounding the feelings of those whom the fate of war has put in our power, you will as far as depends upon you afford those officers every convenience consistent with their safe keeping and a state of close confinement. You will be particularly attentive that the persons confined in the penitentiary house by way of punishment, be kept entirely from the apartments appropriated for the above purposes.[11]

The British officers, thirty in number,[12] were brought to Frankfort in two groups, the first detachment of nineteen arriving on Thursday, December 2, 1813. This group was first confined in a house rented for that purpose in the town, and on December 8 escorted to the penitentiary and assigned to the second floor rooms prepared for them.[13]

[10] Secretary of State to Shelby, November 27, 1813, "Letter Book B," No. 20. Shelby's Correspondence. MSS at Kentucky Historical Society.

[11] Shelby to Miller, December 8, 1813, *ibid.*, "Letter Book A," No. 84.

[12] Richardson, *op. cit.*, p. 268. Their names were: Lieutenant Colonel Warburton; Major Chambers, D.A.Q.M.G.; Major Muir, 41st British; Captain Derenxy, same; Captain McCoy, same; Captain Hill, same; Captain Tallon, same; Captain Dixon, Royal Engineers; Lieutenants Hailes, Watson, Linn, Jeboult, O'Keefe, and Gale, of the 41st; Lieutenants Purvis and Stokoe, Royal Navy; Lieutenants Bremner, Rolette, and Irvine, Provincial Navy; Lieutenant Holmes, Light Dragoons; Ensigns Mompesson, Cochran, and Jones, 41st; A. B. Garden, Gent., Volunteer, Royal Newfoundland Regiment; Ensigns J. Richardson and James Laing, 41st; J. Campbell, Master's Mate, R.P.N.; G. Collins, same; J. Fortier, same; and R. Nelson, Midshipman.

[13] *Reporter*, Dec. 18, 1813; Shelby to Secretary of State, December 13, 1813, "Letter Book A," No. 85, Shelby's Correspondence. MSS at Kentucky Historical Society.

Of the second group, moved from the American prisoner of war base at Chillicothe, a more complete history has been preserved. Major John Richardson, of the 41st Regiment, was one of the latter detachment. He had fought against the Kentuckians at Raisin and again at the Thames where he had been captured along with many of his regiment. His group had been moved from Detroit to Chillicothe and during October and November to the first months of 1814 had been kept in close confinement there. Some two months after the first group of British prisoners arrived in Frankfort this second detachment was prepared for removal to the Kentucky penitentiary.

Moved down the Scioto River to Cincinnati, the escorted prisoners at length entered the Kentucky River and passed up that stream toward Frankfort. Of the trip and confinement Major Richardson wrote in 1842:

> Our progress here was slow and difficult. A thick and apparently impervious wood skirted its banks, and occasionally interweaving its protruding tops, threw a chilling gloom over the scene, while the close under-wood, reaching to the very margin of the waters, seemed to preclude all possibility of a landing. At length a more open space was perceptible, and at this point our journey by water was discontinued. Horses were procured in the adjacent country; and . . . we continued our route towards Frankfort, then at no great distance.
>
> After travelling through a wild and thinly-inhabited country, and along paths which no other than American horses could have trod with safety, a range of lofty and gloomy hills, by which that capital is nearly surrounded, announced the proximity of what we were to consider as our future home. The morning was cold and rainy, and as we wound round the base of a hill which intercepted our view, the towering walls of the penitentiary, situated in that extremity of the town by which we approached, fell suddenly on our gaze. A few minutes brought us in a line with the principal entrance; and as we glanced upwards at the low and narrow windows we beheld our companions thrusting their handkerchiefs through the bars, and saluting us as they could. They were the party that had preceded us from Chillicothe, and consisted chiefly of the officers taken at the Moraviantown. It was a melancholy moment for recognition, and our feelings had imbibed much of the sombre character of the season, as we moved on to the spot appointed for our delivery into the hands of the Marshal of Kentucky.

On entering the prison of the penitentiary, we found our friends distributed into two small rooms little larger than common cells, and crowded together in a distressing manner; but many had reconciled themselves to their situations, and enjoyed a temporary distraction in studying the trades carried on by the convicts in the court, who cheerfully initiated them into the rudiments of their respective arts.[14]

The British officers, however, did not long remain in the penitentiary. The policy of hostages gradually was losing its import and the governments of Great Britain and the United States became lax in the enforcement of confinements of prisoners. Lieutenant Colonel Warburton and Major Chambers were shortly afterward permitted to return to Canada as a result of this policy, a consequence leading to the parole of Major George Madison and Colonel William Lewis a few weeks later.

In the case of the British officers confined at Frankfort the first gesture toward leniency was their removal from the penitentiary to a hotel.

The principal hotel in Frankfort, to which was attached an extensive garden, surrounded by a low wall, was the place selected for our residence, with the express prohibition, however, of out-stepping its limits. Here on the score of personal comfort we had no reason to complain. Three shillings a day was the allowance granted by the American government to each officer, and the sick were entitled to twice that amount. One room was occupied by two prisoners, and our table was abundantly supplied with excellent food. Tea, coffee, eggs, cold meat, and the various 'sweet sauces' to which the Americans are so partial, composed our breakfast; while at dinner we generally found ourselves seated before meats of every description, and succeeded by a plentiful dessert. A number of black slaves were also at our orders, and the preparation of our linen was included in the moderate charge. Such was the revolution effected in our position, and but for the restraint imposed on our liberty, our chains would have been light.[15]

Still later the British officers were ordered placed on parole, and granted permission to return to Canada—provided they pay their own expenses and provide their own horses. This offer

[14]Richardson, *op. cit.*, pp. 254-288.
[15]*Ibid.*

was immediately embraced by those with money sufficient for the trip. The others had to remain in Frankfort to await government transportation provided for exchange and liberation of prisoners of war.

The latter officers, at least, were privileged freedom to come and go where they chose, up to a distance of twenty miles from Frankfort, without escort of any nature.

Major George Madison was among the first to offer these officers the hospitality of his house. Many were frequent visitors in his home, and through him they were introduced to a Mr. Sproule, Frankfort banker, who advanced loans for excursions to nearby estates and towns. Madison accompanied them on these trips, pointing out the beauty of Kentucky in the spring and introducing them to many of central Kentucky's leading families.

All was not so perfect during the latter stages of the confinement however. The people of Frankfort were not inclined to forget on such short notice that Captain Paschal Hickman and the majority of his Franklin County company lay somewhere in the north, their final resting places unknown and not likely ever to be known. One example of this animosity must suffice. Lieutenant Irvine of the Navy, as token for kindnesses shown him by Madison, constructed a miniature boat for the Major's daughter, a novel and finely constructed work which delighted the entire Madison household. Noting the reception of this gift, another of the British officers occupying one of the upper rooms of the hotel, decided upon the same idea—apparently to capture the attentions of another young lady of the town. Unfortunately, however, the young midshipman [J. Campbell] made his model too realistic and mounted the English flag atop his creation before placing the vessel in an open window to dry. A group of Frankfortians soon had gathered below, every eye fixed on the English flag atop the tiny boat. As one they stormed the hotel, dashed the model to the street below and warned, "You British rascals, if you show your tarnation colors here again, we'll throw you after them."[16]

Fortunately for all concerned, shortly after this episode word was received that the whole of the prisoners were to be marched to the frontiers of Canada for immediate exchange. Recalled Major Richardson:

[16]*Ibid.*

The morning of our actual departure from Frankfort was, as will be believed, one of joy and exultation for us all, and at an early hour most of the officers were already up, and with light hearts and cheerful countenance preparing for their journey. Our horses were at length brought to the entrance of the hotel, before which nearly half of the town of Frankfort had collected to witness our departure. Habited in our light and neatly fringed frocks, fastened by silver buckles attached to broad red morocco belts, we soon vaulted into the saddle; and escorted by Lieutenant Mitchell of the rifle service, and Colonel Crockett, the Marshal of the state, a consequential gentleman, who had often vainly sought to subdue our refractory spirits into something like submission to his authority, we commenced our journey. The hand of kindness and the voice of gentlemanly consideration were extended to us by a few, among whom stood principally conspicuous Major Madison and the banker Mr. Sproule; but on the countenances of the many might be traced very different feelings. Even while detesting our presence, they seemed to regret the approaching removal of their victims, and the insolence of their looks and observations bore sufficient testimony of their hostility.

Pursuing a route different from that by which we had reached Frankfort, we soon arrived at Newport . . . opposite to Cincinnati, in the neighborhood of which latter place the prisoners from Chillicothe were awaiting the arrival of their officers. Large boats were procured for the passage of our horses, and having crossed the river the same evening, we were conducted to our old quarters, the principal hotel in Cincinnati.[17]

It was then mid-July, 1814, and with the departure from Kentucky of the last of the British prisoners of war—so closely associated in the minds of the Kentuckians with the battles and massacre at Frenchtown—there was now left only the memory of those who had not returned.

THE DEAD OF RAISIN

Two weeks after the massacre, Alexis Labadie of Frenchtown testified

that the bodies of the Americans killed at the battle of *la Riviere aux Raisins*, of the 22d [and 23d], of January last, remain unburied, and that I have seen the hogs and dogs eating them. The hogs appeared

[17] *Ibid.*

to be rendered mad by so profuse a diet of Christian flesh. I saw the houses of Mr. Jerome and Mr. Godfroy on fire, and have heard that there were prisoners in them. The inhabitants did not dare to bury the dead, on account of the Indians. The inhabitants have been threatened by the Indians, if they did not take up arms against the Americans.[18]

This was borne out by Ensign Isaac L. Baker in his report of February 25 to General Winchester.

The dead of our army are still denied the rites of sepulture. At the time I left Sandwich, I was told the hogs were eating them. A gentleman told me he had seen them running about with the skulls, arms, legs, and other parts of the human system in their mouths. The French people on the Raisin buried Captains Hart, Woolfolk and some others, but it was more than their lives were worth to have been caught paying this last customed tribute to mortality. I several times agitated the subject of burying the dead, when in company with the British officers, but they always answered, that the Indians would not suffer it.[19]

Where rest any of these killed on January 18 and 22 and during the massacre of January 23, 1813, has not definitely been established.

Those killed during the second battle on January 22 and massacred the following day in all probability were buried once and finally October 15, 1813, by Governor Shelby's men who went to Frenchtown for that purpose on their victorious return from the battle of the Thames.

Of that mass burial Major William Trigg wrote the editors of the *Frankfort Argus* on October 22, 1813:

On the 15th we passed the river Raisin—over the field of battle at that place a scene was presented that will be long affecting to the sensibility of Kentuckians—the unburied bones of our countrymen were every where to be seen! By the direction of our governor, Colonel Simral undertook the melancholy duty of interring the remains! By him and some others of the army, the remains of 65 were collected and buried in the best manner our situation would permit,

[18]*American State Papers, Military Affairs*, I, 369.
[19]*Ibid.*, I, 370.

with the customary honors of war. It is some consolation to think that they are buried by the hands that had first, in some degree, revenged their death.

The number buried generally agrees with the number killed on these two days. Where in or near Monroe, newer name of Frenchtown, the interment took place is a matter for still further investigation. Very possibly the exact spot was found in 1904 when the citizens of Monroe and the State of Michigan erected a monument to the slain Kentuckians. During the course of excavating for the base of this monument bones were found, indicating that the plot might have been the same in which Shelby's men first buried their countrymen in 1813.

Of the twelve or thirteen killed in the first battle on January 18, there is a longer and more tragic history.

The latter first received attention when they were buried in a common grave on January 19, immediately after the battle. [See page 56]. This group numbered thirteen men. A similar group, twelve or fourteen, was reburied by Colonel Richard M. Johnson and his troops June 29, 1813, when that force passed through Frenchtown prior to the battle of the Thames. This second interment was violated by the Indians who opened the fresh graves and scattered the bones over a wide area. On their return through the town, September 25, Colonel Johnson's men gathered up the skeletons and again buried them.[20] Granting that these were the killed of January 18, 1813, a listing of their names can be found in the Appendix.

Thereafter the bones of those killed at Frenchtown were not permitted peace. Certain of the remains "were taken up on July 4, 1818, and reinterred in the cemetery at Monroe, Michigan, the town which stands on the site of the battle. In August of the same year they were again taken up and removed to Detroit, and interred in the Protestant Cemetery there. In 1834 they were again taken up and removed to Clinton Street Cemetery, in Detroit; and in September of that year [1834] they were once more, and for the last time, exhumed and placed in boxes marked *Kentucky's Gallant Dead, January 18, 1813, River Raisin,*

[20]Leland Winfield Meyer, *The Life and Times of Colonel Richard M. Johnson of Kentucky* (New York: Columbia University Press, 1932), pp. 113, 121.

Michigan, and at last and forever placed at rest in the State Cemetery, in Frankfort, Kentucky."

The above quoted record of the various moves to which the dead of Raisin were subjected was used, in quotes, by Mr. L. F. Johnson in his *The History of Franklin County, Kentucky* (1912), probably from Mr. Anderson Chenault Quisenberry's *Kentucky in the War of 1812*, the Raisin River chapter of which was first published in *The Register* of January, 1913.

Neither of the above writers indicated the source of the record of these various burials and reburials.

The bones of the twelve or thirteen, more than likely those killed on January 18, were accidentally discovered by citizens of Monroe in 1848. After due consideration these were placed in a box and committed to the charge of Colonel Edward Brooks, who was ordered to deliver them to the nearest point in Kentucky. The Frankfort *Yeoman*, which had announced this information in its issue of October 5, 1848, further stated that "the remains are to be conveyed to Frankfort . . . to be appropriately interred some time hence in the State burying ground."

The next step in the mystery of these Kentucky soldiers of Raisin was provided in *The Military History of Kentucky*, compiled by the Federal Writers' Project and published in 1939. Therein it is stated: "Col. Edward Brooks arrived in Frankfort on September 30, 1848, with those remains which have been found in a common grave, having been unearthed in excavating a street in Monroe, Michigan. An aged Kentuckian, survivor of the massacre, identified them as the bones of his fellow soldiers, having remembered the location of the place of burial." The latter sentence bears up, inasmuch as Joseph Clark who was on the burial detail of January 19 when these twelve or thirteen were buried at Frenchtown in a common grave was still living in Frankfort in September, 1848. He was then only fifty-five years of age.

The above is the only reference discovered to this early removal of the remains from Covington, where Colonel Brooks left them, to the State Capital. The date of the Federal Writers' Project statement is that of September 30, 1848. Yet the *Yeoman*, quoted above, in its issue of a week later stated the remains "are to be conveyed to Frankfort . . . to be interred some time hence."

At any rate the box was still in Covington two years later. On November 14, 1850, John W. Leathers, Senator from Kenton County, told the Kentucky General Assembly that these dead were brought to Covington in September, 1848, and delivered to the Mayor and Common Council of Covington. The remains, he stated further, were deposited by these authorities in the vault of the Baptist Cemetery for further disposition. Mr. Leathers offered at this time a resolution that a committee of five be appointed to take into consideration the propriety of removing these remains from the vault in Covington and giving them a place in the Frankfort Cemetery. This resolution was adopted.[21] It was again offered by Mr. Leathers on December 11, 1850, and again was adopted.[22] During the week following, on December 18, an act was passed allowing Colonel Edward Brooks $105.50 for conveying the remains from Monroe, Michigan, to Covington, Kentucky.[23]

It was not until March 1, 1851, however, that Governor John Larue Helm signed a bill, approved February 17, providing the following significant statements:

> Whereas, it is represented that the governor has caused to be brought to this city the remains of the citizens of Kentucky who fell at Raisin, which remains were recovered and brought to Covington by Col. Brooks . . . the governor is authorized to draw from the treasury on warrant of the second auditor, a sum not exceeding eighty dollars to pay the expenses of the transportation and interment of said remains.[24]

It would appear, therefore, that on some date between December 11, 1850, and February 17, 1851, these few of the dead of Raisin were brought to Frankfort and here buried. Where or on what date must for the present remain unknown. Mr. L. F. Johnson came to the same conclusion after research for his *The History of Franklin County*, above alluded to. He as well failed to produce anything definite. "To the shame of Kentucky be it said that no man knows at this day [1912] where

[21]*Journal of the Senate of the Commonwealth of Kentucky, 1850-51*, p. 50.
[22]*Acts of the General Assembly of Kentucky, 1850-51*, I, 404.
[23]*Ibid.*, II, 70.
[24]*Ibid.*, I, 28.

the bones of these honored dead are buried. The removal to Kentucky was prior to the time the present cemetery was purchased and a part of it dedicated to Kentucky heroes. At that time the cemetery was back of Fort Hill, and even tradition is silent as to whether or not these bones were removed to the new cemetery."[25] Unfortunately, due to fire, the records of the State Cemetery date only to 1876. [Actually the resolution offered in the General Assembly by Mr. Leathers gave rise to the act approved March 15, 1851, authorizing the governor to purchase six lots in the now State Cemetery for use of the state as place of interment of Kentuckians who fell in battle or otherwise were distinguished in the Commonwealth's history.][26]

The bones of the dead at Raisin were next mentioned in 1871. On February 25 of that year new excavations in Monroe unearthed thirty human skulls and various bones,[27] evidently a part of those buried by Governor Shelby and his troops shortly after the battle of the Thames. These apparently were the remains gathered up by citizens of Monroe and reinterred in the old cemetery of that city.

This old burial plot, obviously covering the ground where the dead of Raisin were first interred, was improved in 1904 and converted into a beautiful place of memorial. And here on September 1, 1904, was dedicated with appropriate ceremonies the Raisin Monument erected by the State of Michigan in honor of those who fell in the battles and were massacred. This $10,000 monument must serve as memorial to all the dead of Raisin—until the Commonwealth of Kentucky locates the remains of the twelve brought from Covington in 1850 or 1851 and has them reinterred in the State Cemetery, lots in which were bought 110 years ago to receive them.

[25] Johnson, *op. cit.*, p. 60.
[26] See *Acts of the General Assembly of Kentucky, 1850-51*, II, 398.
[27] Richard H. Collins, *History of Kentucky* . . . (Louisville, Ky.: John P. Morton and Co., 1924), I, 212.

VIII

BIOGRAPHIES

IT HAD BEEN hoped to provide in this section biographical and genealogical accounts of all officers engaged in the River Raisin campaign. Almost three years of research failed, however, to produce materials of interest concerning several of the officers conspicuous at Frenchtown, January 18-23, 1813. Of those about whom little or nothing could be learned were: Pollard Keene, Quartermaster; Captains Robert Edwards, 17th U. S. Infantry; Michael Glaves, 1st Regiment; Henry James, 2nd Regiment; Richard Matson, 1st Rifle Regiment; James Meade, 17th U. S. Infantry; Richard Bledsoe, 1st Rifle Regiment; and Thomas McIlvain, Surgeon or Surgeon's Mate.

For a definitive account of the life and services of General William H. Harrison, commander of the Northwestern Army, the reader is referred to *Old Tippecanoe, William Henry Harrison and His Time*, by Freeman Cleaves, New York, Charles Scribner's Sons, 1939.

JAMES WINCHESTER
Brigadier General, U.S.A., Commanding the Raisin Force

James Winchester was born February 6, 1752, in Carroll County, Maryland, the third child of William and Lydia (Richards) Winchester. William Winchester had come to Maryland from England about thirty years before. His wife was a daughter of Edward Richards of Baltimore County, Maryland. James Winchester and his brother George, after schooling received from tutors and in the local schools of the community, in 1776 enlisted for service in the Revolution. Thereafter the military career of the former was established as a lifetime profession. He became 2nd Lieutenant February 20, 1777; 1st Lieutenant May 27, 1778; taken prisoner at Charleston May 12, 1780, and released December 22 of the same year; transferred to the 3rd Maryland, January 1, 1781; Captain, 1781; served to end of the war in this rank. His commission as Brigadier General, United States Army, bears date of March 27, 1812. He served in this rank until his resignation on March 31, 1815.

Removing to Tennessee in 1785, James Winchester eventually became closely identified with the early growth of that state, serving in the legislature and successively as captain, colonel and brigadier general during Indian campaigns. On the admission of Tennessee into the Union, he was elected state senator and became speaker of the Senate. Growing with the new state, he held various local offices, prospered and gained wealth sufficient to build his still scenic and imposing home, *Cragfont.*

General Winchester's position as commander first of the Army of the Northwest, finally as commander of the Left Wing, his defeat at Frenchtown and captivity by the British are treated in the text. On his exchange and return from captivity, he was placed in command of the Mobile District but when peace was declared he resigned his commission and returned to his home in Tennessee.

From 1816 until 1819 he was occupied in endeavoring to clear himself of charges of neglect and military incompetency, during the course of the Raisin campaign, directed mainly by Robert B. McAfee in his *History of the Late War in the Western Country,* published in 1816. Winchester's answers to the various charges are contained in his *Historical Details, Having Relation to the Campaign of the North-Western Army, under Generals Harrison and Winchester, during the Winter of 1812-13; together with some Particulars Relating to the Surrender of Fort Bowyer,* 1818.

In 1819 General Winchester performed his last public work when he was appointed commissioner to run the Chickasaw Boundary Line between Tennessee and Mississippi. Retiring to *Cragfont* he remained active in public affairs and interests and was prominent in the founding of Memphis, Tennessee. He died on July 26, 1826, and was buried on his plantation.

General Winchester married Susan Black, probably in 1802 or 1803. In the latter year he caused the state legislature to legitimize the four living children of their common law union which had begun in 1792. Fourteen children were born to James and Susan Black Winchester, four of whom were: Caroline E. Winchester, who married in Tennessee January 30, 1825, Orville Shelby; Marcus Winchester, first mayor of Memphis. Marcus has been described as a leading lawyer of that city who married in New Orleans a woman of mixed blood, a beautiful French quadroon, a social drawback which impeded his career but did not keep him from being an excellent mayor and holder of public confidence. A third child was Lucillus Winchester (died 1848) who married in 1838 Elizabeth Farrar (1822-85). Another son, George W. Winchester, married Malvina H. Gaines.

[Edd Winfield Parks, in *Dictionary of American Biography*, v. 20; J. H. DeWitt, "General James Winchester," in *Tennessee Historical Magazine*, 1915; DAR Lineage Books, v. 20, 55, 70. See also bibliographical notes in the text.]

JAMES OVERTON, JR.
Aide-de-Camp to General Winchester

James Overton, Jr., was born in 1785 or 1786, the third son of Waller and Henrietta Ragland Overton. His father removed from Virginia to Mercer then Fayette County, Kentucky. John Overton, brother of Waller, removed to Tennessee where he was Supervisor of Revenue, and Judge on the Supreme Court.

James Overton, Jr., early embarked on a study of medicine in Philadelphia and in the (Lexington) *Kentucky Gazette*, in 1810, advertised that he "will practice Physic in Lexington and will have his shop on Main Street, nearly opposite the Court House. Extensive stock of genuine medicines and assortment of surgeon's instruments. . . ."

He was on the teaching staff at Transylvania University in 1809 and 1816.

He married in Fayette County, Kentucky, April 11, 1816, Eliza H. Dixon, daughter of T. Dixon, and in 1818 removed to Tennessee. His military career extended only from May 27, 1812, when he was appointed from Kentucky a 2nd Lieutenant in the 17th U. S. Infantry, to February 10, 1813, when he resigned.

Dr. James Overton was known as "the father of the Nashville and Chattanooga Railroad," and was active in Tennessee in establishing hospitals for the insane, during the years 1836-1840.

Dr. Overton has been described as a "small, black-eyed man, very hypochondriacal and sarcastic (notoriously so), and yet quite chatty, humorous, and agreeable; telling his class many funny things. . . . He was well educated for his day and plumed himself especially on his Greek. . . ."

His great niece, Mrs. Waller O. Bullock, in speaking of the portrait made of him in Philadelphia before 1815 (the only portrait extant) said of him:

The portrait was done in Philadelphia just as he was completing his medical course, and I think it must have been soon after that he entered upon his work at Transylvania. He took a post-graduate course at Paris, France, and was considered one of the most brilliant men of his day. He had great command of language and his conversation sparkled with wit and humor, nor was he less happy with his pen . . . when distinguished foreigners visited President Jackson at the *Hermitage* it always devolved on Doctor Overton to do the agreeable, his command of French peculiarly fitting him for the post. He early left Kentucky to make his home in Tennessee, where he practiced his profession for many years, dying at an advanced age.

One Dr. James Overton is buried in Mt. Olivet Cemetery, at Nashville. He died October 10, 1865, aged 80 years.

[Harris, Malcolm H., *History of Louisa County, Virginia*, 1936; *Tennessee Historical Quarterly*, III (1944), IX (1950), XV (1956); *East Tennessee Historical Society Publications*, VI (1934); Peters, Robert, *Transylvania University* ("Filson Club Publications," No. 11); McCormick, J. N., *Some Pioneer Kentucky Physicians*, 1917; Acklen, Jeannette T., *Tennessee Records: Tombstone Inscriptions and Manuscripts* . . ., 1934; *Anderson-Overton Genealogy*, q. v., for the children of Dr. James Overton.]

JOHN PAYNE
Brigadier General, Kentucky Militia

John Payne was born April 8, 1764, in Fairfax County, Virginia, the only son of William Payne, Sr., and his second wife, Ann Jennings. He died at his home near Georgetown, Kentucky, September 9, 1837, from injuries received when thrown several months earlier from his horse.

Settling early in Scott County, Kentucky, he served in the militia and commanded a company in Scott's campaign against the Indians in 1791. He was commissioned a Brigadier General in the 6th Brigade, Kentucky Militia, July 16, 1806. Shortly after the Act of Congress of April 10, 1812, authorizing the Governor of Kentucky to raise the "River Raisin Force" of 5,500 men, John Payne was commissioned Brigadier General of the 2nd Brigade, August 6, 1812. Assigned originally to command this force, he was relieved of the command after General Harrison's appointment as Major General in the Kentucky Militia. Thereafter he continued with the army, was present at the destruction September 14, 1812, of the Five Medal's Towns (east of modern Ligon-

Biographies

ier), and was in command at the Rapids just before the battles and massacre at Frenchtown.

After the war General Payne settled at his estate on the Frankfort Road, about three miles from Georgetown. He represented Scott County in the Kentucky Senate in 1830-1832.

He married, June 28, 1787, Elizabeth (Betsey) Johnson, born in Orange County, Virginia, April 16, 1772, a daughter of Suggett and Robert Johnson, and sister of Colonel Richard M. Johnson. Betsey Johnson Payne died in Scott County in November, 1845.

Thirteen children were born to them:

(1) Asa Payne, born March 19, 1788, and died July 10, 1887, served as his father's aide-de-camp during the War of 1812, and was married three times; (2) Robert Payne, born December 20, 1789, married Maria Williams; (3) Nancy Payne, born October 16, 1791, married Zabel Offutt, and died in 1882; (4) Sally Payne, born November 16, 1795, married Charles Tomson who served as a private soldier in Captain Redding's company, was taken prisoner at Frenchtown and carried into Canada before parole; (5) John Payne, born November 16, 1795, married Mary Stevenson, and died in 1887; (6) Betsey Payne, born January 22, 1798, married Uriel Sebree, q. v.; (7) Newton Payne, born January 4, 1800, married, first, Louisa Nuchols, and secondly, Susan Spencer; (8) William J. Payne, born January 26, 1802, and died in 1813; (9) Thomas Jefferson Payne, born February 3, 1804, and died in Howard County, Missouri, in 1880: he married, first, Latitia Thompson, and second, Mary Wright; (10) Franklin Payne, born March 16, 1806, married Polly Rogers and died in 1874; (11) Richard Payne, born February 26, 1808, and died May 27, 1823; (12) Emeline Payne, born March 13, 1810, married James Peak, and died in 1851; (13) Cyrus M. Payne, born November 10, 1812, Sergeant in Company A, Third Regiment, Kentucky Foot Volunteers, Mexican War. He was mustered into service at Louisville October 5, 1847. On the official roster of the company he is listed as "Missing: supposed to be killed by Mexicans June 2, 1848."

[Payne, Brooke, *The Paynes of Virginia*, 1937; Johnston, J. Stoddard, "Colonel Asa Payne," *Register*, XXVI (1928); Clift, G. Glenn, "*Corn Stalk*" *Militia of Kentucky* 1792-1811; Richard H. Collins, *History of Kentucky* . . . 1924; *Report of the Adjutant General of Kentucky: Mexican War Veterans*, 1889; "Original Roster of Officers of War 1812-15," MSS, Kentucky Historical Society.]

SAMUEL WELLS
Colonel, 17th United States Infantry

Samuel Wells was born in Virginia in 1754, probably a son of Charles Wells, whose wife was a Carty. As early as 1775 he was in Mason County, Kentucky, surveying and building cabins with Haydon Wells, Matthew Rust and others. He returned in February of the following year and surveyed more land with the same group. In 1779 he was in the present Shelby County with Captain Bland Ballard and others and about this time built Wells' Station, three and one half miles northwest of the present town of Shelbyville. He was with Colonel John Floyd as an Indian fighter and was credited with saving Floyd's life at the latter's defeat by Indians a few miles east of the present city of Louisville, September 15, 1781.

Colonel Wells' military career in Kentucky became a matter of record with the formation of the State in 1792 and the creation of archival materials. On December 20, 1793, he was appointed by Governor Isaac Shelby as Major of the 9th Regiment, Kentucky Militia, to rank from August, 1792. On December 21, 1794, he was appointed Lieutenant Colonel, Commandant, 1st Regiment of the militia, from July 11, 1792.

Settling in Louisville in the early 1780's he soon became identified with the history of that community, appearing often in the court records of Jefferson County. On April 1, 1795, he was commissioned by Governor Shelby one of the Justices of the Peace for Jefferson County, and given the same post again December 19, 1795. Taking an interest in politics he ran for and was elected to the State House of Representatives, from Jefferson County, in 1795-1796 and again in 1799.

With the outbreak of the War of 1812 Colonel Wells again came forward for military service, and was at once commissioned Major, Battalion Light Dragoons, October 11, 1811, and rendered conspicuous service at the battle of Tippecanoe. On March 12, 1812, he received an appointment in the United States Army as Colonel of the 17th Infantry, recruited largely in Kentucky shortly afterward. He held this rank until honorably discharged June 1, 1814.

Mr. William Graves in his account of the Wells family (see bibliography below) states that Colonel Samuel Wells married a Haden. *DAR Lineage* records indicate that he married, first, in

Biographies

1780, Rebecca Pope. Jefferson County marriage records reveal that he married December 30, 1781, Mary Spear and that the bondsman was Moses Spear. The *Louisville Western Courier* of October 15, 1812, carried the following item: "Mrs. Mary, consort of Col. Samuel Wells, of the 17th U. S. Army, died in Louisville October 10, 1812." Colonel Wells died November 20, 1835, probably at St. Louis. Other sources give the date of his death as 1830.

The known children of Colonel Samuel Wells usually are given as:

Samuel Wells, Jr., born 1784 and died 1859 (other sources give 1788-1853). He married in 1813 Mary Kearney, born in 1788 and died in 1833 (other sources give 1797-1853). They had at least one daughter, Mary Spears Wells.

Levi Wells, Ensign at River Raisin and killed in action there.

Rebecca Wells, born in 1788 and died in 1853 (see Samuel Wells, Jr., above). She married in 1811 Nathan Heald (1755-1832).

[*The Wells Family*, 1 p., n.d., unsigned leaf at Kentucky Historical Society; Clift, G. G., *History of Maysville and Mason County, Kentucky*, v. 1; D.A.R. Lineage Books, v. 66, 145, 160; *Register*, v. 10; *Filson Club History Quarterly*, v. 3, 6, 8; *Executive Journal of Gov. Isaac Shelby*; Pirtle, Alfred, *The Battle of Tippecanoe*; Heitman, Francis B., *Historical Register and Dictionary of the U. S. Army*; Graves, William, *Graves Genealogy*, compiled and presented to the Filson Club, 1943; *William Wells family*, p. 19-29a.]

JOHN ALLEN
Lieutenant Colonel, 1st Rifle Regiment

Colonel Allen was born December 30, 1771, in Rockbridge County, Virginia, the first son of James and Mary Kelsey Allen. Before reaching his eighth birthday he came with his parents to Kentucky, settling at Dougherty's Station on Clark's Run, just below the present site of Danville. Four years later James Allen removed to Nelson County, establishing his family about eight miles from Bardstown.

Here John Allen received his first schooling, before Mr. Shackelford of Bardstown, gaining a thorough knowledge of both Greek and Latin. This school was succeeded by that of Dr. James Priestly, under whom young Allen finished his studies. In this course he knew as schoolmates John Rowan, John Pope, Felix

Grundy and Joseph Hamilton Daviess, all of whom were to share with Allen high places in the local and national life of their times.

In 1791 he began the study of law in the office of Judge Archibald Stuart, of Virginia. It is recorded that while attending court in Lexington on one occasion, Judge Stuart encountered a youth named John Allen and encouraged him to study law, taking him into his office and family.

In 1795 the partnership between Judge Stuart and Allen was dissolved and he later returned to Kentucky, locating in Shelby County. Here he entered into legal practice and eventually earned for himself an enviable name among Kentucky lawyers of his day.

He was elected to represent Shelby County in the Legislature in 1800, and after removing to Frankfort, he represented Franklin County in the House, 1803-1806. During the latter year he was associated with Henry Clay in the defense of Aaron Burr. A year later, in 1807, he was elected to the Kentucky Senate from Franklin and held this position until 1810. In 1808 he was a candidate for governor against the veteran campaigner Charles Scott, and was beaten by Scott only when that seasoned strategist urged the people to send the talented Allen to the United States Congress where his worth would cast glory on Kentucky and himself—and not to the governor's chair, where his brilliance would be wasted.

In 1810 he was elected again to the Senate, from Shelby County, and was in this office at the time of his death.

When the War of 1812 was begun Allen raised one of the first regiments in the state. His commission as Lieutenant Colonel of the 1st Rifle Regiment was dated June 5, 1812. Much original source material concerning the early days of the war in Kentucky is contained in Allen's letters to his wife. These letters recount the day-by-day activities of his regiment; of his first major, Martin D. Hardin, who had married Allen's wife's sister; and of her younger brothers, Dr. Benjamin Logan and Robert Logan. Allen County, created by Act of Assembly approved January 11, 1815, was named in honor of Colonel John Allen.

Colonel Allen married in Shelby County, October 19, 1798, Jane Logan, eldest daughter of General Benjamin Logan and Anne Montgomery Logan. Jane Logan Allen was long hopeful that the Indians had captured her husband and that one day, despite assurances from all that he was no more, he would return. For eight years she watched and waited from their home on the Lex-

Biographies

ington-Louisville road, and each night would throw open the window shutter facing the north and place a candle on the sill. At length her grief and hopelessness wasted away her strength and on February 28, 1821, she died and was buried in the Logan family cemetery near Shelbyville.

Four daughters were born to Colonel John and Jane Logan Allen:

Anna Maria Allen, born August 5, 1802. She married in Shelby County on May 14, 1818, Henry Crittenden, of Frankfort, born May 24, 1792 and died December 31, 1834. After his death Anna Maria Crittenden married David R. Murray, of Cloverport, Kentucky. She died at the latter place April 24, 1877. By her first marriage she had eight children, one of whom was Thomas Theodore Crittenden, governor of Missouri. She had four sons by her second marriage.

Eliza Sarah Allen, second daughter, was born in Shelby County in September, 1806. After the death of her parents she lived with her uncle, Martin D. Hardin. She married in Franklin County, November 26, 1833, Pierce Butler. She died in Maysville, Kentucky, July 28, 1867, surviving her husband who died in Louisville, of cholera, in 1851. For notes on their children see Green's *Historic Families of Kentucky*, pages 267-270.

Jane Logan Allen, third daughter, was born September 24, 1808, in Shelby County. She married there January 8, 1824, Dr. John Todd Parker, then of Woodford County. She died on September 12, 1844, and was buried in the Logan family cemetery near Shelbyville. They had six children, for a list of whom see Green, *op. cit.*, pages 271-275.

Mary Kelsey Allen, fourth daughter, married in Shelby County May 10, 1829, Thomas Willoughby Newton (born Alexandria, Virginia, January 18, 1804, and died in New York City September 22, 1853), member of Congress who served with that body from February 6 to March 3, 1847. They had at least three children: Anna, who married Colonel Richard Johnson, Little Rock, Arkansas, editor and lawyer; Thomas and Robert Newton, officers in the C.S.A.

[Green, Thomas Marshall, *Historic Families of Kentucky* . . . 1st ser., Cincinnati, 1889; *The Crittenden Memoirs*, comp. by H. H. Crittenden, New York, 1936; Willis, George L., Sr., *History of Shelby County*, 1929; *Michigan Pioneer and Historical Collections*, vol. 35; Shelby, Franklin

County marriage records; Cemetery records, Logan Family Cemetery; *Biographical Directory of the American Congress, 1774-1927;* Shinn, Josiah H., *Pioneers and Makers of Arkansas,* 1908.]

WILLIAM LEWIS
Lieutenant Colonel, Commanding, 5th Regiment Kentucky Militia

Born in Virginia in 1767, Colonel Lewis early emigrated to Kentucky and lived for many years in Jessamine County.

His military career began early in the fight to wrest the Virginia country from the Indians. In 1791 he was made captain in the Virginia Levies and as such served in Gaither's Battalion at St. Clair's Defeat. On March 16, 1792, he became Captain in the 3rd Regiment of Infantry and in the Third U. S. Sublegion on September 4 of the same year. He was honorably discharged from this tour on November 1, 1796.

His commission as Lieutenant Colonel of Kentucky Militia was issued under date of August 7, 1812. In this capacity he led his regiment through two battles until his capture by the enemy January 22, 1813. He was held prisoner of war in Quebec until 1814.

Although appointed to the command of the 5th Regiment over senior officers, the appointment was approved by all who knew of his military experience and his ability to lead men. His old friend Governor Charles Scott, who made the appointment, often said of Lewis "that if he were ordered to storm hell he would choose Lewis for one of his men." This confidence was more than borne out during the action at Frenchtown in January, 1813.

Less than a month after his capture, with most of his regiment, all of the surviving Kentucky officers addressed a petition to the Secretary of War, begging that Colonel Lewis' freedom be secured so that his talents could again be of use to the country. In this essay the officers pointed out:

The deportment of Col. Lewis to his brother officers and to the Army presents an example worthy the imitation of every military man. To his inferiors he was dignified, unaccompanying that dignity with any useless pride. To his superiors, you would never know from Lewis that he had a superior, except you saw him in the execution of his orders. He always preserves a respectful distance towards them. With his own command he was popular—not because he courted them, but

Biographies   117

because he always did his duty, and seemed to exert his authority for the good of the country alone. The education of Lewis has not been that of the most polished kind—but if he is deficient in school-learning in some measure he will seldom be found wanting in a knowledge of *men* and *things;* with all, he is well versed in modern history. Military tactics he had made his study for many years; they are the delight of his soul. I suppose Lewis to be between 45 and 50 years of age, and though a man of excellent person, from an inveterate carelessness he has about the frippery of dress, it would never be believed he is the man I have described, unless he was seen in the exercise of military duties.

On his return from captivity Colonel Lewis took up his residence again in Jessamine County. He remained actively in command of Jessamine's 9th Regiment of Militia until 1815. His highest rank as given on September 30 of that year was Colonel.

In 1819 he removed with his family to Arkansas Territory, settling at Pecannerie, then in Pulaski County. He died at his home there during the night of January 17, 1825, in his 58th year. He was buried at Little Rock with full military honors.

Of Colonel Lewis' children, Harriet married on December 28, 1824, Dr. Nimrod Menifee, the great duelling surgeon of early Arkansas. One of Colonel Lewis' sons, William, Jr., died at Pecannerie September 24, 1824.

[Shinn, Josiah H., *Pioneers and Makers of Arkansas*, Little Rock, c1908; *Kentucky Gazette*, 17 Mar. 1825; *Commentator*, 26 Mar. 1825; Heitman, Francis B., *Historical Register and Dictionary of the U. S. Army;* "Colonel William Lewis," in *Reporter*, 5 June 1813; Lossing, *Pictorial Field-Book of the War of 1812;* Young, Bennett H., *History of Jessamine County.*]

JOHN MITCHELL SCOTT
Lieutenant Colonel, Commanding, 1st Regiment

Dr. John M. Scott was born in 1764, a son of Matthew Scott, a captain in the Revolutionary Army, and grandson of John Scott of the French and Indian War. His study and training in medicine was received in New Jersey, under his uncle. When qualified for the profession he received on September 29, 1789, the appointment of Surgeon's Mate in the infantry regiment then commanded by General Josiah Harmar and on duty on the western frontiers. When General Anthony Wayne took over command of the western army, Scott was promoted on April 11, 1792, to Surgeon of the

2nd U. S. Regiment. It was in this capacity that he first met and became intimately acquainted with General William Henry Harrison, then Wayne's aide-de-camp.

After the Treaty of Greenville Dr. Scott returned to Kentucky where he practiced medicine, first in 1796 in Woodford County, later removing to and settling in Frankfort where he became one of the leading practitioners of his day.

Maintaining an active interest in the military, he was appointed Surgeon, 2nd Infantry, November 1, 1796, an office he resigned January 1 of the year following. On March 13, 1797, he became captain in the 22nd Regiment (Franklin County Militia) and on March 22, 1798, major of the 2nd Battalion of this unit.

As personal physician to his old friend, Governor William H. Harrison, Dr. Scott on more than one occasion made the long and perilous trip from his home in Frankfort to that of the governor in Vincennes to attend the latter's wife. When Harrison's third son was born October 4, 1804, on one of these long trips, it was named John Scott Harrison and a son born to Mrs. Scott during the doctor's absence was later to be christened William Henry Harrison Scott.

In 1811 Scott was appointed sheriff of Franklin County, an office he was holding at the time of his death the following year.

For some time prior to the outbreak of the War of 1812 Dr. Scott had been in poor health and fears were entertained for his recovery. It was not Governor Charles Scott's intention, therefore, to appoint the doctor to an active role in the forthcoming campaign. Dr. Scott insisted on his right, as major of the 22nd Regiment, and on August 7, 1812, was officially appointed Lieutenant Colonel, Commandant, of the 1st Regiment, Kentucky Volunteer Militia.

Much to the surprise and delight of his family and friends, who did not expect him to survive the rigors of the campaign, the return to army routines and interests together with the attendant exercise in the open air restored his health. When Scott's regiment was ordered to move out and destroy the Indian villages at Elk Hart his officers recommended that he stay behind and avoid unnecessary fatigue. The commanding general as well asked him to remain in the main camp, assuring him there would be no fighting in that quarter.

Biographies

Colonel Scott made no answer to this but as he approached his horse he was heard to mutter, "As long as I am able to mount you, none but myself shall lead my regiment, either to fight or not to fight."

This detail proved his undoing. The expedition had lasted three days and nights and had exacted much from the colonel and his men. Colonel Scott was barely able to make it back to camp, and despite continued rest and medications he could accompany the army only until it reached Fort Defiance during the night of September 30, 1812. From this camp he was sent back to Frankfort in a litter.

The long trip home ended in November. The harm had been done, however, and Colonel Scott died Sunday evening December 20, 1812. Both branches of the Legislature unanimously adopted a resolution that as a public testimony all members would attend his funeral. He was buried Monday December 21 with full military honors. The military preceded the body, followed by the Governor, Lieutenant-Governor, members of each branch of the Legislature and a large body of the inhabitants of Frankfort.

Dr. Scott had married Catherine Ware, who was born May 1, 1777, a daughter of James Ware, Jr., M.D. (1741-1820) and Catherine Todd Ware (born February 9, 1753). Catherine Ware Scott's will was probated July 15, 1863, in Frankfort. In that instrument are named four of their children:

Elizabeth Scott, who married December 17, 1818, Colonel Solomon P. Sharp. She died in January, 1844.

William Henry Harrison Scott.

Arabella Scott, who married first, December 29, 1831, William M. Davis, of Ohio County, and second, on November 13, 1838, Sylvester Welch.

Catherine Scott, who married June 4, 1834, Johnson Johnson.

A second son, Major John M. Scott, had died before his mother's will was probated. He was born in Frankfort January 8, 1813, and died there October 28, 1850. He entered West Point Military Academy in 1831 and was graduated June 30, 1835, as Second Lieutenant, 1st Infantry. He was promoted to 1st Lieutenant July 7, 1838, Captain June 18, 1846, and Major September 23, 1846, "for gallant and meritorious conduct in the several conflicts at Monterey, Mexico, on the 21st, 22nd, and 23rd September 1846."

[*Kentucky Pioneer Doctors*, published by Daniel M. Hutton, 1934; Heitman, Francis B., *Historical Register and Dictionary of the U. S. Army;* Franklin County marriage and will records; *Lexington Reporter,* January 2, 1813; Cleaves, Freeman, *Old Tippecanoe, William Henry Harrison and His Time;* Dawson, Moses, *William Henry Harrison;* Women's Auxiliary, Franklin County Medical Society, *Doctors of Franklin County, Kentucky,* MS; Johnson, L. F., *The History of Franklin County, Kentucky;* [Frankfort, Ky.] *Daily Commonwealth,* 9 Nov. 1850; *Register of the Officers and Graduates of the U. S. Military Academy* . . . 1850; ALS, John W. Scott, 328 N. Limestone, Lexington, Ky., Oct. 17, 1954.]

BENJAMIN FRANKLIN GRAVES
Major, 2nd Battalion, 5th Regiment

Major Graves was born in Spottsylvania County, Virginia, in 1771, the fourth child and third son of Joseph and Frances (Coleman) Graves. Joseph Graves died at his Spottsylvania County home, *The Red House,* May 12, 1785. Frances (Coleman) Graves, born in Virginia in 1744, died in Fayette County, Kentucky, in December, 1844.

Benjamin F. Graves came to Kentucky with his mother and all of her children, except Joseph, in 1791. They settled in Fayette County where Major Graves spent his life engaged in agricultural pursuits. In 1801 and again in 1804 he was elected to represent his county in the lower house of the General Assembly.

His commission as Major, 2nd Battalion, 5th Regiment, was dated August 7, 1812. One of the wounded left in the houses at Frenchtown following the battle of January 22, 1813, he was made prisoner by the Indians during the massacre which followed on January 23. Ensign Isaac L. Baker in his report to General Winchester of February 25, 1813, reported that Major Graves had been brought to the River Rouge in a sleigh on January 25 or 26, but that no further word was heard of him. Actually he had been carried into captivity by the Potawatomies along with Timothy Mallory, Samuel Ganoe and John Davenport. Mallory and Ganoe successfully made their escape from the Indian camp and brought back word that Major Graves was still with the Indians. He was not heard of again.

Thomas Coleman Graves, youngest brother of Major Benjamin F. Graves and 1st Lieutenant in Captain Richard Hightower's Company, 17th U. S. Infantry, was killed in the action at Frenchtown on January 22, 1813.

Biographies

Graves County, Kentucky, established by Act of Assembly approved December 17, 1823, was named in honor of Major Benjamin F. Graves.

Major Graves married Polly Dudley, born September 6, 1783, a daughter of Ambrose and Ann (Parker) Dudley. They had six children: Ambrose, Lucien, Nancy, Fanny, Elizabeth and Marion Graves.

[Clark, Mrs. Sarah Graves, "Some lines of the Graves family in the Blue Grass," *Register*, v. 34 (1936); Darnell, Elias, *A Journal* . . . for the narrative of Timothy Mallory, captive with Major Graves; Collins, Richard H., *History of Kentucky*, v. 2; *Acts of the General Assembly of Kentucky, 1823-4*; Pratt, Mary B., *Our relations, Dudley-Pratt families*, Indianapolis, Pratt-Foster Co., n.d.]

ELIJAH McCLENAHAN (McCLANAHAN)
Major, 2nd Battalion, 1st Regiment

Major McClenahan was born in Chester County, Pennsylvania, April 14, 1770, and died at his home near Toulon, Stark County, Illinois, July 14, 1851. The inscription on his tombstone there reads: "Elijah McClenahan Died July 14, 1851, aged 81 Years, Three Months."

While it has not yet been proven that John McClenahan, resident of Oxford Township, Chester County, Pennsylvania, and his wife Janet Buchanan (natives of County Armagh, Ireland) were the parents of Major Elijah McClenahan, the following could indicate as much: John McClenahan by his attorney, James Taylor, acting under power of attorney signed in Bourbon County, Kentucky, dated and signed there January 25, 1793, conveyed land in Oxford Township, Chester County, Pennsylvania, which he acquired by Indenture August 10, 1774. John McClenehan was in Chester County in 1799, with 250 acres with improvements, 3 horses, 5 cows, 12 sheep, one Negro, one mill, and then he drops from the returns of that county. In the 1790 census this John McClenahan is not listed as a resident of Pennsylvania. It would seem therefore that he was the father with whom the subject of this sketch migrated, in 1785, to Bourbon County, Kentucky.

In Bourbon at that time the Indians were very troublesome and it was necessary to keep men stationed at the various forts to guard and protect the settlers. Young McClenahan, at the age of eighteen, became one of the Minutemen, stationed at Washington, Mason County, Kentucky. This was an organization commanded by Simon Kenton. He remained a member of this company for two years. In the year 1790 he marched with General Harmar against what was then the Northwestern Indians. They crossed the Ohio River and young McClenahan assisted in cutting the first timber off of where the present city of Cincinnati now stands.

On September 21, 1793 (another reference says 1795) he was married to Elizabeth Kemp, daughter of Reuben Kemp of Bourbon County and later of Pendleton. They reared a family of five sons and six daughters. Two of their children were buried in infancy.

In 1797 Elijah McClenahan moved from Bourbon to Falmouth, Pendleton County, where he hoped to follow his trade as a tanner. The records of the town of Falmouth reveal that a deed from the trustees was made out to McClenahan December 24, 1799. He was a member of the County Court (Justice) when it met September 4, 1799, at the house of Alvin Mountjoy. Members Alvin Mountjoy, Elijah McClenahan and Charles Stern were appointed to fix a place for a "Gaol" and let same to the lowest bidder. (Reuben Kemp is listed as getting a deed from the Trustees of the town of Falmouth in 1800.)

On May 25, 1799, he had been appointed by Governor Garrard a Justice of the Peace for Pendleton County, in place of J. Cook, resigned. On October 8 of the year before he was commissioned Ensign in the 21st Regiment by Governor Garrard. This was followed by commission of Lieutenant in the same regiment, January 19, 1801, and Captain October 3, 1803. He was commissioned Major of the 1st Battalion, 21st Regiment, December 18, 1806, by Governor Greenup.

In 1806 he was elected from Pendleton County to the State Legislature, after which service he returned home and followed his trade as tanner until the outbreak of the War of 1812.

Commissioned Major, 2nd Battalion, 1st Regiment, on August 7, 1812, he marched with Colonel John M. Scott's regiment and as noted in the text succeeded to the command of Colonel Samuel Wells' regiment when that officer returned to the rear on the night preceding the battle of January 22, 1813. Family tradition recounts that he came near to losing his life during the battle when a bullet passed through his hat, cutting the skin and a portion of his hair from the top of his head.

Major McClenahan's account of the battle of January 22 was published in the *Reporter* (Lexington, Ky.) of May 4, 1813: "I was with the troops, and assisted in all the attempts that were made to rally the men," he wrote the editor of that paper. "I conversed with General Winchester on the retreat, after every attempt to rally the troops had proved ineffectual. Subsequent to this conversation with General Winchester I assisted Captain Price, Captain Glaves and others in their retreat. Captain Glaves was wounded, but I succeeded in getting him off, and should have saved Captain Price also, but for the weakness of my horse. . . ."

The old flint lock rifle used by Major McClenahan in the battle is still in the possession of the family of Mr. Frank Clifton McClenahan, Toulon, Illinois.

Returning home from service, Major McClenahan was again, in 1815, elected to the State Legislature from Pendleton County, this time by an almost unanimous vote. Twelve votes only in the county were cast against him.

After this term in the General Assembly he remained a farmer in the community until the fall of 1826, when with his family he moved to Ohio and settled near Sidney, Shelby County. He remained a farmer here until the fall of 1831 when he followed the tide of immigration to Illinois. In the spring of 1833 he settled in Putnam, now Stark County, Illinois.

In his last years Major McClenahan turned his energies to reading, concentrating mainly on the Bible. He made no public profession of religion until after he moved to Illinois and never attached himself to any church until about a year before he died, when both he and his wife joined the Christian Church near Princes Grove, Peoria County, of which church they both remained members until their deaths. Mrs. McClenahan died in September, 1846.

The children of Elijah and Elizabeth (Kemp) McClenahan were:

John McClenahan, born about 1795. He was probably the John McClenahan of Captain Michael Glaves' Company, and with his father during the battle of January 22, 1813. Major McClenahan stated in his report to General Harrison, from Camp on Carrying River, January 26, that "after continuing with the men about half a mile further and finding nothing more could be done I took Capt. Glaves, who was wounded, behind me and my son by the hand and left the road and reached camp with them."

Henry McClenahan, born March 20, 1798; married June 25, 1821, in Pendleton County, Sarah "Sally" Shawhan (October 12,

1803-May 19, 1880), a daughter of Daniel and Mary (McDowell) Shawhan. Henry McClenahan moved in 1826 to Rush County, Indiana, and in 1834 to Goshen Township, Stark County, Illinois, where he died June 16, 1857.

Sarah McClenahan.

Ann McClenahan, born 1802? She married Stephen Worley.

Elizabeth McClenahan, born 1804? She married in 1853 Moses Snodgrass. They removed to Salt Lake City.

Jane McClenahan.

Jemima McClenahan, married in 1830 W. W. Drummond.

Marie McClenahan, married in 1839 Robert Caldwell.

Elsie McClenahan, married a Barnett and migrated west to Oregon.

James McClenahan, married Anne Pollock.

Robert McClenahan, married in 1839 Lucy Richards and settled in Utah.

Elijah McClenahan, Jr., born June 3, 1811, in Pendleton County. He married March 1, 1835, Sarah Emery. She was a native of Ohio and died January 26, 1854.

[Typescript of manuscript by Clarinda McClenahan Bowden, granddaughter of Major McClenahan, contributed by Mrs. Frank Clifton McClenahan, Toulon, Illinois; Collins, Richard H., *History of Kentucky;* Bourbon and Pendleton County court records; *Executive Journal of Governor James Garrard; Harrison's Messages and Letters* (Indiana Historical Collections, vol. 9); "Company Officers," 1799-1804, MS, Kentucky Historical Society; *Executive Journal, 1804-1808, of Governor Christopher Greenup.*]

GEORGE MADISON
Major, 2nd Battalion, 1st Rifle Regiment

Governor George Madison was born in 1763 in Augusta County, Virginia, a son of John and Agatha (Strother) Madison. His father, John Madison, a near relative of President Madison, was first clerk of Augusta County, 1745, member of the vestry and of the Virginia House of Burgesses and House of Delegates. He died in Botetourt County, Virginia, in 1784.

George Madison was a soldier in the American Revolution before he was of age. Removing to Kentucky he entered into the struggle for defense of the country and was thereafter active in the military and official affairs of the new state. He led a company at St. Clair's defeat and was severely wounded during the engagement. His life was saved at this time by John Burnes, a

Frankfort butcher, who rescued Captain Madison and brought him to safety astride his own horse. Madison was again wounded in action the following year during the attack made upon John Adair's force by Little Turtle. In this engagement Madison held the rank of Major.

On the termination of the Indian wars, with Wayne's victory in 1794, Madison returned to private life. Two years later, on March 7, 1796, Governor Isaac Shelby appointed him Auditor of Public Accounts, a post he held until 1816.

The outbreak of the War of 1812 found Madison a settled, successful man of nearly fifty years of age. His old Indian fighting captains Paschal Hickman and Bland Ballard, however, persuaded Madison to join Colonel John Allen's 1st Rifle Regiment as a Major and march with them to the north. His commission as Major, 2nd Battalion, was dated June 17, 1812.

After his capture and confinement in the Fortress at Quebec, Major Madison returned home to Frankfort but with the seeds of early death in his system.

Colonel Orlando Brown, in his *Governors of Kentucky, 1792-1824*, recalled that "Major Madison took with him a very black servant named Peter—or Peter Williams as he was commonly called. Peter had the good fortune to be in the battle, and he came home one of the greatest men who had ever been on a stricken field. Peter was for a long time the oracle with the niggers and boys, and told us how to fight Indians, of whom he had slain so many that he was a marvelous competent teacher of the art. He claimed all the indulgences due a veteran and had them. He pursued the avocation of a hotel cook, and got so fat upon the smell of the kitchen that he could scarcely waddle along, but he talked about the River Raisin to the last."

With Governor Shelby's second term of office about to expire, Major Madison was an almost unanimous choice to succeed him. Colonel James Johnson for a short time was the opposing candidate but he withdrew from the canvas, "declaring that it was perfectly futile for him or any body else to run against a man so popular and so universally beloved as he found his opponent to be."

Madison was elected to the governorship in August, 1816, but the high honor had come too late and found him in the last stages of tuberculosis. He had left only enough strength to take the oath of office and to appoint his Secretary of State, another campaigner in the Northwest, Colonel Charles S. Todd. Governor Madison died in office October 14, 1816, at his home in Paris, Kentucky.

He was first buried in the old burying ground on a hill north of Frankfort. On September 15, 1874, his remains were reinterred in the State Cemetery at Frankfort.

George Madison married Jane Smith, a daughter of Major Francis Smith, of Virginia, who settled later at Frankfort, and Anne (Preston) Smith who was born in 1731 and died in 1813. Jane (Smith) Madison was a granddaughter of the first John Preston, her mother being a daughter of John Preston and Elizabeth (Patton) Preston. Jane (Smith) Madison was born in Botetourt County, Virginia, in 1777 and died in Frankfort, Kentucky, on April 4, 1811, after a long illness.

Four children were born to George and Jane (Smith) Madison, only one of whom, Myra, reached maturity. As named in Governor Madison's will they were Agatha, William, Myra and George. In this instrument the governor appointed Mr. Lewis Marshall to superintend the education of William and George Madison.

Agatha S. Madison died in Woodford County Sunday, June 6, 1819. She was buried near her father, in the old Frankfort cemetery, on the Monday following.

George Madison, Jr., died at the Franklin County residence of Andrew Alexander, his brother-in-law, in October, 1831, after an illness of two or three months.

Of the other son, William, nothing has been learned. Colonel Orlando Brown in his book on the governors stated that "a promising young son of Governor Madison's, Gabriel Madison, was killed by a tame deer at the farm of Doctor Lewis Marshall, in Woodford County." This might have been either George, Jr., or William Madison.

Myra Madison married Andrew Alexander, of Woodford County. (There is a monument in the Scott lot at Frankfort to Andrew J. Alexander, born March 19, 1796, and died December 18, 1833. Also one to William M., son of A. J. and M. Alexander, born January 12, 1827, and died October 27, 1836.) The children of Myra (Madison) and Andrew Alexander were: (a) Appoline Alexander, married Francis P. Blair; (b) Myra Alexander, mar-

Biographies 127

ried Franklin Dick; (c) George M. Alexander, married Mary Campbell, and (d) Andrew J. Alexander, who married Evalinia Martin.

[*Governors of Kentucky, 1792-1824,* by Colonel Orlando Brown, ed. by G. Glenn Clift; *Commentator,* Oct. 18, 1831; *Will Book B,* Franklin County Court; Owen, Thomas McAdory, "William Strother, of Virginia, and his descendants," *Publications of the Southern History Association,* v. 2 (1898); Clift, G. Glenn, *The Governors of Kentucky, 1792-1942* (1942); *Argus of Western America,* April 10, 1811.]

DR. JOHN IRVINE, SENIOR SURGEON

Dr. Irvine, killed during the action of January 22, 1813, was a son of Thomas Irvine, of Clark County, and Jane (Hawkins) Irvine. The mother was a daughter of John Hawkins and widow of Colonel John Todd, killed at the battle of Blue Licks.

Under date of May 5, 1812, Thomas Irvine wrote Governor Charles Scott: "My son John had the honor to serve under your command at Genl. Wayne's Campaign as 1st Surgeon. He desires me to make his most respectful compliments to you and to inform your Excellency that if you thought proper to appoint him Surgeon Genl. or his old appointment that he would accept with pleasure."

His appointment as Senior Surgeon of the Raisin Force was dated August 6, 1812.

John Irvine married February 3, 1800, Ann Bingham Clark (other sources give her name as Nancy Bingham Clark). Five years after the death of her husband at Frenchtown, Ann B. Irvine married, June 30, 1818, William Neely in Clark County. He was a native of Jefferson County, Mississippi, and died at Winchester, Kentucky, August 28, 1818. Mrs. Ann Neely died January 29, 1859, in her 74th year.

Of the children born to Dr. John and Ann Bingham Irvine:

Fanny P. Irvine married on February 22, 1825, Joseph H. January.

Mary Jane Irvine married on February 22, 1825, William C. Sympson.

Eliza H. Irvine, daughter of Dr. John and A. B. Irvine, and wife of A. M. Preston, was born July 2, 1804, and died September 13, 1832. She and her child are buried in Clark County.

Dr. John Irvine and his wife had one son, name unknown to the present investigator, who moved to Illinois.

[Shane Papers, 11CC111; Clark County marriage and cemetery records; *Register*, v. 32 (1934), v. 33 (1935); Letter, Thomas Irvine to Gov. Charles Scott, dated Winchester May 5, 1812, Governor Scott Papers, Kentucky Historical Society, Box 8, jacket 55.]

DR. ALEXANDER MONTGOMERY
Surgeon, 17th United States Infantry

Dr. Montgomery, killed during the action of January 22, 1813, was a son of Major Alexander and Elizabeth Robinson Montgomery. Major Montgomery was born in Virginia in 1750 and died in Fayette County, Kentucky, in late February or early March, 1814. He was juror, Tax Commissioner, Lieutenant in the Washington County, Virginia, militia and fought at King's Mountain. He came to Kentucky with his family in 1790, settling in Fayette County.

Major Alexander and Elizabeth Robinson Montgomery had five sons and two daughters: Major William Montgomery, who served in the War of 1812; Elizabeth "Betsy" Montgomery (1790-1826), who married December 21, 1813, George Coleman (1778-1845), being his second wife; Robinson Montgomery, who removed to Madison County, Missouri; Elijah Montgomery, who likewise served in the War of 1812 on Jackson's staff at New Orleans; Malinda Montgomery, who married a Page; John R. Montgomery; and the subject of this sketch.

Dr. Montgomery was in Transylvania University in 1805. He boarded on Hill Street, Lexington, with 'old Mr. Samuel Price, who lived in a large stone house.' His messmates here were George Robertson, Robert P. Letcher, Alexander M. Edmiston (son of his cousin John Edmiston, *q.v.*), Andrew McMillan and others.

After graduation from Transylvania, Alexander Montgomery studied medicine in Paris, France. In 1809 he was settled in Georgetown for the practice of medicine and was highly esteemed by all who knew him there.

In 1812 he volunteered for service in the war, becoming Surgeon of the 17th U. S. Infantry on March 12, 1812.

Dr. Montgomery was unmarried. He had been engaged to Maria Cecil Gist, daughter of Colonel Nathaniel Gist, since she was sixteen years of age. Maria Cecil Gist was a sister of Captain

Biographies

Nathaniel G. S. Hart's wife. Her mother later became the wife of Governor Charles Scott. After waiting six years Maria Cecil Gist married, on November 24, 1819, Benjamin Gratz whose home now is the present *Mount Hope* in Lexington. She died there November 4, 1841. [Her sister-in-law was Rebekah Gratz, immortalized in Sir Walter Scott's *Ivanhoe*.]

[Data supplied by Miss Julia Spurr, Lexington, Kentucky; *An Outline of the Life of George Robertson, written by himself* . . . (1876); Gaines, *History of Scott County;* Heitman, Francis, *Historical Register, op. cit.;* Fayette County marriage records; *Kentucky Reporter*, March 5, 1814; Clay, Henrietta, *Bits of Family History*, 1932; Simpson, Elizabeth M., *Bluegrass Houses and their Traditions*, 1932.]

DR. ROBERT M. EWING
Surgeon's Mate and Surgeon, 1st Regiment

Dr. Ewing was born in 1787, a son of Colonel Baker Ewing (1750-1808) and Letitia Sorrell Warren, eldest daughter of William and Anne Wilcox Warren. Colonel Baker Ewing was the first Register of the Land Office, Colonel and Deputy Sheriff of Lincoln County but removed to Christian County before 1805. Letitia Sorrell Warren Ewing, mother of Dr. Ewing, was born in 1763/64 and died a widow in Christian County in 1837.

Dr. Ewing was commissioned Surgeon's Mate in the 1st Regiment on August 11, 1812. On December 26, 1812, he was promoted to Surgeon of the Regiment after the resignation of Surgeon William H. Richardson.

Following his service with the Raisin force Dr. Ewing re-enlisted, this time receiving a commission as Surgeon, Colonel Richard M. Johnson's regiment.

After the war he settled near Georgetown where he practiced medicine alone and later as partner with Dr. Gano, of Georgetown. In 1835 he was named one of the trustees to incorporate Georgetown Female College, and two years later was made a Trustee of Georgetown College, this latter office terminating only at his death. He was President of the Board of Trustees of Georgetown College, 1856-1862.

Dr. Robert M. Ewing died October 9, 1862, at his residence near Georgetown in his 76th year. Both he and his wife were buried in the Georgetown Cemetery.

Dr. Ewing married Margaret Gano, daughter of Major Richard Montgomery Gano, of Scott County, and Elizabeth M. Ewing, native of Bedford County, Virginia, who died April 9, 1812, leaving four daughters and three sons.

[Shelby, Cass Knight, *The Family of William Warren of Lincoln County, Ky.* MS, Kentucky Historical Society; Letter, John Allen Gano, Georgetown, to James Ewing, Liberty, Bedford County, Virginia, Feb. 11, 1822. Copy, Kentucky Historical Society; Gaines, *History of Scott County;* Georgetown College *Bulletins; Commonwealth,* Nov. 21, 1862; *Roster of Commissioned Officers War of 1812-16,* MS, Kentucky Historical Society.]

DR. JOHN TODD
Surgeon, 5th Regiment

Dr. Todd was born near Lexington, Kentucky, April 27, 1787, son of General Levi and Jane (Briggs) Todd. His brother, Robert S. Todd, was the father of Mary Todd, wife of Abraham Lincoln. John Todd was one of the earliest graduates of Transylvania University. He next entered the Medical School at Philadelphia, and was graduated there in 1810.

He enlisted in 1812 with his brothers Samuel and Robert S. Todd, his commission as Surgeon of the 5th Regiment being dated July 7, 1812. Taken prisoner by the Indians during the massacre at Frenchtown January 23, 1813, he was later paroled and allowed to return to his home in Lexington.

He practiced medicine in Lexington and later settled for a time at Bardstown. In 1817 he removed to Edwardsville, Illinois. Here and at Springfield he spent the remainder of his life. In 1827 he was appointed by President John Quincy Adams Register of the United States Land Office, at Springfield, and at once moved to that city. He remained in office until he was removed for political reasons in 1829 by President Jackson.

Dr. Todd married in Lexington July 1, 1813, Elizabeth T. B. Smith, daughter of the Reverend John Blair Smith. She was born in Philadelphia on April 17, 1793. Her mother was a daughter of General Francis Nash, Revolutionary soldier.

Dr. John and Elizabeth Smith Todd had six children:

John Blair Smith Todd, born in Lexington April 4, 1814, graduated from West Point July 1, 1837; served in many capacities including service throughout the Mexican War. He resigned his commission in the United States Army September 16, 1856. President Lincoln commissioned him September 19, 1861, Brigadier General of Volunteers. Later he was elected to the United States

Congress. He died at Yankton, Dakota, (now South Dakota), January 5, 1872. He married March 25, 1845, at Fort Smith, Arkansas, Catherine S. Hoffman, daughter of Colonel William Hoffman, U. S. Army.

Francis Walton Todd, born April 17, 1816, at Bardstown, Kentucky, married in California in March, 1851, Mrs. L. M. Jackson, nee Bullitt, of Nachitoches, Louisiana.

William L. Todd, born April 14, 1818, at Edwardsville, Illinois, married in California April 14, 1868, Mrs. Clarissa J. Pike, nee Chase. She was born in 1823 in Duchess County, New York, and died in Sacramento, California, in March, 1874.

Elizabeth J. Todd, born in January, 1825, at Edwardsville, married in Springfield, July 21, 1846, Harrison J. Grimsley. He died in 1865 and she married secondly, in January 1867, the Reverend John H. Brown, who died February 23, 1872.

Lockwood M. Todd, born July 17, 1826, at Edwardsville. He was with General Sherman as commissary on his march to the sea. He married Emily Husband in Virginia City, Montana Territory.

Frances Stuart Todd, born in Springfield December 19, 1832, married there December 18, 1849, Thomas Hart Shelby, of Lexington, Kentucky. She died in Springfield February 1, 1851, leaving one son, John Todd Shelby.

Dr. John Todd died in Springfield, Illinois, January 9, 1865. His wife died there March 11, 1865. Dr. Todd was a Ruling Elder of the First Presbyterian Church in that city at the time of his death.

[Power, John Carroll, *History of the early settlers of Sangamon County, Illinois* (1876); *Illinois State Historical Society Journal*, vol. 9; Townsend, William H., *Lincoln and his wife's home town* (1929); *Commissioned Officers of the War of 1812-16*, MS, Kentucky Historical Society; *Biographical Directory of the American Congress, 1774-1927*.]

DR. THOMAS CHILES DAVIS
Surgeon, 1st Rifle Regiment

Dr. Thomas C. Davis was born December 31, 1779, a son of the pioneer Richard Davis and Ann, or Nancy, Chiles Davis of Virginia. Richard Davis the father was one of the first justices of Hopkins County, Kentucky, and had been a Sergeant in the 1st Regiment, Light Dragoons, Continental Establishment. Later he was Sheriff of Hopkins County. He was born in Stafford County,

Virginia, in 1746 and died in Hopkins County October 8, 1812. Ann Chiles Davis, mother of Dr. Davis, was born December 7, 1755, and died July 28, 1849. They were married in Spottsylvania County, Virginia, in 1773.

Dr. Thomas C. Davis settled in Frankfort after receiving his education in medicine. Three years before, in 1808, he was in Shelby County where he was married. A note in the Kentucky Historical Society's genealogical files points out that the miniature of Dr. Davis, in the Society's museum, he had painted while he was in Canton, China, indicating that he travelled extensively before settling in Frankfort.

He applied to Governor Charles Scott from Frankfort, June 4, 1812, for the post of Surgeon General. On August 15, 1812, he was appointed Surgeon, 1st Rifle Regiment, and with this unit moved into the northwest. The account of his death at Frenchtown is treated in the chapter dealing with the second battle there.

Dr. Davis married in Shelby County, February 15, 1808, Elizabeth Dabney Chiles, daughter of Walter Carr and Phoebe Chiles. After the death of her husband, Mrs. Davis stayed at their home with their infant child. She became a victim of mild melancholia and tradition indicates that she spent much of her time in a grove of trees across Washington Street from the Thomas home, singing softly to herself. This grove was located where the Episcopal Church now stands. On March 13, 1815, she applied for a pension, assigning power of attorney to Charles B. Davis. She was at that time living in Shelby County. This document has a certificate attached, signed by George Madison, which states that "Thos. C. Davis was present on the 22nd January 1813, at the commencement of the action at French Town on the River Raisin, since which time he has not been heard of, and I have every reason to believe he was killed in the action."

Mrs. Elizabeth Davis died about September, 1815, and her only child was reared by Major Thomas Howard, of Richmond, Kentucky.

Dr. Thomas C. and Elizabeth D. Chiles Davis had two children, one of whom died prematurely.

Captain Thomas Chiles Davis, the surviving child, was born in Frankfort November 2, 1811, and died in Texas on April 7, 1891. He married first, April 27, 1834, Anna Maria Carr, daughter of Captain Thomas and Elizabeth Todd Carr. The mother of Anna Davis was a daughter of Colonel Levi Todd. Seven children were born to this union. Captain Davis married second, September 22, 1857, Mrs. Grace, widow of Sir John C. Grace, an English Baronet. She was born Rebecca Fifield Rutherford in 1825. Six children were born to this second marriage.

[Richard Davis family Bible (typescript), Davis family notes in Kentucky Historical Society; Gordon, Major Maurice, *History of Hopkins County* (MS); *Governor Charles Scott's Papers*, Kentucky Historical Society; Shelby County marriage records.]

DR. GUSTAVUS MILLER BOWER
Surgeon's Mate, 5th Regiment

Dr. Bower was born near Culpeper, Culpeper County, Virginia, December 12, 1790, son of Michael and Betsy (Withers) Bower. He attended the public schools of his community and studied medicine in Philadelphia.

Emigrating to Kentucky he settled in Nicholasville in 1810 and began the practice of medicine. Under date of June 3, 1812, Colonel William Lewis in recommending him for a commission in his regiment wrote to Governor Scott: "Doct. Bower is likewise a citizen of our town and lately from Virginia. He attended for some time the lectures in Philadelphia." Shortly afterward Dr. Bower enlisted as a surgeon dresser. His commission as Surgeon's Mate of the 5th Regiment was dated August 7, 1812.

Following the battles and massacre at Frenchtown, he re-enlisted and commanded a company of volunteers at the battle of the Thames.

After the war Dr. Bower moved to Georgetown, Kentucky, where he was one of the early physicians of that place. In 1832 or 1833 he removed to Monroe County, Missouri, settling about one and a half miles from Paris. Here he engaged in the practice of medicine and also in agricultural pursuits. Ten years later he was elected as a Democrat to the Twenty-eighth Congress (March 4, 1843-March 3, 1845). Following this term of service in Washington he resumed the practice of medicine.

Dr. Gustavus M. Bower died at his home near Paris November 17, 1864, and was buried in the family burying ground just north of that city.

He had married first, January 26, 1815, Martha (Patsy) Crockett, who was born in Jessamine County in 1792, a daughter of Colonel Joseph Crockett (May 7, 1742-November 7, 1829). After her death, on April 14, 1830, Dr. Bower married in Kentucky Catherine Long, daughter of James Long also of Kentucky. By this second wife Dr. Bower reared a family of children of whom two are known to the present investigator:

Isabella Bower married December 2, 1857, Brigadier General William Yarnel Slack, being his second wife. General Slack was born in Kentucky August 1, 1816, and mortally wounded in action at the battle of Pea Ridge, Arkansas, his death occurring on March 21, 1862. Isabella Bower Slack lived the remainder of her life at the old Slack homeplace on North Washington Street, Chillicothe, Missouri. They had two children, William Y., and Gustavus Bower Slack.

G. M. Bower, son of Dr. Bower, was a lumber dealer of Paris, Missouri. He was born in Monroe County in October, 1838. Until he was 21 years of age he was kept in school and given a good general education. He was married twice, first in 1873 to a daughter of Major James Ragland who died shortly after their marriage. He married second, in 1878, Anna Levering, a daughter of Frank Levering, of Hannibal, Missouri.

[*Biographical Directory of the American Congress, 1774-1927; Missouri Historical Review*, v. 21, 23; French, Janie Preston Collup, and Zella Armstrong, *The Crockett Family* (Notable Southern Families, v. 5); Young, Bennett H., *The History of Jessamine County, Kentucky;* Letter, Will. Lewis to Gov. Charles Scott, June 3, 1812, Kentucky Historical Society; *History of Monroe and Shelby Counties, Missouri* . . . St. Louis, 1884.]

DR. BENJAMIN LOGAN
Surgeon's Mate, 1st Rifle Regiment

Dr. Logan was born in Lincoln County, Kentucky, January 3, 1789, the fourth son of General Benjamin and Anne Montgomery Logan. He was well educated in the study of medicine and successfully practiced his profession in Shelby County.

His commission as Surgeon's Mate, 1st Rifle Regiment, was dated July 23, 1812. In the same regiment was Robert Logan, fifth son of General Benjamin Logan and brother of Dr. Benjamin Logan, who was killed during the action at Frenchtown. After his capture by the British and Indians on January 22, 1813,

Dr. Benjamin Logan was subsequently paroled and allowed to return home. In 1818 he was a member of the State House of Representatives. In this session he served with his brother John Logan.

Dr. Logan married in Shelby County, February 15, 1820, Eliza L. Winlock, daughter of General Joseph Winlock, also of Shelby. To this union were born five children:

James Knox Logan, their only son, died unmarried.

Ann M. Logan married Judge Zachariah Wheat, being his third wife. They had at least one son.

Eliza Jane Logan married, December 12, 1844, Dr. Robert W. Glass.

Polly (Mary W.) Logan married June 10, 1851, William P. Monroe, her kinsman.

Effie Logan married W. W. Gardiner.

Dr. Benjamin Logan died at his home in Shelby County March 20, 1873, in his 85th year.

[*Daily Kentucky Yeoman*, March 22, 1873; Green, T. M., *Historic families of Kentucky*; Shelby County marriage records; *Biographical encyclopaedia of Kentucky, of the dead and living men of the nineteenth century*.]

CAPTAIN JOHN H. WOOLFOLK
Secretary to General James Winchester

Captain Woolfolk was a son of Sowel and Mary (Harris) Woolfolk, of the Virginia family which came to Woodford County, Kentucky, shortly after the close of the Revolutionary war. Sowel Woolfolk settled on a large estate at Elm Corner, where later was built the Woolfolk home, *Oak Hill*, which was dismantled in 1928.

Of the five children of Sowel and Mary (Harris) Woolfolk, Joseph Harris, John H., and Sowel, Jr., served in the War of 1812.

An account of Captain Woolfolk's death at River Raisin, differing somewhat from that used in the preceding pages was published in *Niles' Weekly Register* of April 10, 1813: "Captain Woolfolk after having been wounded in two places, by some means had got refuge in one of the French houses on the Raisin—he was discovered next day and dragged from his asylum—he was taken to the house of a Mr. Lasselle, where he said he would give one thousand dollars to any who would purchase him. Mr. Lasselle said it was not in his power, but he had no doubt his brother would do it who lived at hand—he directed Woolfolk's owners to the house of his brother, but as they were on their way an Indian from a waste house shot him through the head."

Captain Woolfolk made his will September 12, 1812. It was probated in the July Court, 1813, in Woodford County. The only property mentioned was his library, which he left to his brother Sowel.

[Railey, William E., *History of Woodford County, Kentucky;* Woodford County Will Book D; Davis, William F., *The Genealogy of the male line of the ancestors of Sowyel Woolfolk, born in Virginia, 1744, died in Woodford County, Kentucky, 1830,* MS, Kentucky Historical Society.]

JOHN MOORE McCALLA
Adjutant, 5th Regiment

General John M. McCalla was a son of Andrew McCalla of Philadelphia. The father was a son of William McCalla, born near Philadelphia in 1732 and died there January 26, 1815, and Elizabeth (Means) McCalla. Andrew McCalla removed to Kentucky and was living in Jessamine County on a farm when his son, the Reverend William Latta McCalla was born November 25, 1788. In 1795 Andrew sold his Jessamine County land to Colonel David Meade, on which the latter subsequently erected *La Chaumiere du Prairie,* and moved to Lexington where he opened his Apothecary Store. He was known for his good works and was one of the founders of the Fayette Hospital, later Eastern Lunatic Asylum. Andrew McCalla died in Lexington November 28, 1832, at an advanced age. He had at least two children other than the subject of this sketch: William Latta McCalla, noted above, was a Presbyterian clergyman, Chaplain in the War of 1812, and debater with Alexander Campbell, Abner Kneeland and others. He married on March 30, 1813, Martha Ann Finley, daughter of General Samuel Finley, of Chillicothe, Ohio. Maria McCalla, only daughter of Andrew McCalla, married James Clark, of Nicholasville, lawyer and member of Congress.

John M. McCalla was a student at Transylvania University, 1804-1811, and studied law with his brother-in-law, James Clark, until the outbreak of the War of 1812. He was active in public affairs of Lexington. He early evidenced a passion for books and throughout his life was a collector of items relating to the history of Kentucky and the Middle West.

His commission as Adjutant of the 5th Regiment was dated November 20, 1812. After his capture at Frenchtown and subsequent parole he returned to his home in Lexington. Both William A. Leavy in his *Memoirs of Lexington and its vicinity* and Ranck in his *History of Lexington* state that John M. McCalla built the earlier portions of *Mount Hope*, or the Benjamin Gratz home on Mill Street, in Lexington.

In Lexington John M. McCalla was attorney and U. S. Marshal, for a short time (in 1829) temporary editor of the *Kentucky Gazette* and in 1845 recipient of an appointment as Second Auditor of the U. S. Treasury. Following this appointment he moved to Washington, D. C., held this post in the Treasury Department until 1849, and thereafter lived out his life in that city. He died there in late February or early March, 1873. He left a library of some 3,000 volumes of pamphlets, newspapers and the like pertaining to the history of Kentucky.

General McCalla was a Mason of high standing, having been Grand Master of Lexington Lodge, No. 1, F. & A. M., in 1825, and Grand Master, Grand Lodge of Kentucky in 1830.

He married in Lexington on October 2, 1815, Maria Hogg.

[*Daily Kentucky Yeoman*, March 5, 7, 1873; *Observer & Reporter*, Nov. 29, 1832; Letter, unsigned, to Lockwood Barr, dated Boylestown, Pa., July 14, 1949; Leavy, William A., "Memoir of Lexington and its vicinity," *Register*, v. 40 (1942); Letter Henry M. Clark, Booneville, Mo., to Tarleton E. Clark, dated Nov. 25, 1893; *Concise History of Lexington Lodge No. 1 F. & A. M., Nov. 17, 1788-1913*; Lanman, Charles, *Biographical Annals of the Civil Government of the United States* . . . 1876.]

JAMES GARRARD
Brigade Inspector, 2nd Brigade

General James Garrard was born in Stafford County, Virginia, January 31, 1773, a son of Governor James and Elizabeth Mountjoy Garrard. He was brought to Kentucky when ten years of age and reared at Governor Garrard's home, *Mount Lebanon*, in Bourbon County.

Identifying himself early with the military, agricultural and political life of Bourbon County, he was active in the militia, a prosperous farmer and served in both branches of the General Assembly. He was a Representative in the Lower House in 1808, 1820 and 1831, and in the Senate from 1813 to 1817.

General Garrard's commission as Brigade Inspector (Major) of the 2nd Brigade, the Raisin Force, was dated August 9, 1812. After his capture and parole by the British he returned to Bourbon County and aside from his service in the Legislature devoted himself to agricultural pursuits and the breeding of fine stock. At one time he went to England personally to select from the best stocks, and is considered one of the pioneers in live stock improvement in Kentucky.

His residence, *Fairfield*, was situated on the side of Stoner Creek opposite the home of his father. Here he lived out his life and here died September 1, 1838 after only a few days illness.

James Garrard married in Fayette County, December 18, 1793, Nancy Lewis, daughter of Thomas Lewis who had emigrated from Fairfax County, Virginia, to Kentucky in 1785. Mrs. Garrard's mother was Elizabeth Payne, daughter of Edward Payne and Anne Horden Conyers. Nancy Lewis Garrard died November 17, 1835, and James Garrard married second, September 1, 1836, Mrs. Mary Kerfoot Williams, widow of General Roger Williams. All of General Garrard's children were by his first wife, for a list and genealogy of whom see des Cognets, noted below.

[des Cognets, Anna Russell, *Governor Garrard, of Kentucky, his descendants and relatives*, 1898; *Observer & Reporter*, Sept. 14, 1836; *Niles' Register*, v. 4; *Commissioned Officers of the War of 1812-16*, MS, Kentucky Historical Society.]

BLAND WILLIAMS BALLARD
Captain, 1st Rifle Regiment

Captain Ballard was born in Spottsylvania County, Virginia, October 16, 1759, the eldest son of Bland Ballard, killed March 31, 1788, in the Ballard Massacre, and ———— (Williams) Ballard, his first wife.

Coming to Kentucky with his father in 1779, he joined the militia and was thereafter active in the defense of the western frontiers. He saw service in Colonel Bowman's expedition of May, 1779; in General George Rogers Clark's expedition against the Piqua towns, July, 1780, on which latter excursion he was wounded seriously in the hip. He was again out with General

Clark in 1782 and served as spy for him on the Wabash Expedition of 1786. Later he was guide under Generals Scott and Wilkinson and was with General Wayne at the battle of Fallen Timbers on August 20, 1794. He also filled the post of hunter and spy for General Clark when that officer was stationed at Louisville.

His commission as captain in Lieutenant Colonel John Allen's 1st Rifle Regiment was dated June 6, 1812. In the battle of January 18, 1813, he led the advance guard and was wounded slightly. He was again hit and severely hurt on January 22 by a spent ball. As one of the prisoners taken that day he suffered much during the march through the snow and ice from Malden to Fort George.

The following lines descriptive of Bland W. Ballard and his life and times were penned at the time of his death in 1853:

Of all the remarkable pioneer Indian fighters whose history is identified with Kentucky, few were more distinguished than the deceased. He was a man of wonderful physical powers, of a strong native intellect, of extraordinary sagacity, and of indomitable courage. These qualities eminently fitted him for the pioneer life, and together with the extraordinary circumstances which surrounded him, made his history one of the most romantic in the annals of Kentucky. The whole of his early life abounded in adventures and feats so marvelous that they could scarcely be credited now, were not the truth of some of them attested by others, and the whole of them supported by the deceased's own unquestioned and unquestionable veracity.

Maj. Ballard was an uneducated man, but we have rarely seen one who conversed more fluently or described scenes more graphically. We have often seen him on the street dressed in his buckskin hunting shirt, surrounded by crowds of men and boys listening with breathless attention to his stories. We ourselves have listened to them many an hour, and often through the livelong night without fatigue and wholly unconscious of the approach of morning.

We once heard him asked how many Indians he had killed in one day.

'I kilt,' said he, 'six one morning before breakfast, and it was not a good morning for the business either.'

This reply, given in his peculiarly business-like style, we shall never forget. If we had not recurred to the question we might have thought that the old gentleman was speaking of some morning hunt for squirrels, deer, or buffalo, so singularly calm was his manner; but, on this as on other occasions, Major Ballard never exhibited the slightest compunctions on account of his having killed Indians. His family, and he in his own person, had received too many injuries from the savages for him ever to feel the slightest sympathy for them. He regarded them as a faithless, treacherous race and the enemy of his own, and therefore sorrowed but little over their probable extinction. But he often spoke of some of them as brave, and generous, and for them expressed the warmest admiration.

The history of Major Ballard abounds in many thrilling adventures and anecdotes which we could relate and which might interest our readers, but which the occasion forbids. We cannot, however, close this sketch without referring to one of them. In 1788, the Indians attacked his father's house, situated near the little fork on Tick Creek; a few miles northeast of Shelbyville. The attack was made early in the morning and began by the savages shooting down his brother Benjamin, who had gone out of the house for wood to make a fire. They then assailed the house. The inmates barred the door and prepared for defense. The father of the subject of this sketch was the only man in the house, and he and one old man were the only persons in the fort. Aroused by the guns, he snatched up his own rifle and rushed to the defense of his kindred. He fired and reloaded and fired again as he ran, with good effect. In the meantime, the Indians broke open the house and killed his father, his mother, and two sisters, and tomahawked the youngest sister, a child, who recovered. When the Indians broke into the house, his mother endeavored to escape by the back door, but a savage pursued her and as he raised his tomahawk to strike her the subject of this sketch fired at him, not, however, in time to prevent the fatal blow, and they both fell and expired together. The Indians numbered about fifteen, but, before they completed their work of death and fled, it is supposed that the object of this sketch killed six or seven of them.

But it was not merely as a warrior and soldier that Major Ballard rendered important service to Kentucky. He frequently represented the people of Shelby county in the State Legislature. The State, in appreciation of his services, and to perpetuate his name, have created the county of Ballard, and already in anticipation of his death, is his name inscribed on the beautiful marble shaft erected in her public burying ground in honor of her distinguished dead.

Biographies

The generation now in the sphere of action, and the millions who are to succeed them, will have but an imperfect idea of the character and services of the bold, patriotic men who rescued Kentucky from the forest and the savages. The deceased was a fine specimen of that noble race of men. He was the last of his father's family. His brother James, the companion of his youth, and the sharer of most of his adventures and trials, preceded him but a few years. And now that he is gone, we cannot call to mind a single pioneer of Kentucky, who is left. Who shall snatch their memory from oblivion and give us a true history of Kentucky, with its pages all glowing with life-like sketches of the men who redeemed her from the savage, and with stories of adventures, more romantic than even romance itself can furnish? Without such biographies and sketches the history of Kentucky can no more be written than that of the United States without mentioning the name of Washington.

Major Bland W. Ballard died at his residence in Shelby County September 5, 1853, at the advanced age of 95 years. He was buried on his plantation, about four miles west of Shelbyville, but on November 8, 1854, his remains were reinterred in the State Cemetery at Frankfort, where as noted above his name had already been entered on the State Monument. Reinterred with him at the same time was his first wife.

Major Ballard married first Elizabeth Williamson. She died January 12, 1827, and he married second, in Jefferson County September 10, 1833, Diana Matthews. She died August 17, 1835, and he married third, October 28, 1841, Elizabeth Weaver Garrett, who died in 1854.

Seven children were in the family of Major Ballard: James; Mary; Dorothy or Dolly, who married December 11, 1827, Stephen Stone; Susan; Sally, who married June 13, 1809, Adam Smith; Martha or Patsy, who married a Rounder, and Nancy. One of these named Polly in Bland W. Ballard's will, married December 25, 1810, Luke Hoff or Hough.

[Obituary in *Western Citizen* Sept. 16, 1853, from *Louisville Journal*, quoted above; Jefferson, Shelby county marriage records; *Filson Club History Quarterly*, v. 13 (1939); Willis, George L., Sr., *History of Shelby County, Kentucky; Obituary addresses delivered upon the occasion of the reinterment of the remains of Gen. Chas. Scott, Major Wm. T. Barry, and Capt. Bland Ballard and Wife, In the Cemetery at Frankfort, November 8, 1854* (1855).]

RICHARD BLEDSOE
Captain, 1st Rifle Regiment

Richard Bledsoe, of Fayette County, was commissioned Lieutenant, 1st Rifle Regiment, June 12, 1812. On August 11, a few days before the detachment marched for the northwest, he was made Adjutant. With the resignation, in the field, of Captain John Edmiston, Bledsoe resigned his commission as Adjutant and on October 14, 1812, was promoted to captain and given the command of Captain Edmiston's company which he led in the action at Frenchtown (with John Edmiston in the ranks as private.) Captured January 22, 1813, and later paroled Captain Bledsoe returned to his home near Athens, Fayette County.

One Richard Bledsoe married in Fayette County, January 21, 1807, Sally Gess. There are stones in the Baptist Graveyard, Athens, Fayette County, with the following inscriptions: Sacred to the memory of Richard Bledsoe who was born on the 11th of Nov. 1784 and died on the 22nd of Feb. 1826; Sacred to the memory of Sarah Bledsoe, born 27th Sept. 1785 and died 1st Feb. 1821.

[*Commissioned Officers of the War of 1812-16*, MS, Kentucky Historical Society; *Niles' Register*, v. 4; Fayette County marriage records.]

WILEY R. BRASFIELD
Captain, 5th Regiment

Captain Brasfield, of English lineage, was born in Virginia April 19, 1766. He removed early to Kentucky, settling in Clark County. Here presumably he reared a large family. In 1815 he advertised in the Winchester *Advertiser* for a school teacher willing to attend the children of the community, offering the applicant a house on his plantation.

His commission as captain in the 5th Regiment was dated August 7, 1812. On August 22 of the same year he was commissioned by Governor Charles Scott a major in the 1st Battalion, 36th Regiment. In the field Brasfield resigned his captaincy sometime prior to November 20, 1812, when Joseph Kelly, his Lieutenant, was appointed to the command of Brasfield's company. Records tend to indicate that Captain Brasfield was not present at the action at Frenchtown in January, 1813.

Biographies

On August 26, 1813, he re-enlisted as a private in Captain Isaac Cunningham's company but on the ninth of the month following was promoted to major and served thereafter as Paymaster of the regiment. On this second campaign Major Brasfield went into the final stages of the victorious assault against the British but remained behind the home-coming army to be with his son, James, who was ill.

Major Wiley Brasfield died at his home in Clark County May 19, 1839, aged 74 years.

He had married, in Kentucky, Elizabeth Berry, born November 4, 1771, a daughter of Thomas Berry. She died in Clark County October 21, 1837, aged 66.

Of the children of Wiley R. and Elizabeth Berry Brasfield: James was born in Clark County September 25, 1790, and died in Platte County, Missouri, June 10, 1839. He lost an eye in the War of 1812 service indicated above. He married June 6, 1816, Jane Lafferty, of Scotch parentage, born February 5, 1799, and died January 15, 1880. She was a daughter of Thomas Lafferty (1771-1828) and Eleanor Strode Lafferty (1783-1868). James Brasfield received a good education and was a writer of both prose and poetry. He was sheriff of Clark County for eight years and a surveyor of experience. He removed with his family to Missouri in 1834.

Nancy Brasfield, daughter of Captain Wiley R., married in Clark County December 10, 1818, Henry Lander, who was born there February 28, 1794, served in the War of 1812, removed to Washington County, Illinois, and died there November 28, 1862. Nancy Brasfield Lander died in Trigg County, Kentucky, and Henry Lander married second Mrs. Elizabeth Mimms.

Captain Wiley R. Brasfield was bondsman to the following marriages in Clark County: Polly Brasfield, married Alexander D. Ritchie August 30, 1817; Eliza Brasfield, married July 12, 1820, William Snail.

[Paxton, W. M., *Annals of Platte County, Missouri* . . . (1897); *Clark County Pension List* (typescript); *Commissioned Officers of the War of 1812-16* MS, Kentucky Historical Society; *Kentucky Gazette*, Oct. 26, 1837; *Commonwealth*, June 17, 1839; *Winchester Advertiser*, Jan. 14, 1815; Lander, David, *History of the Lander Family of Virginia and Kentucky*, Chicago, 1926.]

COLEMAN A. COLLIER
Captain, 1st Regiment

Captain Collier was born in Virginia about 1790, a son of Major John Collier born there in Hanover County in 1747. Major John, the father, was the second son of Captain John and Elizabeth Collier. He served in the American Revolution, later moving to Kentucky. He settled for a time in Franklin County, going later to Bourbon and finally to Nicholas County where he died in January, 1820.

Coleman A. Collier was a farmer of Nicholas County when war with Great Britain was declared. He enlisted in Carlisle. His commission as Captain, 1st Regiment, was dated August 7, 1812. He was one of the prisoners taken during the action of January 23, 1813, and was paroled with many of his company a few months afterward. Returning to Kentucky he settled eventually in Harrison County where he died July 13, 1856.

Captain Collier married first, January 30, 1812, Jane Howarton and second on August 11, 1815, Katharine Howarton. He had two sons, one of whom was Robert H. Collier, a farmer of Morning Glory, Nicholas County, who was born there March 17, 1831. Robert H. married in 1849 Eliza Peterson, a daughter of Henry and Annie Peterson. The second son was William J. Collier.

Catharine Howarton (Howerton) applied for a pension August 11, 1856. She was then living in Harrison County. She was a native of Virginia, born there about 1806. She died in 1866.

[Perrin, William H., ed., *History of Bourbon, Scott, Harrison and Nicholas Counties, Kentucky* . . . (1882); Ardery, Mrs. Wm. B., "Collier Family," in *The Kentuckian-Citizen*, Paris, Ky., June 26, 1945; Burns, Annie Walker, comp., *Kentucky Military Pensions, Old War;* Nicholas County marriage records; *Commissioned Officers War of 1812-16* MS, Kentucky Historical Society.]

JOHN MONTGOMERY EDMISTON
Captain, 1st Rifle Regiment

Captain Edmiston was born February 21, 1764 (some sources give 1757) in Washington County, Virginia, eldest son of William and Nancy (or Margaret) Edmiston.

Captain William Edmiston, his father, was born in 1734 in Cecil County, Maryland, a son of Thomas and Martha Camp-

Biographies

belle Edmiston. According to tradition Thomas Edmiston was a younger son of a nobleman and Martha Campbelle, his wife, was a daughter of the Duke of Argyll. On reaching manhood Captain William Edmiston removed to Augusta County, Virginia, where he married and settled on the Holston River in what is now Washington County, Virginia. He was at the Battle of Point Pleasant, commanded a company against the Cherokees in 1776 and served in the Chickamauga expedition of 1779. He was a major at King's Mountain and in 1782 Colonel of the Washington County Militia. He died in 1822.

Eight Edmistons were engaged in the Battle of King's Mountain. Three were killed and one wounded. The survivors were William, major of the regiment, and privates John (subject of this sketch), Samuel and William Edmiston.

Captain John Edmiston, as noted above, was a private in his father's company at King's Mountain. He married his cousin, Margaret Robinson Montgomery, and was for many years Clerk of the Court at Abingdon, Virginia.

In 1790 he moved his family to Kentucky, settling on Boone Creek (?) in the present Fayette County. Here he improved his land and for twenty-two years enjoyed peace and prosperity. When war was declared against Great Britain, although more than fifty years of age, he rallied his friends and neighbors and formed a company. He was elected captain and ultimately assigned with his men to the regiment commanded by Colonel John Allen, who had married a near kins-woman.

Captain Edmiston's commission as Captain, 1st Rifle Regiment, was dated June 12, 1812. He resigned his commission on or prior to October 14 of that year, while in the field, and his Lieutenant, Richard Bledsoe, was promoted to the captaincy of the company. Acting as private in the company he formerly commanded, Edmiston was killed during the action of January 22, 1813. Edmiston (Edmonson) County, created by act of General Assembly approved January 12, 1825, was named in honor of Captain John Edmiston.

C. Frank Dunn writing in the *Sunday Herald-Leader*, June 26, 1949, stated that "Captain Edmiston had asked his friend, Tom Morgan, to burn his body, which he did at an old dry house." Mr. Dunn described and published a photograph of Captain Edmiston's home in the same article. This home, located on the Winchester pike, seven miles from Lexington, was built in 1797 on 250 acres given to him by his father-in-law, James Montgomery, of Washington County, Virginia.

Captain John and Margaret Montgomery Edmiston had three children:

Dr. Alexander M. Edmiston, the only son, married in Garrard County in January, 1812, Faunea Jennings. He settled at Lancaster, Kentucky, where he died July 11, 1812, aged 25 years; Mary R. Edmiston married February 20, 1809, James Richardson, of Fayette County; Margaret Edmiston married September 13, 1809, William C. Pruitt, also of Fayette County.

Mrs. Margaret Edmiston, wife of Captain John, died in Fayette County on October 8, 1834.

[Data supplied by Miss Julia Spurr, Lexington, Kentucky; *Kentucky Gazette*, August 19, 1809, July 21, 1812; *Fayette County Will Book B; Lexington Observer & Reporter*, Oct. 29, 1834; Garrard County marriage records; Fayette County marriage records; Chesney, Mrs. Sarah Ellen James, "Edmonsons-James," *Register*, v. 1 (May, 1903); *Acts of the General Assembly of Kentucky* . . ., 1824-25; *Commissioned Officers of the War of 1812-16* MS, Kentucky Historical Society; *Reporter*, March 6, 1813, which reports Edmiston rejoining his company as a private soldier; Draper, Lyman C., *King's Mountain and Its Heroes* . . . (1929).]

WILLIAM ELLIS
Captain, 1st Rifle Regiment

Captain Ellis, of Harrison County, Kentucky, was born April 6, 1774, the first son and second of eleven children of John and Sarah (Parrish) Ellis. The father John Ellis (January 29, 1749-January 15, 1794) removed from Virginia to Fayette County, Kentucky, when Lexington contained but a single cabin. The mother Sarah (Parrish) Ellis was born April 20, 1751, and died February 1, 1794. She was married to John Ellis October 2, 1770.

At the outbreak of the War of 1812 Captain Ellis raised a company of Harrison and Bourbon county men and offered it for service in response to Governor Scott's call for troops. His commission as captain in the 1st Rifle Regiment was dated June 11, 1812. Shortly before the Raisin detachment began its march through Ohio Captain Ellis "resigned his commission by reason of certain misrepresentations, returned home, corrected them and again returned to the command and re-enlisted as a private, was engaged in scouting along the front with a small party when suddenly they surprised a small body of Indians and a vigorous skirmish ensued. Captain Ellis was virtually disarmed when the breach of his gun was shot away, leaving only the barrel and a small portion of the stock in his hands."

Existing records indicate that Captain Ellis died while the detachment was at Fort Defiance. This is borne out by family Bible entries which list the date of his death as December 12, 1812. The date and place further are substantiated by the appointment of Ellis's lieutenant, Richard Matson, to the command of the company on December 15, 1812, while the unit was at Fort Defiance.

His will, on file in Harrison County, names only his wife, Lucy Ellis. There is record of one Lucy Ellis, widow, marrying in Lexington September 5, 1823, Edward Darnaby, Sr., with Waller Rodes as bondsman. There is no proof, however, that this was the widow of Captain William Ellis.

Two of his brothers also saw service in the War of 1812. Robert Ellis (August 4, 1789-November 15, 1840) was a private in Captain Ellis's company of the first Rifle Regiment, and Timothy Ellis (November 25, 1792-July 6, 1813), the youngest brother, was 4th Sergeant in Captain Manson Seamond's Company of Boswell's Regiment.

[Records from the Joel E. Ellis Bible, typescript on file at the Kentucky Historical Society; *Original Roster of Commissioned Officers of the War of 1812-16*, MS, Kentucky Historical Society; *Commonwealth*, June 9, 1871, from which the quote above was taken; *Biographical Encyclopaedia of Kentucky of the Dead and Living Men of the Nineteenth Century*, Cincinnati, J. M. Armstrong & Co., 1878; *Harrison County Will Book A;* Fayette County Marriage Records.]

WILLIAM GARRARD
Captain, Volunteer Light Dragoons

William Garrard, first child of Governor James Garrard, was born in Stafford County, Virginia, April 20, 1771. He was twelve years of age when his parents settled in Bourbon County, Kentucky.

He was clerk of the Bourbon County Court for many years and represented that county in the Kentucky House of Representatives in 1793, 1796-1800, and again in 1822.

His company of twelve months Light Dragoons, "The Bourbon County Blues," was first called the Bourbon County Company of Mounted Rangers and was first advertised to be formed May 1, 1812. Under a newspaper heading "TWO CHANCES! Volunteer, or be Drafted!!" those inclined to offer their services were informed that "they are offered by their country, one dollar per day, and Rashions furnished them; they find their own horse and equipments, which are to consist of a Rifle, Tomahawk, and Scalping Knife.—Dress to be a Hunting-Shirt and Pantaloons of linen, dyed black, and are to hold themselves in readiness to march at a moment's notice."

Detached from the River Raisin force, "The Bourbon Blues" served under Major James V. Ball in reducing the Indian villages along the Mississinewa River.

Captain Garrard lost both of his horses to Indian fire during the Mississinewa River expedition. William B. Northcutt in his diary of the action tells of Garrard, "the old Captain," that he waddled along through the snow and cold until General Samuel G. Hopkins dismounted one of his men and let the Captain have his horse. Northcutt recalls that

The Captain led the dragoon's horse up by the side of a log to get on him, got on the log and looked all around him and Bawled out at the top of his voice BOURBON BLUES MOUNT, when there was not a single Bourbon Blue there to mount but the old Captain himself, which occasioned some meriment for the boys that heard the order.

William Garrard married January 20, 1818, Susan Dalrymple Peers, daughter of Major Valentine Peers. She was born at Waterside, Loudoun County, Virginia, September 7, 1794, and died at her home near Paris March 8, 1838. To them were born:

(1) William Mountjoy Garrard, born in Paris in 1818, and died at Hot Springs, Arkansas, in 1892. He married Matilda Ann Coburn, of Maysville, Kentucky; (2) Eleanor Orr Garrard, born in 1821, married Joseph H. Holt, of Arkansas; (3) Elizabeth Garrard, born October 18, 1829, married John A. Lyle, of Paris.

[des Cognets, Anna Russell, *Governor Garrard, of Kentucky, His Descendants*, 1898; Northcutt, William B., Diary (MS, Kentucky Historical Society); *The Western Citizen* (Paris, Ky.), May 2, June 27, August 22, 1812.]

JOHN HAMILTON
Captain, 5th Regiment

Captain Hamilton, of Fayette County, Kentucky, was commissioned for the Raisin campaign on August 7, 1812. He commanded the left wing during action at Frenchtown on January 18, 1813, and commanded behind the pickets during the battle of January 22. Captured during the fight on the latter date, he was carried into Canada, later paroled and allowed to return to his home in Lexington.

He married there May 6, 1813, Miss Patsey Gaines, of Bourbon County. He died "at Cape Girardeau, on the Mississippi (where he had gone on business) on September 13, 1815, after a few days illness. He was one of the heroes of this state who gallantly sustained the honor of his country at the Raisin, at the head of his company of volunteers."

[*Kentucky Gazette*, May 11, 1813; September 25, 1815.]

NATHANIEL G. S. HART
Captain, 5th Regiment

Nathaniel Gray Smith Hart was born at Hagerstown, Maryland, about 1784, the second son of Colonel Thomas and Susanna Gray Hart. The father, Colonel Thomas Hart, was a member of the Provincial Congress of North Carolina, a soldier of the Revolution and one of the proprietors of the Transylvania Company. He removed to Hagerstown in 1780 and from thence, in 1794, to Lexington, Kentucky, where he lived until his death on June 23, 1808. Mrs. Susanna Gray Hart survived him until August 26, 1832. She was in her 86th year when she died. Of their other children Lucretia became the wife of Henry Clay; Ann married James Brown, senator, diplomat, first Secretary of State of Kentucky; and Eliza married Dr. Richard Pindell, famed Revolutionary War surgeon.

Nathaniel G. S. Hart studied law under his brother-in-law, Henry Clay, and practiced law for some time in Lexington. (Princeton University has record that one Nathaniel G. Hart was a student there between May 11, 1803, and December 25, 1804.) In 1811, or before, he engaged in the mercantile business in Lexington, running his store in his own name and was a Magistrate for some time before war was declared.

In 1812 he was commander of the Lexington Light Infantry, the town unit of the Fayette County militia, and was about twenty-eight years of age. At the outbreak of the war he and his company of volunteers reported for service and were assigned to the 5th Regiment, commanded by Lieutenant Colonel William Lewis. At Headquarters, Fort Defiance, October 4, 1812, Captain Hart was appointed Deputy Inspector to the left wing of the Northwestern Army. For an account of his death, when forsaken by his school-mate and one-time Lexington guest, Captain William Elliott, see Chapter Six.

On April 6, 1809, Captain Hart married Anna Edwards Gist, daughter of General Nathaniel Gist of the Maryland line in the Revolution, and Mrs. Judith Cary Gist who after General Gist's death married General Charles Scott. The marriage license was issued at Frankfort and it is probable that Captain Hart and Miss Gist were married in the home of the then governor, Charles Scott, the bride's stepfather.

Two children were born to them: Thomas Hart, Jr., who died unmarried in August, 1826; Henry Clay Hart, a midshipman of the United States Navy, who married January 7, 1835, Elizabeth Brent, youngest daughter of Hugh Brent, of Paris, Kentucky.

After the death of Captain Hart the grieving widow and mother was sent by relatives to New Orleans, hoping that a change of scene would tend to alleviate her sorrow. From there she went by boat to New York, arriving on June 1, 1818. Her mother and sister who accompanied her finally acknowledging that recovery was doubtful decided to bring the stricken widow back to Lexington where she might again see her children and friends. She did not go beyond Philadelphia, however, dying there July 10, 1818, in her 27th year.

Hart County, Kentucky, created by Act of Assembly approved January 28, 1819, was named in honor of Captain Nathaniel G. S. Hart. On February 25, 1949, a marker in that county was erected to his memory by the school children of the county, under the auspices of the National Society United Daughters of 1812 in Kentucky.

[Dunn, C. Frank, "Captain Nathaniel G. S. Hart," *Filson Club History Quarterly*, v. 24 (1950); *In Kentucky*, Spring, 1949; Collins, Richard H., *History of Kentucky*, vol. 2; Young, Mrs. Sarah S., *Genealogical narrative of the Hart family in the United States* (1882); "The Lexington Light Infantry Company War of 1812," *Register*, v. 42 (1944); Leavy, William A., "A Memoir of Lexington and its vicinity," *Register* v. 40 (1942).]

PASCHAL HICKMAN
Captain, 1st Rifle Regiment

A son of the celebrated Reverend William Hickman, Paschal Hickman came to Kentucky with his family when very young. Reverend Hickman settled in Franklin County in 1784 and on January 17, 1788, moved to the Forks of Elkhorn where he was pastor and where he reared his large family. The mother of Captain Hickman was a Shackelford according to Reverend Hickman's manuscript account of his life. Of her he wrote: "Sorely distressed in mind about the massacre of her son at the Raisin, she pined away and died June 9, 1813." She was the Reverend Hickman's first wife.

It is known that Paschal the son served in most of the Indian campaigns waged from Kentucky, was a spy or scout under General Wayne in 1794 and that at this time he was a moderately sized man of 160 pounds. His home was near the railroad tunnel in Frankfort. He lived there in 1812 and his family continued to dwell there in 1813 but the house undoubtedly was built some time prior to 1812. The stone foundation was massive and "had the appearance of having been done by honest hands." The nails by which the woodwork was joined were all of wrought iron, and the window and door frames were fastened together by locust pins. The home was torn down in 1879 and Colonel J. W. Smith built a warehouse on the site.

In due course Paschal Hickman amassed considerable holdings in land and other property. From 1797 until 1812 Franklin County tax books list him as owning 5,984 acres of land in sixteen Kentucky counties. An inventory of his slaves and personal estate, approved in the May Court, 1813, valued his property at $9,217.85.

Early records of the 22nd (Franklin County) Regiment, Kentucky Militia, show that Hickman was an ensign in 1802 and promoted to lieutenant on September 24, 1803. He was listed in L. F. Johnson's *History of Franklin County* as a man prominent in the county before 1800. In 1808 he was appointed jailor of the county, a post he held at the time he enlisted for service against Great Britain. Mr. Johnson described him as "six feet two inches tall and weighing over two hundred pounds. He was a very handsome man and one of the most popular of that day."

On June 8, 1812, ten days before the United States declared

war against Great Britain, Paschal Hickman was commissioned captain in the First Rifle Regiment. At the same time Peter Dudley was commissioned lieutenant and Peter G. Voorhies ensign. In June and July Captain Hickman, then described as a man of 220 pounds, recruited his company of Franklin County men and began the difficult process of arming and drilling the group into a military unit.

By late June his company was able to make a creditable public appearance. On July 1, 1812, the Frankfort *Palladium* reported that

> On Saturday last the volunteer company of this county, commanded by Capt. Paschal Hickman, and the volunteer company of Woodford County, commanded by Capt. Virgil M'Cracken, and both attached to Col. John Allen's volunteer rifle regiment, met in a very handsome piece of woods near Major W. Graham's, about 4 miles from this place, for the purpose of being instructed in military manoeuvring, camp duty, &c. and remained encamped until Monday. On Sunday a very large concourse of ladies and gentlemen collected at the camp, where two very animating discourses were delivered by the Rev. Mr. Shannon and the Rev. Mr. Mitchell. His excellency Governor Harrison visited the camp, and by permission of the officers, practiced the troops in a variety of manoeuvres and evolutions peculiarly well adapted to Indian warfare, marching through woods, &c. to the great satisfaction of all present.

An account of Captain Hickman's participation in the Raisin campaign and of his death at Frenchtown is given elsewhere in this study. Hickman County, Kentucky, formed by Act of Assembly approved December 19, 1821, was named in his honor.

Paschal Hickman married, March 11, 1797, Elizabeth "Betsy" F. Hall, daughter of William Hall (died 1865) and Mary "Pattie" Hall, his first wife. Three daughters were born to them: Sally, who married June 22, 1820, George W. Chambers, of Louisville; Patsy, who married first October 31, 1818, John Sproul, and second on January 20, 1825, Colonel Benjamin Estill, of Abingdon, Virginia; and Susan Hall Hickman, who married William K. Trigg and removed to Missouri.

After the death of Captain Hickman, Elizabeth (Hall) Hickman married on December 9, 1823, William Littell, noted Ken-

Biographies   153

tucky lawyer and author of *Political Transactions in and Concerning Kentucky,* etc.

[*Commonwealth,* May 26, 1871; Darnell, Ermina Jett, *Forks of Elkhorn Church* (1946); Woodson, Mrs. Mary Willis Renick, *My Recollections of Frankfort* (MS, Kentucky Historical Society); *Tri-Weekly Yeoman,* July 1, 1879; *Will and Settlement Book B,* Franklin County, Ky.; *Register of Commissions issued . . . 1799-1804* (MS, Kentucky Historical Society); *Official Roster of Officers of War 1812-15* (MS, Kentucky Historical Society); Hickman, William, "A Short Account of my Life and Travels," . . . (typescript, Kentucky Historical Society.)]

RICHARD HIGHTOWER
Captain, 17th United States Infantry

Captain Hightower, of Jessamine County, Kentucky, was a son of George Hightower, Sr., according to the latter's will on file in Jessamine County. The plantation mentioned in that instrument was probably the home now owned by Mrs. George Faig and Mrs. Walter Moffett, in that county. The parents of Richard Hightower it is thought were buried in the basement of this old home.

In 1810 Richard Hightower had in his Jessamine County household one male under sixteen and one aged twenty-six to forty-five. He also owned eight slaves. Two years later, on the outbreak of war, he enlisted in the United States Army and was commissioned a captain in the newly formed 17th United States Infantry on March 12, 1812. In this capacity he served at Frenchtown and was captured. Paroled and back in the service, he transferred May 12, 1814, to the 19th United States Infantry when the 17th Infantry was consolidated with the 19th, 26th and 27th Regiments to form the 17th and 19th regiments of infantry. Captain Hightower resigned from the army on June 29, 1814.

Joshua Hightower, his brother, enlisted in the volunteer militia and saw service as 1st Sergeant in Captain Gustavus M. Bower's company, Colonel George Trotter's Regiment.

That Richard Hightower experienced financial difficulties after the War of 1812 is evidenced throughout deeds recorded in Jessamine County. In 1833 he deeded his farm to the President and Board of Directors of the Bank of the Commonwealth of Kentucky and shortly afterward, in 1834, removed to Mississippi.

He died on Monday, November 4, 1838, at the Columbus, Mississippi, home of John T. Connell, in his 71st year.

The Columbus Democrat in its comment on the death of Captain Hightower noted in part:

Those best acquainted with his biography state that at an early age he bore arms in the Revolutionary conflict, and that at a later period, when his character was fully developed, he was entrusted with the command of a company of riflemen, raised in Kentucky, his adopted State, during the American War. This company he commanded at the Thames, and it is said by those who shared with him that victory over a foreign foe, which shed much lustre on the American arms, that he was ever foremost in the fight. It must be gratifying to those friends of Captain Hightower who live at a distance to learn that though comparatively amongst strangers, he received during his illness all the attention that it was possible or necessary to bestow, and that after his death, his remains were paid all the respect that his warmest friends could desire. His body was conveyed to the grave accompanied by a large number of our most respectable citizens, together with the Columbus Rifle Company and Band. The late Captain Hightower was buried with all the honors of war.

[*Columbus Democrat*, Columbus, Miss., Nov. 10, 1838; Heitman, Francis B., *Historical Register and Dictionary of the United States Army* . . .; Data contributed by Mary Lee Mahin, Keene, Ky.; U. S. Census of Kentucky, Jessamine County, 1810; Jessamine County court records.]

JOSEPH H. KELLY
Captain, 5th Regiment

Captain Kelly was born in Spottsylvania County, Virginia, January 29, 1767, a son of Major William Kelly (born in Ireland, 1735, died in 1783), a Revolutionary soldier of the First Virginia Regiment, and Redsy (Smith) Kelly, who was born in 1737.

Shortly after Major Kelly's death in 1783 his widow with her two sons, Joseph H. and Griffin Kelly and her younger daughters removed to Kentucky, settling near Winchester. Three years later Joseph Kelly was out with General George Rogers Clark. He enlisted in the Raisin Force and was commissioned August 14, 1812, a lieutenant in Captain Wiley R. Brasfield's company of the 5th Regiment. His promotion to captain of the company, on November 16 of the same year, followed Captain Brasfield's resignation. Captured during the action of January 22, 1813, Captain Kelly drew pay for subsistence to March 25, 1813.

After parole by the British he returned to Clark County but

Biographies

subsequently removed to Henry County, settling on a large tract of land between Eminence and Pleasureville. Here he reared his large family, lived out his life and died October 16, 1853. He was buried on his farm. A tall shaft from which the inscription long since disappeared marks his final resting place.

Captain Kelly married in 1787 Elizabeth Mallory, born March 24, 1771, and died March 30, 1830. To them were born six sons and six daughters:

(1) Samuel Kelly, born September 22, 1788, married Patsy (Sarah) Sutton, who died May 4, 1857. Samuel Kelly died February 26, 1871; (2) Permelia Kelly, born June 18, 1791, married James Sams (1785-Feb. 26, 1849) on December 24, 1806. She died July 26, 1855; (3) James Kelly, born July 1, 1793; (4) Elizabeth Kelly, born October 10, 1795, married first Fielding Lacklin, second Thomas Showmaker (Shoemaker); (5) Sarah Kelly, born January 29, 1798; (6) William Kelly, born April 12, 1800, married Susan Hayden; (7) Jane Kelly, born May 30, 1802, married first William Kelly, second a Dr. Whitehead; (8) Joseph Kelly, born June 13, 1804, married first Nancy Smith, second Harriet Jones; (9) Ariel (Uriel) Kelly, born June 20, 1806, died in 1807; (10) Polly (Mary) Kelly, born September 18, 1807, married in 1821 Joel P. Thomasson. She died in April, 1879; (11) Griffin Kelly, born January 15, 1810, married Rebecca Jane Smith; (12) Nancy Kelly, born April 28, 1812, married Burgess Acton (Ecton).

[Drane, Maude Johnston, *History of Henry County, Kentucky* (1948); General Winchester's *Orderly Book; Militia Officers, 1812-16* (MS, Kentucky Historical Society); Records from Bible of Major William Kelly and Redsy Smith Kelly, Bible of Joseph Kelly and Elizabeth Mallory Kelly, the latter in Acklen, Jeannette T., *Bible Records and Marriage Bonds (Tennessee Records)*, c1933.]

MAURICE LANGHORNE
Captain, 1st Rifle Regiment

Captain Langhorne was born February 10, 1775, a son of John Langhorne (October 8, 1751-March 14, 1784) and Sarah Bell Langhorne. The latter, born August 24, 1754, was a daughter of Judith Cary and David Bell, who lived and died near Lynchburg, Virginia. Sarah Bell and John Langhorne, parents of Captain Maurice Langhorne, were married April 30, 1774. After her death he married Cary Harrison. A sister of Sarah Bell Langhorne was Judith Bell who married first Nathaniel Gist (1735-1796) and second Governor Charles Scott. One of her daughters, Ann Gist, married Captain Nathaniel Hart, killed at the River Raisin.

Maurice Langhorne lived early in Bourbon County, Kentucky, and represented that county in the Kentucky House of Representatives in 1808 and again in 1810. With the outbreak of war he volunteered and received his commission as captain, 1st Rifle Regiment, June 10, 1812. Research indicates that he was not present for the battles and massacre at Frenchtown. Men were drawn on detail from his company for both battles, however, and he was in position on January 25, 1813, to make up and send to the *Western Citizen*, at Paris, a list of his men killed, wounded and missing in action.

Following his service with the Raisin Force, Captain Langhorne settled at Maysville, Mason County, Kentucky. (His commission as captain of a rifle company in Bourbon County's 71st Regiment had been resigned by November, 1813.)

In Maysville he operated Langhorne's Tavern or Hotel, famed in the early annals of that city. As early as 1817 subscriptions were opened in Maysville for the new Bank of Limestone under the direction of Captain Langhorne. In 1825 he was one of the committee appointed to greet General Lafayette and it was in Langhorne's Hotel that the General was dined.

Shortly after this Captain Maurice Langhorne moved to Jefferson County where he continued to make his home until his death on June 3, 1841. (His grave stone in Old Western Cemetery, Louisville, says June 23, 1841.)

He had married first, in Bourbon County on July 4, 1799, Nancy Johnson who died in July, 1826. He married second, in Lexington on June 14, 1827, Paulina Ann Brook, daughter of Mann Satterwhite, of Lexington, and widow of Benjamin M. Brook whom she had married July 25, 1812.

Three children were born to Captain Langhorne: John H. (Jack) Langhorne, Robert, and Victoria Langhorne.

[Paxton, W. M., *The Marshall Family* . . . (1885); Clift, G. G., *History of Maysville and Mason County*, v. 1 (1936); *Commissioned Officers of the War of 1812-16* (MS, Kentucky Historical Society); Bourbon and Fayette county marriage records; *Western Citizen*, Feb. 13, 1813; *Commonwealth*, July 6, 1841; Jefferson County Will Book 3; Collins, Richard H., *History of Kentucky*.]

VIRGIL McCRACKEN
Captain, 1st Rifle Regiment

Captain McCracken, of Woodford County, was a son of Cyrus and Elizabeth McCracken. His father was one of the first settlers of the Woodford County region and with Hancock Lee built cabins one mile below Frankfort and named the site Leestown. Cyrus McCracken lost his life during the course of General George Rogers Clark's expedition of 1782 against the Piqua towns. He died November 4, 1782, from wounds received during the action and was buried "near the block-house at the mouth of Licking, on the Kentucky side." Elizabeth McCracken, his mother, was living in Woodford County in 1810, her family at that time containing eight members. The McCracken home was on McCracken's Mill Road, on Glenn Creek.

Virgil McCracken was named for his uncle who died in 1780. He has been described as an intelligent, patriotic and fearless man. He represented Woodford County in the lower house of the Legislature in 1810 and 1811. With the outbreak of war with Great Britain he raised a company and was commissioned its captain June 13, 1812. Left behind with the wounded, on January 23, 1813, Captain McCracken was taken prisoner by the Indians and carried from Frenchtown. Ensign Isaac L. Baker in his report to General Winchester of February 25, 1813, noted: "About the 10th instant, an Indian brought captain M'Cracken's commission to Sandwich; the paper was bloody. The fellow said he took the captain in trust, but some time after when stripped and examined, he found an Indian scalp in his bosom, which induced him to kill him. This you cannot but be assured is an humbug of the fellow's own making to screen himself from the odium of barbarity. The captain's character and the danger that attended his carrying such furniture in a disastrous battle, gives it to the lie."

McCracken County, Kentucky, created by Act of Assembly approved for date of January 15, 1825, was named in honor of Captain Virgil McCracken.

He had married in Woodford County, December 31, 1800, Sally Caldwell, daughter of Henry C. Caldwell of that county. Their children were:

Mary Bird McCracken, born in 1801 and died in 1885. She married on November 5, 1817, Thomas R. Jesse; Martha M. "Pattie" McCracken married January 2, 1822, John Williams; Cyrus, Virgil, and George McCracken, all who died before attaining the age of twenty-five.

[*McCracken family* (one page, unsigned, undated, at Kentucky Historical Society); Woodford County marriage records; Collins, Richard H., *History of Kentucky*, vol. 2; *Niles' Weekly Register*, vol. 4; *Commissioned Officers of the War of 1812-16* (MS, Kentucky Historical Society); Railey, William E., *History of Woodford County* (1938).]

JOHN MARTIN
Captain, 5th Regiment

Captain John "Jack" Martin was born in Clark County, Kentucky, March 6, 1797. In 1810-11 he built the Clark House, later known as the Webster House, in Winchester. He was the first to keep this hotel which was razed in April, 1880. Soon after finishing the Webster House war against Great Britain was declared and Captain Martin raised a company of Clark County men for the Raisin campaign. His commission was dated July 29, 1812. While records indicate that he was not present for the battles or massacre at Frenchtown many of his men were. Following this tour, he raised another company and continued in the service.

Remaining active in the militia, he was Lieutenant Colonel of the 17th Regiment (Clark County) on April 9, 1814, and Colonel, Commandant, on May 2, 1814.

He died in Clark County January 28, 1877, and was buried on the Martin home ten miles east of Winchester, near the Winchester and Mt. Sterling pike.

Captain Martin married Mary F. _____, who was born July, 1809, and died April 25, 1881. Of their children, Kate Bell was born July 4, 1845, and died October 24, 1851; Nannie was born October 13, 1838, and died June 14, 1856; John G., died at the age of 37 years, one month and eleven days. All were buried in the family cemetery at the Martin home.

[*Officers of the War of 1812-16* (MS, Kentucky Historical Society); *Clark County Democrat*, Apr. 14, 1880; Martin family cemetery records; Clark County Historical Society, *Clark County Chronicles* (newspaper clippings, Kentucky Historical Society).]

JAMES MEADE
Captain, 17th U. S. Infantry

Little concerning the life of Captain Meade has been discovered. According to Collins he was a native of Woodford County. Captain Peter Funk in his diary of the Tippecanoe action notes that Captain Meade came to the service from Fayette County. It has been accepted that he was very young when he volunteered for military duty under Colonel Joseph H. Daviess late in 1811. He was a member of either Captain Funk's or Captain Frederick Geiger's companies when he established a reputation for bravery and daring during the course of the battle of Tippecanoe. This record led to his appointment, on March 12, 1812, as captain in the 17th United States Infantry.

With his men on the exposed right flank at Frenchtown, he received the first enemy onslaught and was killed early in the action of January 22, 1813.

Meade County, Kentucky, formed by Act of Assembly approved December 17, 1823, was named in his honor. In the Act describing the new county and designating its name he is called Captain James M. Meade.

[Pirtle, Capt. Alfred, *The Battle of Tippecanoe* . . . (1900); Collins, Richard H., *History of Kentucky; Acts* . . . 1823-24; Heitman, Francis B., *Historical Register and Dictionary of the United States Army* . . .]

JAMES C. PRICE
Captain, 5th Regiment

Captain Price was born in Halifax County, Virginia, in 1779, the eldest son of Colonel William Price. The latter was born in Stafford County, Virginia, in 1755, and died October 10, 1808, in Jessamine County, Kentucky. After the surrender of Lord Cornwallis in October, 1781, Colonel Price removed from Stafford to Halifax County. In 1782 he visited Kentucky and entered land on warrants received for his services as a Revolutionary War soldier. In 1787 he removed with his family to Kentucky, settling in the limits of the present county of Jessamine. His wife was Mary Cunningham who died in 1839.

Captain James C. Price was in command of the Jessamine Blues, one of the most noted military companies in its day, when war was declared against Great Britain. This company's uniform was blue, with light facings, and was considered in those days a marvel of beauty. Immediately after the call for volunteers, Captain Price offered his company and was elected to lead it into the northwest.

Eight years before, in 1804, he had married Susannah Barkley. His son, mentioned below, was Kleber F. Price, a child of two years when his father was killed at Frenchtown. The son was born in Jessamine County and died there in October, 1863. He married Elizabeth Neal Singleton, born in 1809, a daughter of Mason and Fannie (Garnet) Singleton, natives of Jessamine County.

A few days before the first battle at River Raisin Captain Price composed the following letter to his wife, the last presumably ever written by him to his family. As a document it must rank high among the constantly growing heritage of American war letters; as indication of the type of citizen-soldier of the War of 1812, it is possibly more faithful than the best of portraits.

In Camp, near River Raisin
Jan. 16, 1813.

Dear Susan:

I have only time to inform you that we expect to have a battle tomorrow with the British and Indians. On the eve of battle I have believed it proper to address you these lines.

As you are aware that the object nearest to my heart is your welfare and that of my children, and so far as I have been able I have provided everything in my power for your comfort and that of my children. I feel in no unhappy mood about my girl children; I know they are in your company at all hours of the day. You know where they visit and who are their associates.

My only son, I feel a great interest in his future and welfare. Early impressions are lasting and often, perhaps always, tend to give a permanent cast to the leading principles of the heart, and to the general character of the mind. Teach my boy to love truth, to speak truth at all times. He must not be allowed to associate with children or other persons who indulge in swearing or misrepresentations. He must be taught to bear in mind that 'an honest man is the noblest work of God;' he must be rigidly honest in his dealings. He must be taught to attend church every Sabbath. Never allow him to run about on Sabbath days, fishing. Teach my son the habits of industry. Industry and virtue are twin brothers, but indolence and vice are closely associated. Indolence leads to every vice and every other evil. Industry leads to virtue and every other good. Not a day must be lost in teaching him how to work, and the great principles of our holy religion must be on all occasions impressed on his mind. It may be possible I may fall in battle and my only boy must know that his father, next to God, loves his country, and is now risking his life in defending that country against a barbarous and cruel enemy. Be sure and teach my son, with Pope, to say and feel that—

> Vice is a monster of such frightful mein
> As to be hated needs but to be seen.
> Yet seen, too oft, familiar with her face,
> We first endure, then pity, then embrace.

Teach him these lines of the great poet; they will do him good when he grows older. Pray for me that you may be with me once more.

Your affectionate husband,
James C. Price

Susanah Price,
   Near Nicholasville, Ky.

Post Script.—The snow is two feet deep, the crust is very hard and we walk over it and ride upon it on horseback. We often sleep under such deep snow, we cover up in our blankets and we sleep warm during the night. Eb. has been sick, but is now on duty.
               J.C.P.

Captain Price's body was never recognized among those found after the battle of January 22, 1813.

Mrs. Susannah Price, a daughter of John and Susannah Barkley, died a few years after the Raisin battle. Her will was probated in Jessamine County in November, 1819. In this instrument she names her parents and her four children: Kleber, Martha A., Mary and Eliza Price.

[Jessamine County wills; Perrin, W. H., J. H. Battle and G. C. Kniffin, *Kentucky. A History of the State* (1887); Young, Bennett H., *History of Jessamine County, Kentucky*.]

URIEL SEBREE
Captain, 1st Regiment

A native of Virginia, Captain Sebree settled early in Kentucky, establishing Boone County as his home. He represented that county in the Kentucky House of Representatives in 1806-1807, and in the Senate from 1813-1817. In 1818 he was apparently a resident of Lexington, Kentucky, the *Lexington Directory* of that year listing him as a merchant, with a residence on Second Street. Prior to this he had been active in the early history of Covington, and was one of the original trustees of the city in 1815.

Commissioned as captain, 1st Regiment, on August 7, 1812, he led his company at Raisin and was captured when the detachment was surrendered to Proctor on January 22, 1813.

In 1819, then a Major, he was engaged by Colonel Richard M. Johnson, a near kinsman, to command the ship *Calhoun* on Johnson's Yellowstone Expedition.

Shortly after this expedition he removed, in 1821, to Missouri, locating in Howard County. Here he became County Judge in 1828, was at one time Register of the Land Office at Fayette, and one of the first moderators of the Baptist Association of Missouri. He died in Missouri.

Captain Sebree married, while a resident of Lexington, Kentucky, in September, 1817, Elizabeth Payne, of Scott County. She was a daughter of General John Payne (Apr. 8, 1764-Sept. 9, 1837) and Elizabeth Johnson Payne (1772-1845), daughter of Robert and Jemima Suggett Johnson and sister of Colonel Richard M. Johnson.

Of the children of Uriel and Elizabeth Payne Sebree: John P. Sebree was in both branches of the Missouri Legislature and warden of the State Penitentiary, 1873-77. He married Louise Daly. One of their nine children was Admiral Uriel Sebree. John P. Sebree died in 1882; a daughter married William Augustus Hall (1815-1888), United States Representative from Missouri and father of Uriel Sebree Hall, also a Representative from that State.

[Payne family materials, Kentucky Historical Society; Conrad, Howard L., *Encyclopaedia of the History of Missouri* (1901), vol. 5; *History of Howard and Cooper Counties, Missouri* (1883); *Commissioned Officers of the War of 1812-16* (MS, Kentucky Historical Society); Lexington, Ky., *Reporter*, Sept. 17, 1817; Meyer, Leland Winfield, *The Life and Times of Colonel Richard M. Johnson of Kentucky* (1932).]

JOHN SIMPSON
Captain, 1st Rifle Regiment

John Simpson, lawyer and soldier, was a Virginian by birth. At an early date in the history of the Commonwealth he migrated with his father to Lincoln County, Kentucky. In the new country he became a prominent lawyer, member and Speaker of the House of Representatives and was elected to the United States Congress—yet beyond his record of public appearance little is known of him.

His first taste of Indian warfare came in 1794 when he was out with General Anthony Wayne and fought in the Battle of Fallen Timbers. Three years later he was attending the school of Mr. Mahan, on Salt River, with Robert B. McAfee. The latter at this time found him "a young man six feet seven inches high of Shelby County." When Mr. Mahan moved his school to Danville in 1799, both McAfee and Simpson continued with him there. It is stated that he also attended Dr. Priestly's school at Bardstown, where his classmates were John Allen, John Rowan, Felix Grundy, John Pope and others destined to head the legal profession in Kentucky.

Urged and encouraged by John Allen, lawyer Simpson moved to Shelby County after completing his law studies and entered upon the practice there. His first entrance into politics came in 1806 when he successfully ran for a seat in the House of Representatives. He was elected to the same seat again in 1808-1811, and was elected Speaker of the House in 1810-1811.

The War of 1812, declared early in the year, disrupted and eventually closed the career of John Simpson. In this year he became candidate for United States Representative from the 8th District to the Thirteenth Congress, winning the election over Stephen Ormsby. (Later Ormsby was elected to fill the vacancy caused by the death at Raisin of Representative-elect Simpson.)

At the outbreak of war Simpson was Captain of Grenadiers, 18th Regiment (Shelby County). His commission as Captain, First Rifle Regiment, under his old friend and advisor Lieutenant Colonel John Allen, was dated June 13, 1812. An account of his death, during the action at Frenchtown on January 22, 1813, is given elsewhere in this study.

Simpson County, formed by Act of Assembly approved January 28, 1819, was named in his honor. Simpsonville, on the Midland Trail in Shelby County, was also named for him. The town was laid out in 1816 but not incorporated until 1832.

[Collins, Richard H., *History of Kentucky; Commissioned Officers of the War of 1812-16* (MS, Kentucky Historical Society); *Biographical Directory of the American Congress, 1774-1927;* McAfee, Robert B., "The Life and Times of Robt. B. McAfee and his family connections," *Register,* v. 25 (1927).]

LYNN WEST
Captain, 1st Regiment

Captain West was born in Virginia in 1770 or 1771. He came to Kentucky with his Uncle Edward West in 1784, settling in Georgetown and working with his kinsman in the gunsmith business until 1797. In the latter year he returned to Prince William County, Virginia, to marry. Returning to Georgetown and the home he had built on the corner of Hamilton and what is now Bourbon Street he continued the manufacture of guns and other implements.

He was fond of fine-blooded horses and was an early breeder and racer. He is credited with establishing one of the first race courses in Scott County. At one time he was a member of the Board of Trustees of Georgetown.

Already active in Scott County's 77th Regiment before war against Great Britain was declared, Captain West offered his military abilities and training to the war effort and was commissioned captain in the 1st Regiment August 7, 1812. Records indicate that men from his company were detailed for the Raisin march but that Captain West did not accompany them to Frenchtown.

After this tour he returned to Scott County and there lived out his life. He resigned his commission as captain, 77th Regiment, May 6, 1815. He died in Georgetown January 26, 1836, aged 66 years.

In Prince William County, Virginia, Lynn West married on January 26, 1797, Susan Jackson who was born there in 1777 and died in Georgetown August 8, 1860. Of the nine children born to them: Susan was born in Georgetown February 28, 1812. She married a Crockett and on May 28, 1843, George Griffith Steffee. She died January 25, 1887; Captain Lewis West was born in Georgetown in 1800. He learned the gunsmith trade from his father and followed it until the age of seventy-nine. He married

Sarah Mahoney, daughter of Captain James H. Mahoney. She died in 1874 leaving five children.

[Perrin, William Henry, ed., *History of Bourbon, Scott, Harrison and Nicholas Counties* . . . (1882); Gaines, B. O., *History of Scott County*; Kentucky Historical Society membership certificate of George McCalla Spears, dated 1916; Lexington *Observer & Reporter*, Jan. 27, 1836; *Commissioned Officers of the War of 1812-16* (MS, Kentucky Historical Society.)]

SAMUEL L. WILLIAMS
Captain, 5th Regiment

Samuel Luttrell Williams was born October 22, 1781, a son of Rolla (Walter Raleigh) and Rebecca (Luttrell) Williams. The father was born in Culpeper County, Virginia, in 1754, of Welsh descent. He was a soldier of the American Revolution and removed to Kentucky in 1784, settling in the present Montgomery County. He died there in 1827.

Samuel L. Williams was commissioned captain in the 5th Regiment on August 7, 1812. Following his capture at River Raisin and parole he returned to Montgomery County where he reared his large family and took an active part in community and State activities. He represented Montgomery County in the Kentucky House of Representatives in 1814 and 1818, and was sent to the Kentucky Senate in 1820-24, 1828-32, and in 1840-1844. He died on his farm September 3, 1872.

He had married Fanny Cluke in 1811. To this union were born twelve children:

Eliza Ann Williams (1812-1881) married James Hutchcraft (1800-1863); Maria Louisa Williams; General John Stuart "Cerro Gordo" Williams, born July 10, 1818, and died July 17, 1898, was a Colonel in the Mexican War, Brigadier General in the Confederate States Army, and member of the United States Senate. He was twice married, first on April 18, 1843, to Ann P. Harrison who died in 1844, and second, in 1870, to Mrs. Henrietta Hamilton. He had but one child, Mary, who married Colonel James H. Holloway, of Clark County; Nancy L. Williams; General Richard Luttrell Williams, also a soldier, was in the Union Army during the Civil War. General Dick Williams was married twice, his second wife being Minerva Tribble Stoner Grubbs, widow of John Grubbs; Frances Amanda Williams; Thomas Jefferson Williams; Henry Clay Williams, who also served in the C.S.A., in the 6th

Kentucky Cavalry. He married Lue Rogers. He was a school teacher; Caroline Frances Williams; Harriet Amanda Williams; Benjamin Warfield Williams; and James Williams, soldier in the Mexican War.

[Levin, H., ed., *The Lawyers and Lawmakers of Kentucky* (1897); *Biographical Directory of the American Congress, 1774-1927; Biographical encyclopaedia of the dead and living men of the nineteenth century* (1878); Reid, Richard, *Historical sketches of Montgomery County* . . . (1926); Collins, Richard H., *History of Kentucky;* Hutchcraft, H. D., "The Williams and Hutchcraft Genealogy and History," *Register,* v. 2. No. 5 (May, 1904); Hawthorne, Bess L., *Williams family data* (typescript, Kentucky Historical Society); Williams, John Augustus, *In Memoriam: Remarks on the life and character of General Samuel L. Williams.* Cincinnati, Robert Clarke & Co., 1872.]

THE BRITISH AND INDIAN LEADERS

HENRY A. PROCTOR was born in Wales in 1787 (other sources say 1765). He joined the army at an early age and at the outbreak of the War of 1812 was sent to Canada as Colonel of the 42nd Regiment. He was dispatched by General Sir Isaac Brock to Amherstburg to prevent the landing of General William Hull, and subsequently gained the victory of Brownstown, which exploits contributed much to the fall of Detroit and the capitulation of Hull.

He opened the campaign of 1812 by defeating General Winchester on the River Raisin, for which services he was promoted to Brigadier General. He was repelled from Fort Meigs by General Harrison in May, 1813, from Fort Stephenson (Lower Sandusky, Ohio) by Major Croghan on August 2 and was totally defeated by Harrison at the Battle of the Thames October 5, 1813.

For his conduct in America, especially at the River Raisin and the defeat at the Thames, he was afterwards court-martialed and sentenced to be suspended from rank and pay for six months. He was reinstated, commanded again during the war and rose to the rank of Lieutenant General. He was much admired by the people of Canada, and the sentence passed upon him was regarded as arbitrary and unmerited.

General Proctor died in Liverpool, England, in 1859.

[*Appleton's cyclopaedia of American Biography,* v. 5; *Harper's encyclopaedia of American History,* v. 7; *Michigan Pioneer and Historical Collections,* v. 15.]

Biographies

COLONEL JAMES BABY of the Essex Militia and member and for some time President of the Legislative Council of Upper Canada, was born at Detroit in 1763, the eldest son of Duperon Baby. Colonel Baby's house at Sandwich, standing as late as 1890, was used by Hull as his headquarters when he invaded Canada, July 12, 1812. The house was also used by Generals Brock and Harrison. Baby performed many useful services for the British cause, and justly held a high station socially and intellectually. McAfee noted in his history of the war: "On the part of the British, Colonel James Baby acted with generosity and friendship, and Colonel Elliott with Major Muir were likewise found on the side of humanity in many serviceable acts (during and after the battles and massacre at Frenchtown)." Colonel Baby was colonel of militia, western district, and was awarded a land grant. He died in Toronto, Canada, in 1833.
[*Michigan Pioneer and Historical Collections*, vol. 16.]

CAPTAIN MATTHEW ELLIOTT, Jr., of the Indian Department, was present at the battle of River Raisin fought January 22, 1813. He was given a land grant for his services. His father, Colonel Matthew Elliott, also served as captain in the Royal Indian Department, 1777-84, and fought at Blue Licks and Sandusky in the Indian massacres of the Revolution. He died near Burlington Heights on May 7, 1814, aged 75 years. His wife, mother of Captain Elliott, was Marie Louise Sans Chagrin, who died July 9, 1826, aged sixty years. [*Ibid.*, vol. 16.]

CAPTAIN WILLIAM ELLIOTT, of the 1st Essex Militia and Caldwell's Rangers, was a son of Colonel Matthew Elliott, Deputy Superintendent of the Indian Department. Captain William Elliott was present at Detroit, where he was given medal and clasp, and was at Frenchtown and Miami. The family lived at Amherstburg. Captain Elliott has been referred to in these pages as the one-time Lexington, Kentucky, guest of Captain Nathaniel G. S. Hart whose life the Englishman did not save on January 23, 1813. [*Ibid.*, vol. 16.]

GEORGE FREDERICK RAPP, interpreter for the western nations, 1812, was at the capture of Detroit, the massacre at River Raisin, at the defeat of Proctor at the Thames and at Lewiston on the Niagara River. [*Ibid.*, vol. 16.]

MAJOR EBENEZER REYNOLDS, who led the British forces into the first battle at Frenchtown on January 18, and was present at the battle of January 22, 1813, was major of flank companies, 1st and 2nd Essex Militia, and Lieutenant Colonel on September 21, 1813. He was present at Detroit, receiving the medal and clasp; at Frenchtown January 18 and 22, 1813, as noted above. He was sheriff for Kent County, Upper Canada, 1833, and awarded a pension after the war. [*Ibid.*, vol. 16.]

LIEUTENANT COLONEL THOMAS BLIGH ST. GEORGE was born in England about 1765 and died in London November 6, 1837. He entered the army as an ensign, became a lieutenant in 1790, captain four years later, major in 1804 and lieutenant colonel the year following. During the period of his promotions he served in France, Portugal, Corsica and in the Mediterranean area. In March, 1809, he went to Upper Canada, having been appointed inspecting field officer of the militia there. He commanded at Amherstburg when it was attacked by Hull, led the militia at the capture of Detroit in August, 1812, and again at Frenchtown. In the struggle on River Raisin he received four wounds "in a gallant attempt to occupy a Building favourably situated for the Enemy's Annoyance." He became colonel in 1813, major general in 1819, was appointed a Companion of the Bath in 1815 and knighted in 1835. [*Appleton's Cyclopaedia of American Biography*, vol. 5.]

BLACK HAWK was born at Kaskaskia, Illinois, in 1767 and died near the river Des Moines, Iowa, October 3, 1838. An American Indian chosen principal chief of the Sacs, about 1788, he was leader of the revolt of the Sacs and Foxes, in 1832, which brought about the Black Hawk War (last uprising east of the Mississippi River). He was present with his warriors on the British side at River Raisin, Fort Meigs, Fort Stephenson and Moraviantown. His autobiography was published in Boston, 1834. [*Michigan Pioneer and Historical Collections*, v. 16.]

CAPTAIN BILLY CALDWELL was a natural son, by a Shawnee Indian mother, of Colonel William Caldwell. He was an accepted chief of the tribe to which his mother belonged. "Billy" first showed his usefulness to the British in 1810, and was given a good position in the Indian Department. In 1812 he was commissioned a captain in the militia and as such was present at the battles of River Raisin, January, 1813. His father, Colonel William Caldwell, was a loyalist resident of the Pennsylvania back settlements; commissioned captain December 24,

1781, he served in the noted partisan troop "Butler's Rangers." It was Colonel William Caldwell, sent out by Detroit commander Colonel De Peyster, who defeated Colonel Crawford of the Ohio militia near Sandusky, June 4, 1782, and permitted him to be tortured before he was burned at the stake. [*Ibid*, vol. 16.]

ROUND HEAD was a Wyandot (Huron) chief who fought for the British, being connected chiefly with Colonel Proctor's command. He was with Major Muir, of Proctor's command, on the Miami near Fort Miami, Ohio, September 27-28, 1812, and urged in vain that the English commander make a stand here against the American forces. In October following he accompanied Major Muir to River Raisin and a few months later met his death in battle. General Proctor in a letter dated October 23, 1813, stated that "the Indian cause and ours experienced a serious loss in the death of Round Head."

Shortly before the Americans reached Frenchtown in January, 1813, Round Head and his warrior companion Walk-in-the-Water sent the following note to the inhabitants of the village:

> The Hurons and the other tribes of Indians, assembled at the Miami Rapids, to the inhabitants on the river Raisin—
> FRIENDS! LISTEN!
> You have always told us you would give us any assistance in your power.
> We, therefore, as the enemy is approaching us, within twenty-five miles, call upon you all to rise up and come here immediately, bringing your arms along with you.
> Should you fail at this time, we will not consider you in future as friends, and the consequences may be very unpleasant.
> We are well convinced you have no writings forbidding you to assist us. We are your friends at present.
> (Signed) ROUND HEAD
> *By an emblem resembling a horse.*
> WALK IN THE WATER
> *By an emblem resembling a turtle.*

[*Handbook of American Indians* (Bureau of American Ethnology, Bulletin 30); *Niles' Weekly Register*, vol. 5.; *Barbarities of the enemy. Exposed in a Report* . . . Troy, Printed by Francis Adancourt, 1813.]

SPLIT LOG, the Huron chief, first appears in the War of 1812 with the force of Major A. H. Muir in the neighborhood of Fort Wayne, in September, 1812. He was at the battles and massacre on River Raisin, January, 1813. In May, 1814, with Blackbird he became disgusted with the short allowances made his warriors, being then near the Niagara frontier, cut loose from the command, retired toward Lake Huron, and was believed to have expressed wishes to make peace with the Americans.

[*Michigan Pioneer and Historical Collections*, vol. 16.]

WALK-IN-THE-WATER, was a Wyandot chief serving with the British 41st Regiment during the River Raisin campaign. His residence was at Maguaga. He has been described as "a fine, commanding person, near six feet in height, and well-proportioned, and as straight as an arrow. He was mild and pleasant in his deportment." He was friendly to the United States and desired to join them at the beginning of the war; but the instructions of his government not to employ savages and his own humane impulses would not allow Hull to accept his services. Soon after this Walk-in-the-Water and his band of Wyandots joined the British at Malden. Their hands were in that service if their hearts were not. Walk-in-the-Water died about 1817. His *totem* or arms as noted above was a *turtle*.

[Lossing, Benson J., *The Pictorial Field-Book of the War of 1812* . . . (1869); *Michigan Pioneer and Historical Collections*, vol. 26.]

APPENDIX

Rolls of troops engaged in the battles and massacre at Frenchtown, on the River Raisin, Michigan Territory, January 18 - 23, 1813

LIST OF ABBREVIATIONS IN APPENDIX

Capt.—Captain
Cpl.—Corporal
D.M.—Drum Major
dischd.—discharged
F.M.—Fife Major
Hon. Disch.—Honorable Discharge, Honorably Discharged
KIA—Killed in action
Lt., Lieut.—Lieutenant
Lt. Col.—Lieutenant Colonel
MIA—Missing in action
POW—Prisoner of war
QM—Quartermaster
Qm. Sgt., Qr. M. Sgt.—Quartermaster Sergeant
"R" Service—U. S. Army, regular service
resg.—resigned
S.M., Sgt. Maj.—Sergeant Major
Sgt.—Sergeant
Sub.—Substitute
Surg. Mate—Surgeon's Mate
trfd.—transferred
Vice—In the place of
WIA—Wounded in action

17th United States Infantry

(Rosters of 1812-13 not found. Only known participants at Raisin listed.)

NAME	RANK	REMARKS
Samuel Wells	Colonel	See biographical section.
Alexander Montgomery	Surgeon	KIA Jan. 22. (1)
Caleb H. Holder*	1st Lt.	POW Jan. 22. (1)
Robert Logan*	1st Lt.	KIA Jan. 22. (1)
James Overton, Jr.*	2nd Lt.	Resigned Feb. 10, 1813. (1)
James Liggett*	Ensign	Killed Sept. 25, 1812. (1)
Philip S. Sharer*	"	KIA Jan. 22. (1)
Levi Wells	"	KIA Jan. 22. (1). 7th U.S. Inf.
Blake, Braxton*	Private	KIA Jan. 22. (2)
Gardner, John*	"	KIA Jan. 22. (2)
Redding, William*	"	KIA Jan. 22. (2)
Wells, Thomas K.*	"	KIA Jan. 22. (2)

* Regimental unit unknown.
(1) Heitman, Francis B., *Historical Register . . . of the U. S. Army* . . . .
(2) U. S. Pensions, Statements of Heirs. Sen. Doc. 514.

Captain Robert Edwards's Company, 17th United States Infantry

(Roster of 1812-13 not found. Only known participants at Raisin listed.)

NAME	RANK	REMARKS
Robert Edwards	Captain	KIA Jan. 22. (2)
Alexander Robertson	1st. Lt.	Hon. Disch. 1 June 1814. (1,2)
Joshua Norvell	2nd. Lt.	Resigned 1 Sept. 1812 (2)
Isaac L. Baker	Ensign	POW Jan. 22. (3) 2nd. Inf.
William Luckett	Ensign	(1)
R. L. Stewart	Sgt. Maj.	POW Jan. 22. (3)
Anders, Robert	Rank unknown	POW Jan. 22. (3)
Casey, John or Joshua	"	POW Jan. 22. (3)
Ceasar, Thomas	"	POW Jan. 22. (3)
Delany, Willis	"	POW Jan. 22. (3)
Downey, Henry	"	KIA Jan. 24. (4)
Dyne, Andrew	"	POW Jan. 22. (3)
Farm, Isom	"	POW Jan. 22. (3)
Grindstaff, Isaac	"	POW Jan. 22. (3)
Hobach, Marcus	"	(5)
Kamp, William	"	POW Jan. 22. (3)
Maxfield, John	"	POW Jan. 22. (3)
Mayfield, Southerland	"	Trfd. to Capt. Hightower's Co.
Poage, John	"	POW Jan. 22. (3)

Captain Robert Edwards's Company, 17th United States Infantry
(Continued)

NAME	RANK	REMARKS
Ship, George	Rank unknown	POW Jan. 22. (3)
Tiller, John	"	POW Jan. 22. (3)
Walker, Jeremiah	"	WIA Jan. 18. (6)

(1) *Argus*, 1 Apr. 1812.
(2) Heitman, *Historical Register . . . of the U. S. Army* . . . .
(3) *Palladium*, 24 Mar. 1813.
(4) *American State Papers, Military Affairs*, vol. I.
(5) Winchester's *Orderly Book*, 5 Nov. 1812.
(6) Official Report of the Killed, Wounded and Missing, January 18, 1813. (Copy of original from National Archives, Washington, D. C.)

Captain Richard Hightower's Company, 17th U. S. Infantry
(Jessamine County)

NAME	RANK	REMARKS
Richard Hightower	Captain	POW Jan. 22. (2)
Thomas C. Graves	1st Lt.	KIA Jan. 22. (2)
Ashton Garrett	2nd Lt.	POW Jan. 22. (1)
William O. Butler	Ensign	Attached 11/23/1812; POW Jan. 22 (1)
James Gray	"	Lived. See *Argus*, 1 Apr. 1813
Lucius C. Pleasants	1st Sgt.	
Benjamin Segar	2nd Sgt.	POW Jan. 22. (1)
Jesse Denilhess	3rd Sgt.	
Thomas Childers	Corporal	POW Jan. 22. (1)
Samuel Jones	"	POW Jan. 22. (1)
Acton, William	Private	
Allison, John	"	
Andrews, Robert	"	
Barton, Karswell	"	
Bates, Alfred	"	POW Jan. 22. (1)
Blake, Beverly A.	"	KIA Jan. 22. (3)
Blythe, William	"	
Byron, John	"	
Camp, William	"	
Carter, John	"	POW Jan. 22. (1)
Carter, William	"	POW Jan. 22. (1)
Casey, Joshua	"	
Ceasar, Thomas	"	See Capt. Robert Edwards's Co.
Childers, Thomas	"	
Cook, Matthew	"	
Cooly, John	"	POW Jan. 22. (1)

Rosters of Troops

Captain Richard Hightower's Company, 17th U. S. Infantry *(Continued)*

NAME	RANK	REMARKS
Craig, Walter	Private	
Davis, William	"	POW Jan. 22. (1)
Delaney, Willis	"	
Denore, Baldwin	"	
Dobbs, John	"	
Dyne, Andrew	"	
Emmerson, William	"	POW Jan. 22. (1)
Farrow, Isham	"	
Fisher, John	"	POW Jan. 22. (1)
Fowler, James	"	
Fowler, Thomas	"	
Gentry, Zebedee	"	
Gohagen, William	"	
Goodlett, William	"	POW Jan. 22. (4)
Grigsby, James	"	POW Jan. 22. (1)
Grindstaff, Isaac	"	
Hanley, Thomas H.	"	
Hobson, Bennett	"	
Hope, George	"	POW Jan. 22. (1)
Ingsley, James	"	
James, Samuel	"	
Johnson, William	"	
Lane, John	"	
McCarty, David	"	
McDaniel, William	"	
McKenzie, John	"	
McLin, Frederick	"	McNitt? POW Jan. 22. (4)
Martin, James	"	
Mathews, Philip	"	
Maxwell, John	"	
Mayfield, Southerland	"	POW Jan. 22. (3)
Morgan, J.	"	
Morris, George	"	POW Jan. 22. (1)
Murphy, David	"	POW Jan. 22. (1)
Murrane, J.	"	
Murrane, Mark	"	
Murrane, Tom	"	
Pagget, James	"	
Pagget, Thomas	"	
Pogue, John	"	
Prewitt, Edmund	"	
Price, John	"	
Ralston, Alexander	"	
Reed, Adam	"	POW Jan. 22. (1)
Reed, Robert	"	KIA Jan. 22. (3)
Rice, John	"	POW Jan. 22. (1)

Captain Richard Hightower's Company, 17th U. S. Infantry *(Continued)*

NAME	RANK	REMARKS
Scroggins, William	Private	
Shaw, John	"	
Shimp, George	"	
Shover, Simon	"	
Smith, Richard	"	
Stewart, Rice	"	
Summerfield, Ephraim	"	POW Jan. 22. (1)
Thompson, James	"	POW Jan. 22. (1)
Tiller, John	"	See also Capt. Robert Edwards's Co.
Walker, Jeremiah	"	
Webb, Adam	"	
White, Charles	"	
Williams, Silas	"	POW Jan. 22. (1)
Winchester, Peter	"	Winchell? POW Jan. 22. (4)
Wood, John	"	

(1) *Palladium*, 24 Mar. 1813.
(2) Heitman, *Historical Register* . . . *of the U. S. Army* . . . .
(3) Sen. Doc. 514.
(4) *Palladium*, 31 Mar. 1813.

Captain James Meade's Company, 17th U. S. Infantry

(Roster of 1812-13 not found. Only known participants at Raisin listed.)

NAME	RANK	REMARKS
James Meade	Captain	KIA Jan. 22. (1)
Thomas J. Overton	1st Lt.	KIA Jan. 22. (1)
John C. Richardson	2nd Lt.	(1)
James Munday	Ensign	POW Jan. 22. (1)
Henry Agnew	Sgt.	Reduced to ranks 21 Oct. 1812. (3)
John McKenzie	"	POW Jan. 22. (2)
Walter Craig	Corporal	POW Jan. 22. (2)
Charles White	"	POW Jan. 22. (2)
Barton, Roswell	Private	POW Jan. 22. (2)
Cook, Matthew	"	POW Jan. 22. (2)
Devers, Baldwin	"	POW Jan. 22. (2)
Fowler, James	"	POW Jan. 22. (2)
Gohagan, William	"	POW Jan. 22. (2) Also Capt. Hightower's.
McCardy, David	"	POW Jan. 22. (2)
Morgan, John	"	POW Jan. 22.(2)

Rosters of Troops

Captain James Meade's Company, 17th U. S. Infantry *(Continued)*

NAME	RANK	REMARKS
Paggett, Thomas	Private	POW Jan. 22. (2) Also Capt. Hightower's.
Scroggin, William	"	POW Jan. 22. (2) Also Capt. Hightower's.
Smith, Thomas	"	(3)

(1) *Argus*, Apr. 1, 1812.
(2) *Palladium*, Mar. 24, 1813.
(3) Winchester's *Orderly Book*, this date.

Captain Angus Lewis Langham's Company, 19th U. S. Infantry
(Roster of 1812-13 not found. Only known participants at Raisin listed.)

NAME	RANK	REMARKS
Angus Lewis Langham	Captain	
Simon Shover	Sergeant	POW Jan. 22. (1)
John Ellerton (Ellerson)	Corporal	POW Jan. 22. (1)
Clark, Thomas	Private	POW Jan. 22. (1)
French, John	"	Murdered 21 Oct. 1812. (2)
Martin, James	"	POW Jan. 22. (1)
Smith, Richard	"	POW Jan. 22. (1)

(1) *Palladium*, Mar. 24, 1813.
(2) Winchester's *Orderly Book*, this date.

1st Regiment, Kentucky Militia (Scott's Regiment)
August 15–October 14, 1812

NAME	RANK	REMARKS
John M. Scott	Lt. Col.	Died Dec., 1812.
Richard M. Gano	Major, 1st Bn.	Succeeded Lt. Col. Scott
Elijah McClanahan	Major, 2nd Bn.	

Staff Officers

William H. Richardson	Surgeon	Resigned.
Robert Ewing	Surg. Mate	Promoted to Surgeon 26 Dec. 1812.
George C. Patrick	"	Appointed 26 Dec. 1812.
Samuel Shannon	Chaplain	Commissioned 29 June 1812.
John Branham	Adjutant	Commissioned 15 Aug. 1812.
Alfred Sandford	"	Commissioned 26 Aug. 1812.
James King	Quar. Master	Commissioned 15 Aug. 1812.

1st Regiment, Kentucky Militia (Scott's Regiment) *(Continued)*

NAME	RANK	REMARKS
Barnett Williams	Paymaster	Commissioned 15 Aug. 1812.
Alexander McCoy	QM Sgt.	
John Feltz	S.M.	
William Fee	D.M.	
James Miller	F.M.	

[Original Roster Officers of the War of 1812-16, MS, Kentucky Historical Society. Report of the Adjutant General . . . Soldiers of Kentucky in the War of 1812.]

Captain Thomas Morris's Company, 1st Regiment
August 15—October 14, 1812
(Bourbon County)

NAME	RANK	REMARKS
Thomas Morris	Captain	
Edward B. Rule	Lieutenant	POW Jan. 22. (1)
Joseph Bowles	Ensign	
Francis Irwin	Sergeant	
John Henry	"	POW Jan. 22. (1)
William Rogers	"	
Levi Parker	"	
George Mozer	Corporal	POW Jan. 22. (1)
John Hamilton	"	
Raucer Spicer	"	
Richard Swanson	"	
Baker, Jacob	Private	
Balyell, John	"	
Barton, Joshua	"	POW Jan. 22. (1)
Bay, Joseph	"	
Beckett, Samuel	"	
Bell, Thomas	"	Right arm injured about Jan. 1, 1812. (3)
Biggs, John	"	
Blakeney, William	"	
Bould, Peter	"	
Busey, William	"	POW Jan. 22. (1)
Cassaday, Thomas	"	
Chadd, Samuel	"	
Clay, William W.	"	
Croffort, Alexander B.	"	
Dickerson, William S.	"	POW Jan. 22. (1)
Dougherty, Jarrett	"	POW Jan. 22. (2)
Duckett, Caleb M.	"	
Ferguson, David	"	
Frakes, Nathan	"	

Rosters of Troops

Captain Thomas Morris's Company, 1st Regiment *(Continued)*

NAME	RANK	REMARKS
Geers, Jesse	Private	POW Jan. 22. (1)
Gill, Robert	"	
Greer, Thomas	"	POW Jan. 22. (1)
Harris, Willie	"	
Hebber, John	"	
Heddleston, Robert	"	(Huddleston) POW Jan. 22. (1)
Henry, John	"	POW Jan. 22. (1)
Irwin, John	"	
Jacks, William	"	
Johnson, John	"	
Johnson, Robert	"	POW Jan. 22. (1)
Johnson, Silas	"	
Jones, Jesse	"	
Jones, Willis	"	
Kenny, James	"	
McBee, John	"	POW Jan. 22. (1)
McGinnis, Thomas	"	
Manford, John	"	POW Jan. 22. (1)
Marshall, Timothy P.	"	POW Jan. 22. (1)
Meenach, Samuel	"	POW Jan. 22. (1)
Morgan, Hugh	"	
Morris, Thales	"	POW Jan. 22. (1)
Mulholm, William	"	
Myers, George	"	POW Jan. 22. (1)
Parker, Garland	"	
Parrish, Anderson	"	
Percell, Thomas	"	
Pierson, Bartholomew	"	
Plummer, George	"	
Rule, Matthew	"	
Sodosky, Isaac	"	(Sandusky) POW Jan. 22. (1)
Sparks, Joseph	"	
Spurgin, Moses	"	
Stadler, John	"	
Stewart, Joseph	"	POW Jan. 22. (1)
Tooks, William	"	
Townsend, William	"	POW Jan. 22. (1)
Trammell, James	"	
Wills, David	"	POW Jan. 22. (1)
Wilson, John	"	

This company sent a detail to Frenchtown; the remainder of the unit stayed behind to guard the baggage of the Raisin Force.

(1) *Palladium,* 24 Mar. 1813.
(2) *Argus,* 1 Jan. 1814.
(3) Franklin County Pension List.

Captain Joseph Redding's Company, 1st Regiment
August 15–October 14, 1812
(Scott County)

NAME	RANK	REMARKS
Joseph Redding	Captain	
Joseph McCalla	Lieutenant	
Barnett Williams	Ensign	
John Lemon	Sergeant	
Daniel Long	"	
Thomas Ogburn	"	
Alvan Motherhead	"	
William Lindsay	Corporal	POW Jan. 22. (1)
James Minor	"	
Hugh Montgomery	"	
James McCauley	"	
John Luke	Musician	
Abbott, Edward T.	Private	
Abbott, H. G.	"	
Adkins, James	"	
Alexander, William	"	
Allen, Robert	"	
Bagby, John	"	
Baldwin, ———	"	POW Jan. 22. (1)
Burbridge, John (or Jesse)	"	POW Jan. 22. (1)
Clinton, Samuel	"	
Collins, Richard	"	
Cooke, William	"	WIA, POW Jan. 22. (2)
Criswell, Robert	"	POW Jan. 22. (1)
Cury, John	"	POW Jan. 22. (1)
Davis, Lodowick	"	
Dehoney, Thomas	"	POW Jan. 22. (1)
Deterson, John	"	
Dick, John	"	
Dickey, Benjamin	"	
Dickey, William	"	
Downing, William	"	POW Jan. 22. (1)
Ducker, John	"	POW Jan. 22. (1)
Foster, John	"	POW Jan. 22. (1)
Galloway, Samuel	"	
Grimes, Willis	"	POW Jan. 22. (1)
Hammond, James	"	
Hanna, Andrew	"	
Jack, Allen	"	
Lee, Robert	"	
Lee, William	"	
Long, Thomas	"	
McCormick, Francis	"	
Moore, Clark	"	

Rosters of Troops

Captain Joseph Redding's Company, 1st Regiment *(Continued)*

NAME	RANK	REMARKS
Nolin, William	Private	
Osborn, Jesse	"	
Osborn, Reuben	"	
Osborn, William	"	
Perkins, Jeremiah	"	
Price, William	"	POW Jan. 22. (1)
Reading, Joseph	"	
Redding, J. W.	"	
Robertson, Willis	"	
Rogers, John	"	POW Jan. 22. (1)
Rogers, William	"	
Sebastian, Elijah	"	
Sharp, Armistead	"	
Shirley, Robert	"	
Smith, Reuben	"	
Snell, Robert	"	POW Jan. 22. (1)
Sullivan, James	"	
Thompson, Charles	"	POW Jan. 22. (1) [Thomson]
Threlkeld, Thomas	"	
Toom, Benjamin	"	
Turner, Julius	"	POW Jan. 22. (1)
Viley, Warren	"	
Ward, Thomas	"	Massacred Jan. 23. (4)
Ward, William	"	
White, Brockman	"	
Wiley, Nathaniel	"	
Williams, Bennett	"	
Williamson, John	"	
Wright, James	"	POW Jan. 22. (1)
Yates, William	"	

This company furnished a detail for the River Raisin march.
(1) *Palladium*, 24 Mar. 1813.
(2) *Ibid*, 31 Mar. 1813.
(3) *Reporter*, 27 Mar. 1813.
(4) *American State Papers. Military Affairs*, I.

Captain George Pugh's Company, 1st Regiment
August 15–October 14, 1812
(Bath County)

NAME	RANK	REMARKS
George Pugh	Captain	
James Johnson	Lieutenant	
Daniel Ralls	Ensign	
William T. Kincaid	Sergeant	POW Jan. 22. (1)
Solomon D. King	"	

Captain George Pugh's Company, 1st Regiment *(Continued)*

NAME	RANK	REMARKS
Asa Maxey	Sergeant	POW Jan. 22. (1)
Edward Davis	"	
John Roach	"	WIA Jan. 18. (2); POW Jan. 22. (1)
William Miller	Corporal	POW Jan. 22. (1)
John P. Okely (Oakley)	"	
Thomas Owings	"	
James Poor	"	
Charles Lyman	Drummer	
John Burkes	Fifer	
Adjutant, Ebenezer	Private	
Bashaw, Cuthbert	"	POW Jan. 22. (1)
Bashaw, William	"	
Blackburn, William	"	POW Jan. 22. (1)
Breckinridge, Alexander	"	
Bresto, Ezra	"	
Burbridge, Jesse	"	POW Jan. 22. (1)
Burbridge, William	"	
Cartmell, David	"	
Cave, William	"	POW Jan. 22. (1)
Cook, John	"	
Cooper, James H.	"	POW Jan. 22. (1)
Cooper, Robert	"	
Davis, Luke	"	
Dunlap, John	"	
Eliot, James	"	
Emmet, Alexander	"	
Evans, William	"	
Ewing, Patrick	"	POW Jan. 22. (3)
Ferrel, Thomas	"	
Forsythe, John	"	
Forsythe, Samuel	"	
Fort, Noble	"	
Gilkison, William	"	
Goodpasture, Cornelius	"	
Gragg, Jesse	"	POW Jan. 22. (1)
Hamilton, Alexander	"	POW Jan. 22. (1). Also Andrew.
Hamilton, Robertson	"	
Hammelton, William	"	
Howard, James	"	
Hughard, Thomas	"	
Jamison, James	"	
Jamison, William	"	
Johnson, James	"	
Johnson, John	"	POW Jan. 22. (1)
Jones, James	"	POW Jan. 22. (1)

Rosters of Troops

Captain George Pugh's Company, 1st Regiment *(Continued)*

NAME	RANK	REMARKS
Kincaid, William	Private	
Lemmons, William	"	
Lockridge, James	"	WIA Jan. 22, POW Jan. 22. (1)
Lyon, Noah	"	
Lyon, Samuel	"	
McClanahan, James	"	
McClellen, Robert	"	
McClure, Samuel	"	
McCollister, Mark	"	
McKennen, Solomon	"	
McKinney, Charles	"	
McLane, John	"	
McNat, Abner	"	
Manley, James	"	
Manley, William	"	
Morgan, John	"	POW Jan. 22. (1)
Morris, Joseph	"	
Oakley, Thomas	"	Died at Miami Rapids, Feb., 1813. (4)
Overly, Peter	"	
Owings, John	"	
Parker, Joel	"	
Power, Jeremiah	"	
Ray, William	"	
Rayburn, Henry	"	
Rayburn, John	"	
Richardson, David	"	
Roberts, John	"	
Rogers, James	"	
Runyan, Benjamin	"	
Said, James	"	
Silrey (Silvey), John	"	POW Jan. 22. (1)
Simmons, John	"	
Thompson, Samuel	"	
Trimble, Robert	"	
Varvel, Andrew	"	POW Jan. 22. (1)
Ward, Armistead	"	WIA Jan. 18. (2)
Watson, Julius	"	
White, James	"	
White, John D.	"	
White, William	"	POW Jan. 22. (1)
Williams, Wesley	"	
Young, Eli	"	

This company furnished a detail for the River Raisin march.
(1) *Palladium*, 24 Mar. 1813.
(2) *Official Report of killed, wounded and missing Jan. 18, 1813.*
(3) *Argus*, Jan. 1, Feb. 12, 1814.
(4) Bath County *Will Book A.*

Captain Lynn West's Company, 1st Regiment
August 15–October 14, 1812
(Scott County)

NAME	RANK	REMARKS
Lynn West	Captain	
Tarenor R. Branham	Lieutenant	
David Grishom	"	POW Jan. 22. (2)
Mason Moss	"	
Thomas Story	"	
George Bradford	Sergeant	POW Jan. 22. (2)
James Carroll	"	
Joseph Cox	"	
John Fetty	"	
Abraham Short	"	POW Jan. 22. (2)
James Cox	Corporal	POW Jan. 22. (2)
John McCallister	"	
Jesse Oldham	"	
Elias Tapp	"	
Allen, Samuel	Private	
Armstrong, James	"	
Breedlove, Major	"	
Campbell, William	"	
Carter, William	"	
Cope, William	"	
Cummins, Thomas	"	
Danner, Samuel	"	POW Jan. 22. (2)
Eve, Benjamin	"	POW Jan. 22. (2)
Eve, Jabez	"	POW Jan. 22. (2)
Ford, A.	"	
Frayer, Joseph	"	
Giles, Samuel	"	
Graves, Thomas H.	"	WIA Jan. 18. (1); POW Jan. 22. (2)
Griffith, Belfield	"	POW Jan. 22. (2)
Griffith, George	"	WIA, POW Jan. 22. (2)
Harris, Thomas	"	
Henderson, Samuel	"	
Henderson, Thomas	"	
Hogan, James	"	
Hunt, James	"	
Ireland, Alexander	"	
James, Wiley	"	
Johnson, Isaac	"	
Kindrie, Benjamin	"	
Lacy, Stephen	"	
Lemon, Alexander	"	
Loury, John	"	
Lowry, William	"	

Rosters of Troops

Captain Lynn West's Company, 1st Regiment *(Continued)*

NAME	RANK	REMARKS
Lynn, William P.	Private	
McCandless, John	"	POW Jan. 22. (2)
McCormack, James	"	
McDaniel, John	"	
McGohie, Daniel	"	
McHatton, James	"	
Merrill, James	"	
Mit, Samuel	"	
Monteath, William	"	POW Jan. 22. (2)
Montgomery, John	"	
Mosby, William	"	
Nafe, Daniel	"	
Peek, Thomas	"	
Powers, Robert	"	
Prue, Isiah	"	
Rainey, Abraham	"	
Ratchford, William	"	
Rogers, Valentine	"	
Scofield, Stephen	"	
Scott, Abram	"	
Scruggs, James	"	
Self, James	"	
Sharon, Samuel	"	WIA. (3)
Sharron, James F.	"	
Short, Cyrus	"	KIA Jan. 18. (1)
Short, George	"	
Short, Obediah	"	
Smith, John	"	
Smith, William	"	
Sutton, Thomas	"	
Tarlton, Thomas	"	
Thompson, Peter	"	
Tilford, Alexander	"	
Todd, Abel	"	
Tyree, Tarlton	"	POW Jan. 22. (2)
Ward, John	"	WIA Jan. 18. (1)
Wells, Derit	"	
Wickersham, James	"	
Wiggins, Thomas	"	
Williams, Silas	"	
Wolf, Henry	"	
Worrel, Jonathan	"	
Young, William	"	

(1) *Official report of killed, wounded and missing . . . Jan. 18, 1813.*
(2) *Palladium,* 24 Mar. 1813.
(3) *Scott County Pension List.*

Captain Coleman A. Collier's Company, 1st Regiment
August 15–October 14, 1812
(Nicholas County)

NAME	RANK	REMARKS
Coleman A. Collier	Captain	POW Jan. 22. (2)
James W. Gillispie	Lieutenant	
Jesse Daugherty	Ensign	POW Jan. 22. (2)
Thomas Corbin	Sergeant	Sub. for Daniel Snap
William Dingle	"	
William Fleet	"	Ens., 12/29/1812. (3); WIA 1/18, POW 1/22. (1, 5)
Thomas Griffith	"	Sub. for Geo. Fryman; POW Jan. 22. (2)
James Brown	Corporal	
James Fryman	"	
David Gray	"	
William Kenton	"	POW Jan. 22. (2)
Bailey, Benjamin	Private	Sub. for Abraham Miller
Bannister, John	"	
Bellows, Jacob	"	POW Jan. 22. (2)
Bennett, George	"	Sub. for Wm. Conway; POW Jan. 22. (2)
Blain, John	"	
Burns, Ignatius	"	
Burns, Robert	"	
Camel, Robert	"	
Carr, James	"	POW Jan. 22. (2)
Colvin, Bennett	"	
Cord, Ashkery	"	
Crawford, Alexander	"	
Davis, Thomas	"	POW Jan. 22. (2)
Dudley, Ambrose	"	Sub. for John Brown
Endicott, William	"	
Erwin, John	"	
Fielder, John	"	
Gray, William	"	
Howard, Mathew	"	
Hurley, James	"	
Johnson, Jonathan	"	
Kincart, James	"	POW Jan. 22. (2)
Layton, Robert	"	
Louder, Nathaniel	"	
McAnnelly, John	"	
McDowell, Alexander	"	
McLaughlin, John	"	POW Jan. 22. (2)
McMichael, Robert	"	Sub. for Abraham Darling; WIA Jan. 15. (4)
Mars, Samuel	"	

Captain Coleman A. Collier's Company, 1st Regiment *(Continued)*

NAME	RANK	REMARKS
Mires, David	Private	
Morgan, John	"	POW Jan. 22. (2)
Oliver, John	"	
Overfield, Mose	"	
Pope, Jacquillin A.	"	Sub. for John Smith; POW Jan. 22. (2)
Powell, William	"	Sub. for Chas. Powell
Smart, Humphrey	"	
Smith, William	"	
Stevenson, Robert	"	
Weaver, Abram	"	
Wheeler, Joshua	"	Sub. for William Wheeler
Williamson, John	"	Sub. for Joseph Parks

(1) *Official report of killed, wounded and missing . . . Jan. 18, 1813.*
(2) *Palladium*, 24 Mar. 1813.
(3) *Original Roster, 1812-16*, MS, Kentucky Historical Society.
(4) *Gallatin County Pension List.*
(5) *Niles' Weekly Register*, X, 10.

Captain Michael Glaves's Company, 1st Regiment
August 15—October 14, 1812
(Pendleton County)

NAME	RANK	REMARKS
Michael Glaves	Captain	WIA Jan. 18 or 22; escaped Jan. 22. (3)
Thomas Coleman	Lieutenant	Deceased by 23 Dec. 1812. (4)
James King	Ensign	Lt., 23 Dec. 1812 in place of Thomas Coleman (4)
William Bryan	Sergeant	
David Craig	"	
John Dawson	"	WIA, POW Jan. 22. (5)
Martin Fugate	"	
Thomas Bryan	Corporal	
John Goodwin	"	Sub. for John Lawrence; POW Jan. 22. (2)
James Henry	"	
Daniel McClain	"	
John Walker	"	

Captain Michael Glaves's Company, 1st Regiment *(Continued)*

NAME	RANK	REMARKS
Ammerman, Albert	Private	WIA Jan. 18. (1); POW Jan. 22. (7)
Baker, Thomas	"	
Beard, George N.	"	
Browning, James	"	POW Jan. 22. (2)
Bryan, Luke	"	
Burns, James	"	
Childers, Abraham	"	
Coleman, Ambrose	"	
Colvin, James B.	"	
Dance, John	"	
Dance, William	"	
Ellis, Elijah	"	
Ellis, James	"	
Ellis, John	"	
Erwin, Robert	"	
Ewing, Thomas	"	
Gibson, James	"	WIA, POW Jan. 22. (2)
Glen, Richard O.	"	
Green, Edward G.	"	
Green, Jesse P.	"	WIA, POW Jan. 22. (6)
Hawkins, Abner	"	
Homes, James	"	
Huffman, Jacob	"	POW Jan. 22. (2, 6)
Hutchinson, James	"	
Jones, Hillery	"	
Jump, Joseph	"	
Jump, Valentine	"	
Know, Samuel	"	
Law (Love), Thomas	"	POW Jan. 22. (2)
Luckett, William	"	
McCarty, Reuben	"	
McClanahan, John	"	
McIntosh, John	"	Sub. for Griffin Theobald
Minor, John L.	"	POW Jan. 22. (2)
Mountjoy, John	"	
Norton, George	"	Sub. for John N. Clarke
Owens, John	"	
Pollard, John	"	
Pollard, Thomas	"	POW Jan. 22. (2)
Riddle, William	"	
Sanders, John H.	"	
Sanders, William	"	
Spencer, John J.	"	
Stewart, James	"	
Walker, Alexander	"	

Captain Michael Glaves's Company, 1st Regiment *(Continued)*

NAME	RANK	REMARKS
Wilson, Samuel	Private	
Woodyard, Alexander	"	
Zimmerman, Philip	"	

(1) *Official report of killed and wounded* . . . Jan. 18, 1813.
(2) *Palladium*, 24 Mar. 1813.
(3) *Indiana Historical Collections*, IX.
(4) *Original Roster of Officers 1812-15*, MS, Kentucky Historical Society.
(5) *American State Papers. Military Affairs*, vol. 1.
(6) *Palladium*, 31 Mar. 1813.
(7) *Barbarities of the enemy* . . . Troy, 1813.

Captain Uriel Sebree's Company, 1st Regiment
August 15–October 14, 1812
(Boone County)

NAME	RANK	REMARKS
Uriel Sebree	Captain	POW Jan. 22. (2)
Robert Kirtley	Lieutenant	Resigned by 22 Dec. 1812. (3)
Barnett Rogers	Ensign	
William Campbell	Sergeant	POW Jan. 22. (2)
Uriel Cave	"	
Joel Garrett (Garnet)	"	Lt., vice Robert Kirtley, Dec. 22, 1812. (3)
E. Hawkins	"	POW Jan. 22. (2)
Allen Morgan	"	
John Dulany	Corporal	
John Ellis	"	
Richard Gainer	"	
Johnston Watts	"	POW Jan. 22. (2)
Mills Wilks	"	WIA Jan. 18. (4); POW Jan. 22. (2)
Nathan Underwood	Fifer	POW Jan. 22. (2)
Simeon Christy	Drummer	Discharged
Alphen, Ransom	Private	POW Jan. 22. (2)
Alloway, John	"	
Barbee, John	"	POW Jan. 22. (2)
Barnum, Barney	"	
Cherry, John	"	POW Jan. 22. (2)
Conly, Robert	"	POW Jan. 22. (2)
Cornelius, Terrill	"	
Crow, Thomas S.	"	WIA Jan. 18. (1); KIA Jan. 23. (5)
Day, Joseph	"	WIA Jan. 18. (1)

Captain Uriel Sebree's Company, 1st Regiment *(Continued)*

NAME	RANK	REMARKS
Dickerson, Samuel	Private	POW Jan. 22. (2)
Estes, John	"	
Fitzgerald, Jesse	"	
Flint, Simeon	"	
Green, Nathaniel	"	
Gilmore, James	"	
Grimsley, Silas	"	Discharged
Hawkins, Gabriel	"	POW Jan. 22. (2)
Holler, John	"	
Hughes, Hugh	"	
Jones, John	"	POW Jan. 22. (6)
Lane, Martin	"	POW Jan. 22. (2)
Marshall, John	"	
Merit, James	"	
Mosby, Daniel	"	
Mosby, Thomas	"	POW Jan. 22. (2)
O'Neal, David	"	POW Jan. 22. (2)
O'Neal, William	"	
Polly, John	"	
Porter, Thomas	"	
Rowen, John	"	POW Jan. 22. (2)
Royell (Russell), Abednego	"	POW Jan. 22. (2)
Royster, James	"	
Sanford, Lawrence	"	
Seals, Barnet (Bernard)	"	
Searcy, Berry	"	
Smith, Benjamin C.	"	
Smith, John (Johnston)	"	POW Jan. 22. (2)
Smith, William I.	"	
Stephens, Thomas	"	
Terrell, Robert	"	WIA Jan. 18 (1); POW Jan. 22. (2)
Thomas, James O. W.	"	
Tour, John	"	WIA Jan. 18. (1)
Vickers, William	"	
Vinsant, John	"	KIA Jan. 18. (1)
Watson, Laban	"	
White, Willis	"	

(1) *Official report of killed and wounded . . . Jan. 18, 1813.*
(2) *Palladium*, 24 Mar. 1813.
(3) *Original Roster War of 1812-15*, MS, Kentucky Historical Society.
(4) *Boone County Pension List.*
(5) *American State Papers. Military Affairs*, I.
(6) *Argus*, Jan. 1, Feb. 12, 1814.

5th Regiment, Kentucky Volunteer Regiment
August 15–October 14, 1812

NAME	RANK	REMARKS
	Field Officers	
William Lewis	Lieut. Col.	POW Jan. 22.
Joseph Robb	Maj. 1st Bn.	
Benjamin Graves	Maj. 2nd Bn.	KIA Jan. 25 or 26.
	Staff Officers	
John Todd	Surgeon	POW Jan. 23.
Gustavus M. Bower	Surg. Mate	POW Jan. 23.
Pollard Keene	Quartermaster	POW Jan. 22.
Richard Blanton	Paymaster	
James Suggett	Chaplain	
John McCalla	Adjutant	Appointed Nov. 20, 1812; POW Jan. 22.
Alexander Ferguson	QM Sgt.	
Thomas Fant	Chief Musician	See also Captain Hart's Company.
Thomas Cox	"	

[Commissioned Officers of the War of 1812-16, MSS, Kentucky Historical Society; Adjutant General's Report . . . *Soldiers of Kentucky in the War of 1812.*]

Captain Nathaniel G. S. Hart's Company, 5th Regiment
August 15–October 14, 1812
(Fayette County)

NAME	RANK	REMARKS
Nathaniel G. S. Hart	Captain	WIA, KIA Jan. 23. (2)
Lyndon Comstock	Lieutenant	POW Jan. 22. (2)
James L. Herron	Ensign	POW Jan. 22. (3)
Fielding Gosney	Sergeant	POW Jan. 22. (2)
Thomas Smith	"	
Levi L. Todd	"	POW Jan. 22. (2)
John Whitney	"	Not in action. (4)
Charles F. Allen	Corporal	Not in action. (4)
William O. Butler	"	WIA, POW Jan. 22. (3)
Thomas Chamberlain	"	WIA, POW Jan. 22. (2)
Robert S. Todd	"	
Adams, Daniel	Private	POW Jan. 22. (2)
Allen, Francis I.	"	POW Jan. 22. (2)
Allen, Francis W.	"	
Allen, Hugh	"	POW Jan. 22. (2)
Allison, Andrew	"	POW Jan. 22. (2)
Anderson, Thomas	"	

Captain Nathaniel G. S. Hart's Company, 5th Regiment *(Continued)*

NAME	RANK	REMARKS
Beard, Henry	Private	POW Jan. 22. (2)
Bell, William C.	"	POW Jan. 22. (2)
Bickley, John	"	Beckley. WIA Jan. 18 (1); POW Jan. 22. (2)
Blythe, James Ebenezer	"	KIA Jan. 23. (3)
Bradford, Charles	"	WIA Jan. 18 (1); POW Jan. 22. (6)
Calker, Solomon	"	Not in action. (4)
Campbell, Robert T.	"	POW Jan. 22. (2)
Charles, Lewis	"	POW Jan. 22. (2)
Chinn, Richard H.	"	POW Jan. 22. (2)
Cock, Samuel P.	"	POW Jan. 22. (2)
Collins, Elisha	"	POW Jan. 22. (2)
Cope, Malcolm T.	"	Not in action. (4)
Crawford, Alexander	"	KIA (5)
Dailey, Lawrence	"	POW Jan. 22. (2)
Davis, Benjamin	"	Not in action. (4)
Davis, William	"	WIA Jan. 18. (1); KIA Jan. 22. (5)
Dunn, Philip	"	Not in action. (4)
Elder, Edward	"	POW Jan. 22. (2)
Elder, Samuel M.	"	KIA. (5)
Fant, Thomas	"	POW, KIA (5)
Francis, Enoch	"	Not in action. (4)
Francis, Jesse	"	Not in action. (4)
Gilpin, Ralph	"	Not in action. (4)
Goodloe, Kemp M.	"	POW Jan. 22. (2)
Hagert, John	"	Not in action. (4)
Hickman, James L.	"	POW Jan. 22. (2)
Higgins, James	"	POW Jan. 22. (2)
Hines, Bennett M.	"	POW Jan. 22. (2)
Holding, Samuel	"	POW Jan. 22. (2)
How, Jacob	"	Not in action. (4)
Huston, James	"	Not in action. (4)
John, Armstrong	"	
Johnston, James M.	"	POW Jan. 22. (2)
Kay, John	"	
Kelly, Robert E.	"	WIA Jan. 18.(1); POW Jan. 22. (2)
King, Thomas W.	"	KIA. (5)
Lake, Adam	"	Not in action. (4)
Lewis, Charles	"	POW Jan. 22. (2)
Lewis, William	"	
Lingenfelter, Daniel	"	POW Jan. 22. (2)
McChesney, John	"	Not in action. (4)
Mathers, Robert	"	Not in action. (4)
Maxwell, James D.	"	

Captain Nathaniel G. S. Hart's Company, 5th Regiment *(Continued)*

NAME	RANK	REMARKS
Maxwell, John	Private	
Mesmer, Peter	"	KIA. (5)
Monks, Thomas	"	POW Jan. 22. (2)
Moon, John A.	"	POW Jan. 22. (2)
Neal, Charles	"	Not in action. (4)
Neal, James	"	WIA Jan. 18. (1); POW Jan. 22. (2)
Norville, Joshua	"	POW Jan. 22. (2)
Parker, James P.	"	POW Jan. 22. (2)
Pritchart, William	"	
Rawlings, Robert	"	
Reiley, James	"	KIA Jan. 18. (1)
Rolls, James	"	Ralls? Not in action. (4)
Ross, George G.	"	Lieut., attached.
Schwing, Jacob	"	POW Jan. 22. (2)
Searls, Charles	"	WIA Jan. 18. (1)
Shindlebower, George	"	KIA. (5)
Smith, Stephen	"	KIA. (5)
Snalley, Valentine	"	POW Jan. 22. (2)
Stephen, Bela	"	
Stewart, Armstrong	"	KIA Jan. 22. (5)
Talbot, Daniel	"	
Templeman, Jesse C.	"	Not in action. (4)
Todd, Samuel N. (or B.)	"	WIA, POW Jan. 22. (2)
Townley, John	"	
Vance, John W.	"	POW Jan. 22. (2)
Vance, Joseph	"	
Vanpelt, Derick	"	POW Jan. 22. (2)
Verdon, William	"	
Williams, Zephaniah	"	POW Jan. 22. (2)

(1) *Official Report of killed and wounded . . . January 18, 1813.*
(2) *Palladium,* 24 Mar. 1813.
(3) *Niles' Weekly Register,* IV; *American State Papers. Military Affairs,* I.
(4) *Reporter,* 13 Feb. 1813.
(5) Ranck, G. W., *History of Lexington.*
(6) *Barbarities of the enemy . . .* Troy, 1813.

Captain James C. Price's Company, 5th Regiment
August 15–October 14, 1812
(Jessamine County)

NAME	RANK	REMARKS
James C. Price	Captain	KIA Jan. 22. (5)
William Caldwell	Lieutenant	POW Jan. 22. (5)
Daniel Bourne	Ensign	

Captain James C. Price's Company, 5th Regiment *(Continued)*

NAME	RANK	REMARKS
William E. Price	Sergeant	POW Jan. 22. (2)
David Richardson	"	
John Scott	"	POW Jan. 22. (2)
John Shanklin	"	
Nathaniel H. Caldwell	Corporal	POW Jan. 22. (2)
John Ficklin	"	
Solomon Smith	"	POW Jan. 22. (2)
Elisha Williams	"	
Barkley, William	Private	
Barr, George	"	WIA Jan. 18. (1); POW Jan. 22. (2)
Bennett, James	"	Burnett? POW Jan. 22 (2)
Brice, John T.	"	Escaped Jan. 22. (3)
Brown, Thomas	"	
Callender, Jacob	"	
Carlton, George	"	
Carlton, Isaac	"	
Carlton, Noah	"	
Conner, Rice	"	
Daugherty, John	"	POW Jan. 22. (2)
Dedman, James	"	POW Jan. 22. (2)
Easley, Pleasant	"	
East, Elijah	"	
Edwards, Thomas	"	
Elkin, Benjamin	"	POW Jan. 22. (2)
Farrow, John	"	POW Jan. 22. (2)
Finney, James	"	
Forsee, Stephen	"	Frost? POW Jan. 22. (2)
Frost, James	"	
Goin, John	"	
Haggard, John	"	Discharged Dec. 16, 1812. (4)
Hews, Charles	"	
Hicks, James	"	
Hushman, Matthew	"	
Kindred, Edward	"	
Krickbaum, John	"	
Lewis, William A.	"	
Lillard, Thomas	"	POW Jan. 22. (2)
Linkhorn, George	"	POW Jan. 22. (2)
McConnell, M. G.	"	
McGrath, Terrance	"	
Morgan, W.	"	
Moss, Pleasant	"	
Neal, George	"	POW Jan. 22. (2)
Netherland, John	"	POW Jan. 22. (2)
Overstreet, W.	"	

Rosters of Troops 195

Captain James C. Price's Company, 5th Regiment *(Continued)*

NAME	RANK	REMARKS
Ramsey, John or James	Private	POW Jan. 22. (2)
Rice, George	"	POW Jan. 22. (2)
Rice, Joseph	"	POW Jan. 22. (2)
Richards, Alexander	"	
Richardson, Robert	"	
Scott, Joseph	"	POW Jan. 22. (2)
Simmons, David	"	
Skeene, William	"	
Taylor, John	"	
Underwood, Edward	"	WIA Jan. 18. (1)
Walker, James	"	
Ward, George S.	"	
Ward, William	"	POW Jan. 22. (2)
Webber, Benjamin	"	
Wilson, Thomas	"	POW Jan. 22. (2)
Woodson, Obediah	"	WIA Jan. 18. (1); POW Jan. 22. (2)
Young, Joel	"	
Young, Richard	"	

"Eight of this company in addition to Captain Price were massacred January 22, 1813. About 30 escaped the action of that day." (5)

(1) *Official list of killed and wounded . . . Jan. 18, 1813.*
(2) *Palladium,* 24 Mar. 1813.
(3) *History of Pike County, Missouri* (1883).
(4) Darnell, Elias, *Journal . . .*
(5) Young, Bennett H., *History of Jessamine County, Kentucky.*

Captain Wiley R. Brasfield's Company, 5th Regiment
August 15–October 14, 1812
(Clark County)

NAME	RANK	REMARKS
Wiley R. Brasfield	Captain	Resigned by Nov. 27, 1812. (3)
Joseph Kelly	Lieutenant	Captain Nov. 27, 1812. (3); POW Jan. 22. (2)
Stephen Rash	Ensign	
William Donaldson	Sergeant	POW Jan. 22. (2)
John Oram	"	
William Rash (or Nash)	"	Ensign 27 Nov. 1812. (3); POW Jan. 22. (4)
Edward Young	"	

Captain Wiley R. Brasfield's Company, 5th Regiment *(Continued)*

NAME	RANK	REMARKS
Cornelius Barrow	Corporal	
Richard Chiles	"	
Daniel Coleman	"	POW Jan. 22. (2)
William Weldon	"	POW Jan. 22. (2)
Thomas Wood	"	WIA Jan. 18. (1); POW Jan. 22. (2)
Joseph Young	"	
James W. Whitehurst	Musician	
Samuel Kelly	"	
Athens, James	Private	
Athers, Nathaniel	"	
Balance, Proctor	"	
Barr, James B.	"	
Bean, William	"	POW Jan. 22. (2)
Berry, George	"	
Blake, John	"	
Blake, Peyton	"	
Brinigan, John	"	
Campbell, John	"	
Capps, Caleb	"	
Chrisholm, Nathaniel	"	
Crockett, James	"	
Crosthwait, Warning	"	
Cummings, Cal	"	
Dyke, John	"	
Fandric, Joseph	"	Fandree? POW Jan. 22. (5)
Fandric, William	"	Fandree?
Goff, Levi	"	
Hackney, Hightower	"	
Hamilton, John	"	
Harris, Claiborne	"	
Harvey, John	"	POW Jan. 22. (2)
Jones, John	"	POW Jan. 22. (2)
Kelley, James	"	POW Jan. 22. (2)
Lacklin, Fielding	"	
Lusk, John	"	
Lusk, Silas	"	
McDonald, George	"	
McDonald, James	"	
McDonald, John	"	
McGonnigle, John	"	
Martin, Nathan	"	POW Jan. 22. (2)
Morris, William G.	"	
Morrison, Boswell	"	
Murphy, Zachariah	"	
Paul, Michael	"	POW Jan. 22. (2)

Captain Wiley R. Brasfield's Company, 5th Regiment *(Continued)*

NAME	RANK	REMARKS
Peebles, James	Private	WIA Jan. 18. (1)
Petty, William	"	
Pruett, John	"	
Ramsey, William	"	POW Jan. 22. (2)
Rash, John	"	POW Jan. 22. (2)
Redman, Thomas	"	
Samuel, Isiah	"	
Samuel, John	"	
Sanders, Constant	"	POW Jan. 22. (2)
Scothorn, Nathan	"	POW Jan. 22. (2)
Smith, George	"	
Smith, Philip	"	
Stuart, James	"	POW Jan. 22. (2)
Suddeth, Ezekiel	"	Lieutenant 27 Nov. 1812. (3) MIA?
Suddeth, Lewis	"	
Thompson, Andrew	"	POW Jan. 22. (2)
Valandingham, Richard	"	
Vinage, John	"	POW Jan. 22. (2)
Webb, James C.	"	POW Jan. 22. (2)
Westbrook, Thomas	"	
Williams, Olly	"	POW Jan. 22. (2)
Wilson, James	"	
Wilson, Mathias	"	
Wright, Jacob	"	
Wright, Morgan	"	POW Jan. 22. (2)
Young, John	"	
Young, Robert C.	"	
Young, William	"	POW Jan. 22. (2)

(1) *Official report of killed and wounded . . . Jan. 18, 1813.*
(2) *Palladium,* 24 Mar. 1813.
(3) *Original roster of officers, 1812-16,* MS, Kentucky Historical Society.
(4) *Niles' Weekly Register,* IV.
(5) *Michigan Pioneer and Historical Collections,* XVI.

Captain Samuel L. Williams's Company, 5th Regiment
August 15–October 14, 1812
(Montgomery County)

NAME	RANK	REMARKS
Samuel L. Williams	Captain	POW Jan. 22. (2)
Benjamin Warfield	Lieutenant	Resigned by Nov. 28, 1812. (5)
John Higgins	Ensign	Lt., Nov. 28, 1812 (5); POW Jan. 22. (2)
William Ficklin	Sergeant	WIA Jan. 18. (1)

Captain Samuel L. Williams's Company, 5th Regiment *(Continued)*

NAME	RANK	REMARKS
Joseph Harrow	Sergeant	Ensign Nov. 28, 1812. (5); POW Jan. 22. (3)
William J. Simpson	"	WIA Jan. 18. (1); POW Jan. 22. (2)
Thaddeus Williams	"	
Samuel W. Brown	Corporal	
Jacob Irwin	"	James? POW Jan. 22. (2)
Levi Pritchett	"	Pritchard? WIA, POW Jan. 22. (2)
Henry Ringo	"	POW Jan. 22. (2)
Enoch Yates	"	POW Jan. 22. (2)
Asa Ballenger	Musician	
Zenas Darnold	"	Darnell?
Adkerson, Isiah	Private	
Allen, David	"	
Allen, James	"	POW Jan. 22. (2)
Allen, John	"	POW Jan. 22. (2)
Anderson, John	"	
Anderson, Thomas	"	
Armstrong, Samuel	"	
Bell, Patterson	"	
Biggs, Landy	"	
Blythe, Charles	"	
Carter, Kenyon	"	
Cook, Alexander	"	
Daniel, John W.	"	
Darnell, Allen	"	WIA Jan. 18. (1) KIA Jan. 22. (6)
Darnell, Daniel	"	KIA Jan. 23. (4)
Darnell, Elias	"	POW Jan. 22. (2). Author of *Journal*.
Darnold, Hezekiah	"	Darnell?
Darnold, Samuel	"	Darnell?
Davenport, John	"	WIA Jan. 18. (1)
Davis, Benjamin	"	
Digernell, John	"	
Drain, John	"	
Farrow, Alexander S.	"	POW Jan. 22. (2)
Feathercoil, George	"	
Fowke, Jared	"	
Frakes, Barnabas	"	
Frakes, Joseph	"	
Frame, Samuel	"	POW Jan. 22. (2)
Frame, William	"	KIA Jan. 18. (1)
Frazier, Alexander	"	
Harlan, Joshua	"	
Harlon, Nelson	"	

Captain Samuel L. Williams's Company, 5th Regiment *(Continued)*

NAME	RANK	REMARKS
Hensley, Joseph	Private	
James, Alexander D.	"	POW Jan. 22. (2)
Jeffries, Enoch	"	
Jamerson, Daniel C.	"	
Jimerson, John	"	
Jones, Wiley	"	
King, Henry	"	
Macdonald, John	"	McDaniel? KIA Jan. 18. (1)
McIlrain, James	"	
McMillan, John	"	POW Jan. 22. (2)
Marshall, Joseph	"	
Mason, John	"	
Matier, Samuel	"	
Morton, Jacob	"	
Myers, John	"	
Oxen, George	"	
Priest, Elias	"	
Priest, George	"	POW Jan. 22. (2)
Pritchard, Benjamin B.	"	POW Jan. 22. (2)
Rector, Daniel	"	
Ricketts, Thomas	"	
Ringo, Robert	"	WIA Jan. 18. (1); POW Jan. 22. (2)
Rings, William	"	
Rogers, Harris	"	
Rogers, Larkin	"	
Rogers, Thomas	"	
Said, Jesse	"	Sale? POW Jan. 22. (2)
Sears, Alexander D.	"	
Shortridge, Charles	"	
Simms, Josiah	"	
Sprouce, Samuel L.	"	
Wells, James Q.	"	
Westbrook, Thomas	"	POW Jan. 22. (2)
Wheeler, Samuel	"	
Whitsett, Samuel	"	
Williamson, Jesse	"	
Wilson, Abraham	"	
Wilson, James	"	
Wilson, John	"	POW Jan. 22. (2)

(1) *Official report of killed and wounded . . . Jan. 18, 1812.*
(2) *Palladium,* 24 Mar. 1813.
(3) *Ohio Historical and Archaeological Quarterly,* XVI.
(4) *American State Papers. Military Affairs,* I.
(5) *Original roster Officers of the War of 1812-15,* MS, Kentucky Historical Society.
(6) Darnell, Elias, *A Journal . . .*

Captain John Hamilton's Company, 5th Regiment
August 15–October 14, 1812
(Fayette County)

NAME	RANK	REMARKS
John Hamilton	Captain	POW Jan. 22. (2)
William H. Moore	Lieutenant	POW Jan. 22. (2)
Robert Hamilton	Ensign	
Thomas Dickerson	Sergeant	
Jesse Durur	"	
William Gray	"	
Tobias Pennington	"	POW Jan. 22. (2)
Ira Barbee	Corporal	WIA, POW Jan. 22. (2)
Thomas Barker	"	WIA Jan. 18. (1); POW Jan. 22. (2)
Robert McCullough	"	POW Jan. 22. (2)
George F. Muldraugh	"	
William Patterson	"	
John Smedley	"	
Samuel Smedley	"	
Barbie, John	Private	
Chinn, Alfred	"	WIA Jan. 18. (1); KIA Jan. 22/23. (4)
Chinn, Humphrey	"	WIA, POW Jan. 22. (2)
Chinn, Nathaniel	"	WIA Jan. 18. (1); POW Jan. 22. (2)
Cleyton, George	"	
Colbert, William (Willis)	"	WIA Jan. 18. (1); POW Jan. 22. (3)
Corman, George	"	POW Jan. 22. (2)
Crowder, William	"	
Doyle, William	"	POW Jan. 22. (2)
Fields, Luke	"	KIA Jan. 18. (1)
Fisher, James	"	
Fisher, Thomas	"	
Fisher, William	"	
Fry, William	"	
Goodright, Michael	"	
Gordon, Lewis M.	"	
Gray (or Gragg), James	"	POW Jan. 22. (2)
Hamilton, Thomas	"	POW Jan. 22. (2)
Harris, Samuel	"	
Hicks, Abraham	"	
Hicks, Samuel	"	POW Jan. 22. (2)
Jones, Harwell	"	
Jones, Philip	"	POW Jan. 22. (2)
Kice, John	"	Rice?
Kidd, Edmond I.	"	

Captain John Hamilton's Company, 5th Regiment *(Continued)*

NAME	RANK	REMARKS
Knau (Rau ?), George	Private	
Lawrence, John	"	
Lemon, James	"	
Long, Harwell	"	POW Jan. 22. (2)
Love, John S.	"	
McClane, Jonathen	"	POW Jan. 22. (2)
Maunel, Abraham	"	
Mifford, Andrew	"	
Moore, Gasland (Garland?)	"	
Moore, Samuel T.	"	
Muldrough, John	"	Died of typhoid fever, Nov., 1812. (5)
Musgrove, William	"	POW Jan. 22. (2)
Patterson, John	"	
Patterson, Thomas	"	
Patterson, William	"	POW Jan. 22. (2)
Patterson, William D.	"	POW Jan. 22. (2)
Price, Cosby	"	
Ritchie, James	"	
Rogers, Richard	"	
Russell, Hendley	"	
Russell, Thomas A.	"	POW Jan. 22. (2)
Sanderson, George	"	
Simpson, Anderson	"	POW Jan. 22. (2)
Simpson, Andrew	"	POW Jan. 22. (2)
Smedley, Samuel	"	
Spellers, James	"	
Tandy, Linton	"	POW Jan. 22. (2)
Tandy, Willis	"	WIA, POW Jan. 22. (6)
Tucker, Robert	"	
Venard, Absalom	"	
Venard, Thomas	"	
Wallace, William	"	
Wheeler, George N.	"	
Wilhite, John	"	POW Jan. 22. (2)
Williamson, Lucas	"	
Wood, Benjamin B.	"	POW Jan. 22. (2)

(1) *Official report of killed and wounded . . . Jan. 18, 1813.*
(2) *Palladium,* 24 Mar. 1813.
(3) *Boone County Pension List.*
(4) Chinn Family notes, MS, Kentucky Historical Society.
(5) *Palladium,* 2 Dec. 1812.
(6) *Honor Roll . . . of Soldiers of 1812 buried in Illinois,* I.

Captain Stewart W. Megowan's Company, 5th Regiment
August 15—October 14, 1812
(Fayette County)

NAME	RANK	REMARKS
Stewart W. Megowan	Captain	
Martin Wymore	Lieutenant	
Charles S. Todd	Ensign	Trfd. to QM-General's Dept. (2)
Jonathan Davis	Sergeant	
Thomas Gatewood	"	
Bernard Harvey	"	POW Jan. 22. (1)
Beverly Pilcher	"	
Richard Roach	"	POW Jan. 22. (1)
Ira Stout	"	
Thomas Key	Corporal	
Joseph Lonkart	"	
Joel Porter	"	
Samuel McMicken	Musician	McMeekin? POW Jan. 22. (1)
Andrew Summers	"	
Alsop, Alexander	Private	
Armstrong, John	"	
Ballard, Anderson	"	
Barker, John, Jr.	"	
Blackburn, Thomas H.	"	Blackwell? POW Jan. 22. (1)
Boyer, Ezra (Ira)	"	POW Jan. 22. (1)
Butler, John	"	
Cummings, James	"	POW Jan. 22. (1)
Eares, John	"	Eves? POW Jan. 22. (1)
Fair, James	"	
Gatewood, Thomas R.	"	
Geter, Barnett	"	POW Jan. 22. (1)
Giltner, Bernard	"	POW Jan. 22. (1)
Gindron, James I.	"	
Grider, Moses	"	
Hogan, John P.	"	
Kinney, Benjamin	"	POW Jan. 22. (1)
Kirby, Zachariah	"	
Liggins, William	"	
Lithell, John	"	
McCall, John	"	
McCamant, John	"	
McDaniel, E.	"	
Mahon, Alexander	"	
Masterson, Richard	"	
Miller, John P.	"	
Mitchell, William	"	
Napper, James	"	
Nichols, John	"	POW Jan. 22. (1)
Peachy, William	"	Preacher? POW Jan. 22. (1)

Rosters of Troops 203

Captain Stewart W. Megowan's Company, 5th Regiment *(Continued)*

NAME	RANK	REMARKS
Pettitt, John	Private	
Porter, Samuel	"	
Price, William	"	POW Jan. 22. (1)
Robinson, Isaac	"	
Servant, Charles	"	
Shire, John	"	
Shirerry, George	"	
Tally, John	"	
Watkins, Thomas	"	
York, Bartlett	"	

This company furnished a detail for the Raisin march.
(1) *Palladium*, 24 Mar. 1813.
(2) Griffin, G. W., *Memoir of Charles S. Todd*.

Captain John Martin's Company, 5th Regiment
August 15–October 14, 1812
(Clark County)

NAME	RANK	REMARKS
John Martin	Captain	
William McGuire	Lieutenant	POW Jan. 22. (2)
Jonathan Taylor	Ensign	
James Holloday	Sergeant	
William Morton	"	
Roger Quisenberry	"	POW Jan. 22. (2)
John D. Snydor	"	WIA Jan. 18. (1); KIA Jan. 22/23. (3)
Benjamin Antrebus	Corporal	POW Jan. 22. (2)
Alfred Barnes	"	
Abner T. Crow	"	
Thomas Ricketts	"	POW Jan. 22. (2)
William Smith	"	POW Jan. 22. (2)
George McManama	Musician	
Ashbrook, John	Private	POW Jan. 22. (2)
Barney, William	"	
Baxter, George	"	
Baxter, John	"	
Bernett, B.	"	Burnett?
Biddle, Caleb	"	POW Jan. 22. (2)
Bookshire, Benjamin	"	
Booth, Elijah	"	
Brandge, Bartlett	"	
Bruce, Durrett	"	

Captain John Martin's Company, 5th Regiment *(Continued)*

NAME	RANK	REMARKS
Burmun, Peter M.	Private	
Bush, Tilman	"	
Chism, James	"	
Ciddle, Cal	"	
Clawson, Peter	"	POW Jan. 22. (2)
Cooper, John	"	
Daniel, John	"	
Davies, James	"	
Dewitt, Frederick	"	POW Jan. 22. (2)
Dyke, Stephen	"	
Elsbery, William	"	
Emerson, James	"	POW Jan. 22. (2)
Eubank, George	"	POW Jan. 22. (2)
Eubanks, William	"	
Evans, George	"	
Ewell, William	"	
Fowler, Thomas	"	
Gore, Nathan	"	
Guin, John	"	Gwinn? POW Jan. 22. (2)
Hammer, William	"	
Holder, Gava	"	
Holloday, Eliot H.	"	POW Jan. 22. (2) Holladay.
Hopkins, Mordecai	"	
Hull, James	"	
Johnston, Joshua	"	POW Jan. 22. (2)
Kinciad, Charles	"	
Lammons, John	"	POW Jan. 22. (2)
Landers, James	"	
Lane, Mordecai	"	POW Jan. 22. (2)
Lisle, Samuel	"	
McGee, William	"	
Marks, Hastings	"	
Marks, Nathaniel	"	
Martin, John	"	
Maxwell, John	"	
Montgomery, Jesse	"	
Moore, William	"	
Morris, B.	"	WIA Jan. 18. (1)
Owings, Boswell	"	
Patrick, John	"	
Piggs, William	"	
Richardson, Philip T.	"	POW Jan. 22. (2)
Routt, William	"	
Sammons, John	"	
Sams, Daniel	"	
Shortridge, Elisha	"	

Rosters of Troops 205

Captain John Martin's Company, 5th Regiment *(Continued)*

NAME	RANK	REMARKS
Store, Francis	Private	Stone? POW Jan. 22. (2)
Strode, Stephen	"	POW Jan. 22. (2)
Tinsley, John	"	
Tolin, Morgan	"	
Tuggle, John	"	
Vallandingham, Hugh	"	
Wilson, Alexander	"	POW Jan. 22. (2)
Wilson, David A.	"	POW Jan. 22. (2)
Wise, William	"	

(1) *Official report of killed and wounded . . . Jan. 18, 1813.*
(2) *Palladium,* 24 Mar. 1813.
(3) *Niles' Weekly Register,* V: Lists John Sidney KIA. This report also lists as killed Jan. 22 Thomas S. Crow, unit not identified.

Captain Patrick Gray's Company, 5th Regiment
August 15–October 14, 1812
(Jessamine County)

NAME	RANK	REMARKS
Patrick Gray	Captain	His will probated March, 1813. (5)
James Fletcher	Lieutenant	
James Clark	Ensign	Resigned by 26 Nov. 1812. (2)
John Botts	Sergeant	Ensign 26 Nov. 1812. (2); POW Jan. 22. (6)
George Chrisman	"	
Thomas Reed	"	
William Sechrest	"	POW Jan. 22. (1)
Robert Dinwiddie	Corporal	POW Jan. 22. (1)
Samuel Huckstep	"	
James Norrel	"	
Anderson, Oliver	Private	WIA (3); POW Jan. 22. (1)
Armstrong, Levy	"	
Arnett, John	"	
Bagwell, Cary	"	
Bishop, John	"	POW Jan. 22. (1)
Bradshaw, Smith	"	
Brown, Samuel	"	POW Jan. 22. (1)
Burk, Benjamin	"	
Campbell, James	"	
Cardwell, James	"	
Cardwell, Samuel	"	POW Jan. 22. (1)
Cary, Mefford	"	

Captain Patrick Gray's Company, 5th Regiment *(Continued)*

NAME	RANK	REMARKS
Clark, George W.	Private	
Croslin, Benjamin	"	
Dickerson, David	"	POW Jan. 22. (1)
Dickerson, William	"	POW Jan. 22. (1)
Downes, Benore P.	"	
Duncan, Robert	"	
Elmore, David	"	
Finney, James	"	POW Jan. 22. (1)
Hopkins, Thomas	"	POW Jan. 22. (1)
Howard, Achilles	"	
Hunter, Charles	"	POW Jan. 22. (1)
Hutcherson, Samuel	"	
Jeter, Henry	"	POW Jan. 22. (1)
Jimmerson, David	"	Jamison? POW Jan. 22. (1)
Jimmerson, John	"	Jamison?
Jimmerson, William	"	Jamison?
Johnson, John	"	POW Jan. 22. (1)
Kennady, William	"	
Lana, Henry	"	
Leon, Moses	"	Lair? He died of typhus 7 Nov. 1812. (4)
Lusk, James	"	POW Jan. 22. (1)
McClure, Martin	"	
Marshall, James	"	
Marshall, William	"	
May, Lindsay	"	
Messick, Nathan	"	
Miller, Francis	"	
Morris, Henry	"	
Myers, John	"	POW Jan. 22. (1)
Nevins, Henry	"	POW Jan. 22. (1)
Newal, Armstrong	"	Noel? POW Jan. 22. (1)
Patterson, John	"	
Pilcher, Lewis	"	
Pollock, William	"	POW Jan. 22. (1)
Read, Peter	"	
Robinson, Michael	"	
Rusk, Robert	"	
Sales, Thomas F.	"	
Shelton, Thomas	"	
Smith, Peter	"	
Spencer, Absalom	"	
Spires, Greenbury	"	
Stype, John	"	
Summers, James	"	
Summers, Thomas	"	

Rosters of Troops

Captain Patrick Gray's Company, 5th Regiment (Continued)

NAME	RANK	REMARKS
Thompson, Pitman	Private	
Venable, Hamden S.	"	
Wager, Absalom	"	POW Jan. 22. (1)
Wallace, Abraham	"	
Wallace, James	"	
Waters, Lewis	"	
Welsh, Alexander	"	Lieut. 26 Nov. 1812. (2)
Wharton, Joseph	"	
Willis, John	"	
Willis, William	"	

(1) *Palladium*, 24 Mar. 1813.
(2) *Official roster of officers war of 1812-16*, MS, Kentucky Historical Society.
(3) *Kentucky Yeoman*, 6 Feb. 1873.
(4) *Draper MSS*, 5CC69. (Kentucky Historical Society photostats).
(5) *Jessamine County Will Book A*.
(6) *Niles' Weekly Register*, IV.

First Rifle Regiment
August 15–October 14, 1812

NAME	RANK	REMARKS
	Field Officers	
John Allen	Lieut. Col.	KIA Jan. 22.
Martin D. Hardin	Maj. 1st Bn.	
George Madison	Maj. 2nd Bn.	POW Jan. 22.
	Staff Officers	
Thomas Mitchell	Chaplain	Adjutant Oct. 14, 1812.
Thomas C. Davis	Surgeon	KIA Jan. 22.
Benjamin Logan	Surg. Mate	POW Jan. 22.
Richard Bledsoe	Adjutant	See Capt. Edmiston's Company.
Peter Dudley	Paymaster	
Peter G. Voorhies	Quartermaster	
George C. Patrick	Sgt. Major	Vice Wm. McClanahan resg. Aug. 18, 1812.
James Stewart	Qr. M. Sgt.	Resigned.
James Hamilton	Drum Major	
William Kelly	Fife Major	
John Christopher	Sgt. Major	Vice G. C. Patrick, resgd. Oct. 2, 1812.
Benjamin Bridges	Qr. M. Sgt.	Vice James Stewart, resgd. Sept. 6, 1812.

[Official Roster Officers War of 1812-16, MS, Kentucky Historical Society; Adjutant General's Report . . . *Kentucky Soldiers in the War of 1812*; *Palladium*, Feb. 24, Mar. 24, 1813.]

Captain William Kerley's Company, 1st Rifle Regiment
August 15–October 14, 1812
(Madison County)

NAME	RANK	REMARKS
William Kerley	Captain	
Harrison Monday	Lieutenant	Resigned by Oct. 14, 1812. (1)
Davis Hardin	Ensign	Resigned by Dec. 15, 1812. (1)
Richard C. Holder	1st Sgt.	
Hudson Martin	2nd Sgt.	Ensign Dec. 15, 1812. (1)
Richard Gentry	3rd Sgt.	Vice John A. Gaines from ranks.
George C. Patrick	4th Sgt.	
James D. Dickey	1st Cpl.	
Esrane Tipton	2nd Cpl.	Esmon?
Robert D. Maupin	3rd Cpl.	
Thomas G. Jones	4th Cpl.	
Jesse Cock	Drummer	KIA. (4)
Akers, James	Private	
Amarine, George	"	Vice Archibald Woods, Esq.
Amarine, Jonathan	"	Vice Benjamin Midner.
Barnes, James	"	
Barnes, Thomas	"	Vice George Williams.
Bassnet, William	"	
Bettersworth, Fielding	"	
Bettersworth, Jesse	"	Vice R. A. Sturgus.
Bingham, George	"	
Blackwell, David	"	Vice Ezekiel Blackwell; POW Jan. 22. (2)
Boggs, James	"	
Boggs, John W.	"	
Bratton, Joseph	"	
Brown, Arthur	"	
Brunett, Elijah	"	
Burnan, Bennett	"	
Burrass, James	"	Died of typhus about Nov. 7, 1812. (3)
Burton, David	"	
Canon, James H.	"	
Cavenaugh, Thomas	"	
Chapman, John	"	Vice Pleasant Watkins.
Chinn, James	"	Vice A. W. Rollings.
Cock, Henry D.	"	Vice Thomas J. Sturman.
Cornelison, Aaron	"	
Curles, Morgan	"	
Donaho, Jesse	"	
Dougherty, Cornelius	"	
Emmett, Matthais	"	Died of typhus about Nov. 7, 1812. (3)
Estes, William	"	

Rosters of Troops

Captain William Kerley's Company, 1st Rifle Regiment *(Continued)*

NAME	RANK	REMARKS
Fox, Charles	Private	
Francis, Lewis	"	
Freeman, Samuel	"	
Fullalove, Larkin	"	
Gentry, James	"	Vice William Munday.
Goding, Hugh	"	
Greening, John	"	
Haden, Tyrel	"	
Hall, David	"	Vice John Gregg.
Hanson, Thomas	"	POW Jan. 22. (2)
Harris, Western	"	
Harrison, Williby	"	
Haveline, Jesse	"	
Hill, Archibald	"	
Johnson, Gersham	"	Vice John Daniels.
Jones, Samuel D.	"	
McCall, Thomas	"	
McGuire, Willis	"	
Million, Benson	"	
Morton, William	"	
Noble, William	"	
Owens, John	"	
Owens, Philip	"	
Profet, Anderson	"	
Profet, James	"	
Quinn, Hiram	"	
Redman, Washington	"	
Reese, John	"	
Richardson, Thomas	"	
Sale, Samuel	"	
Simpson, John	"	
Simpson, Robert	"	
Smallwood, Russell	"	
Swope, John	"	
Thompson, Richard L.	"	
Thompson, Thomas	"	
Turner, James	"	
Turner, Tarlton	"	
Virgus, Jordan	"	
Wayne, William	"	
Williams, Squire	"	
Woodruff, Benjamin	"	
Woodruff, William B.	"	

Captain William Kerley's Company, 1st Rifle Regiment *(Continued)*

NAME	RANK	REMARKS
Woods, Andrew W.	Private	
Woods, Archibald	"	
Young, John M.	"	

This company furnished a detail for the Raisin march.

(1) *Original roster of Officers of the War of 1812-15*, MS, Kentucky Historical Society.
(2) *Palladium*, 24 Mar. 1813.
(3) *Draper MSS*, 5CC69.
(4) *Kentucky Gazette*, 8 Aug. 1835.

Captain William Ellis's (Richard Matson's) Company, 1st Rifle Regiment
August 15–October 14, 1812
(Bourbon and Harrison Counties)

NAME	RANK	REMARKS
William Ellis	Captain	Died at Fort Defiance by 15 Dec. 1812 (1,12)
Richard Matson	Lieutenant	Capt. 15 Dec. 1812. (1); WIA Jan. 18. (2)
Francis Chinn	Ensign	Lieut. 15 Dec. 1812. (1) WIA Jan. 18. (2)
David Cone	1st Sgt.	Coone? POW Jan. 22. (3)
William E. Boswell	2nd Sgt.	POW Jan. 22. (3)
William B. Chinn	3rd Sgt.	POW Jan. 22. (3)
Hugh Brown	4th Sgt.	
Jeremiah Morgan	1st Cpl.	POW Jan. 22. (3)
John P. Chinn	2nd Cpl.	POW Jan. 22. (3)
Basil R. L. Holliday	3rd Cpl.	
James Martin	4th Cpl.	
James Foxworthy	Bugler	POW Jan. 22. (3)
Adams, James	Private	POW Jan. 22. (3)
Adams, John	"	POW Jan. 22. (3)
Adams, William	"	WIA Jan. 18. (2); POW Jan. 22. (3)
Bails, Russell	"	
Barnes, Oliver	"	
Black, Robert	"	
Blair, James	"	
Blair, Samuel	"	
Breckenridge, Eddy L.	"	
Bridges, John	"	WIA Jan. 18. (2); Returned. (9)
Brown, Irwin	"	

Rosters of Troops 211

Captain William Ellis's (Richard Matson's) Company, 1st Rifle Regiment *(Continued)*

NAME	RANK	REMARKS
Brown, John	Private	
Chinn, Rawleigh	"	
Chinn, Thomas W.	"	Ensign 15 Dec. 1812. (1) POW Jan. 22. (11)
Coone, Jone (John)	"	
Craig, James	"	POW Jan. 22. (3)
Craig, William	"	
Dear, Jesse	"	
Eades, Horatio	"	
Edwards, Jessie	"	
Ellis, Robert	"	WIA, POW Jan. 22. (4) Brother of Captain Ellis.
Fewel, Ephraim	"	
Fightmaster, John	"	Deserted; POW with Indians. (5)
Fowler, John H.	"	
George, Alfred	"	POW Jan. 22. (3)
George, William	"	
Gray, William	"	
Grooms, Horatio	"	POW Jan. 22. (3)
Hailey, Daniel	"	WIA Jan. 22. (6)
Hamilton, Alexander	"	
Hamilton, William	"	
Harmon, John	"	
Herring, Jonathan	"	
Herring, Samuel	"	
Hibs, Adam	"	
Houster, William	"	
Hull, Thomas	"	POW Jan. 22. (3)
Jessup, Samuel B.	"	
Jones, Ambrose	"	
Jones, Cully	"	
Jones, Isaac, Sr.	"	Jones, Isaac, POW Jan. 22. (3)
Jones, Isaac, Jr.	"	
Kenning, David	"	
Lewis, Aaron	"	POW Jan. 22. (3)
Lewis, Alexander	"	
McClure, John	"	
McKinsey, John	"	POW Jan. 22. (3)
McKitrick, David	"	
McKitrick, Robert	"	
Martin, David	"	
Masters, John	"	POW Jan. 22. (8)
Matthias, Amont	"	
Millner, Joseph	"	Miller? POW Jan. 22. (3)

Captain William Ellis's (Richard Matson's) Company,
1st Rifle Regiment (Continued)

NAME	RANK	REMARKS
Morgan, Moses	Private	KIA Jan. 18. (7)
Morrell, John	"	
Newell, Hugh	"	Escaped Jan. 22. (10)
Norman, Caleb	"	
Porter, William	"	
Riley, James	"	
Ritter, John	"	POW Jan. 22. (3)
Roberts, William	"	
Rowland, Joseph	"	Returned. (9)
Sanders, James	"	
Scott, William B.	"	POW Jan. 22. (3)
Sellers, Jonathan	"	
Shoemaker, Spencer	"	WIA Jan. 18, POW Jan. 22. (6)
Sidnor, Robert T.	"	POW Jan. 22. (3)
Townsend, George	"	
Vanding, Stephen	"	
Wells, Basil	"	
Wells, Benjamin	"	
Wells, John	"	
Wolf, John	"	
World, Robert	"	Worles? Returned. (9)

(1) *Official roster of officers war of 1812-15*, MS, Kentucky Historical Society.
(2) *Report of killed and wounded . . . Jan. 18, 1813.*
(3) *Palladium*, 24 Mar. 1813.
(4) *Ibid.*, 31 Mar. 1813.
(5) Darnell, Elias, *Journal* . . . .
(6) *Harrison County Pension Records*.
(7) *Indiana Historical Collections*, IX.
(8) *Argus*, 12 Feb. 1814.
(9) *Palladium*, 24 Feb. 1813.
(10) *History of Bourbon, Scott, Harrison . . . Counties*, 1882.
(11) *Niles' Weekly Register*, IV.
(12) *Biographical Encyclopaedia of Kentucky* . . . J. M. Armstrong & Co., 1878.

Captain John Simpson's Company, 1st Rifle Regiment
August 15—October 14, 1812
(Lincoln County)

NAME	RANK	REMARKS
John Simpson	Captain	KIA Jan. 22. (2)
Thomas Mitchell	Lieutenant	
George Cardwell	Ensign	WIA, POW Jan. 22. (2)
Benjamin Porter	1st Sgt.	
Samuel Demearee	2nd Sgt.	

Rosters of Troops   213

Captain John Simpson's Company, 1st Rifle Regiment *(Continued)*

NAME	RANK	REMARKS
James Sill	3rd Sgt.	
Abraham Smith	4th Sgt.	
Robert Radford	1st Cpl.	
Jeremiah Long	2nd Cpl.	Sgt. Sept. 4, 1812, vice Abraham Smith.
Lazarus Tilly	3rd Cpl.	POW Jan. 22. (2)
Thomas Griffith	4th Cpl.	
Ashby, Henderson	Private	
Ashby, Willoughby	"	POW Jan. 22. (2)
Atherton, Henry	"	
Atherton, William	"	WIA Jan. 18. (1); POW Jan. 22. (3)
Bartine, Nicholas	"	
Berry, Robert	"	
Bird, Henry	"	
Birk, Samuel	"	Burk? POW Jan. 22. (2)
Bollas, James W.	"	POW Jan. 22. (2)
Burwell, William	"	Burnett? POW Jan. 22. (2)
Carr, John	"	
Cline, Aaron	"	
Collete, Aaron	"	
Conally, Daniel	"	
Daniel, John	"	
Dowdle, John	"	POW Jan. 22. (2)
Dowell, Fauntleroy	"	Dowdle? POW Jan. 22. (2)
Ducker, Nathan	"	
Duncan, Richard	"	
Faught, George	"	Fant?
Faught, William	"	Fant? POW Jan. 22. (2)
Fisher, Jesse	"	WIA Jan. 18. (1)
Fitzgerald, Henry	"	
Gibbons, David	"	
Glasscock, Peter	"	POW Jan. 22. (2)
Hill, Foster	"	
Hoddin, Abraham	"	
Hollis, James W.	"	
Horbeson, Samuel	"	Harbison?
Kelso, Elijah	"	Died of typhus Nov., 1812. (4)
Kerrill, James	"	
Lee, Zachariah	"	WIA Jan. 18. (1)
Lock, John	"	
McClelland, Joseph	"	
McCormick, James	"	
McCullom, Jacob	"	POW Jan. 22. (2)
McGrimes, John	"	POW Jan. 22. (2)
Mahurine, John	"	

Captain John Simpson's Company, 1st Rifle Regiment *(Continued)*

NAME	RANK	REMARKS
Miller, John	Private	
Mitchell, Samuel	"	
Mullikin, Benjamin	"	
Mullikin, Charles	"	Mulligan? POW Jan. 22. (2)
Osburn, George	"	
Pearson, William	"	
Roberts, Jesse	"	
Roberts, John	"	POW Jan. 22. (2)
Rodman, John	"	POW Jan. 22. (2)
Rogers, George	"	
Ross, John	"	
Senly, Tucker	"	
Shannon, John	"	
Sharp, Thomas	"	
Sills, John A.	"	
Simpson, Joseph	"	KIA Jan. 18. (1)
Teralt, John	"	
Truman, John	"	
Tucker, William W.	"	
Tylor, William	"	
Watson, Bartholomew	"	
Williby, Ashby	"	
Wright, Reuben	"	

(1) *Report of killed and wounded* . . . Jan. 18, 1813.
(2) *Palladium*, 24 Mar. 1813.
(3) *Argus*, Jan. 1, Feb. 12, 1814.
(4) *Palladium*, 2 Dec. 1812.

Captain Bland W. Ballard's Company, 1st Rifle Regiment
August 15–October 14, 1812
(Shelby County)

NAME	RANK	REMARKS
Bland W. Ballard	Captain	WIA Jan. 18. (1); POW Jan. 22. (2)
John Williamson	Lieutenant	KIA, MIA, 15 Feb. 1813. (State Monument)
John W. Nash	Ensign	WIA, POW Jan. 22. (2)
James M. Ackran	1st Sgt.	McAchran
Martin Jackson	2nd Sgt.	
William Cooper	3rd Sgt.	POW Jan. 22. (2)
Amariah A. McGrig	4th Sgt.	POW Jan. 22. (2)
Bland Ballard	Corporal	Died of swamp fever, Jan., 1813. (3)

Rosters of Troops 215

Captain Bland W. Ballard's Company, 1st Rifle Regiment *(Continued)*

NAME	RANK	REMARKS
Thomas Garnett	Corporal	
William Harrold	"	
Burton Mulligan	"	
Akin, Alexander	Private	POW Jan. 22. (2)
Arnold, Robert	"	
Austin, George	"	
Beal, Henry	"	
Beale, Robert	"	POW Jan. 22. (2)
Bennett, Jacob	"	
Bennett, Lavoler	"	
Blandford, John B.	"	
Boone, Josiah	"	
Boyd, William	"	
Bridges, Benjamin, Sr.	"	
Brooks, Thomas	"	
Bruner, Jacob	"	
Caplinger, John	"	
Caplinger, Samuel	"	
Caplinger, Solomon	"	
Chapman, John	"	POW Jan. 22. (2)
Cline, Nicholas	"	
Cole, Pleasant	"	
Cooper, Benjamin	"	
Dailey, Francis	"	
Dailey, John	"	
Davis, John	"	
Garnett, Harris H.	"	
Grant, Robert	"	
Graves, Samuel	"	
Hall, George	"	Returned. (4)
Hamlin, William A.	"	Hamblen?
Hill, Hardy	"	POW Jan. 22. (2)
Howard, William	"	
Howell, Lewis	"	POW Jan. 22. (2)
Huddleston, Allen	"	
Huff, Abraham	"	Hart? POW Jan. 22. (2)
Hunter, John	"	
Jamison, Isaac	"	
Kinder, George	"	
Kinder, Jacob	"	
Lambert, Moses	"	
Lessler, Jacob	"	Returned. (4)
Leforce, Robertson	"	POW Jan. 22. (2)
Logan, James W.	"	
McComsey, John	"	McCurnsey? POW Jan. 22. (2)

Captain Bland W. Ballard's Company, 1st Rifle Regiment *(Continued)*

NAME	RANK	REMARKS
Metcalfe, Enoch	Private	
Montgomery, Alexander	"	POW Jan. 22. (5)
Moore, John	"	
Neal, James	"	
Patterson, John	"	POW Jan. 22. (2)
Potts, Thomas	"	
Quarles, Samuel	"	
Redd, Mordecai	"	
Redding, Thomas	"	POW Jan. 22. (2)
Rice, Abraham	"	POW Jan. 22. (2)
Roberts, Pleasant M.	"	
Robins, Gerades R.	"	
Rutledge, Joshua	"	
Samples, Samuel	"	
Shackleford, Edmond	"	
Shepherd, Ezekiel	"	
Simpson, James	"	POW Jan. 22. (2)
Thralkeld, Thomas	"	
Thralkeld, William	"	
Tombs, Benjamin	"	
Tyler, John	"	
Vancleave, Benjamin	"	
Vancleave, Thomas	"	
Walker, John	"	POW Jan. 22. (2)
Warren, Joel	"	POW Jan. 22. (2)
Watts, Jeremiah	"	
Webb, Richard	"	
Wetherford, Elijah	"	
Wetherford, Martin	"	POW; died Feb. 1, 1813, at Sandwich. (6)
Whitaker, Aquilla	"	
Whitaker, John	"	POW Jan. 22. (2)
Williams, Elias	"	
Williams, John	"	

(1) *Report of killed and wounded* . . . *Jan. 18, 1813.*
(2) *Palladium,* 24 Mar. 1813.
(3) *Filson Club History Quarterly,* XIII.
(4) *Palladium,* 24 Feb. 1813.
(5) *Ibid.,* 31 Mar. 1813.
(6) *Niles' Weekly Register,* IV.

Captain Maurice Langhorne's Company, 1st Rifle Regiment
August 15–October 14, 1812
(Bourbon County)

NAME	RANK	REMARKS
Maurice Langhorne	Captain	
Abraham Keller	Lieutenant	
Joseph Morin	Ensign	WIA Jan. 22. (1); MIA, POW Jan. 25. (4)
Edward M. McConnell	1st Sgt.	WIA Jan. 18. (2); POW Jan. 22. (3)
Thomas S. Benson	2nd Sgt.	KIA Jan. 18. (2)
Hezekiel Elgin	3rd Sgt.	
Lewis Reno	4th Sgt.	
Levin P. Scroggin	1st Cpl.	
Merit Valandingham	2nd Cpl.	
William Delany	3rd Cpl.	
Richard Keith	4th Cpl.	POW Jan. 22. (3)
Thornton Wilson	Drummer	
Cumberland Wilson	"	
Allenthorp, Jacob	Private	Vice Middleton Day; POW Jan. 22. (3)
Ames, Nicholas	"	Amos? POW Jan. 22. (3)
Armstrong, William	"	Vice Geo. Cleveland; WIA Jan. 18. (2)
Baldwin, Ira	"	POW Jan. 22. (3)
Beckett, Joseph	"	MIA Jan. 25. (4)
Bell, William	"	POW Jan. 22. (3)
Booth, Harrison	"	WIA Jan. 18. (2); POW Jan. 22. (3)
Bowen, John	"	
Boyle, John	"	Vice Job Tillett; POW Jan. 22. (3)
Brice, Benoni	"	
Butler, William	"	MIA Jan. 25. (4); KIA Jan. 22. (7)
Byrd, Abraham	"	MIA Jan. 25. (4)
Byrd, John	"	
Chadd, William	"	Vice Elijah Current; POW Jan. 22. (3)
Corbin, Nicholas	"	Vice Nathan Corbin; POW Jan. 22. (3)
Craver, George	"	
Crawford, Robert	"	
Crawford, William	"	MIA Jan. 25. (4)
Davis, Nathaniel	"	
Eadsi, Robert	"	

Captain Maurice Langhorne's Company, 1st Rifle Regiment *(Continued)*

NAME	RANK	REMARKS
Edwards, William M.	Private	POW Jan. 22. (3)
Ellis, Thomas	"	MIA Jan. 25. (4)
Estis, George W.	"	
Feamster, Charles	"	POW Jan. 22. (3)
Givens, John	"	Gwinn? POW Jan. 22. (3)
Grant, Daniel	"	POW Jan. 22. (3)
Hamilton, Andrew	"	MIA Jan. 25. (4)
Harrison, Robert	"	KIA Jan. 18. (2)
Hayden, Nathaniel	"	POW Jan. 22. (3)
Hill, Fountain	"	
Hinkson, John	"	Vice John B. Lucker.
Hughes, William	"	POW Jan. 22. (3)
Hull, Corbin R.	"	
Humble, Jesse	"	KIA Jan. 18. (2)
Humphrey, Benjamin	"	
Jacobs, Daniel	"	Vice Edward Waller.
Johnston, William	"	MIA Jan. 25. (4)
Jump, John	"	POW Jan. 22. (3)
Keith, George	"	WIA Jan. 18. (2)
Kemp, Charles	"	
Legabeck, Saint	"	
Lighter, Christian	"	Lyter? POW Jan. 22. (3)
Link, Jacob	"	
Ludspeth, David	"	POW Jan. 22. (3)
McClanahan, William	"	Resgd. as Sgt. Maj. and re-enlisted.
McConnell, William	"	POW Jan. 22. (3)
McCormick, John	"	MIA Jan. 25. (4)
McCune, James	"	Vice Jesse Yelton; POW Jan. 22. (3)
McDowell, William	"	MIA Jan. 25. (4)
Menefee, Benjamin P.	"	POW Jan. 22. (3)
Menick, John	"	Returned. (1)
Myers, Jacob	"	
Parmer, Thomas	"	Deserted at Dayton. (6)
Phemister, Charles	"	POW Jan. 22. (3)
Pugh, William	"	POW Jan. 22. (3)
Riddle, Abraham	"	Ruddle? POW Jan. 22. (3)
Ruth, Richard	"	Returned. (1)
Sapp, James	"	
Shingleton, William	"	MIA Jan. 25. (4)
Shoemaker, James	"	
Sidner, Frederick	"	
Smith, Abraham	"	POW Jan. 22. (3)
Smith, Jacob	"	POW Jan. 22. (3)

Rosters of Troops 219

Captain Maurice Langhorne's Company, 1st Rifle Regiment *(Continued)*

NAME	RANK	REMARKS
Stephens, Dawson	Private	POW Jan. 22. (3)
Thomas, William	"	MIA Jan. 25. (4)
Tucker, Joseph	"	
Underwood, Bennett	"	POW Jan. 22. (3)
Whitledge, Lyne	"	POW Jan. 22. (3)
Whitledge, Thomas	"	
Wilmott, Charles P.	"	POW Jan. 22. (3)
Yokum, Solomon	"	
Taken from the ranks:		
Chinn, Joseph R.	"	Crippled.
Clark, Benjamin L.	"	Joined the "R" service.

(1) *Palladium*, 24 Feb. 1813.
(2) *Report of killed and wounded . . . Jan. 18, 1813.*
(3) *Palladium*, 24 Mar. 1813.
(4) List of killed, wounded and missing prepared by Capt. Langhorne Jan. 25, 1813. Published in *The Western Citizen*, 13 Feb. 1813.
(5) *Indiana Historical Collections*, IX.
(6) Letter, Capt. Langhorne, 18 Sept. 1812, in *The Western Citizen*, 13 Feb. 1813.
(7) *Niles' Weekly Register*, V.

Captain Paschal Hickman's Company, 1st Rifle Regiment
August 15–October 14, 1812
(Franklin County)

NAME	RANK	REMARKS
Paschal Hickman	Captain	WIA Jan. 18. (2); KIA Jan. 23. (3)
Peter Dudley	Lieutenant	Paymaster 11 Aug. 1812; QM 22 Oct. 1812. (1)
Peter G. Voorhies	Ensign	QM 11 Aug. 1812; resigned by 22 Oct. 1812. (1)
David Quinn	1st Sgt.	KIA. (5)
Benjamin Head	2nd Sgt.	
George Nicholas	3rd Sgt.	Nicholson? POW Jan. 22. (3)
John Nailor	4th Sgt.	KIA. (5)
Alexander Rennick	1st Cpl.	
William T. Pemberton	2nd Cpl.	
Richard Chism	3rd Cpl.	KIA. (5)
Benjamin B. Johnson	4th Cpl.	
Armstrong, Joseph	Private	POW Jan. 22. (3)
Arnold, Berrisford	"	KIA. (5)

Captain Paschal Hickman's Company, 1st Rifle Regiment *(Continued)*

NAME	RANK	REMARKS
Arnold, Scott	Private	Listed in original roster. Returned. (4)
Bassett, James	"	POW Jan. 22. (3)
Biscoe, James	"	KIA. (5)
Blackburn, Samuel	"	Vice Charles Humphrey.
Boone, Isaac	"	KIA. (5)
Bratton, William	"	POW Jan. 22. (3)
Brock, John	"	Vice Hugh Brock. POW Jan. 22. (3)
Brown, Overton	"	WIA Jan. 18. (2)
Brown, William	"	
Calvert, Martin	"	Colbert? POW Jan. 22. (3)
Clark, Joseph	"	WIA Jan. 18. (6); POW Jan. 22. (3)
Clark, Philip	"	KIA. (5)
Cosby, Garland	"	
Cox, John	"	WIA Jan. 18. (2); KIA (5)
Davis, Lemuel, Sr.	"	
Davis, Lemuel, Jr.	"	
Dudley, Thomas P.	"	WIA, POW Jan. 22. (3)
Fenwick, Lewis B.	"	POW Jan. 22. (2)
Goodrich, Nathan	"	
Hays, John	"	
Head, Moses	"	
Hensley, William D.	"	
Herndon, Elisha	"	
Holton, John A.	"	WIA Jan. 18. (2); POW Jan. 22. (3)
Humphreys, James B.	"	
Johnston, George T.	"	
Kenton, Simon	"	KIA. (5)
King, Gideon	"	WIA, POW Jan. 22. (3)
Koons, John	"	
Lane, John	"	KIA. (5)
Lewis, Zachariah W.	"	POW Jan. 22. (3)
Lively, Jacob	"	Vice B. Botts.
McBride, Lapsley	"	KIA. (5)
McCracken, Otho	"	
Marshall, Timothy	"	
Mathews, David E.	"	
Mayhall, Francis	"	KIA Jan. 18. (6)
Mayhall, John	"	
Moore, Joshua	"	KIA Jan. 18. (2)
Moore, Timothy T.	"	
Moseley, Joseph	"	Moxley in original roster.

Rosters of Troops

Captain Paschal Hickman's Company, 1st Rifle Regiment *(Continued)*

NAME	RANK	REMARKS
Mulligan, John G.	Private	
Noland, John	"	WIA Jan. 18. (2); POW Jan. 22. (3)
Owen, Robert D.	"	POW Jan. 22. (3)
Pannell, Benjamin	"	
Parker, James	"	KIA. (5)
Phillips, John	"	KIA. (5)
Pitts, Joseph	"	KIA. (5)
Poe, Jesse	"	
Poindexter, Meriwether	"	KIA. (5)
Prewitt, William F.	"	KIA. (5)
Reading, Samuel	"	
Richardson, James A.	"	POW Jan. 22. (3)
Richardson, John C.	"	
Robertson, Alexander	"	Robinson? KIA. (5)
Robertson, George	"	Robinson? KIA. (5) Geo. Rogers Robinson according to a descendant
Rosson, John	"	
Sanders, John	"	POW Jan. 22. (3)
Sanders, William	"	POW Jan. 22. (3)
Slaughter, Francis	"	Returned. (4)
Smiley, Jesse	"	
Smith, John	"	KIA. (5)
Smith, Samuel	"	WIA Jan. 18. (2); KIA (5)
Sparks, Reuben	"	
Steele, Rankin	"	Returned. (4)
Stevens, William	"	KIA. (5)
Tate, John	"	KIA. (5)
Tate, Thomas	"	
Throckmorton, Samuel	"	KIA. (5)
Underwood, Benjamin	"	
Updike, William	"	
West, Van	"	
West, William	"	
Wilson, James	"	KIA. (5)
Yancy, George	"	

(1) *Original roster of officers of the war of 1812-15*, MS, Kentucky Historical Society.
(2) *Report of killed and wounded . . . Jan. 18, 1813*.
(3) *Palladium*, 24 Mar. 1813.
(4) *Ibid.*, 24 Feb. 1813.
(5) MS roster, Captain Hickman's Company. No dates given for deaths in action.
(6) Joseph Clark in *Commonwealth*, 9 Jan. 1871.

Captain Virgil McCracken's Company, 1st Rifle Regiment
August 15—October 14, 1812
(Woodford County)

NAME	RANK	REMARKS
Virgil McCracken	Captain	KIA after Jan. 23. (6)
Thomas Brooks	Lieutenant	
Henry Stone	Ensign	
George W. McClary	1st Sgt.	Listed MIA, KIA Feb. 15, 1813.
James H. Bomar	2nd Sgt.	Died at Fort Defiance in Dec., 1812. (3)
Samuel Steele	3rd Sgt.	
Nathaniel Mitchell	4th Sgt.	
James Brooks	1st Cpl.	
Edward B. Meredith	2nd Cpl.	
George Pugh	3rd Cpl.	
Willis Brown	4th Cpl.	Vice John Payton.
William Rearden	Bugler	
Atwood, Robert	Private	Volunteered 10 August 1812.
Bell, John P.	"	
Bell, Robert	"	
Bell, Thomas P.	"	
Bevis, William	"	
Brooks, Alexander	"	
Brown, Anderson	"	
Brown, John	"	
Bryan, Augustus	"	
Buchannon, Abraham	"	
Caldwell, James	"	
Christopher, John	"	
Collins, Bartlett	"	WIA, POW Jan. 22. (4)
Cook, Seth	"	
Daugherty, Thomas	"	
Dickey, William	"	
Ellis, Lee	"	
Ford, Reuben	"	
Hawkins, Francis	"	
Henton, George	"	
Latta, Alexander	"	
McCracken, Ovid	"	
McGuire, Samuel	"	Substituted in place of Lewis Endicott.
McKnight, James	"	
Mitchell, Archibald	"	
Mitchell, Solomon	"	
Morgan, Jarrett	"	POW Jan. 22. (2)
Mosley, John	"	
Nall, William H.	"	
Pace, Joel	"	

Captain Virgil McCracken's Company, 1st Rifle Regiment *(Continued)*

NAME	RANK	REMARKS
Pace, Joseph	Private	
Palmer, Lewis	"	
Peacock, William	"	WIA, POW Jan. 22. (2)
Pitman, Asa	"	POW Jan. 22. (2)
Railey, George	"	
Railey, Silas	"	
Railey, William, Jr.	"	
Read, John	"	
Reddin, Nehemiah	"	
Resler, Abraham	"	
Rooney, William	"	
Rowland, Henry L.	"	
Scearcy, Leonard	"	
Scearcy, Merritt	"	Returned. (1)
Scroggins, John	"	
Scroggins, Robert	"	
Slocomb, James	"	
Smith, George	"	Returned. (1)
Spencer, Calmer	"	
Spicer, Henry	"	POW Jan. 22. (2)
Stansberry, Thomas	"	
Stapp, Wyatt	"	
Steele, John	"	
Stevenson, Robert	"	
Stone, John	"	
Stucker, George	"	
Summers, Thomas G.	"	
Todd, Lewis S.	"	
Tutt, Lewis Y.	"	
Vasvil, Daniel	"	
Williams, John B.	"	POW Jan. 22. (2)
Williams, William	"	
Willmin, James	"	
Wooldridge, Robert	"	
Young, Merritt	"	
Young, Richard M.	"	

(1) *Palladium*, 24 Feb. 1813.
(2) *Ibid.*, 24 Mar. 1813.
(3) *Ibid.*, 10 Feb. 1813.
(4) *Grant County Pension Records.*
(5) *Original roster of officers of the war of 1812-15*, MS, Kentucky Historical Society.
(6) *Niles' Weekly Register*, IV.

Captain John Edmiston's (Richard Bledsoe's) Company, 1st Rifle Regiment
August 15—October 14, 1812
(Fayette County)

NAME	RANK	REMARKS
John Edmiston	Captain	Resigned by Oct. 14, 1812; (1) Re-enlisted as Pvt., (2); KIA Jan. 22. (4)
Richard Bledsoe	Lieutenant	Capt. 14 Oct. 1812. (1); POW Jan. 22. (2)
Vanallen Prewitt	Ensign	
James Frarey	1st Sgt.	Ensign 14 Oct. 1812. (1)
Thomas Gist	2nd Sgt.	Lieut., 15 Dec. 1812. (1)
William Cravins	3rd Sgt.	
Stapleton C. Burch	4th Sgt.	POW Jan. 22. (4)
John M. Davis	1st Cpl.	POW Jan. 22. (4)
John Welch	2nd Cpl.	
Clement Estes	3rd Cpl.	WIA Jan. 18. (3)
B. S. Cockrill	4th Cpl.	
German Britterham	Drummer	John? POW Jan. 22. (4)
Fielding Mahoney	Fifer	
Adams, Feathergill	Private	
Adams, John	"	POW Jan. 22. (4)
Allen, Beverly	"	
Ansberry, Thomas	"	
Ball, Jacob.	"	Returned. (2)
Beeturn, Adam	"	Beatum? POW Jan. 22. (4)
Bittingham, John	"	Brittingham?
Blackwell, James	"	
Bradley, Samuel	"	POW Jan. 22. (4)
Brink, Ephraim	"	Vice Hezekiah Ellis.
Brink, Samuel	"	
Bryant, Morgan	"	POW Jan. 22. (4)
Buckner, George	"	
Bynes, Andrew	"	Burns?
Caw, Walter E.	"	
Chandler, Richard	"	
Chinn, Charles	"	
Clegett, T. Y.	"	Clagget?
Cockrill, Benjamin	"	
Cotton, John E.	"	
Estes, Abraham	"	WIA Jan. 18. (3); POW Jan. 22. (5)
Estes, William	"	
Ewing, James	"	
Flournoy, Hoy B.	"	POW Jan. 22. (4)
Forbes, Jacob	"	
Foster, Thomas	"	

Rosters of Troops

Captain John Edmiston's (Richard Bledsoe's) Company, 1st Rifle Regiment *(Continued)*

NAME	RANK	REMARKS
Fry, George	Private	
Gillespie, David	"	
Goodloe, Henry	"	Vice Francis Preston.
Grimes, John	"	POW Jan. 22. (4)
Hawkins, S. O.	"	
Hendley, Elkhanna	"	Wounded Sept., 1812; dischd. 30 Oct. 1812. (6)
Henney, Robert P.	"	
Hudson, Dudley	"	WIA Jan. 18. (3); POW Jan. 22. (4)
Hundley, Charles	"	
Jenkins, Richard	"	
McCrosky, Elijah	"	POW Jan. 22. (4)
McDowell, John	"	
McDowell, Richard	"	
Morgan, Moses	"	KIA Jan. 18. (3)
Nailor, Francis	"	
Nicholas, Robert	"	
Nunnelly, Robert	"	WIA, POW Jan. 22. (4)
Owens, Nathaniel	"	
Parker, B. W.	"	
Peel, Hugh	"	
Pogue, Thomas	"	
Prewitt, Robert	"	
Price, Williamson	"	WIA Jan. 18. (3); POW Jan. 22. (4)
Rankin, Benjamin	"	
Robinson, John	"	
Rutherford, Robert	"	Vice Henry H. Prewitt.
Sanders, John	"	
Shryock, Christian	"	Died of typhus Nov., 1812. (7)
Smith, Joseph	"	POW Jan. 22. (4)
South, Rowland H.	"	
Summers, Robert	"	
Summers, William	"	
Sutton, Samuel	"	POW Jan. 22. (4)
Tericks, Samuel	"	Tetricks? POW Jan. 22. (4)
True, William	"	POW Jan. 22. (4)
Varble, Jacob	"	POW Jan. 22. (2)
Veale, James	"	POW Jan. 22. (4)
Whittington, John	"	POW Jan. 22. (4)
Williamson, Anderson	"	POW Jan. 22. (4)
Wilson, William	"	POW Jan. 22. (4)

Captain John Edmiston's (Richard Bledsoe's) Company,
1st Rifle Regiment *(Continued)*

NAME	RANK	REMARKS
Winn, Adam	Private	
Winn, Thomas, Jr.	"	
Yates, George	"	

(1) *Official roster of Officers of the war of 1812-15*, MS, Kentucky Historical Society.
(2) *Palladium*, 24 Feb. 1813.
(3) *Official report of killed and wounded . . . Jan. 18, 1813.*
(4) *Palladium*, 24 Mar. 1813.
(5) *Ibid.*, 31 Mar. 1813.
(6) *Fayette County Pension Records.*
(7) *Palladium*, 2 Dec. 1812.

Captain Henry James's Company (Spies)
2nd Regiment, Kentucky Militia
September 1–October 1, 1812
(Pulaski County)

NAME	RANK	REMARKS
Henry James	Captain	POW Jan. 22. (2)
James Kennedy	Lieutenant	
David Farr	Ensign	Fain in Pulaski County tax lists.
William Carman	Sergeant	Cowan?
Joseph Girdley	"	Girdler in Pulaski County tax lists.
Robert Kennedy	"	
John Wiles	"	Whiles?
William C. Carter	Corporal	
Thomas Ferrell	"	POW Jan. 22. (1)
William Murphy	"	
John Scott	"	
Adams, James	Private	POW Jan. 22. (1)
Adams, Nathaniel	"	POW Jan. 22. (1)
Adams, Nimrod	"	
Adams, Thomas	"	
Ashley, John	"	
Barron, John	"	
Blunt, Miles	"	
Bundy, Reuben	"	
Chambers, Hugh	"	
Clifton, Isiah	"	
Clifton, Nehemiah	"	
Cook, Richard	"	

Rosters of Troops

Captain Henry James's Company (Spies)
2nd Regiment, Kentucky Militia *(Continued)*

NAME	RANK	REMARKS
Crouch, Aaron	Private	
Davis, William	"	
Depau, Charles	"	POW Jan. 22. (1)
Dixon, Timothy	"	POW Jan. 22. (1)
Dooling, Daniel	"	
Dooling, James	"	
Dooling, John	"	POW Jan. 22. (1)
Dooling, Thomas	"	
Dotson, Thomas	"	
Drummons, James	"	
Earles, Samuel	"	
Ellison, John	"	POW Jan. 22. (1)
Ferguson, David	"	
Fisher, John	"	POW Jan. 22. (1)
Fisher, Nathaniel	"	POW Jan. 22. (1)
Gabbert, William	"	
Gill, Richard	"	
Gilmore, Robert	"	POW Jan. 22. (1)
Girdley, James	"	Girdler? POW Jan. 22. (1)
Graves, John	"	
Griffin, Squire	"	
Hamilton, James	"	
Harring, Levi	"	
Harris, Barnabas	"	
Hendricks, James	"	
Hendricks, John	"	POW Jan. 22. (1)
Henson, Elijah	"	
Hite, Burton	"	POW Jan. 22. (1)
Holloway, Levy	"	
Jones, Jonathan	"	
Lewis, Mathew	"	POW Jan. 22. (1)
Long, Tackley	"	
Lynch, John	"	
McAllaster, George	"	
McClure, Eleazer	"	
McFall, Robert	"	POW Jan. 22. (1)
McGall, William	"	
McKinsey, James	"	
McWherter, Jesse	"	
Moore, William	"	POW Jan. 22. (1)
Murphy, John	"	POW Jan. 22. (1)
Nash, William	"	POW Jan. 22. (1)
Nichols, Alexander	"	
Noble, Mark	"	

Captain Henry James's Company (Spies)
2nd Regiment, Kentucky Militia *(Continued)*

NAME	RANK	REMARKS
Phelkins, John	Private	Felkins in Pulaski County tax lists.
Randle, Nimrod	"	
Ray, Elijah	"	
Raynolds, Henry	"	
Rife, Abraham	"	
Royalty, William	"	POW Jan. 22. (1)
Simpson, John	"	
Smith, John	"	POW Jan. 22. (1)
Spencer, Samuel	"	
Stephens, Thomas	"	
Stephens, William	"	
Sutherland, Daniel	"	
Toms, Anderson	"	Tombs in Pulaski County tax lists.
Upton, Benjamin	"	
Vanhook, Aaron	"	
Vanhook, Lawrence	"	
Walls, Gabriel	"	
Walls, Isaac S.	"	
Walls, Jacob	"	
Ware, John	"	
Warren, Gabriel	"	
Warren, Joel	"	

(1) *Palladium,* 24 Mar. 1813.
(2) *Niles' Weekly Register,* IV.

Captain William Garrard's Volunteer Light Dragoons
May, 1812–April, 1813
(Bourbon County)

NAME	RANK	REMARKS
William Garrard	Captain	
Edmund Baisey	1st Lieut.	WIA
David M. Hickman	2nd Lieut.	
Thomas McClanahan	3rd Lieut.	
Walker Thornton	Cornet	
Strawder J. Hawkins	Quarter Master	
Benjamin W. Edwards	Sgt. Major	
John Finch	Q. M. Sgt.	
Charles M. Clarkson	1st Sgt.	
William Barton	2nd Sgt.	

Rosters of Troops

Captain William Garrard's Volunteer Light Dragoons (Continued)

NAME	RANK	REMARKS
Edward McGuire	3rd Sgt.	
James Benson	4th Sgt.	
William Walton	1st Cpl.	
John S. Bristow	2nd Cpl.	
James Conn	3rd Cpl.	
John Metcalf	4th Cpl.	
Lewis Hutchinson	5th Cpl.	
James W. Bryant	6th Cpl.	
Nicholas Bryant	Sadler	
Joseph McConnel	Farrier	WIA
William Benear	Gunsmith	
Jacob Sharer	Blacksmith	
Ephraim Wilson	Trumpeter	
Baisman, John	Private	WIA
Ball, John	"	
Barton, Stephen	"	
Barton, Thomas	"	
Baylor, William	"	
Bedford, Stephen	"	
Bedford, Thomas	"	KIA
Bolding, Jesse	"	
Boswell, John E.	"	KIA
Brest, John	"	WIA
Brown, Beverly	"	KIA
Brown, Henry O.	"	
Brown, James	"	
Calwell, Samuel I.	"	
Clark, James	"	
Clark, John	"	Died in service.
Clinkenbeard, Jonathan	"	
Counts, Jacob	"	
Davis, William	"	
Duncan, Lewis	"	
Eastin, Thomas	"	WIA
Edwards, Gustavis	"	
Field, Silas	"	
Finch, James	"	
Funston, John	"	
Henderson, Samuel	"	Died in service.
Hickman, Thomas	"	
Hill, James	"	Died in service.
Hunt, James	"	
Johnston, James	"	
Jones, Garrard	"	
Jones, Lewis	"	

Captain William Garrard's Volunteer Light Dragoons *(Continued)*

NAME	RANK	REMARKS
Jones, William	Private	
Jones, William	"	
Kendrick, James	"	
Kerchivill, Thomas	"	
Langhorn, David	"	
Logson, John	"	
Loring, Fredic	"	"A little Frenchman."
Marshal, Thomas	"	
Metcalf, Charles	"	
Moore, George	"	
Moore, Horatio	"	
Mountjoy, William	"	
Neal, William P.	"	
Northcutt, William B.	"	
Owens, Stephen	"	
Owens, Wiatt	"	
Pepper, Abel	"	
Prewitt, Price	"	
Prichard, Talifona	"	
Reading, James Y.	"	
Richardson, Moses	"	WIA
Robinson, Garrard	"	
Robinson, John M.	"	Died in service.
Roland, Daniel	"	
Roy, Beverly	"	
Sanders, Isaac	"	WIA
Scott, Alexander	"	
Scott, William	"	WIA
Scott, William	"	
Shamblin, George	"	
Shelton, Colvin	"	
Shropshire, John	"	
Shy, Jacob	"	Badly frostbitten.
Smedley, Daniel	"	WIA
Smith, Charles	"	
Snody, John	"	
Terrel, John	"	
Thomas, Jacob	"	
Thomas, Robert	"	
Timberlake, Richard	"	
Todd, Jesse	"	
Toles, Henry	"	WIA
Waller, Edward	"	
Webb, James	"	
Webster, Thomas	"	WIA twice.
West, Roger P.	"	

Rosters of Troops

Captain William Garrard's Volunteer Light Dragoons *(Continued)*

NAME	RANK	REMARKS
Wilson, Henry	Private	WIA
Wilson, John	"	
Wilson, William	"	
Winn, John	"	
Woodyard, Walter	"	

"This Company is Composed of one hundred and Six men and but two Maried Men in it and twenty of them were own Cousins.

"Uniform of the Company. Deep Blue Broad Cloth Coatee and pantiloons trimed with White Lace. Red Velvet Vest trimed with the Same. Jacked Leather Cap with Bear Skin over the top. Black Cockade with a Silver Eagle in the Center. Black plume tiped with Red, Boots, and Spurs, &c." Roster and comment from the War of 1812 diary of William B. Northcutt. [Owned by the Kentucky Historical Society.]

BIBLIOGRAPHY
and INDEX

BIBLIOGRAPHY

In addition to many county court records, genealogical compilations, and personal correspondence files, the main sources below were consulted.

PRINTED SOURCES

Acklen, Jeannette Tillotson. *Tennessee Records: Bible Records and Marriage Bonds.* Nashville: Cullom & Ghertner, 1933.

_____ *Tennessee Records: Tombstone Inscriptions and Manuscripts, Historical and Biographical.* Nashville: Cullom & Ghertner, 1933.

American Historical Association. *Annual Report, 1896.* Washington, D.C., 1896.

American State Papers: Documents, Legislative and Executive, of the Congress of the United States . . . Class V, Military Affairs, Vol. 1. Washington: Gales and Seaton, 1832.

Anderson, W. P. *Anderson-Overton: A Continuation of Anderson Family Records Published in 1936* . . . Cincinnati: The Gibson and Perin Co., 1945.

Appleton's Cyclopaedia of American Biography. 6 vols. New York: D. Appleton and Co., 1888-89.

Armstrong, John. *Notices of the War of 1812.* 2 vols. New York: Wiley & Putnam, 1840.

Atherton, William. *Narrative of the Sufferings & Defeat of the North-Western Army, under General Winchester: Massacre of the Prisoners.* . . . Frankfort, Ky.: A. G. Hodges, 1842.

Barbarities of the Enemy, Exposed in A Report of the Committee of the House of Representatives of the United States, Appointed to enquire into the spirit and manner in which the war has been waged by the enemy: And the Documents Accompanying Said Report. Troy, N. Y.: Printed by Francis Adancourt, 1813.

Biographical Directory of the American Congress, 1774-1927. . . . (Sixty-ninth Congress, Second Sess. House Doc. 783.) Washington: Government Printing Office, 1928.

Biographical Encyclopaedia of Kentucky of the Dead and Living Men of the Nineteenth Century. Cincinnati: J. M. Armstrong & Co., 1878.

Brown, Orlando. "The Governors of Kentucky," *Register of the Kentucky Historical Society,* XLIX (1951).

Butler, Mann. *A History of the Commonwealth of Kentucky.* . . . 2nd ed. Cincinnati: J. A. James, etc., 1836.

Clark, Sarah Graves. "Some Lines of the Graves Family in the Blue Grass," *Register of the Kentucky Historical Society,* XXXIV (1936).

Clay, Henrietta. *Bits of Family History.* [Lexington, Ky.: Clay Printing Co., 1933.]

Cleaves, Freeman. *Old Tippecanoe: William Henry Harrison and His Time.* New York: Charles Scribner's Sons, 1939.

Clift, G. Glenn. *"Corn Stalk" Militia of Kentucky, 1792-1811.* Frankfort: Kentucky Historical Society, 1957.

_____ *The Governors of Kentucky, 1792-1942.* Cynthiana, Ky.: Hobson Press, 1942.

_____ *History of Maysville and Mason County, Kentucky.* Vol. 1. Lexington: Transylvania Printing Co.; 1936.

Coffin, William F. *1812: The War, and its Moral: A Canadian Chronicle.* Montreal: John Lovell, 1864.

Collins, Richard H. *History of Kentucky* . . . 2 vols. Louisville: John P. Morton & Co., 1924.

Conrad, Howard L. *Encyclopaedia of the History of Missouri.* . . . 5 vols. New York: The Southern History Co., 1901.

Crittenden, H. H. (comp.). *The Crittenden Memoirs.* New York: G. P. Putnam's Sons, 1936.

Cullum, George W. *Register of the Officers and Graduates of the U. S. Military Academy . . . To January 1, 1850.* New York: J. F. Trow, 1850.

Darnall (Darnell, Darnold), Elias. *A Journal Containing an Accurate & Interesting Account of the Hardships, Sufferings, Battles, Defeat and Captivity of Those Heroic Kentucky Volunteers and Regulars, Commanded by General Winchester in the Years 1812-1813.* Paris, Ky.: Joel R. Lyle, 1813.

Darnell, Ermina Jett. *Forks of Elkhorn Church.* Louisville, Ky.: Standard Printing Co., 1946.

Dawson, Moses. *A Historical Narrative of the Civil and Military Services of Major-General William H. Harrison.* Cincinnati: n.p., 1824.

Dembitz, Lewis N. *Kentucky Jurisprudence . . . with An Introduction on the Sources of Kentucky Law.* Louisville: John P. Morton & Co., 1890.

Bibliography and Index 237

des Cognets, Anna Russell. *Governor Garrard of Kentucky, His Descendants and Relatives.* Lexington, Ky.: James M. Byrnes, 1898.

DeWitt, John H. "General James Winchester, 1752-1826," *Tennessee Historical Magazine,* I (1915).

Dictionary of American History. Vol. IV. New York: Charles Scribner's Sons, 1946.

Drane, Maude Johnston. *History of Henry County, Kentucky.* [Louisville: Franklin Printing Co., 1948.]

Draper, Lyman C. "Biographical Field Notes," *Quarterly Bulletin of The Historical Society of Northwestern Ohio,* V (1933).

_____ *King's Mountain and Its Heroes: History of the Battle of King's Mountain, October 7th, 1780. . . .* New York: Dauber & Pine Bookshops, Inc., 1929.

Dudley, Thomas P. "Battles and Massacre at Frenchtown, Michigan, January, 1813," *Western Reserve Historical Society, Historical and Archaeological Tracts,* No. 1, 1893.

Dunn, C. Frank. "Captain Nathaniel G. S. Hart," *The Filson Club History Quarterly,* XXIV (1950).

Esarey, Logan (ed.). *Messages and Letters of William Henry Harrison.* 2 vols. ("Indiana Historical Collections," VII, IX.) Indianapolis: Indiana Historical Commission, 1922.

Federal Writers' Project. *Kentucky: A Guide to the Bluegrass State.* ("American Guide Series.") New York: Hastings House, 1954.

Fish, Carl R. *American Diplomacy.* New York: Henry Holt and Co., 1923.

French, Janie Preston Collup, and Zella Armstrong. *The Crockett Family.* ("Notable Southern Families," V.) Bristol, Tenn.: The King Printing Co., 1928.

Gaines, B. O. *The B. O. Gaines History of Scott County [Kentucky].* 2 vols. Georgetown, Ky.: B. O. Gaines Printery, 1905.

Gordon, Major Maurice. *History of Hopkins County, Kentucky.* (Typescript, Kentucky Historical Society.)

Green, Thomas Marshall. *Historic Families of Kentucky. . . .* Cincinnati: Robert Clarke & Co., 1889.

Griffin, G. W. *Memoir of Col. Chas. S. Todd.* Philadelphia: Claxton, Remsen & Haffelfinger, 1873.

Harris, Malcolm H. *History of Louisa County, Virginia.* Richmond: The Dietz Press, 1936.

Heitman, Francis B. *Historical Register and Dictionary of the United States Army, From Its Organization, September 29, 1789, to March 2, 1903.* 2 vols. Washington: Government Printing Office, 1903.

_____ *Historical Register of the Officers of the Continental Army during the War of the Revolution.* . . . Rev. Ed. Washington: Rare Book Shop Publishing Co., 1914.

History of Howard and Cooper Counties, Missouri. . . . St. Louis: National Historical Co., 1883.

History of Monroe and Shelby Counties, Missouri. . . . St. Louis: National Historical Co., 1884.

History of Pike County, Missouri: An Encyclopedia of Useful Information and a Compendium of Actual Facts. Des Moines, Iowa: Mills & Co., 1883.

Hodge, Frederick Webb (ed.). *Handbook of American Indians.* 2 vols. ("Smithsonian Institution, Bureau of American Ethnology," Bull. 30.) Washington: Government Printing Office, 1907, 1910.

Johnson, L. F. *The History of Franklin County, Kentucky.* Frankfort: Roberts Printing Co., 1912.

Johnston, J. Stoddard. "Colonel Asa Payne," *Register of the Kentucky Historical Society,* XXVI (1928).

Kentucky. Adjutant General. *Report of the Adjutant General of the State of Kentucky: Soldiers of the War of 1812.* Frankfort: Capital Office: E. Polk Johnson, 1891.

_____ *Report of the Adjutant General of the State of Kentucky: Mexican War Veterans.* Frankfort: Capital Office: John D. Woods, 1889.

Kentucky. General Assembly. *Acts,* 1809, 1812, 1823-24, 1824-25, 1850-51.

_____ *Journal of the Senate,* 1850-51.

Kentucky Pioneer Doctors. Harrodsburg: Daniel M. Hutton, 1934.

Lander, David. *History of The Lander Family of Virginia and Kentucky.* Chicago: Regan Printing House, 1926.

Lanman, Charles. *Biographical Annals of the Civil Government of the United States.* Washington: Government Printing Office, 1876.

Leavy, William A. "A Memoir of Lexington and its Vicinity," *Register of the Kentucky Historical Society,* XL (1942).

Levin, H. (ed.) *The Lawyers and Lawmakers of Kentucky.* Chicago: The Lewis Publishing Co., 1897.

Bibliography and Index 239

"The Lexington Light Infantry Company, War of 1812," *Register of the Kentucky Historical Society*, XLII (1944).

Lossing, Benson John (ed.). *Harper's Encyclopedia of United States History from 458 A.D. to 1915.* 10 vols. New York: Harper and Brothers, 1901-15.

_____ *The Pictorial Field-Book of the War of 1812.* New York: Harper and Brothers, 1869.

McAfee, Robert B. *History of the Late War in the Western Country.* ... Lexington, Ky.: Worsley and Smith, 1816.

_____ "The Life and Times of Robt. B. McAfee and his Family Connections," *Register of the Kentucky Historical Society*, XXV (1927).

McCormack, J. N. *Some of the Medical Pioneers of Kentucky.* Bowling Green, Ky.: The Times-Journal Publishing Co., 1917.

McElroy, Robert M. *Kentucky in the Nation's History.* New York: Moffat, Yard and Co., 1909.

McMaster, John B. *History of the People of the United States.* ... 8 vols. New York: D. Appleton and Co., 1883-1913.

Marshall, Humphrey. *History of Kentucky.* ... 2 vols. Frankfort: Geo. S. Robinson, 1824.

Meyer, Leland Winfield. *The Life and Times of Colonel Richard M. Johnson of Kentucky.* New York: Columbia University Press, 1932.

Michigan Pioneer and Historical Society Collections. 40 vols. Lansing: The Society, etc., 1877-1929.

Narrative of the Life of General Leslie Combs: Embracing Incidents in the Early History of the Northwestern Territory. Washington: J. T. and Lem. Towers, 1855.

Nolte, Vincent. *Fifty Years on Both Hemispheres.* ... New York: J. S. Redfield, 1854.

Obituary Addresses Delivered upon the Occasion of the Re-interment of the Remains of Gen. Chas. Scott, Maj. Wm. T. Barry, and Capt. Bland Ballard and Wife, In the Cemetery at Frankfort, November 8, 1854. Frankfort, Ky.: A. G. Hodges, 1855.

Owen, Thomas McAdory. "William Strother, of Virginia, and his Descendants," *Publications of The Southern History Association*, 1898.

"Papers and Orderly Book of Brigadier General James Winchester," *Historical Collections, Collections and Researches made by the Michigan Pioneer and Historical Society*, 1902.

Paxton, W. M. *Annals of Platte County, Missouri.* . . . Kansas City: Hudson-Kimberly Publishing Co., 1897.

-------- *The Marshall Family.* Cincinnati: Robert Clarke & Co., 1885.

Payne, Brooke. *The Paynes of Virginia.* Richmond: William Byrd Press, 1937.

Perrin, William Henry (ed.). *History of Bourbon, Scott, Harrison and Nicholas Counties, Kentucky: With an Outline Sketch of the Blue Grass Region,* by Robert Peter, M.D. Chicago: O. L. Baskin & Co., 1882.

-------- *Kentucky. A History of the State.* . . . Louisville, Chicago: F. A. Battey & Co., 1888.

Peter, Robert. *Transylvania University: Its Origin, Rise, Decline, and Fall.* ("Filson Club Publications," No. 11.) Louisville, Ky.: John P. Morton and Co., 1896.

Pirtle, Alfred. *The Battle of Tippecanoe.* ("Filson Club Publications," No. 15.) Louisville, Ky.: John P. Morton and Co., 1900.

Power, John Carroll. *History of the Early Settlers of Sangamon County, Illinois.* Springfield: Edwin A. Wilson and Co., 1876.

Pratt, Mary B. *Our Relations: Dudley-Pratt Families.* Indianapolis: Pratt-Foster Co., n.d.

Quaife, Milo M. (ed.). *The John Askin Papers.* 2 vols. ("Burton Historical Records.") Detroit: Detroit Library Commission, 1928, 1931.

Railey, William E. *History of Woodford County [Kentucky].* Frankfort: Roberts Printing Co., 1928.

Ranck, George W. *History of Lexington, Kentucky: Its Early Annals and Recent Progress.* . . . Cincinnati: Robert Clarke & Co., 1872.

Reid, Richard. *Historical Sketches of Montgomery County [Kentucky].* . . . *Read at the Fourth of July Celebration, 1876.* n.p., n.d.

Richardson, John. *Richardson's War of 1812: With Notes and a Life of the Author,* by Alexander Clark Casselman. Toronto: Historical Publishing Co., 1902.

Robertson, George. *An Outline of the Life of George Robertson, written by Himself.* Lexington, Ky.: Transylvania Printing Co., 1876.

Shaler, Nathaniel S. *A General Account of the Commonwealth of Kentucky.* . . . Cambridge, Mass.: John Wilson and Son, 1876.

Shinn, Josiah H. *Pioneers and Makers of Arkansas.* [Little Rock: Democrat Printing & Lithographing Co., 1908.]

Bibliography and Index 241

Simpson, Elizabeth M. *Bluegrass Houses and their Traditions.* Lexington, Ky.: Transylvania Press, 1932.

Slocum, Charles E. "The Origin, Description and Service of Fort Winchester...," *Ohio Archaeological and Historical Society Publications,* 1900-01.

Todd, Charles S., and Benjamin Drake. *Sketches of the Civil and Military Services of William Henry Harrison.* Rev. and Enl. by James H. Perkins. Cincinnati: J. A. and U. P. James, 1847.

Townsend, William H. *Lincoln and His Wife's Home Town.* Indianapolis: The Bobbs-Merrill Co., 1929.

United States. Senate. *Report From the Secretary of War, In Obedience to Resolutions of the Senate of the 5th and 30th of June, 1834, and the 3rd of March, 1835, In Relation to the Pension Establishment of the United States.* (Senate Doc. 514.) 3 vols. Washington: Printed by Duff Green, 1835.

Williams, John Augustus. *In Memoriam: Remarks on the Life and Character of General Samuel L. Williams.* Cincinnati: Robert Clarke & Co., 1872.

Willis, Geo. L., Sr. *History of Shelby County, Kentucky.* Shelby County Genealogical-Historical Society's Committee on Printing, 1929.

[Winchester, James.] *Historical Details, having Relation to the Campaign of the North-Western Army under Generals Harrison and Winchester, during the Winter of 1812-13, together with Some Particulars relating to the Surrender of Fort Bowyer, &c.* Lexington, Ky.: Worsley & Smith, 1818.

Witherell, B. F. H. "Reminiscences of the North-West," *Third Annual Report and Collections of the State Historical Society of Wisconsin, for the Year 1856.* Madison: Calkins & Webb, 1857.

Young, Bennett H. *The Battle of the Thames.* ("Filson Club Publications," No. 18.) Louisville, Ky.: John P. Morton and Co., 1903.

_____ *History of Jessamine County, Kentucky.* Louisville, Ky.: Courier-Journal Job Printing Co., 1898.

NEWSPAPERS

Argus of Western America [Frankfort, Kentucky].
Clark County Democrat [Winchester, Kentucky].
The Commonwealth [Frankfort, Kentucky].
Daily Kentucky Yeoman [Frankfort, Kentucky].

Kentucky Gazette [Lexington, Kentucky].
Lexington [Kentucky] *Observer and Reporter.*
Louisville [Kentucky] *Western Courier.*
The Palladium [Frankfort, Kentucky].
Reporter [Lexington, Kentucky].
Trump of Fame [Warren, Ohio].
The Western Citizen [Paris, Kentucky].
The Western Spy [Cincinnati, Ohio].
Winchester [Kentucky] *Advertiser.*

PERIODICALS

East Tennessee Historical Society's Publications [Knoxville, Tennessee].
The Filson Club History Quarterly [Louisville, Kentucky]
Historical and Archaeological Tracts, Western Reserve Historical Society [Cleveland, Ohio].
Journal of the Illinois State Historical Society [Springfield, Illinois].
Missouri Historical Review [Columbia, Missouri].
Niles' Weekly Register [Baltimore, Maryland].
Ohio Archaeological and Historical Society Publications [Columbus, Ohio].
Ohio Historical and Philosophical Quarterly [Cincinnati, Ohio].
Quarterly Bulletin of The Historical Society of Northwestern Ohio [Toledo, Ohio].
Register of the Kentucky Historical Society [Frankfort, Kentucky].
Tennessee Historical Magazine [Nashville, Tennessee].

MANUSCRIPT SOURCES

Abstract of the Killed Wounded and Missing in the Action at French Town on the River Raisin 22nd of January 1813, James Garrard, Jr. (photostat)

Thomas Bodley Papers [Kentucky Historical Society]. (1 folder)

Commissioned Officers War of 1812-16 [Kentucky Historical Society]. (1 volume)

Draper MSS, State Historical Society of Wisconsin [Madison, Wisconsin].

Bibliography and Index 243

C. Frank Dunn Manuscripts [Kentucky Historical Society]. (130 volumes)

General and Field Officers of Kentucky 1812-1816 [Kentucky Historical Society]. (1 volume)

William Henry Harrison Papers [Kentucky Historical Society]. (1 folder)

Kentucky. Governor, 1800-1804 (Garrard). Executive Journal, 1800-1804 [Kentucky Historical Society]. (1 volume)

_____ Governor, 1804-1808 (Greenup). Papers Pertaining to the Militia, 1804-1808 [Kentucky Historical Society, Section 1, Box 7, Jackets 38-46].

_____ Governor, 1808-1812 (Scott). Papers Relating to Volunteers, War of 1812 [Kentucky Historical Society, Section 1, Box 8, Jackets 53-55]; Executive Journal, 1808-1812 [Kentucky Historical Society]. (1 volume)

_____ Governor, 1812-1816 (Shelby). Executive Journal, 1812-1816; Letter Book "A"; Letter Book "B" [Kentucky Historical Society]. (3 volumes)

William B. Northcutt Diary [Kentucky Historical Society]. (1 volume)

Official Roster of Officers of the War 1812-15 [Kentucky Historical Society]. (1 volume)

Register of Commissions issued to Captains, Lieutenants and Ensigns, August, 1799–December, 1804 [Kentucky Historical Society]. (1 volume)

INDEX

INDEX

Abbott, Edward T., 180
Abbott, H. G., 180
Ackran, Sergeant James M., 214
Acton, Burgess, 155
Acton, Nancy Kelly, 155
Acton, William, 174
Adair, John, 125
Adams, Daniel, 191
Adams, Feathergill, 224
Adams, James, 210, 226
Adams, John, 210, 224
Adams, President John Quincy, 130
Adams, Nathaniel, 226
Adams, Nimrod, 226
Adams, Thomas, 226
Adams, William, 210
Adjutant, Ebenezer, 182
Adkerson, Isiah, 198
Adkins, James, 180
Advertiser, Winchester, Ky., 142
Agnew, Sergeant Henry, 176
Akers, James, 208
Akin, Alexander, 215
Alexander, A. J., 126
Alexander, Andrew, 126
Alexander, Andrew J., 126-27
Alexander, Appoline, 126
Alexander, Evalinia Martin, 127
Alexander, George M., 127
Alexander, M., 126
Alexander, Mary Campbell, 127
Alexander, Myra, 126-27
Alexander, William, 180
Alexander, William M., 126
Allen, Anna Maria, 115
Allen, Beverly, 224
Allen, Corporal Charles F., 191
Allen, David, 198
Allen, Eliza Sarah, 115
Allen, Francis I., 191
Allen, Francis W., 191
Allen, Hugh, 191
Allen, James, 113, 198
Allen, Jane Logan, 114-15
Allen, John, 198
Allen, Lieutenant Colonel John, 17-18, 37, 50, 61, 91, 125, 139, 145, 152, 163; account of troop movements, 30-34; advances toward Frenchtown, 47ff; appointed to command, 16; biography, 113-16; county named for, 87, 114; death, 64n, 65-66, 79; in first battle at River Raisin, 53ff; letter, 61; marches to St. Marys, 24-25; quells revolt among militiamen, 35-36; regiment of, 207-26; reinforces regulars at River Raisin, 64-65; servant of, 95
Allen, Mary Kelsey, 113, 115
Allen, Robert, 180
Allen, Samuel, 184
Allen County, Kentucky, origin of name, 114
Allenthorp, Jacob, 217
Allison, Andrew, 191
Allison, John, 174
Alloway, John, 189
Alphen, Ransom, 189
Alsop, Alexander, 202
Amarine, George, 208
Amarine, Jonathan, 208
Ames, Nicholas, 217
Amherstburg, Canada, 62-63, 89, 166-68; *see also* Fort Malden
Ammerman, Albert, 83-84, 86, 87n, 188
Amos, Nicholas, 217
Anders, Robert, 173
Anderson, John, 198
Anderson, Colonel John, 80n
Anderson, Oliver, 205
Anderson, Thomas, 191, 198
Andrews, Colonel John, 58
Andrews, Robert, 174
Ansberry, Thomas, 224
Antrebus, Corporal Benjamin, 203
Argus of Western America, 102
Arkansas Territory, 117
Armstrong, James, 184
Armstrong, John, 202
Armstrong, Joseph, 219
Armstrong, Levy, 205
Armstrong, Samuel, 198
Armstrong, William, 217
Arnett, John, 205
Arnold, Berrisford, 219
Arnold, Robert, 215
Arnold, Scott, 220
Ashbrook, John, 203
Ashby, Henderson, 213
Ashby, Willoughby, 213
Ashley, John, 226
Askin, John, 71n, 89n
Athens, James, 196
Athers, Nathaniel, 196
Atherton, Henry, 213
Atherton, William, 75, 85, 213

Atwood, Robert, 222
Auglaize River, 32, 37
Austin, George, 215

Baby, Duperon, 167
Baby, Colonel James, biography, 167
Bagby, John, 180
Bagwell, Cary, 205
Bailey, Benjamin, 186
Bails, Russell, 210
Baisey, Lieutenant Edmund, 228
Baisman, John, 229
Baker, Ensign Isaac L., 87, 120, 157, 173; report on dead at River Raisin, 102; takes charge of prisoners, 93-94
Baker, Jacob, 178
Baker, Thomas, 188
Balance, Proctor, 196
Baldwin, ------, 180
Baldwin, Ira, 217
Ball, Jacob, 224
Ball, Major James V., 148
Ball, John, 229
Ballard, Anderson, 202
Ballard, Bland, 214
Ballard, Captain Bland Williams, 112, 125, 138; advances toward River Raisin, 51ff; appointed to command, 16; at Fort Defiance, 32-34; biography, 138-41; company of, 214-16; county named for, 87, 140
Ballard, Diana Matthews, 141
Ballard, Dorothy, 141
Ballard, Elizabeth Weaver Garrett, 141
Ballard, Elizabeth Williamson, 141
Ballard, James, 141
Ballard, Martha, 141
Ballard, Mary, 141
Ballard, Nancy, 141
Ballard, Sally, 141
Ballard, Susan, 141
Ballard Massacre, 140
Ballengall, David, 5
Ballenger, Asa, 198
Balyell, John, 178
Bank of Kentucky, 21
Bank of Limestone, 156
Bannister, John, 186
Baptist Association of Missouri, 162
Barbee, Corporal Ira, 200
Barbee, John, 189
Barbee, Lieutenant Colonel Joshua, 37
Barbie, John, 200
Bardstown, Ky., 113, 163
Barker, John, Jr., 202

Barker, Corporal Thomas, 200
Barkley, John, 161
Barkley, Susannah, 160-61
Barkley, William, 194
Barnes, Corporal Alfred, 203
Barnes, James, 208
Barnes, Oliver, 210
Barnes, Thomas, 208
Barnett, ------, 124
Barnett, Elsie McClenahan, 124
Barney, William, 203
Barnum, Barney, 189
Barr, George, 194
Barr, James B., 196
Barron, John, 226
Barrow, Corporal Cornelius, 196
Bartine, Nicholas, 213
Barton, Joshua, 178
Barton, Karswell, 174
Barton, Roswell, 176
Barton, Stephen, 229
Barton, Thomas, 229
Barton, Sergeant William, 228
Bashaw, Cuthbert, 182
Bashaw, William, 182
Bassett, James, 220
Bassnet, William, 208
Bates, Alfred, 174
Bath County, Ky., militia company from, 181-83
Baxter, George, 203
Baxter, John, 203
Bay, Joseph, 178
Baylor, William, 229
Beal, Henry, 215
Beale, Robert, 215
Bean, William, 196
Beard, George N., 188
Beard, Henry, 192
Beatum, Adam, 224
Beckett, Joseph, 217
Beckett, Samuel, 178
Beckley, John, 192
Beckner, Colonel Lucien, xii
Bedford, Stephen, 229
Bedford, Thomas, 229
Beeson, Lewis, xii
Beeturn, Adam, 224
Bell, David, 155
Bell, John P., 222
Bell, Judith, 155
Bell, Judith Cary, 155
Bell, Patterson, 198
Bell, Robert, 222
Bell, Sarah, 155

Bibliography and Index

Bell, Thomas, 178
Bell, Thomas P., 222
Bell, William, 217
Bell, William C., 192
Bellair, Oliver, 92-93
Bellows, Jacob, 186
Benear, William, 229
Bennett, George, 186
Bennett, Jacob, 215
Bennett, James, 194
Bennett, Lavoler, 215
Benson, Sergeant James, 229
Benson, Sergeant Thomas S., 217
Bernett, B., 203
Berry, Elizabeth, 143
Berry, George, 196
Berry, Robert, 213
Berry, Thomas, 143
Bettersworth, Fielding, 208
Bettersworth, Jesse, 208
Bevis, William, 222
Bickley, John, 192
Biddle, Caleb, 203
Big Spring, Ky., 20
Biggs, John, 178
Biggs, Landy, 198
Bingham, George, 208
Bird, Henry, 213
Birk, Samuel, 213
Biscoe, James, 220
Bishop, John, 205
Bittingham, John, 224
Black, Robert, 210
~Black, Susan, 108
~Black Hawk, biography, 168
Black Hawk War, 168
Black Swamp, Ohio, 40, 42-43, 68
Blackbird (Potawatomi), 170
Blackburn, Samuel, 220
Blackburn, Thomas H., 202
Blackburn, William, 182
Blackwell, David, 208
Blackwell, Ezekiel, 208
Blackwell, James, 224
Blackwell, Thomas H., 202
Blain, John, 186
Blair, Appoline Alexander, 126
Blair, Francis P., 126
Blair, James, 210
Blair, Samuel, 210
Blake, Beverly A., 174
Blake, Braxton, 173
Blake, John, 196
Blake, Peyton, 196
Blakeney, William, 178

Blandford, John B., 215
Blanton, Richard, 191
Bledsoe, Captain Richard, 51, 61, 66, 107, 207; assumes command of Captain Edmiston's company, 142; biography, 142; company of, 224-26
Bledsoe, Sally Gess, 142
Bledsoe, Sarah, 142
Blue Jacket, George, 58
Blue Licks, Battle of, 127, 167
Blunt, Miles, 226
Blythe, Charles, 198
Blythe, Reverend James, 20
Blythe, James Ebenezer, 192; death, 84
Blythe, William, 174
Bodley, Major Thomas, 40-41
Boggs, James, 208
Boggs, John W., 208
Bolding, Jesse, 229
Bollas, James W., 213
Bomar, Sergeant James H., 222
~Boone, Isaac, 220
~Boone, Josiah, 215
Boone County, Ky., militia company from, 189-90
Booth, Elijah, 203
Booth, Harrison, 217
Boswell, John E., 229
Boswell, General William, 147
Boswell, Sergeant William E., 210
Botts, B., 220
Botts, Sergeant John, 205
Boulard, Antoine, 83
Bould, Peter, 178
"Bourbon County Blues," 17, 24, 31-34, 147-48, 228-31
Bourbon County, Ky., militia companies from, 178-79, 210-12, 217-19; Volunteer Light Dragoons, 228-31
Bourne, Ensign Daniel, 193
Bowen, John, 217
Bower, Anna Levering, 134
Bower, Betsy Withers, 133
Bower, Catherine Long, 134
Bower, Dr. Gustavus Miller, 84, 85n, 87, 134, 153, 191; biography, 133-34; cares for wounded at Frenchtown, 74ff; court-martialed, 39; takes charge of prisoners, 93
Bower, Isabella, 134
Bower, Martha Crockett, 134
Bower, Michael, 133
Bowles, Ensign Joseph, 51, 178
Bowman, Colonel John, 138
Boyd, William, 215

Boyer, Ezra, 202
Boyer, Ira; see Ezra Boyer
Boyle, John, 217
Bradford, Charles, 84, 192
Bradford, Sergeant George, 184
Bradley, Samuel, 224
Bradshaw, Smith, 205
Brandge, Bartlett, 203
Brandy Jack, 68
Branham, John, 177
Branham, Lieutenant Tarenor R., 184
Brasfield, Eliza, 143
Brasfield, Elizabeth Berry, 143
Brasfield, Elizabeth Mimms, 143
Brasfield, James, 143
Brasfield, Jane Lafferty, 143
Brasfield, Nancy, 143
Brasfield, Polly, 143
Brasfield, Captain Wiley R., 25; appointed to command, 16; biography, 142-43; company of, 195-97; resigns his commission, 154
Bratton, Joseph, 208
Bratton, William, 220
Breckenridge, Eddy L., 210
Breckinridge, Alexander, 182
Breedlove, Major, 184
Bremner, Lieutenant ——, 97n
Brent, Elizabeth, 150
Brent, Hugh, 150
Brest, John, 229
Bresto, Ezra, 182
Brice, Benoni, 217
Brice, Private John J., escapes Indians at Frenchtown, 68
Brice, John T., 194
Bridges, Benjamin, Sr., 215
Bridges, Sergeant Benjamin, 207
Bridges, John, 210
Briggs, Jane, 130
Brinigan, John, 196
Brink, Ephraim, 224
Brink, Samuel, 224
Bristow, Corporal John S., 229
British, at River Raisin, 166-68; attack Frenchtown, 63ff; flag at Frankfort, Ky., 100; forces at Frenchtown, 49-50; killed at Frenchtown, 70n; losses at Frenchtown, 71; prisoners at Frankfort, Ky., 96ff; release American prisoners, 92ff
Britterham, German, 224
Brittingham, John, 224
Brock, Hugh, 220

Brock, General Sir Isaac, 24, 166-67; surrender of Detroit, 22
Brock, John, 220
Brook, Benjamin M., 156
Brook, Paulina Ann, 156
Brooks, Alexander, 222
Brooks, Colonel Edward, 104-06
Brooks, Corporal James, 222
Brooks, Thomas, 215
Brooks, Lieutenant Thomas, 222
Brookshire, Benjamin, 203
Brown, Anderson, 222
Brown, Ann Hart, 149
Brown, Arthur, 208
Brown, Beverly, 229
Brown, Elizabeth (Todd) Grimsley, 131
Brown, Henry O., 229
Brown, Sergeant Hugh, 210
Brown, Irwin, 210
Brown, James, 149, 186, 229
Brown, John, 186, 211, 222
Brown, Reverend John H., 131
Brown, Colonel Orlando, 18, 125-26
Brown, Overton, 220
Brown, Samuel, 205
Brown, Corporal Samuel W., 198
Brown, Thomas, 194
Brown, William, 220
Brown, Corporal Willis, 222
Browning, James, 188
Brownstown, Michigan Territory, 62, 85, 166
Bruce, Durrett, 203
Bruner, Jacob, 215
Brunett, Elijah, 208
Bryan, Augustus, 222
Bryan, Luke, 188
Bryan, Corporal Thomas, 187
Bryan, Sergeant William, 187
Bryant, Corporal James W., 229
Bryant, Morgan, 224
Bryant, Nicholas, 229
Buchanan, Janet, 121
Buchannon, Abraham, 222
Buckner, George, 224
Buffalo, New York, prisoners reach, 95
Bullitt, Miss ——, 131
Bullock, Mrs. Waller O., 109-10
Bundy, Reuben, 226
Burbridge, Jesse, 180, 182
Burbridge, John, 180
Burbridge, William, 182
Burch, Sergeant Stapleton C., 224
Burk, Benjamin, 205

Bibliography and Index 251

Burk, Samuel, 213
Burkes, John, 182
Burmun, Peter M., 204
Burnam, Bennett, 208
Burnes, John, 124-25
Burnett, B., 203
Burnett, James, 194
Burnett, William, 213
Burns, Andrew, 224
Burns, Ignatius, 186
Burns, James, 188
Burns, Robert, 186
Burr, Aaron, 6, 114
Burrass, James, 208
Burton, David, 208
Burwell, William, 213
Busey, William, 178
Bush, Tilman, 204
Butler, Eliza Allen, 115
Butler, John, 202
Butler, Mann, 35n
Butler, Pierce, 115
Butler, William, 217
Butler, Ensign William O., 51, 174, 191; heroism on River Raisin, 54-55, 69; poem by, 76-79
Butler's Rangers, 169
Bynes, Andrew, 224
Byrd, Abraham, 217
Byrd, John, 217
Byron, John, 174

Caldwell, Ensign ———, 51
Caldwell, Captain Billy, biography, 168-69
Caldwell, Henry C., 157
Caldwell, James, 222
Caldwell, Marie McClenahan, 124
Caldwell, Corporal Nathaniel H., 194
Caldwell, Robert, 124
Caldwell, Sally, 157
Caldwell, William, 65
Caldwell, Colonel William, 168-69
Caldwell, Lieutenant William, 193
Caldwell's Rangers, 167
Calhoun, John C., 8
Calhoun, 162
Calker, Solomon, 192
Callender, Jacob, 194
Calvert, Martin, 220
Calwell, Samuel I., 229
Camel, Robert, 186
Camp, William, 174
Camp Carron River, 87, 88n; see also Camp on Carrying Back

Camp on Carrying Back, 90n, 123; see also Camp Carron River
Campbell, Reverend Alexander, 136
Campbell, J., 97n, 100
Campbell, James, 205
Campbell, John, 196
Campbell, John Douglas Sutherland, 9th Duke of Argyll, 145
Campbell, Mary, 127
Campbell, Robert T., 192
Campbell, William, 184
Campbell, Sergeant William, 189
Canada, annexation question, 7-8; militia at Frenchtown, 48
Cannon, fired when survivors came home, 95
Canon, James H., 208
Canton, China, 132
Caplinger, John, 215
Caplinger, Samuel, 215
Caplinger, Solomon, 215
Capps, Caleb, 196
Cardwell, Lieutenant ———, 40
Cardwell, Ensign George, 212
Cardwell, James, 205
Cardwell, Samuel, 205
Carlisle, Ky., 144
Carlton, George, 194
Carlton, Isaac, 194
Carlton, Noah, 194
Carman, Sergeant William, 226
Carneal, Thomas Davis, 17
Carr, Anna Maria, 132-33
Carr, Elizabeth Todd, 133
Carr, James, 186
Carr, John, 213
Carr, Nanon L., xii
Carr, Captain Thomas, 133
Carroll, Sergeant James, 184
Carter, John, 174
Carter, Kenyon, 198
Carter, William, 174, 184
Carter, Corporal William C., 226
Cartmell, David, 182
Cary, Mefford, 205
Casey, John, 173
Casey, Joshua, 174; see also John Casey
Cassady, Thomas, 178
Cave, Sergeant Uriel, 189
Cave, William, 182
Cavenaugh, Thomas, 208
Caw, Walter E., 224
Ceasar, Thomas, 173-74
Chadd, Samuel, 178

Chadd, William, 217
Chagrin, Marie Louise Sans, 167
Chamberlain, Corporal Thomas, 191
Chambers, Major ——, 97n, 99
Chambers, George W., 152
Chambers, Hugh, 226
Chambers, Major Peter, 32, 34
Chambers, Sally Hickman, 152
Chandler, Richard, 224
Chapman, John, 208, 215
Charles, Lewis, 192
Chase, Miss ——, 131
Chaumiere du Prairie, 136
Cherokee Indians, 145
Cherry, John, 189
Chesapeake, 1
Cheves, Langdon, 8
Chickamauga Indians, 145
Chickasaw Boundary Line, 108
Childers, Abraham, 188
Childers, Thomas, 174
Chiles, Ann, 131-32
Chiles, Elizabeth Dabney, 132
Chiles, Nancy; *see* Ann Chiles
Chiles, Phoebe, 132
Chiles, Corporal Richard, 196
Chiles, Walter Carr, 132
Chillicothe, Ohio, 98, 101
Chinn, Alfred, 200
Chinn, Charles, 224
Chinn, Ensign Francis, 210; death, 66-67n; in command at River Raisin, 54
Chinn, Humphrey, 200
Chinn, James, 208
Chinn, Corporal John P., 210
Chinn, Lieutenant John T., 51
Chinn, Joseph R., 219
Chinn, Nathaniel, 200
Chinn, Rawleigh, 211
Chinn, Richard H., 192
Chinn, Ensign Thomas, 51
Chinn, Ensign Thomas W., 211
Chinn, Sergeant William B., 210
Chism, James, 204
Chism, Corporal Richard, 219
Chrisholm, Nathaniel, 196
Chrisman, Sergeant George, 205
Christopher, John, 222
Christopher, Sergeant John, 207
Christy, Simeon, 189
Ciddle, Cal, 204
Cincinnati, Ohio, 101, 122
Clagget, T. Y., 224
Clark, Ann Bingham, 127
Clark, Benjamin L., 219

Clark, General George Rogers, 138-39, 154, 157
Clark, George W., 206
Clark, James, 136, 205, 229
Clark, John, 229
Clark, Joseph; 49, 56-57, 104, 220
Clark, Maria McCalla, 136
Clark, Nancy Bingham, 127
Clark, Philip, 220
Clark, Thomas, 177
Clark County, Ky., militia companies from, 158, 195-97, 203-05
Clark House; *see* Webster House
Clark's Run, Ky., 113
Clarke, John N., 188
Clarkson, Sergeant Charles M., 228
Clawson, Peter, 204
Clay, Henry, 4, 8, 21, 58, 114; addresses troops at Georgetown, Ky., 20; on Canadian annexation, 7-8; recommends Harrison for Major General, Kentucky Militia, 23; wife, 149
Clay, Lucretia Hart, 149
Clay, William W., 178
Cleaves, Freeman, 107
Clegett, T. Y., 224
Cleveland, George, 217
Cleyton, George, 200
Clift, Virginia Diller Gilmore, vii
Clifton, Isiah, 226
Clifton, Nehemiah, 226
Cline, Aaron, 213
Cline, Nicholas, 215
Clinkenbeard, Jonathan, 229
Clinton, Samuel, 180
Clothing for troops, 39-40
Cloverport, Ky., 115
Cluke, Fanny, 165
Coburn, Matilda Ann, 148
Cochran, Ensign ——, 97n
Cock, Henry D., 208
Cock, Jesse, 208
Cock, Samuel P., 192
Cockrill, Corporal B. S., 224
Cockrill, Benjamin, 224
Colbert, Martin, 220
Colbert, William, 200
Colbert, Willis, 200
Cole, Pleasant, 215
Coleman, Ambrose, 188
Coleman, Corporal Daniel, 196
Coleman, Elizabeth Montgomery, 128
Coleman, Frances, 120
Coleman, George, 128
Coleman, Mrs. Horace W., xii

Bibliography and Index   253

Coleman, Lieutenant Thomas, 187
Collete, Aaron, 213
Collier, Captain Coleman A., 25, 51, 61; appointed to command, 16; biography, 144; company of, 186-87; court-martialed, 39
Collier, Eliza Peterson, 144
Collier, Elizabeth, 144
Collier, Jane Howarton, 144
Collier, John, 144
Collier, Katharine Howarton, 144
Collier, Robert H., 144
Collier, William J., 144
Collins, Bartlett, 222
Collins, Elisha, 192
Collins, G., 97n
Collins, Richard, 180
Collins, Richard H., 159
Columbus (Miss.) *Democrat*, 154
Columbus, Miss., Rifle Company and Band, 154
Colvin, Bennett, 186
Colvin, James B., 188
Combs, Leslie, 42-43; in retreat at Frenchtown, 68
Comstock, Lieutenant Lyndon, 52, 191
Conally, Daniel, 213
Cone, Sergeant David, 210
Confederate States Army, 165
Conly, Robert, 189
Conn, Corporal James, 229
Connell, John T., 153
Conner, Rice, 194
Conway, William, 186
Conyers, Anne Horden, 138
Cook, Alexander, 198
Cook, J., 122
Cook, John, 182
Cook, Matthew, 174, 176
Cook, Richard, 226
Cook, Seth, 222
Cooke, William, 180
Cooly, John, 174
Coone, Sergeant David; see Sergeant David Cone
Coone, John, 211
Coone, Jone, 211
Cooper, Benjamin, 215
Cooper, James H., 182
Cooper, John, 204
Cooper, Robert, 182
Cooper, Sergeant William, 214
Cope, Malcolm T., 192
Cope, William, 184
Corbin, Nathan, 217

Corbin, Nicholas, 217
Corbin, Sergeant Thomas, 186
Cord, Ashkery, 186
Corman, George, 200
Cornelison, Aaron, 208
Cornelius, Terrill, 189
Cornwallis, Charles, 1st Marquis, 159
Cosby, Garland, 220
Cotgreave, Major W. W., 58
Cotton, John E., 224
Coulter, Dr. E. Merton, xiii
Counties, Kentucky, named for soldiers at River Raisin, 87, 114, 121, 140, 145, 150, 152, 157, 159, 163
Counts, Jacob, 229
Covington, Ky., Baptist Cemetery, 105; dead of Raisin at, 104-05
Cowan, Sergeant William, 226
Cox, Corporal James, 184
Cox, John, 220
Cox, Sergeant Joseph, 184
Cox, Thomas, 191
Cragfont, 108
Craig, Sergeant David, 187
Craig, James, 211
Craig, Walter, 175-76
Craig, William, 211
Craig's Hill, Ky., 20
Craver, George, 217
Cravins, Sergeant William, 224
Crawford, Alexander, 186, 192
Crawford, Robert, 217
Crawford, William, 169, 217
Criswell, Robert, 180
Crittenden, Anna Allen, 115
Crittenden, Henry, 115
Crittenden, Thomas Theodore, 115
Crockett, ———, 101, 164
Crockett, James, 196
Crockett, Colonel Joseph, 134
Crockett, Martha, 134
Crockett, Susan West, 164
Croffort, Alexander B., 178
Croghan, Major George, 166
Croslin, Benjamin, 206
Crosthwait, Warning, 196
Crouch, Aaron, 227
Crow, Corporal Abner T., 203
Crow, Thomas S., 189, 205
Crowder, William, 200
Cummings, Cal, 196
Cummings, James, 202
Cummins, Thomas, 184
Cunningham, Captain Isaac, 143
Cunningham, Mary, 159

Curles, Morgan, 208
Current, Elijah, 217
Cury, John, 180

Dailey, Francis, 215
Dailey, John, 215
Dailey, Lawrence, 192
Daly, Louise, 162
Dance, John, 188
Dance, William, 188
Daniel, John, 204, 213
Daniel, John W., 198
Daniels, John, 209
Danner, Samuel, 184
Danville, Ky., 113, 163
Darling, Abraham, 186
Darnaby, Edward, Sr., 147
Darnaby, Lucy Ellis, 147
Darnall; see Darnell, Darnold
Darnell, Allen, 198; death, 85
Darnell, Daniel, 198
Darnell, Elias, 22, 43-44, 48-49, 58, 80, 85, 198
Darnell; see also Darnold
Darnold, Hezekiah, 198
Darnold, Samuel, 198
Darnold, Zenas, 198
Darnold; see also Darnell
Daugherty, Ensign Jesse, 186
Daugherty, John, 194
Daugherty, Thomas, 222
Davenport, John, captivity, 120; 198
Davies, James, 204
Daviess, Joseph Hamilton, 6, 12, 114, 159
Davis, Ann Chiles, 131-32
Davis, Anna Carr, 132-33
Davis, Arabella Scott, 119
Davis, Benjamin, 192, 198
Davis, Charles B., 132
Davis, Sergeant Edward, 182
Davis, Elizabeth Chiles, 132
Davis, John, 215
Davis, Corporal John M., 224
Davis, Sergeant Jonathan, 202
Davis, Lemuel, Jr., 220
Davis, Lemuel, Sr., 220
Davis, Lodowick, 180
Davis, Luke, 182
Davis, Nancy Chiles; see Ann Chiles Davis
Davis, Nathaniel, 217
Davis, Rebecca Rutherford (Grace), 133
Davis, Richard, 131-32

Davis, Dr. Thomas Chiles, 132-33, 186, 207; biography, 131-33; death, 67, 132
Davis, William, 175, 192, 227, 229
Davis, William M., 119
Dawson, Sergeant John, 187
Day, Joseph, 189
Day, Middleton, 217
Dayton, Ohio, 218; army arrives at, 23-24
Dear, Jesse, 211
Dedman, James, 194
Defiance, Ohio, 37
Dehoney, Thomas, 180
Delaney, Willis, 175
Delany, Corporal William, 217
Delany, Willis, 173
Delaware Indians, 86
Demearee, Sergeant Samuel, 212
Denilhess, Sergeant Jesse, 174
Denore, Baldwin, 175
Depau, Charles, 227
DePeyster, Colonel Arnet S., 169
Derenxy, Captain ———, 97n
des Cognets, Anna Russell, 138
Deterson, John, 180
Detroit, Michigan Territory, 21-24, 32, 41, 44, 55, 62, 98, 166-68; Clinton Street Cemetery, 103; General Hull at, 17; prisoners sent to, 93; Protestant Cemetery, 103; see also Fort Malden
Detroit River, 63
Devers, Baldwin, 176
Dewitt, Frederick, 204
Dick, Franklin, 127
Dick, John, 180
Dick, Myra Alexander, 126-27
Dickerson, David, 206
Dickerson, Samuel, 190
Dickerson, Sergeant Thomas, 200
Dickerson, William, 206
Dickerson, William S., 178
Dickey, Benjamin, 180
Dickey, Corporal James D., 208
Dickey, William, 180, 222
Dickson, Robert, 89
Digernell, John, 198
Dingle, Sergeant William, 186
Dinwiddie, Corporal Robert, 205
Dixon, Captain ———, 97n
Dixon, Eliza H., 109
Dixon, T., 109
Dixon, Timothy, 227
Dobbs, John, 175

Bibliography and Index 255

Doctors, River Raisin Force, 127-34
Donaho, Jesse, 208
Donaldson, Sergeant William, 195
Dooling, Daniel, 227
Dooling, James, 227
Dooling, John, 224
Dooling, Thomas, 227
Dotson, Thomas, 227
Dougherty, Cornelius, 208
Dougherty, Jarrett, 178
Dougherty's Station, Ky., 113
Dowdle, Fauntleroy, 213
Dowdle, John, 213
Dowell, Fauntleroy, 213
Downes, Benore P., 206
Downey, Henry, 173
Downing, William, 180
Doyle, William, 200
Drain, John, 198
Draper, Mrs. _____, tavern of, 62
Drummond, Jemima McClenahan, 124
Drummond, W. W., 124
Drummons, James, 227
Ducker, John, 180
Ducker, Nathan, 213
Duckett, Caleb M., 178
Dudley, Ambrose, 121, 186
Dudley, Ann Parker, 121
Dudley, Lieutenant Peter, 152, 207, 219
Dudley, Polly, 121
Dudley, Reverend Thomas Parker, 59, 81-82, 220
Dulany, Corporal John, 189
Duncan, Lewis, 229
Duncan, Richard, 213
Duncan, Robert, 206
Dunlap, John, 182
Dunn, C. Frank, xii, 145-46
Dunn, Philip, 192
Durocher, Judge L., 86n
Durur, Sergeant Jesse, 200
Duvall, William P., 13
Dyke, John, 196
Dyke, Stephen, 204
Dyne, Andrew, 173, 175

Eades, Horatio, 211
Eadsi, Robert, 217
Eares, John, 202
Earles, Samuel, 227
Easley, Pleasant, 194
East, Elijah, 194
Eastern Lunatic Asylum, 136
Eastin, Thomas, 229
Ecton; see Acton

Edmiston, Dr. Alexander M., 128, 146
Edmiston, Faunea Jennings, 146
Edmiston, Captain John Montgomery, 33, 128, 207; appointed to command, 17; biography, 144-46; company of, 224-26; county named for, 87, 145; death, 65, 79, 145; home, 145-46; resigns command of his company, 142, 145
Edmiston, Margaret, 144, 146
Edmiston, Margaret Montgomery, 145
Edmiston, Martha Campbelle, 144-45
Edmiston, Mary R., 146
Edmiston, Nancy, 144
Edmiston, Samuel, 145
Edmiston, Thomas, 144-45
Edmiston, Captain William, 144-45
Edmiston; see also Edmonson
Edmonson County, Ky., origin of name, 145
Edmonson; see also Edmiston
Edwards, Sergeant Benjamin W., 228
Edwards, Gustavis, 229
Edwards, Jessie, 211
Edwards, Captain Robert, 61, 107, 176; company of, 173-74; death, 65
Edwards, Thomas, 194
Edwards, William M., 218
Edwardsville, Illinois, 130
Elder, Edward, 192
Elder, Samuel M., 192
Elgin, Sergeant Hezekiel, 217
Eliot, James, 182
Elk Hart, 118
Elkhart River, 30
Elkin, Benjamin, 194
Ellerson, Corporal John; see Corporal John Ellerton
Ellerton, Corporal John, 177
Elliott, Marie Louise Sans Chagrin, 167
Elliott, Colonel Matthew, 50, 167
Elliott, Captain Matthew, Jr., 167
Elliott, Captain William, 150; biography, 167; deserts Frenchtown, 75-76; promises sleds for wounded at Frenchtown, 74
Ellis, Elijah, 188
Ellis, Hezekiah, 224
Ellis, James, 188
Ellis, John, 146, 188-89
Ellis, Lee, 222
Ellis, Lucy, 147
Ellis, Robert, 147, 211
Ellis, Sarah Parrish, 146
Ellis, Thomas, 218

Ellis, Timothy, 147
Ellis, Captain William, appointed to command, 16; biography, 146-47; company of, 210-12; death, 147; resigns commission, 146
Ellison, John, 227
Elmore, David, 206
Elsbery, William, 204
Emerson, James, 204
Emery, Sarah, 124
Emmerson, William, 175
Emmet, Alexander, 182
Emmett, Matthais, 208
Endicott, Lewis, 222
Endicott, William, 186
Equipment of volunteers, 19
Erie, Penn., prisoners reach, 95
Erskine, David Montague, 2, 4
Erwin, John, 186
Erwin, Robert, 188
Esker, Mrs. Jerome A., xii
Essex Militia, 49-50, 55, 167-68
Estes, Abraham, 224
Estes, Corporal Clement, 224
Estes, John, 190
Estes, William, 208, 224
Estill, Colonel Benjamin, 152
Estill, Patsy Hickman Sproul, 152
Estis, George W., 218
Eubank, George, 204
Eubanks, William, 204
Evans, George, 204
Evans, William, 182
Eve, Benjamin, 184
Eve, Jabez, 184
Eves, John, 202
Ewell, William, 204
Ewing, Colonel Baker, 129
Ewing, Elizabeth M., 129
Ewing, James, 224
Ewing, Mrs. Katherine W., xii
Ewing, Letitia Warren, 129
Ewing, Margaret Gano, 129
Ewing, Patrick, 182
Ewing, Dr. Robert M., 177; biography, 129-30
Ewing, Thomas, 188

Faig, Mrs. George, 153
Fain, Ensign David, 226
Fair, James, 202
Fairfield, 138
Fallen Timbers, Battle of, 139, 163
Falmouth, Ky., 122
Fandree, Joseph; see Joseph Fandric

Fandree, William; see William Fandric
Fandric, Joseph, 196
Fandric, William, 196
Fant, George, 213
Fant, Thomas, 191-92
Fant, William, 213
Farm, Isom, 173
Farr, Ensign David, 226
Farrar, Elizabeth, 109
Farrow, Alexander S., 198
Farrow, Isham, 175
Farrow, John, 194
Faught, George, 213
Faught, William, 213
Fayette County, Ky., militia companies from, 191-93, 200-03, 224-26
Fayette Hospital, 136
Feamster, Charles, 218
Feathercoil, George, 198
Fee, William, 178
Felkins, John, 228
Feltz, Sergeant John, 178
Fenwick, Lewis B., 220
Ferguson, Sergeant Alexander, 191
Ferguson, David, 178, 227
Feris, Dr. ------, 38
Ferrell, Corporal Thomas, 182, 226
Fetty, Sergeant John, 184
Fewel, Ephraim, 211
Ficklin, Corporal John, 194
Ficklin, Sergeant William, 197
Field, Silas, 229
Fielder, John, 186
Fields, Luke, 200
5th Regiment, Kentucky Militia, Adjutant, 135-36; composition, 16, 18; rosters, 191-207; surgeon, 130-31
Fightmaster, John, 211
Filson Club, The, xi
Finch, James, 229
Finch, Sergeant John, 228
Finley, Martha Ann, 136
Finley, General Samuel, 136
Finney, James, 194, 206
1st Regiment, Kentucky Militia, composition, 16; rosters, 177-90; surgeon, 129-30
1st Rifle Regiment, Kentucky Militia, at Fort Defiance, 32-34; composition, 16, 18, 24-25; rosters, 207-26; surgeon, 131-33
Fisher, James, 200
Fisher, Jesse, 213
Fisher, John, 175, 227
Fisher, Nathaniel, 227

Bibliography and Index
257

Fisher, Thomas, 200
Fisher, William, 200
Fitzgerald, Henry, 213
Fitzgerald, Jesse, 190
Five Medal's Towns, 110
Flag, of Kentuckians, 72
Fleet, William, 51, 186
Fletcher, Lieutenant James, 205
Flint, Simeon, 190
Flournoy, Hoy B., 224
Floyd, Colonel John, 112
Forbes, Jacob, 224
Ford, A., 184
Ford, Reuben, 222
Forsee, Stephen, 194
Forsythe, John, 182
Forsythe, Samuel, 182
Fort, Noble, 182
Fort Barbee, Ohio, 40
Fort Bowyer, Ala., 108
Fort Defiance, Ohio, 32, 34, 119, 147, 150, 210, 222; description, 37; rechristened Fort Winchester, 37; see also Fort Winchester
Fort George, Canada, 139
Fort Hill, Frankfort, Ky., 106
Fort Jennings, Ohio, 44
Fort McArthur, Ohio, 42-43, 46
Fort Malden, Upper Canada, 62 see also Amherstburg
Fort Meigs, Ohio, 166, 168
Fort Miami, Ohio, 169
Fort Michilimackinac, Michigan Territory, 17, 63n
"Fort Starvation," 43; see also Fort Winchester
Fort Stephenson, Ohio, 166, 168; see also Lower Sandusky, Ohio
Fort Wayne, Indiana Territory, 23-27, 34, 41, 170; description, 28; destroyed by Indians, 27-28; soldiers buried at, 38
Fort Winchester, Ohio, 37, 41; see also Fort Defiance, "Fort Starvation"
Fortier, J., 97n
Foster, John, 180
Foster, Thomas, 224
Fowke, Jared, 198
Fowler, James, 175-76
Fowler, John H., 211
Fowler, Thomas, 175, 204
Fox, Charles, 209
Foxworthy, James, 210
Frakes, Barnabas, 198
Frakes, Joseph, 198
Frakes, Nathan, 178
Frame, Samuel, 198
Frame, William, 198
Francis, Enoch, 192
Francis, Jesse, 192
Francis, Lewis, 209
Frankfort, Ky., 17, 118-19, 125-26; British prisoners at, 96ff; cannon fired at to greet survivors, 95; cemetery, 104-06, 126, 141; Episcopal Church, 132; hotel, 99ff; news of Raisin defeat reaches, 89-90; receives declaration of war, 16; war fever at, 10-11
Franklin County, Ky., history, 104-05; militia company from, 18-19, 95, 100, 151-52, 219-21; women of send clothing to troops, 39-40
Frarey, Sergeant James, 224
Frayer, Joseph, 184
Frazier, Alexander, 198
Freeman, Samuel, 209
French, John, 177
French, of Frenchtown, 47; warn Winchester of British advance, 59
Frenchtown, Michigan Territory (Monroe, Michigan), 46, 94, 103, 108, 111, 116, 120; British at, 47; captured, 53; murder of wounded at, 88-89; occupied by Americans, 55; residents warned, 169; wounded Kentuckians at, 80ff; see also Monroe, Michigan; River Raisin
Frost, James, 194
Fry, George, 225
Fry, William, 200
Fryman, George, 186
Fryman, Corporal James, 186
Fugate, Sergeant Martin, 187
Fullalove, Larkin, 209
Funk, Captain Peter, 159
Funston, John, 229

Gabbert, William, 227
Gainer, Corporal Richard, 189
Gaines, John A., 208
Gaines, Malvina H., 109
Gaines, Patsey, 149
Gaither's Battalion, 116
Gale, Lieutenant _____, 97n
Galloway, Samuel, 180
Gano, Dr. _____, 129
Gano, Elizabeth Ewing, 129-30
Gano, Reverend John, 88n
Gano, General John Stites, 87-88

Gano, Margaret, 129
Gano, Major Richard Montgomery, 129, 177; biography, 88n; letter, 87
Gano; *see also* Ganoe
Ganoe, Samuel, captivity, 120
Ganoe, *see also* Gano
Garden, A. B., 97n
Gardiner, Effie Logan, 135
Gardiner, W. W., 135
Gardner, John, 173
Garnet, Fannie, 160
Garnet, Sergeant Joel, 189
Garnett, Harris H., 215
Garnett, Corporal Thomas, 215
Garrard, Eleanor Orr, 148
Garrard, Elizabeth, 148
Garrard, Elizabeth Mountjoy, 137
Garrard, Governor James, 122, 137, 147
Garrard, Major James, 26-27, 37, 48n, 53-54, 61; biography, 137-38
Garrard, Mary Kerfoot Williams, 138
Garrard, Matilda Coburn, 148
Garrard, Nancy Lewis, 138
Garrard, Susan Peers, 148
Garrard, Captain William, 17, 24, 31; at Fort Defiance, 32-34; biography, 147-48; company of, 228-31
Garrard, William Mountjoy, 148
Garrett, Lieutenant Ashton, 174; account of escape, 67n; assists in retreat at Frenchtown, 66
Garrett, Elizabeth Weaver, 141
Garrett, Sergeant Joel, 189
Gates, ------, 63
Gatewood, Sergeant Thomas, 202
Gatewood, Thomas R., 202
Geers, Jesse, 179
Geiger, Captain Frederick, 159
Gentry, James, 209
Gentry, Sergeant Richard, 208
Gentry, Zebedee, 175
George, Alfred, 211
George, William, 211
Georgetown, Ky., xi, 3, 18, 110-11; College, 129; Female College, 129; troops march from, 21-22; troops rendezvous at, 20
Gess, Sally, 142
Geter, Barnett, 202
Gibbons, David, 213
Gibson, James, 188
Giles, Samuel, 184
Gilkison, William, 182
Gill, Richard, 227
Gill, Robert, 179

Gillespie, David, 225
Gillispie, Lieutenant James W., 186
Gilmore, James, 190
Gilmore, Robert, 227
Gilpin, Ralph, 192
Giltner, Bernard, 202
Gindron, James I., 202
Girdler, James, 227
Girdler, Sergeant Joseph, 226
Girdley, James, 227
Girdley, Sergeant Joseph, 226
Gist, Anna Edwards, 150, 156
Gist, Judith Cary, 150, 155
Gist, Maria Cecil, 128-29
Gist, Colonel Nathaniel, 128, 150, 155
Gist, Sergeant Thomas, 224
Givens, John, 218
Glass, Eliza Logan, 135
Glass, Dr. Robert W., 135
Glasscock, Peter, 213
Glaves, Captain Michael, 64n, 67n, 83, 107; advances toward River Raisin, 51ff; appointed to command, 16; company of, 187-89; escape, 88; in retreat at Frenchtown, 65, 123
Glen, Richard O., 188
Godfroy, ------, 102
Godfroy, Gabriel, Jr., 84
Goding, Hugh, 209
Goff, Levi, 196
Gohagen, William, 175-76
Goin, John, 194
Goodlett, William, 175
Goodloe, Henry, 225
Goodloe, Kemp M., 192
Goodpasture, Cornelius, 182
Goodrich, Nathan, 220
Goodright, Michael, 200
Goodwin, Corporal John, 187
Gordon, Lewis M., 200
Gore, Nathan, 204
Goshen Township, Illinois, 124
Gosney, Sergeant Fielding, 191
Grace, Sir John C., 133
Grace, Rebecca Rutherford, 133
Gragg, James, 200
Gragg, Jesse, 182
Graham, Major W., 152
Grant, Daniel, 218
Grant, Robert, 215
Gratz, Benjamin, 129, 137
Gratz, Maria C. Gist, 129
Gratz, Rebekah, 129
Graves, Ambrose, 121

Bibliography and Index

Graves, Major Benjamin Franklin, 20, 50, 61, 76, 91, 191; advances toward Frenchtown, 48ff; biography, 120-21; captivity, 120; county named for, 87, 121; death, 79, 81-82; wounded, 72
Graves, Elizabeth, 121
Graves, Fanny, 121
Graves, Frances Coleman, 120
Graves, John, 227
Graves, Joseph, 120
Graves, Lucien, 121
Graves, Marion, 121
Graves, Nancy, 121
Graves, Polly Dudley, 121
Graves, Samuel, 215
Graves, Lieutenant Thomas Coleman, 174; death, 65, 120
Graves, Thomas H., 184
Graves, William, 112
Graves County, Ky., origin of name, 121
Gray, Corporal David, 186
Gray, James, 174, 200
Gray, Captain Patrick, 49; appointed to command, 16; company of, 205-07
Gray, William, 186, 200, 211
Green, Edward G., 188
Green, Jesse P., 188
Green, Nathaniel, 190
Green, Thomas Marshall, 115
Greening, John, 209
Greenup, Governor Christopher, 23, 122
Greenville, Treaty of, 118
Greenville, Ohio; see Grenville, Ohio
Greer, Thomas, 179
Gregg, John, 209
Grenville, Ohio, 24
Grider, Moses, 202
Griffin, Squire, 227
Griffith, Belfield, 184
Griffith, George, 184
Griffith, Thomas, 186, 213
Grigsby, James, 175
Grimes, John, 225
Grimes, Willis, 180
Grimsley, Elizabeth Todd, 131
Grimsley, Harrison J., 131
Grimsley, Silas, 190
Grindstaff, Isaac, 173, 175
Grishom, Lieutenant David, 184
Grooms, Horatio, 211
Grubbs, John, 165
Grubbs, Minerva Tribble Stoner, 165
Grundy, Felix, 8, 113-14, 163

Guin, John, 204
Gunsmiths, 164
Gwinn, John, 204, 218

Hackney, Hightower, 196
Haden, ------, 112
Haden, Tyrel, 209
Hagert, John, 192
Haggard, John, 194
Hailes, Lieutenant ------, 97n
Hailey, Daniel, 211
Hall, David, 209
Hall, Elizabeth F., 152
Hall, George, 215
Hall, Mary, 152
Hall, Uriel Sebree, 162
Hall, William, 152
Hall, William Augustus, 162
Halladay, Mordecai, 204
Hamblen, William A., 215
Hamilton, Alexander, 182, 211
Hamilton, Andrew, 182, 218
Hamilton, Mrs. Henrietta, 165
Hamilton, James, 207, 227
Hamilton, John, 196
Hamilton, Captain John, 51; appointed to command, 16; biography, 149; company of, 200-01
Hamilton, Corporal John, 178
Hamilton, Patsey Gaines, 149
Hamilton, Ensign Robert, 200
Hamilton, Robertson, 182
Hamilton, Thomas, 200
Hamilton, William, 211
Hamlin, William A., 215
Hammelton, William, 182
Hammer, William, 204
Hammond, James, 180
Hanley, Thomas H., 175
Hanna, Andrew, 180
Hanson, Thomas, 209
Harbison, Samuel, 213
Hardin, Ensign Davis, 208
Hardin, Major Martin D., 12-13, 15, 35n, 114-15, 207
Harlan, Joshua, 198
Harlon, Nelson, 198
Harmar, General Josiah, 117, 122
Harmon, John, 211
Harring, Levi, 227
Harris, Barnabas, 227
Harris, Claiborne, 196
Harris, Mary, 135
Harris, Samuel, 200
Harris, Thomas, 184

Harris, Western, 209
Harris, Willis, 179
Harrison, Ann P., 165
Harrison, Cary, 155
Harrison, John Scott, 118
Harrison, Robert, 218
Harrison, Governor and Major General William Henry, 7, 12, 21, 25, 74-76, 110, 118, 123, 152; abandons campaign, 89; appointed Major General of Kentucky Militia, 22-23; at Battle of Thames, 90; at Fort Meigs, 166; authorizes Winchester to march to Rapids, 41; biography, 107; commands Northwestern Army, 32; leads troops through Ohio, 24ff; physician, 17; popularity, 21-22, 24, 28, 30-31; reappointed to command, 36; recommends Winchester to abandon march to Rapids, 44-45; surrenders command, 30; takes command of army, 22-23; turns over command to Winchester, 31; Wabash Campaign, 5-6
Harrison, Williby, 209
Harrison County, Ky., militia company from, 210-12
Harrold, Corporal William, 215
Harrow, Sergeant Joseph, 51, 198
Hart, Abraham, 215
Hart, Ann, 149
Hart, Anna Gist, 150, 156
Hart, Eliza, 149
Hart, Elizabeth Brent, 150
Hart, Henry Clay, 150
Hart, Lucretia, 149
Hart, Nathaniel, Sr., 21-22
Hart, Captain Nathaniel G. S., 58-59, 61, 69n, 75-76, 156, 167; appointed to command, 16; biography, 149-50; burial, 102; company of, 191-93; county named for, 87, 150; death, 79, 81, 86-87; sends Colonel Wells with message to Harrison, 60-61; servant of, 95
Hart, Mrs. Nathaniel G. S., 129
Hart, Susanna Gray, 149
Hart, Colonel Thomas, 149
Hart, Thomas, Jr., 150
Hart County, Ky., origin of name, 150
Harvey, Sergeant Bernard, 202
Harvey, John, 196
Haveline, Jesse, 209
Hawkins, Abner, 188
Hawkins, Sergeant E., 189
Hawkins, Francis, 222
Hawkins, Gabriel, 190
Hawkins, Jane, 127
Hawkins, John, 127
Hawkins, S. O., 225
Hawkins, Strawder J., 228
Hayden, Nathaniel, 218
Hayden, Susan, 155
Hays, John, 220
Head, Sergeant Benjamin, 219
Head, Moses, 220
Heald, Rebecca Wells, 113
Hebber, John, 179
Heddleston, Robert, 179
Helm, Governor John Larue, 105
Henderson, Samuel, 184, 229
Henderson, Thomas, 184
Hendley, Elkhanna, 225
Hendricks, James, 227
Hendricks, John, 227
Henney, Robert P., 225
Henry, Corporal James, 187
Henry, John, 178-79
Henry Plot, 15
Hensley, Joseph, 199
Hensley, William D., 220
Henson, Elijah, 227
Henton, George, 222
Hermitage, 110
Herndon, Elisha, 220
Heron, Ensign James, 51
Herring, Jonathan, 211
Herring, Samuel, 211
Herron, Ensign James L., 191
Hews, Charles, 194
Hibs, Adam, 211
Hickman, Lieutenant David M., 228
Hickman, Elizabeth Hall, 152
Hickman, James L., 192
Hickman, Captain Paschal, 19, 35-36, 49, 75-76, 81, 91, 100, 125; advances toward River Raisin, 51ff; appointed to command, 16; biography, 151-53; company of, 18-19, 219-21; county named for, 87, 152; death, 82-83; home, 151; procures flour for army, 41; Wayne's Campaign, 25; wounded, 53
Hickman, Patsy, 152
Hickman, Sally, 152
Hickman, Susan Hall, 152
Hickman, Thomas, 229
Hickman, Reverend William, 151
Hickman County, Ky., origin of name, 152,
Hicks, Abraham, 200

Bibliography and Index

Hicks, James, 194
Hicks, Samuel, 200
Higgins, James, 192; bravery at Frenchtown, 69n
Higgins, John, 51, 197
Hightower, George, Sr., 153
Hightower, Joshua, 153
Hightower, Captain Richard, 51, 61, 120, 177; biography, 153-54; company of, 174-76; death, 153-54
Hill, Captain ------, 97n
Hill, Archibald, 209
Hill, Foster, 213
Hill, Fountain, 218
Hill, Hardy, 215
Hill, James, 229
Hines, Bennett, M., 192
Hinkson, John, 218
Hite, Burton, 227
Hobach, Marcus, 173
Hobson, Bennett, 175
Hoddin, Abraham, 213
Hoff, Luke, 141
Hoffman, Catherine S., 131
Hoffman, Colonel William, 131
Hogan, James, 184
Hogan, John P., 202
Hogg, Maria, 137
Hogs, eat dead at Frenchtown, 101-02
Holder, Lieutenant Caleb H., 51, 173
Holder, Gava, 204
Holder, Sergeant Richard C., 208
Holding, Samuel, 192
Holler, John, 190
Holliday, Corporal Basil R. L., 210
Hollis, James W., 213
Holloday, Eliot H., 204
Holloday, Sergeant James, 203
Holloway, Colonel James H., 165
Holloway, Levy, 227
Holloway, Mary Williams, 165
Holmes, Lieutenant ------, 97n
Holt, Eleanor Garrard, 148
Holt, Joseph H., 148
Holton, John A., 220
Homes, James, 188
Hope, George, 175
Hopkins, Mordecai, 204
Hopkins, Major General Samuel, 13, 23, 148
Hopkins, Thomas, 206
Horbeson, Samuel, 213
Horses, thoroughbred, 164
Hough, Luke; see Luke Hoff
Houster, William, 211

How, Jacob, 192
Howard, Achilles, 206
Howard, James, 182
Howard, Mathew, 186
Howard, Major Thomas, 132
Howard, William, 215
Howarton, Jane, 144
Howarton, Katharine, 144
Howell, Lewis, 215
Howerton, Catharine; see Katharine Howarton
Huckstep, Corporal Samuel, 205
Huddleston, Allen, 215
Huddleston, Robert; see Robert Heddleston
Hudson, Dudley, 225
Huff, Abraham, 215
Huffman, Jacob, 188
Hughard, Thomas, 182
Hughes, Hugh, 190
Hughes, William, 218
Hull, Corbin R., 218
Hull, James, 204
Hull, Thomas, 211
Hull, Brigadier General William, 13, 17-18, 20-21, 90, 166-68, 170; commissioned Brigadier General, 16; surrenders Detroit, 22-24
Hull's Road, 42-44, 58
Humble, Jesse, 218
Humphrey, Benjamin, 218
Humphrey, Charles, 220
Humphreys, James B., 220
Hundley, Charles, 225
Hunt, James, 184, 229
Hunter, Charles, 206
Hunter, John, 215
Hurley, James, 186
Huron Indians, 66, 170
Husband, Emily, 131
Hushman, Matthew, 194
Huston, James, 192
Hutchcraft, Eliza Williams, 165
Hutchcraft, James, 165
Hutcherson, Samuel, 206
Hutchinson, James, 188
Hutchinson, Corporal Lewis, 229

Indians, at Frenchtown, 48-50, 168-70; in battles at Frenchtown, 63ff; in Bourbon County, Ky., 121; in first battle on River Raisin, 55-56; plunder prisoners, 73; rout Americans at Battle of River Raisin 65ff; supplied by British, 6-7; threaten inhabitants

of Frenchtown, 102; treatment of at Frenchtown, 81; victory celebration after Raisin battles, 76
Ingsley, James, 175
Ireland, Alexander, 184
Irvine, Lieutenant ——, 97n, 100
Irvine, Ann Clark, 127
Irvine, Eliza H., 127
Irvine, Fanny P., 127
Irvine, Jane Hawkins, 127
Irvine, Dr. John, 38; arrives at Frenchtown, 59; biography, 127-28; in retreat at Frenchtown, 67
Irvine, Mary Jane, 127
Irvine, Thomas, 127
Irwin, Sergeant Francis, 178
Irwin, Corporal Jacob, 198
Irwin, Corporal James, 198
Irwin, John, 179
Ivanhoe, 129

Jack, Allen, 180
Jacks, William, 179
Jackson, President Andrew, 110, 128, 130
Jackson, Francis James, 2, 4
Jackson, Mrs. L. M., 131
Jackson, Sergeant Martin, 214
Jackson, Susan, 164
Jacobs, Daniel, 218
Jamerson, Daniel C., 199
James, Alexander D., 199
James, Captain Henry, 52, 107; company of spies, 226-28
James, Samuel, 175
James, Wiley, 184
Jamison, David, 206
Jamison, Isaac, 215
Jamison, James, 182
Jamison, John, 206
Jamison, William, 182, 206
January, Fanny Irvine, 127
January, Joseph H., 127
Jay Treaty, 12
Jeboult, Lieutenant ——, 97n
Jefferson, President Thomas, 1, 81n
Jeffries, Enoch, 199
Jenkins, Richard, 225
Jennings, Ann, 110
Jennings, Faunea, 146
Jennings, Colonel William, 32, 34, 37
Jereaume, Jean Baptiste, 84
Jerome, ——, 102
"Jessamine County Blues," 65, 159

Jessamine County, Ky., militia companies from, 159-60, 193-95, 205-07
Jesse, Mary Bird McCracken, 158
Jesse, Thomas R., 158
Jessup, Samuel B., 211
Jeter, Henry, 206
Jimmerson, David, 206
Jimmerson, John, 199, 206
Jimmerson, William, 206
John, Armstrong, 192
Johnson, ——, 28
Johnson, Anna Newton, 115
Johnson, Corporal Benjamin B., 219
Johnson, Catherine Scott, 119
Johnson, Elizabeth, 111, 162
Johnson, Gersham, 209
Johnson, Isaac, 184
Johnson, James, 125, 181-82
Johnson, Jemima Suggett, 162
Johnson, John, 179, 182, 206
Johnson, Johnson, 119
Johnson, Jonathan, 186
Johnson, L. F., 104-05, 151
Johnson, Nancy, 156
Johnson, Colonel Richard M., 8, 21, 111, 115, 129, 162; author of anti-British resolutions, 3; buries dead of Raisin, 103; letter, 30; militia company, 13; Mounted Riflemen, 28; recommends Harrison for Major General, Kentucky Militia, 23; Yellowstone Expedition, 162
Johnson, Robert, 111, 162, 179
Johnson, Silas, 179
Johnson, Suggett, 111
Johnson, William, 175
Johnston, George T., 220
Johnston, James, 229
Johnston, James M., 192
Johnston, Joshua, 204
Johnston, William, 218
Jones, Ensign ——, 97n
Jones, Ambrose, 211
Jones, Cully, 211
Jones, Garrard, 229
Jones, Harriet, 155
Jones, Harwell, 200
Jones, Hillery, 188
Jones, Isaac, Jr., 211
Jones, Isaac, Sr., 211
Jones, James, 182
Jones, Jesse, 179
Jones, John, 190, 196
Jones, Jonathan, 227
Jones, Lewis, 229

Bibliography and Index 263

Jones, Philip, 200
Jones, Corporal Samuel, 174
Jones, Samuel D., 209
Jones, Corporal Thomas G., 208
Jones, Wiley, 199
Jones, William, 230
Jones, Willis, 179
Jordan, Captain ——, 40
Jump, John, 218
Jump, Joseph, 188
Jump, Valentine, 188

Kamp, William, 173
Kay, John, 192
Kearney, Mary, 113
Keene, Pollard, 61, 191
Keith, George, 218
Keith, Corporal Richard, 217
Keller, Lieutenant Abraham, 217
Kelley, James, 196
Kelly, Ariel, 155
Kelly, Elizabeth, 155
Kelly, Elizabeth Mallory, 155
Kelly, Griffin, 154-55
Kelly, Harriet Jones, 155
Kelly, James, 155
Kelly, Jane, 155
Kelly, Captain Joseph, 51, 61, 155, 195; assumes command Captain Brasfield's company, 142; biography, 154-55
Kelly, Mary, 155
Kelly, Nancy, 155
Kelly, Nancy Smith, 155
Kelly, Patsy Sutton, 155
Kelly, Permelia, 155
Kelly, Rebecca Smith, 155
Kelly, Redsy Smith, 154
Kelly, Robert E., 192
Kelly, Samuel, 155, 196
Kelly, Sarah, 155
Kelly, Susan Hayden, 155
Kelly, Uriel; see Ariel Kelly
Kelly, William, 154-55, 207
Kelsey, Mary, 113
Kelso, Elijah, 213
Kemp, Charles, 218
Kemp, Elizabeth, 122
Kemp, Reuben, 122
Kendrick, James, 230
Kennady, William, 206
Kennedy, Lieutenant James, 226
Kennedy, Sergeant Robert, 226
Kenning, David, 211
Kenny, James, 179
Kenton, Simon, 122, 220

Kenton, Corporal William, 186
Kentucky, causes of war in, 2-14; counties named for River Raisin soldiers; see Counties, Kentucky; declaration of war, 8-10; General Assembly, anti-British resolutions of, 2-4, 6-7; volunteers from, 13
Kentucky Gazette, 8, 10-11, 109, 137
Kentucky Historical Society, 79, 104, 132, 231
Kentucky River, 98
Kentucky Yeoman, 104
Kerchivill, Thomas, 230
Kerley, Captain William, 32; appointed to command, 16; company of, 208-10; court-martialed, 39
Kerr, Judge Charles, 14n
Kerrill, James, 213
Key, Corporal Thomas, 202
Kice, John, 200
Kidd, Edmond I., 200
Kincaid, William, 183
Kincaid, Sergeant William T., 181
Kincart, James, 186
Kinciad, Charles, 204
Kinder, George, 215
Kinder, Jacob, 215
Kindred, Edward, 194
Kindrie, Benjamin, 184
King, Gideon, 220
King, Henry, 199
King, James, 177, 187
King, Sergeant Solomon D., 181
King, Thomas W., 192
King's Mountain, Battle of, 13, 128, 145
Kinkead, Ludie J., xii
Kinney, Benjamin, 202
Kirby, Zachariah, 202
Kirtley, Lieutenant Robert, 189
Kitson, Bombadier ——, 55
Knau, George, 201
Kneeland, Abner, 136
Know, Samuel, 188
Koons, John, 220
Korea, xi
Krickbaum, John, 194

Labadie, Alexis, 101-02
Labadie, Medard, 72
Lacklin, Elizabeth Kelly, 155
Lacklin, Fielding, 155, 196
Lacy, Stephen, 184
Lafayette, Marquis de, 156
Lafferty, Eleanor Strode, 143

Lafferty, Jane, 143
Lafferty, Thomas, 143
Laing, Ensign James, 97n
Lair, Moses, 206
Lake, Adam, 192
Lake Erie, 50
Lake Ontario, 94
Lake St. Clair, 94
Lambert, Moses, 215
Lammons, John, 204
Lana, Henry, 206
Lander, Henry, 143
Lander, Nancy Brasfield, 143
Landers, James, 204
Lane, John, 175, 220
Lane, Martin, 190
Lane, Mordecai, 204
Langham, Captain Angus Lewis, 60; company of, 177
Langhorn, David, 230
Langhorne, Cary Harrison, 155
Langhorne, John, 155
Langhorne, John H., 156
Langhorne, Captain Maurice, appointed to command, 16; biography, 155-56; company of, 217-19; letter, 27-28
Langhorne, Nancy Johnson, 156
Langhorne, Paulina Brook, 156
Langhorne, Robert, 156
Langhorne, Sarah Bell, 155
Langhorne, Victoria, 156
Langhorne's Hotel, 156
Lascelle, Jacques, 58
Lascelle, Nannette, 58
Lasselle, ——, 135-36
Lasselle, Francois, 86
Latta, Alexander, 222
Law, Thomas, 188
Lawrence, John, 187, 201
Layton, Robert, 186
Leathers, John W., 105-06
Leavy, William A., 137
Lebanon, Ohio, 23
Lee, Hancock, 157
Lee, Robert, 180
Lee, William, 180
Lee, Zachariah, 213
Leestown, Ky., 157
Leforce, Robertson, 215
Legabeck, Saint, 218
Lemmons, William, 183
Lemon, Alexander, 184
Lemon, James, 201
Lemon, Sergeant John, 180
Leon, Moses, 206

Leopard, 1
Lessler, Jacob, 215
Letcher, Robert P., 128
Levering, Anna, 134
Levering, Frank, 134
Lewis, Aaron, 211
Lewis, Alexander, 211
Lewis, Charles, 192
Lewis, Elizabeth Payne, 138
Lewis, Harriet, 117
Lewis, Mathew, 227
Lewis, Nancy, 138
Lewis, Thomas, 138
Lewis, Lieutenant Colonel William, 18, 25, 37, 61, 133, 150, 192; advances toward Frenchtown, 47ff; appointed to command, 16; at Fort Defiance, 32-34; biography, 116-17; captured by Indians, 68; in retreat at Frenchtown, 67; on the Wabash River, 30; paroled, 99; regiment of, 191-207; released from captivity, 95; servant of, 95; victory at River Raisin, 62
Lewis, William, Jr., 117
Lewis, William A., 194
Lewis, Zachariah W., 220
Lewiston, N. Y., 167
Lexington, Ky., 15-16, 20, 23; anti-British meetings at, 4; *Directory*, 1818, 162; Light Infantry, 58, 150; Lodge No. 1, F.&A.M., 137; war fever in, 10-11
Liggett, Ensign James, 173; death, 33
Liggins, William, 202
Lighter, Christian, 218
Ligonier, Indiana Territory, 110-11
Lillard, Thomas, 194
Lincoln, Abraham, 130
Lincoln, Mary Todd, 130
Lincoln County, Ky., militia company from, 212-14
Lindsay, Corporal William, 180
Lingenfelter, Daniel, 192
Link, Jacob, 218
Linkhorn, George, 194
Linn, Lieutenant ——, 97n
Lisle, Samuel, 204
Lithell, John, 202
Littell, Elizabeth Hickman, 152
Littell, William, 152
Little Rock, Ark., 117
Little Turtle, 125
Lively, Jacob, 220
Liverpool, England, 166
Lock, John, 213

Bibliography and Index 265

Lockridge, James, 183
Logan, Anne Montgomery, 114, 134-35
Logan, Dr. Benjamin, 114, 134, 207; biography, 134-35
Logan, General Benjamin, 114, 134
Logan, Effie, 135
Logan, Eliza Jane, 135
Logan, Eliza Winlock, 135
Logan, James Knox, 135
Logan, James W., 215
Logan, Jane, 114-15
Logan, John, 135
Logan, Mary W., 135
Logan, Robert, 114, 134, 173
Logan, Judge William, 25n, 30n, 34n
Logson, John, 230
Long, Catherine, 134
Long, Sergeant Daniel, 180
Long, Harwell, 201
Long, James, 134
Long, Sergeant Jeremiah, 213
Long, Tackley, 227
Long, Thomas, 180
Lonkart, Corporal Joseph, 202
Loring, Fredic, 230
Louder, Nathaniel, 186
Louisville, Ky., 112
Louisville Western Courier, 113
Loury, John, 184
Love, John S., 201
Love, Thomas, 188
Lower Sandusky, Ohio, 166; see also Fort Stephenson
Lowndes, William, 8
Lowry, William, 184
Lucker, John B., 218
Luckett, William, 173, 188
Ludspeth, David, 218
Luke, John, 180
Lusk, James, 206
Lusk, John, 196
Lusk, Silas, 196
Luttrell, Rebecca, 165
Lyle, Elizabeth Garrard, 148
Lyle, John A., 148
Lyman, Charles, 182
Lynch, John, 227
Lynn, William P., 185
Lyon, Noah, 183
Lyon, Samuel, 183
Lyter, Christian, 218

McAchran, Sergeant James M.; see Sergeant James M. Ackran
McAfee, Robert B., 40, 108, 163, 167

McAllaster, George, 227
McAnnelly, John, 186
McBee, John, 179
McBride, Lapsley, 220
McCall, John, 202
McCall, Thomas, 209
McCalla, Andrew, 136
McCalla, Elizabeth Means, 136
McCalla, John Moore, 61, 191; at surrender of Kentuckians, 71; biography, 136-37; library, 137
McCalla, Lieutenant Joseph, 180
McCalla, Maria, 136
McCalla, Maria Hogg, 137
McCalla, Martha Finley, 136
McCalla, Reverend William Latta, 136
McCallister, Corporal John, 184
McCamant, John, 202
McCandless, John, 185
McCardy, David, 176
McCarty, David, 175
McCarty, Reuben, 188
McCauley, Corporal James, 180
McChesney, John, 192
McClain, Corporal Daniel, 187
McClanahan, Major Elijah, 67n, 177; arrives at Frenchtown, 59; assists in retreat, 65; commands 17th U. S. Infantry at Frenchtown, 61; reinforces regulars at River Raisin, 64-65; rifle of, 123; see also Major Elijah McClenahan (same person)
McClanahan, James, 183
McClanahan, John, 188
McClanahan, Lieutenant Thomas, 228
McClanahan, William, 207, 218
McClanahan; see also McClenahan
McClane, Jonathen, 201
McClary, Sergeant George W., 51, 222
McClelland, Joseph, 213
McClellen, Robert, 183
McClenahan, Ann, 124
McClenahan, Anne Pollock, 124
McClenahan (McClanahan), Major Elijah, biography, 121-124; escape, 88; see also Major Elijah McClanahan (same person)
McClenahan, Elijah, Jr., 124
McClenahan, Elizabeth, 124
McClenahan, Elizabeth Kemp, 122
McClenahan, Elsie, 124
McClenahan, Mrs. Frank C., xii
McClenahan, Frank Clifton, 123
McClenahan, Henry, 123-24
McClenahan, James, 124

McClenahan, Jane, 124
McClenahan, Janet Buchanan, 121
McClenahan, Jemima, 124
McClenahan, John, 121, 123
McClenahan, Lucy Richards, 124
McClenahan, Marie, 124
McClenahan, Robert, 124
McClenahan, Sarah, 124
McClenahan, Sarah Emery, 124
McClenahan, Sarah Shawhan, 123-24
McClenahan; see also McClanahan
McClure, Eleazer, 227
McClure, John, 211
McClure, Martin, 206
McClure, Samuel, 183
McCollister, Mark, 183
McComsey, John, 215
McConnel, Joseph, 229
McConnell, Edward, 67
McConnell, Sergeant Edward M., 217
McConnell, M. G., 194
McConnell, William, 218
McCormack, James, 185
McCormick, Francis, 180
McCormick, James, 213
McCormick, John, 218
McCoy, Captain ———, 97n
McCoy, Sergeant Alexander, 178
McCracken, Cyrus, 157-58
McCracken, Elizabeth, 157
McCracken, George, 158
McCracken, Martha M., 158
McCracken, Mary Bird, 158
McCracken, Otho, 220
McCracken, Ovid, 222
McCracken, Sally Caldwell, 157
McCracken, Captain Virgil, 34, 49, 51, 61, 64n, 152; appointed to command, 17; biography, 157-58; company of, 222-23; county named for, 87, 157; death, 157
McCracken, Virgil, Jr., 158
McCracken County, Ky., origin of name, 157
McCracken's Mill Road, 157
McCrosky, Elijah, 225
McCullom, Jacob, 213
McCullough, Corporal Robert, 200
McCune, James, 218
McCurnsey, John, 215
McDaniel, E., 202
McDaniel, John, 185; see also John Macdonald
McDaniel, William, 175
McDonald, George, 196

McDonald, James, 196
Macdonald, John, 199
McDonald, John, 196
McDonall, Lieutenant Colonel ———, 63n
McDowell, Alexander, 186
McDowell, John, 225
McDowell, Mary, 124
McDowell, Richard, 225
McDowell, William, 218
McFall, Robert, 227
McGall, William, 227
McGee, William, 204
McGinnis, Thomas, 179
McGohie, Daniel, 185
McGonnigle, John, 196
McGrath, Terrance, 194
McGrig, Sergeant Amariah A., 214
McGrimes, John, 213
McGuire, Sergeant Edward, 229
McGuire, Samuel, 222
McGuire, William, 51, 203
McGuire, Willis, 209
McHatton, James, 185
McIlrain, James, 199
McIlvain, Dr. Thomas, 38, 107; death, 65, 78
McIntosh, John, 188
McKee, Samuel, 13, 17
McKeehan, Dr. Samuel, 93
McKennen, Solomon, 183
McKenzie, John, 175-76
McKinney, Charles, 183
McKinsey, James, 227
McKinsey, John, 211
McKitrick, David, 211
McKitrick, Robert, 211
McKnight, James, 222
McLane, John, 183
McLaughlin, John, 186
McLin, Frederick, 175
McManama, George, 203
McMeekin, Samuel, 202
McMichael, Robert, 186
McMicken, Samuel, 202
McMillan, Andrew, 128
McMillan, John, 199
McNat, Abner, 183
McNitt, Frederick, 175
McWherter, Jesse, 227

Macon Bill No. 2, 2
Mad River, 24
Madison, ———, 85
Madison, Agatha Strother, 124-26

Bibliography and Index

Madison, Gabriel, 126
Madison, Major George, 17, 35n, 47, 50, 61, 101, 132, 207; advances toward Frenchtown, 48ff; at surrender of Kentuckians, 71-73; biography, 124-27; death, 126; elected governor of Kentucky, 125-26; entertains, British prisoners, 100f; paroled, 99; released from captivity, 95-96; senior officer at Frenchtown, 69
Madison, George, Jr., 126
Madison, President James, 8, 13, 30, 124; orders British prisoners confined at Frankfort, Ky., 96
Madison, Jane Smith, 126
Madison, John, 124
Madison, Myra, 126-27
Madison, William, 126
Madison County, Ky., militia company from, 208-10
Mahan, ——, 163
Mahon, Alexander, 202
Mahoney, Fielding, 224
Mahoney, Captain James H., 165
Mahoney, Sarah, 165
Mahurine, John, 213
Malden, Upper Canada, 22, 25, 32, 41, 47, 50, 58, 66, 73, 83, 85-86, 139; 170; prisoners at, 92-94
Mallory, Elizabeth, 155
Mallory, Timothy, 120
Manford, John, 179
Manley, James, 183
Manley, William, 183
Marks, Hastings, 204
Marks, Nathaniel, 204
Mars, Samuel, 186
Marshall, Humphrey, 11
Marshall, James, 206
Marshall, John, 190
Marshall, Joseph, 199
Marshall, Dr. Lewis, 126
Marshall, Thomas, 230
Marshall, Timothy, 220
Marshall, Timothy P., 179
Marshall, William, 206
Martin, David, 211
Martin, Evalinia, 127
Martin, Sergeant Hudson, 208
Martin, James, 175, 177, 210
Martin, John, 204
Martin, Captain John, appointed to command, 16; biography, 158; company of, 203-05
Martin, John G., 158

Martin, Kate Bell, 158
Martin, Mary F., 158
Martin, Nannie, 158
Martin, Nathan, 196
Mason, John, 199
Mason County, Ky., 112, 121
Masons, 137
Masters, John, 211
Masterson, Richard, 202
Mathers, Robert, 192
Mathews, David E., 220
Mathews, Philip, 175
Matier, Samuel, 199
Matson, Captain Richard, 51, 64n; account of escape, 67n; assumes command of Captain Ellis's company, 147; company of, 210-12; escapes at Frenchtown, 65, 67
Matthews, Diana, 141
Matthias, Amont, 211
Maumee Bay, 50
Maumee Rapids, 29, 34
Maumee River, 33-34, 38-39
Maunel, Abraham, 201
Maupin, Corporal Robert D., 208
Maxey, Sergeant Asa, 182
Maxfield, John, 173
Maxwell, James D., 192
Maxwell, John, 175, 193, 204
May, Lindsay, 206
Mayfield, Southerland, 173, 175
Mayhall, Francis, 220
Mayhall, Frank, 49
Mayhall, John, 220
Maysville, Ky., prisoners reach, 95
Meade, Colonel David, 136
Meade, Captain James M., 61; biography, 159; company of, 176-77; county named for, 87, 159; death, 65, 77, 159
Meade County, Ky., origin of name, 159
Meadville, Pa., 95
Means, Elizabeth, 136
Medical Department, River Raisin Force, 127-34
Meenach, Samuel, 179
Megowan, Captain Stewart W., appointed to command, 16; company of, 202-03
Memphis, Tenn., 108
Menefee, Benjamin P., 218
Menick, John, 218
Menifee, Harriet Lewis, 117
Menifee, Dr. Nimrod, 117
Meredith, Corporal Edward B., 222

Merit, James, 190
Merrill, James, 185
Mesmer, Peter, 193
Messick, Nathan, 206
Metcalf, Charles, 230
Metcalf, Corporal John, 229
Metcalfe, Enoch, 216
Mexican War, 111, 130, 165-66
Michigan, 55; erects monument to River Raisin soldiers, 103, 106
Midland Trail, 163-64
Midner, Benjamin, 208
Mifford, Andrew, 201
Miller, Abraham, 186
Miller, Major Anderson, 97
Miller, Francis, 206
Miller, James, 178
Miller, John, 214
Miller, John P., 202
Miller, Corporal William, 182
Million, Benson, 209
Millner, Joseph, 211
Mimms, Mrs. Elizabeth, 143
Minor, Corporal James, 180
Minor, John L., 188
Minutemen, Mason County, Ky., 121
Mires, David, 187
Mississinewa River, 148
Mit, Samuel, 185
Mitchell, Lieutenant ——, 101
Mitchell, Reverend ——, 152
Mitchell, Archibald, 222
Mitchell, Sergeant Nathaniel, 222
Mitchell, Samuel, 214
Mitchell, Solomon, 222
Mitchell, Lieutenant Thomas, 212
Mitchell, Reverend Thomas, 207
Mitchell, William, 202
Mobile District, 108
Moffett, Mrs. Walter, 153
Mompesson, Ensign ——, 97n
Monday, Lieutenant Harrison, 208; *see also* Lieutenant Harrison Munday
Monks, Thomas, 81, 193
Monroe, James, 30-31
Monroe, Mary Logan, 135
Monroe, William P., 135
Monroe, Michigan, 103-06; *see also* Frenchtown, River Raisin
Monteath, William, 185
Monterey, Mexico, 119
Montgomery, Alexander, 216
Montgomery, Dr. Alexander, 61, 128, 173; arrives at Frenchtown, 59; biography, 128-29; death, 65, 78
Montgomery, Anne, 114, 134
Montgomery, Elijah, 128
Montgomery, Elizabeth "Betsy," 128
Montgomery, Elizabeth Robinson, 128
Montgomery, Corporal Hugh, 180
Montgomery, James, 146
Montgomery, Jesse, 204
Montgomery, John, 185
Montgomery, John R., 128
Montgomery, Malinda, 128
Montgomery, Margaret Robinson, 145
Montgomery, Robinson, 128
Montgomery, Thomas, 13, 17
Montgomery, Major William, 128
Montgomery County, Ky., militia company from, 69n, 197-99
Moon, John A., 193
Moore, Clark, 180
Moore, Garland, 201
Moore, Gasland, 201
Moore, George, 230
Moore, Horatio, 230
Moore, John, 216
Moore, Joshua, 220
Moore, Samuel T., 201
Moore, Timothy T., 220
Moore, William, 204, 227
Moore, Lieutenant William H., 51, 200
Moraviantown, Upper Canada, 98, 168
Morgan, Sergeant Allen, 189
Morgan, Hugh, 179
Morgan, J., 175
Morgan, Jarrett, 222
Morgan, Corporal Jeremiah, 210
Morgan, John, 176, 183, 187
Morgan, Moses, 212, 225
Morgan, Tom, 145
Morgan, W., 194
Morin, Ensign Joseph, 217
Morning Glory, Ky., 144
Morrell, John, 212
Morris, B., 204
Morris, George, 175
Morris, Henry, 206
Morris, Joseph, 183
Morris, Thales, 179
Morris, Captain Thomas, 49; appointed to command, 16; company of, 178-79
Morris, William G., 196
Morrison, Ensign ——, 51
Morrison, Boswell, 196
Morton, J. H., 67n
Morton, Jacob, 199
Morton, William, 203, 209
Mosby, Daniel, 190

Bibliography and Index

Mosby, Thomas, 190
Mosby, William, 185
Moseley, Joseph, 220
Mosley, John, 222
Moss, Lieutenant Mason, 184
Moss, Pleasant, 194
Motherhead, Sergeant Alvan, 180
Mount Hope, 129, 137
Mount Lebanon, 137
Mt. Sterling, Ky., 16, 69n; war fever in, 11
Mountjoy, Alvin, 122
Mountjoy, John, 188
Mountjoy, William, 230
Moxley, Joseph, 220
Mozer, Corporal George, 178
Muir, Major Adam, 97n, 167, 170
Muldraugh, Corporal George F., 200
Muldrough, John, 201
Mulholm, William, 179
Mulligan, Corporal Burton, 215
Mulligan, Charles, 214
Mulligan, John G., 221
Mullikin, Benjamin, 214
Mullikin, Charles, 214
Munday, Lieutenant Harrison, 32-33
Munday, Ensign James, 176
Munday, William, 209
Munday; see also Monday
Murphy, David, 175
Murphy, John, 227
Murphy, Corporal William, 226
Murphy, Zachariah, 196
Murrane, J., 175
Murrane, Mark, 175
Murrane, Tom, 175
Murray, Anna Allen Crittenden, 115
Murray, David R., 115
Musgrove, William, 201
Myers, George, 179
Myers, Jacob, 218
Myers, John, 199, 206

Nafe, Daniel, 185
Nailor, Francis, 225
Nailor, Sergeant John, 219
Nall, William H., 222
Napper, James, 202
Nash, General Francis, 130
Nash, Ensign John W., 51, 214
Nash, William, 51, 195, 227
Nashville and Chattanooga Railroad, 109
Navarre, Colonel Francis, 64n
Navarre, Robert, 64n

Neal, Charles, 193
Neal, George, 194
Neal, James, 193, 216
Neal, William P., 230
Neely, Ann Irvine, 127
Neely, William, 127
Negroes, at River Raisin, 95, 125
Nelson, R., 97n
Netherland, John, 194
Nevins, Henry, 206
New Orleans, Battle of, xi, 128
New York (State), prisoners enter, 94-95
Newal, Armstrong, 206
Newell, Hugh, 67, 212
Newfoundland Fencibles, 63
Newport, Ky., 17-18, 24; British prisoners at, 101; reached by troops, 22
Newton, Anna, 115
Newton, Mary Allen, 115
Newton, Robert, 115
Newton, Thomas, 115
Newton, Thomas Willoughby, 115
Niagara, 93
Niagara Falls, 95
Niagara River, 94-95, 167
Nicholas, Sergeant George, 219
Nicholas, Robert, 225
Nicholas County Ky., militia company from, 186-87
Nicholasville, Ky., 16; war fever in, 11
Nichols, Alexander, 227
Nichols, John, 202
Nicholson, Sergeant George, 219
Night View of the Battle of Raisin, 76-79
Niles' Weekly Register, 11, 87-88, 135
19th United States Infantry, 36; roster, 177
Noble, Mark, 227
Noble, William, 209
Noel, Armstrong, 206
Noland, John, 221
Nolin, William, 181
Norman, Caleb, 212
Norrel, Corporal James, 205
Northcutt, William B., 31, 148, 230-31
Norton, George, 188
Norvell, Joshua, 173
Norville, Joshua, 193
Nuchols, Louisa, 111
Nunnelly, Robert, 225
Nuvel, ———; see Hugh Newell

Oak Hill, 135
Oakley, Corporal John P., 182
Oakley, Thomas, 183
Offutt, Nancy Payne, 111
Offutt, Zabel, 111
Ogburn, Sergeant Thomas, 180
Ohio militia, at surrender of Detroit, 24
Ohio River, 22, 95, 122; troops cross, 23
O'Keefe, Lieutenant ———, 97n
Okely, Corporal John P., 182
Oldham, Corporal Jesse, 184
Oliver, John, 187
Olliwochica, Indian prophet, 5
O'Neal, David, 190
O'Neal, William, 190
Oram, Sergeant John, 195
Ormsby, Stephen, 163
Osborn, Jesse, 181
Osborn, Reuben, 181
Osborn, William, 181
Osburn, George, 214
Overfield, Mose, 187
Overly, Peter, 183
Overstreet, W., 194
Overton, Eliza Dixon, 109
Overton, Henrietta Ragland, 109
Overton, Major James, Jr., 173; biography, 109-10; captured by Indians, 68; negotiates surrender of Kentuckians, 71
Overton, John, 109
Overton, Lieutenant Thomas J., 176; death, 65
Overton, Waller, 109
Owen, Colonel Abraham, 6
Owen, Robert D., 221
Owens, John, 188, 209
Owens, Nathaniel, 225
Owens, Philip, 209
Owens, Stephen, 230
Owens, Wiatt, 230
Owings, Boswell, 204
Owings, John, 183
Owings, Corporal Thomas, 182
Oxen, George, 199
Oxford Township, Pa., 121

Pace, Joel, 222
Pace, Joseph, 223
Page, ———, 128
Page, Malinda Montgomery, 128
Pagget, James, 175
Pagget, Thomas, 175, 177
Palladium, 152
Palmer, Lewis, 223

Pannell, Benjamin, 221
Paris, France, 110, 128
Parker, Ann, 121
Parker, B. W., 225
Parker, Garland, 179
Parker, James, 221
Parker, James P., 193
Parker, Jane Logan Allen, 115
Parker, Joel, 183
Parker, Dr. John Todd, 115
Parker, Sergeant Levi, 178
Parks, Joseph, 187
Parmer, Thomas, 28, 29, 218
Parrish, Anderson, 179
Parrish, Sarah, 146
Patrick, Dr. George C., 67, 177
Patrick, Sergeant George C., 207, 208
Patrick, John, 204
Patterson, John, 201, 206, 216
Patterson, Thomas, 201
Patterson, William, 200-01
Patterson, William D., 201
Patton, Elizabeth, 126
Paul, Michael, 196
Payne, Ann Jennings, 110
Payne, Anne Conyers, 138
Payne, Asa, 111
Payne, Betsey, 111
Payne, Cyrus M., 111
Payne, Edward, 138
Payne, Elizabeth, 138, 162
Payne, Elizabeth Johnson, 111, 162
Payne, Emeline, 111
Payne, Franklin, 111
Payne, John, 111
Payne, Brigadier General John, 32, 45, 162; appointed to command, 18; biography, 110-11; on the Wabash River, 30; relieved by Harrison, 23
Payne, Latitia Thompson, 111
Payne, Louisa Nuchols, 111
Payne, Maria Williams, 111
Payne, Mary Stevenson, 111
Payne, Mary Wright, 111
Payne, Nancy, 111
Payne, Newton, 111
Payne, Polly Rogers, 111
Payne, Richard, 111
Payne, Robert, 111
Payne, Sally, 111
Payne, Susan Spencer, 111
Payne, Thomas Jefferson, 111
Payne, William, Sr., 110
Payne, William J., 111
Payton, John, 222

Pea Ridge, Battle of, 134
Peachy, William, 202
Peacock, William, 223
Peak, Emeline Payne, 111
Peak, James, 111
Pearson, William, 214
Pecannerie, Arkansas Territory, 117
Peebles, James, 197
Peek, Thomas, 185
Peel, Hugh, 225
Peers, Susan Dalrymple, 148
Peers, Major Valentine, 148
Pemberton, Corporal William T., 219
Pendleton County, Ky., militia company from, 187-89
Penitentiary, Kentucky, British prisoners in, 97ff
Pennington, Sergeant Tobias, 200
Pepper, Abel, 230
Percell, Thomas, 179
Perkins, Jeremiah, 181
Peterson, Annie, 144
Peterson, Eliza, 144
Peterson, Henry, 144
Pettitt, John, 203
Petty, William, 197
Phelkins, John, 228
Phemister, Charles, 218
Philadelphia, Pa., 21, 109-10, 133; Medical School, 130
Phillips, John, 221
Picqua; see Piqua, Ohio
Pierson, Bartholomew, 179
Piggs, William, 204
Pike, Mrs. Clarissa J., 131
Pilcher, Sergeant Beverly, 202
Pilcher, Lewis, 206
Pilcher, William S., 55n
Pindell, Eliza Hart, 149
Pindell, Dr. Richard, 149
Piqua Indians, 157
Piqua, Ohio, 24-25, 32
Pirogues, 43
Pitman, Asa, 223
Pitts, Joseph, 221
Pittsburgh, Pa., prisoners reach, 95
Pleasants, Sergeant Lucius C., 174
Plummer, George, 179
Poage, John, 173
Poe, Jesse, 221
Pogue, John, 175
Pogue, Lieutenant Colonel Robert, 37
Pogue, Thomas, 225
Poindexter, Meriwether, 221
Point Pleasant, Battle of, 145
Pollard, John, 188
Pollard, Thomas, 80, 188
Pollock, Anne, 124
Pollock, William, 206
Polly, John, 190
Poor, Corporal James, 182
Pope, John, 11-12, 16, 113, 163
Pope, Jacquillin A., 187
Pope, Rebecca, 113
Porter, Sergeant Benjamin, 212
Porter, Corporal Joel, 202
Porter, Peter B., 8
Porter, Samuel, 203
Porter, Thomas, 190
Porter, William, 212
Potawatomi Indians, 27, 30, 55-56, 63n, 120
Potts, Thomas, 216
Powell, Charles, 187
Powell, William, 187
Power, Jeremiah, 183
Powers, Robert, 185
Preacher, William, 202
Presque Isle, 49-50
Presque Isle Hill, 45
Presquille; see Presque Isle
Preston, A. M., 127
Preston, Anne, 126
Preston, Eliza Preston, 127
Preston, Elizabeth Patton, 126
Preston, Francis, 225
Preston, John, 126
Prewitt, Edmund, 175
Prewitt, Henry H., 225
Prewitt, Price, 230
Prewitt, Robert, 225
Prewitt, Ensign Vanallen, 224
Prewitt, William F., 221
Price, Cosby, 201
Price, Eliza, 161
Price, Elizabeth Singleton, 160
Price, Captain James C., 25, 61, 67-68; appointed to command, 16; biography, 159-61; company of, 193-95; death, 65, 161; in retreat at River Raisin, 123; letter, 160-61
Price, John, 175
Price, Kleber F., 160-61
Price, Martha A., 161
Price, Mary, 65n, 161
Price, Mary Cunningham, 159
Price, Samuel, 128
Price, Susannah Barkley, 160-61
Price, William, 159, 181, 194, 203
Price, Williamson, 225

Prichard, Talifona, 230
Priest, Elias, 199
Priest, George, 199
Priestly, Dr. James, 113, 163
Princes Grove, Illinois, 123
Princeton University, 149
Prisoners at River Raisin, appearance, 74; treatment by Indians, 75ff
Pritchard, Benjamin B., 199
Pritchard, Corporal Levi; see Corporal Levi Pritchett
Pritchart, William, 193
Pritchett, Corporal Levi, 198
Proctor, Colonel Henry A., xiii, 58-59, 83, 92, 169; at Battle of River Raisin, 62ff; at Battle of Thames, 90-91; biography, 166; censored for deserting wounded, 74; court-martialed, 166; Kentuckians surrender to, 71-73; reinstated to command, 166; tactics in battle at Frenchtown, 70
Profet, Anderson, 209
Profet, James, 209
Prue, Isiah, 185
Pruett, John, 197
Pruitt, Margaret Edmiston, 146
Pruitt, William C., 146
Pugh, Captain George, 49; appointed to command, 16; company of, 181-83
Pugh, Corporal George, 222
Pugh, William, 218
Pulaski County, Ky., militia company from, 226-28
Purvis, Lieutenant ——, 97n
Putnam, Illinois, 123

Quaife, Milo M., xiii
Quarles, Samuel, 216
Quebec, Canada, 116, 125
Queen Charlotte, 55, 62
Quinn, Sergeant David, 219
Quinn, Hiram, 209
Quisenberry, Anderson Chenault, 104
Quisenberry, Sergeant Roger, 203

Radford, Corporal Robert, 213
Ragland, Henrietta, 109
Ragland, Major James, 134
Railey, George, 223
Railey, Silas, 223
Railey, William, Jr., 223
Rainey, Abraham, 185
Raisin River; see River Raisin, Michigan Territory; see also Frenchtown, Michigan Territory, Monroe, Michigan

Ralls, Ensign Daniel, 181
Ralls, James, 193
Ralston, Alexander, 175
Ramsey, James, 195
Ramsey, John, 195
Ramsey, William, 197
Ranck, George W., 137
Randle, Nimrod, 228
Rankin, Benjamin, 225
Rapids of the Maumee, 111
Rapp, George Frederick, biography, 167
Rash, John, 197
Rash, Ensign Stephen, 195
Rash, Sergeant William, 195
Ratchford, William, 185
Rau, George, 201
Rawlings, Robert, 193
Ray, Elijah, 228
Ray, William, 183
Rayburn, Henry, 183
Rayburn, John, 183
Raynolds, Henry, 228
Read, John, 223
Read, Peter, 206
Reading, James Y., 230
Reading, Joseph, 181
Reading, Samuel, 221
Rearden, William, 222
Rector, Daniel, 199
Red House, 120
Redd, Mordecai, 216
Reddin, Nehemiah, 223
Redding, J. W., 181
Redding, Captain Joseph, 49, 111; appointed to command, 16; company of, 180-81
Redding, Thomas, 216
Redding, William, 173
Redman, Thomas, 197
Redman, Washington, 209
Reed, Adam, 175
Reed, Robert, 175
Reed, Sergeant Thomas, 205
Reese, John, 209
Register of The Kentucky Historical Society, 104
Reiley, James, 193
Rennick, A. H., 25, 219
Reno, Sergeant Lewis, 217
Reporter, 3, 11, 122
Resler, Abraham, 223
Reynolds, Major Ebenezer, 49-50, 55; biography, 167-68
Reynolds, Squire, 62-64, 68, 74, 89
Rice, Abraham, 216

Bibliography and Index 273

Rice, George, 195
Rice, John, 175
Rice, Joseph, 195
Richards, Alexander, 195
Richards, Edward, 107
Richards, Lucy, 124
Richards, Lydia, 107
Richardson, David, 183, 194
Richardson, Ensign J., 97n
Richardson, James, 146
Richardson, James A., 221
Richardson, John, 70, 98, 100
Richardson, John C., 176, 221
Richardson, Mrs. Judith L., 27n
Richardson, Mary Edmiston, 146
Richardson, Moses, 230
Richardson, Philip T., 204
Richardson, Robert, 195
Richardson, Dr. Robert, 70-71, 89
Richardson, Thomas, 209
Richardson, William H., 27n, 129, 177
Richmond, Ky., 16
Ricketts, Thomas, 199, 203
Riddle, A., 42
Riddle, Abraham, 218
Riddle, William, 188
Rife, Abraham, 228
Riley, James, 212
Ringo, Corporal Henry, 198
Ringo, Robert, 199
Rings, William, 199
Ritchie, Alexander D., 143
Ritchie, James, 201
Ritchie, Polly Brasfield, 143
Ritter, John, 212
River Raisin, Michigan Territory, 32; Brigade Inspector, 137-38; composition of battle force, 16-17; dead of, 56-57, 101ff; defenses, 58; first battle on, 46ff; killed, wounded, missing on, 48n; living and dead of, 92ff; massacre at, 80ff; Medical Department, 127-34; monument, 106; rosters of troops at, 171ff; second battle on, 62ff; *see also* Frenchtown, Michigan Territory, Monroe, Michigan
Roach, Sergeant John, 182
Roach, Sergeant Richard, 202
Robb, Major Joseph, 191
Robert, Joseph, 81n, 84n
Roberts, Jesse, 214
Roberts, John, 183, 214
Roberts, Pleasant M., 216
Roberts, William, 212
Robertson, Alexander, 173, 221

Robertson, George, 128, 221
Robertson, Willis, 181
Robins, Gerades R., 216
Robinson, Alexander, 221
Robinson, Elizabeth, 128
Robinson, Garrard, 230
Robinson, George, 221
Robinson, George Rogers, 221
Robinson, Isaac, 203
Robinson, John, 225
Robinson, John M., 230
Robinson, Michael, 206
Roche De Baut, 44
Rodes, Waller, 147
Rodman, John, 214
Rogers, Ensign Barnett, 189
Rogers, George, 214
Rogers, Harris, 199
Rogers, James, 183
Rogers, John, 181
Rogers, Larkin, 199
Rogers, Lue, 166
Rogers, Polly, 111
Rogers, Richard, 201
Rogers, Thomas, 199
Rogers, Valentine, 185
Rogers, William, 178, 181
Roland, Daniel, 230
Rolette, Lieutenant _____, 97n
Rollings, A. W., 208
Rolls, James, 193
Rooney, William, 223
Ross, George G., 193
Ross, John, 214
Rosson, John, 221
Rouge River, Michigan Territory, 120
Round Head (Wyandot), 63ff, 68; biography, 169
Rounder, _____, 141
Rounder, Martha Ballard, 141
Routt, William, 204
Rowan, John, 6, 113, 163
Rowen, John, 190
Rowland, Henry L., 223
Rowland, Joseph, 212
Roy, Beverly, 230
Royal Indian Department, 167
Royalty, William, 228
Royell, Abednego, 190
Royster, James, 190
Ruddle, Abraham, 218
Rule, Lieutenant Bryan, 51
Rule, Lieutenant Edward B., 178
Rule, Matthew, 179
Runyan, Benjamin, 183

Rusk, Robert, 206
Russell, Abednego, 190
Russell, Hendley, 201
Russell, Thomas A., 201
Rust, Matthew, 112
Ruth, Richard, 218
Rutherford, Rebecca Fifield, 133
Rutherford, Robert, 225
Rutledge, Joshua, 216

Said, James, 183
Said, Jesse, 199
St. Clair, General Anthony, 116, 124
St. George, Lieutenant Colonel Thomas, 62; biography, 168; wounded at River Raisin, 74
St. Joseph's River, 32
St. Louis, Mo., 113
St. Mary's, Ohio, 25-27
St. Mary's River, 40-41
Sale, Samuel, 209
Sales, Thomas F., 206
Salt Lake City, Utah, 124
Salt River, 163
Sammons, John, 204
Sampels, Samuel, 216
Sams, Daniel, 204
Sams, James, 155
Sams, Permelia, 155
Samuel, Isiah, 197
Samuel, John, 197
Sanders, Constant, 197
Sanders, Isaac, 230
Sanders, James, 212
Sanders, John, 221, 225
Sanders, John H., 188
Sanders, William, 188, 221
Sanderson, George, 201
Sandford, Alfred, 177
Sandusky, Isaac; see Isaac Sodosky
Sandusky, Ohio, 167
Sandwich, Upper Canada, 17, 66, 167, 216; prisoners reach, 94
Sandy Creek, 84, 86
Sanford, Lawrence, 190
Sapp, James, 28, 218
Satterwhite, Mann, 156
Satterwhite, Paulina Ann, 156
Scearcy, Leonard, 223
Scearcy, Merritt, 223
Schwing, Jacob, 193
Scioto River, 98
Scofield, Stephen, 185
Scothorn, Nathan, 197
Scott, Abram, 185

Scott, Alexander, 230
Scott, Arabella, 119
Scott, Catherine, 119
Scott, Catherine Ware, 119
Scott, General and Governor Charles, 3-4, 13, 16, 110, 114, 116, 118, 127, 132-33, 139, 142, 146, 150; appoints Harrison Major General, 22-23; bids troops farewell, 19-20; orders mobilization, 15; orders relief of Hull, 17; wife, 129, 156
Scott, Elizabeth, 119
Scott, John, 117, 194, 226
Scott, Major John M., 119
Scott, Lieutenant Colonel John Mitchell, 7n, 17-18, 23-25, 37, 88n, 122; appointed to command, 16; at Fort Defiance, 32-34; at the Potawatomi towns, 30; biography, 117-20; death, 119; regiment of, 177-90
Scott, Mrs. John M., 118
Scott, Joseph, 195
Scott, Judith Cary Gist, 150
Scott, Matthew, 117
Scott, Sir Walter, 129
Scott, William, 230
Scott, William B., 212
Scott, William Henry Harrison, 118-19
Scott County, Ky., militia companies from, 180-81, 184-85
Scroggin, Corporal Levin P., 217
Scroggin, William, 177
Scroggins, John, 223
Scroggins, Robert, 223
Scroggins, William, 176
Scruggs, James, 185
Seals, Barnet, 190
Seals, Bernard; see Barnet Seals
Seamond, Captain Manson, 147
Searcy, Berry, 190
Searles, Charles, 193; death, 84-85
Sears, Alexander D., 199
Sebastian, Elijah, 181
Sebree, Elizabeth Payne, 111, 162
Sebree, John P., 162
Sebree, Louise Daly, 162
Sebree, Admiral Uriel, 162
Sebree, Captain Uriel, 51, 61, 111; appointed to command, 16; biography, 162; company of, 189-90
Sechrest, Sergeant William, 205
2nd Brigade, Kentucky Militia, Brigade Inspector, 137-38
2nd Regiment, Kentucky Militia, rosters, 226-28

Bibliography and Index

Segar, Sergeant Benjamin, 174
Self, James, 185
Sellers, Jonathan, 212
Senly, Tucker, 214
Servant, Charles, 203
17th United States Infantry, 51; at Frenchtown, 61; at St. Mary's, 27-28; history, 153; placed under Winchester's command, 36; rosters, 173-77; surgeon, 128-29
Shackelford, _____, 113, 151
Shackleford, Edmond, 216
Shamblin, George, 230
Shane's Crossing, 40
Shanklin, Sergeant John, 194
Shannon, Reverend _____, 152
Shannon, John, 214
Shannon, Reverend Samuel, 177
Sharer, Jacob, 229
Sharer, Ensign Philip S., 173
Sharon, Samuel, 185
Sharp, Armistead, 181
Sharp, Elizabeth, Scott, 119
Sharp, Colonel Solomon P., 119
Sharp, Thomas, 214
Sharron, James F., 185
Shaw, John, 176
Shawhan, Daniel, 124
Shawhan, Mary McDowell, 124
Shawhan, Sarah, 123-24
Shelby, Caroline Winchester, 108
Shelby, Frances Todd, 131
Shelby, Governor Isaac, 87, 106, 112, 125; at Battle of the Thames, 90; buries dead at Frenchtown, 102; elected governor, 12-13; learns of defeat at River Raisin, 89-90; letter, 30-31; receives British prisoners in Frankfort, 96-97; recommends Harrison for Major General, Kentucky Militia, 23
Shelby, John Todd, 131
Shelby, Orville, 108
Shelby, Thomas Hart, 131
Shelby County, Ky., militia company from, 214-16
Shelbyville, Ky., 112, 115
Shelton, Colvin, 230
Shelton, Thomas, 206
Shepherd, Ezekiel, 216
Sherman, General William T., 131
Shimp, George, 176
Shindlebower, George, 193
Shingleton, William, 218
Ship, George, 174

Shire, John, 203
Shirerry, George, 203
Shirley, Robert, 181
Shoemaker, James, 218
Shoemaker, Spencer, 212
Shoemaker; *see also* Showmaker
Short, Sergeant Abraham, 184
Short, Cyrus, 185
Short, George, 185
Short, Obediah, 185
Shortridge, Charles, 199
Shortridge, Elisha, 204
Shover, Simon, 176-77
Showmaker, Elizabeth Lacklin, 155
Showmaker, Thomas, 155
Showmaker; *see also* Shoemaker
Shropshire, John, 230
Shryock, Christian, 225
Shy, Jacob, 230
Sidner, Frederick, 218
Sidney, John, 205
Sidnor, Robert T., 212
Sill, Sergeant James, 213
Sills, John A., 214
Silrey, John, 183
Silvey, John; *see* John Silrey
Simmons, David, 195
Simmons, John, 183
Simms, Josiah, 199
Simpson, Anderson, 201
Simpson, Andrew, 201
Simpson, James, 216
Simpson, John, 209, 228
Simpson, Captain John, 17, 61, 91; appointed to command, 17; biography, 163-64; company of, 212-14; county named for, 87, 163; death, 65, 79; militia volunteer, 13; town named for, 163
Simpson, Joseph, 214
Simpson, Robert, 209
Simpson, Sergeant William J., 198
Simpson County, Ky., origin of name, 163
Simpsonville, Ky., origin of name, 163
Simrall, Lieutenant Colonel James, 30; buries dead at Raisin, 102
Singleton, Elizabeth Neal, 160
Singleton, Fannie Garnet, 160
Singleton, Mason, 160
Skeene, William, 195
Slack, Gustavus Bower, 134
Slack, Isabella Bower, 134
Slack, William Y., 134

Slack, Brigadier General William Yarnel, 134
Slaughter, Francis, 221
Slocomb, James, 223
Slocum, Dr. Charles F., 37
Smallwood, Russell, 209
Smart, Humphrey, 187
Smedley, Daniel, 230
Smedley, Corporal John, 200
Smedley, Samuel, 200-01
Smiley, Jesse, 221
Smith, Abraham, 213, 218
Smith, Adam, 141
Smith, Anne Preston, 126
Smith, Benjamin C., 190
Smith, Charles, 230
Smith, Elizabeth T. B., 130
Smith, Major Francis, 126
Smith, George, 197, 223
Smith, Colonel J. W., 151
Smith, Jacob, 218
Smith, Jane, 126
Smith, John, 185, 187, 190, 221, 228
Smith, Reverend John Blair, 130
Smith, Johnston; see John Smith
Smith, Joseph, 225
Smith, Nancy, 155
Smith, Peter, 206
Smith, Philip, 197
Smith, Rebecca Jane, 155
Smith, Redsy, 154
Smith, Reuben, 181
Smith, Richard, 176-77
Smith, Sally Ballard, 141
Smith, Samuel, 221
Smith, Corporal Solomon, 194
Smith, Stephen, 193
Smith, Thomas, 177, 191; biography, 29n; letter, 29
Smith, William, 185, 187, 203
Smith, William I., 190
Snail, Eliza Brasfield, 143
Snail, William, 143
Snalley, Valentine, 193
Snap, Daniel, 186
Snell, Robert, 181
Snodgrass, Elizabeth McClenahan, 124
Snodgrass, Moses, 124
Snody, John, 230
Snydor, Sergeant John D., 203
Sodosky, Isaac, 179
Solomon (servant), 95
South, Rowland H., 225
Sparks, Joseph, 179
Sparks, Reuben, 221

Spear, Mary, 113
Spear, Moses, 113
Spellers, James, 201
Spencer, Absalom, 206
Spencer, Calmer, 223
Spencer, John J., 188
Spencer, Samuel, 228
Spencer, Susan, 111
Spicer, Henry, 223
Spicer, Corporal Raucer, 178
Spies, 226-28
Spires, Greenbury, 206
Split Log (Huron), 170
Spring Hill, 21
Springfield, Illinois, 130; First Presbyterian Church, 131
Springfield, Ky., 4n
Sprouce, Samuel L., 199
Sproul, John, 152
Sproul, Patsy Hickman, 152
Sproule, _____, 100-01
Spurgin, Moses, 179
Spurr, Julia Patton Hughes, xii
Stadler, John, 179
Stansberry, Thomas, 223
Stapp, Wyatt, 223
Steele, John, 223
Steele, Rankin, 221
Steele, Sergeant Samuel, 222
Steffee, George Griffith, 164
Steffee, Susan Crockett, 164
Stephen, Bela, 193
Stephens, Dawson, 219
Stephens, Thomas, 190, 228
Stephens, William, 228
Stern, Charles, 122
Stevens, William, 221
Stevenson, Mary, 111
Stevenson, Robert, 187, 223
Stewart, Armstrong, 193
Stewart, James, 188, 207
Stewart, Joseph, 179
Stewart, Sergeant Major, R. L., 173
Stewart, Rice, 176
Stokoe, Lieutenant _____, 97n
Stone, Dorothy Ballard, 141
Stone, Francis, 205
Stone, Ensign Henry, 222
Stone, John, 223
Stone, Stephen, 141,
Stony Creek, 59, 76
Store, Francis, 205
Story, Lieutenant Thomas, 51, **184**
Stout, Sergeant Ira, 202
Strode, Eleanor, 143

Bibliography and Index 277

Strode, Stephen, 52, 205
Strother, Agatha, 124
Stuart, A. H. H., 61n
Stuart, Judge Archibald, 61n, 114
Stuart, James, 197
Stucker, George, 223
Sturgus, R. A., 208
Sturman, Thomas J., 208
Stype, John, 206
Suddeth, Ezekiel, 197
Suddeth, Lewis, 197
Suggett, Reverend James, 191
Suggett, Jemima, 162
Sullivan, James, 181
Summerfield, Ephraim, 176
Summers, Andrew, 202
Summers, James, 206
Summers, Robert, 225
Summers, Thomas, 206
Summers, Thomas G., 223
Summers, William, 225
Surgeons, River Raisin Force, 127-34
Sutherland, Daniel, 228
Sutton, Patsy, 155
Sutton, Samuel, 225
Sutton, Sarah; see Patsy Sutton
Sutton, Thomas, 185
Swanson, Corporal Richard, 178
Swope, John, 209
Sympson, Mary Irvine, 127
Sympson, William C., 127

Talbot, Daniel, 193
Tallon, Captain _____, 97n
Tally, John, 203
Tandy, Linton, 201
Tandy, Willis, 201
Tapp, Corporal Elias, 184
Tarlton, Thomas, 185
Tate, John, 221
Tate, Thomas, 221
Taylor, James, 121
Taylor, John, 195
Taylor, Ensign Jonathan, 203
Tecumseh, 5, 32, 34, 45; not at River Raisin, 89
Templeman, Jesse C., 193
Tennessee, 107-08
Teralt, John, 214
Tericks, Samuel, 225
Terrel, John, 230
Terrell, Robert, 190
Tetricks, Samuel, 225
Thames River, 94

Thames River, Battle of, xi, 87, 90-91, 98, 102-03, 106, 133, 166-67
Theatre, Frankfort, Ky., 90
Theobald, Griffin, 188
Thomas, Jacob, 230
Thomas, James O. W., 190
Thomas, Robert, 230
Thomas, William, 219
Thomasson, Joel P., 155
Thomasson, Mary Kelly, 155
Thompson, Andrew, 197
Thompson, Charles, 181
Thompson, James, 176
Thompson, Latitia, 111
Thompson, Peter, 185
Thompson, Pitman, 207
Thompson, Richard L., 209
Thompson, Samuel, 183
Thompson, Thomas, 209
Thomson, Charles; see Charles Thompson
Thornton, Walker, 228
Thralkeld, Thomas, 216
Thralkeld, William, 216
Threlkeld, Thomas, 181
Throckmorton, Samuel, 221
Tick Creek, 140
Tilford, Alexander, 185
Tiller, John, 174, 176
Tillett, Job, 217
Tilly, Corporal Lazarus, 213
Timberlake, Richard, 230
Tinsley, John, 205
Tippecanoe, Battle of, xi, 5-6, 12, 112, 159
Tipton, Corporal Esmon, 208
Tipton, Corporal Esrane, 208
Todd, Abel, 185
Todd, Catherine, 119
Todd, Catherine Hoffman, 131
Todd, Charles, S., 41, 72n, 126, 202
Todd, Elizabeth, 133
Todd, Elizabeth J., 131
Todd, Elizabeth T. B. Smith, 130
Todd, Emily Husband, 131
Todd, Frances Stuart, 131
Todd, Francis Walton, 131
Todd, Jane Briggs, 130
Todd, Jesse, 230
Todd, Dr. John, 61, 83n, 87, 127, 191; biography, 130-31; cares for wounded at Frenchtown, 74ff
Todd, John Blair Smith, 130
Todd, Levi, 130, 133
Todd, Sergeant Levi L., 191

Todd, Lewis S., 223
Todd, Lockwood M., 131
Todd, Mary, 130
Todd, Robert S., 130, 191
Todd, Samuel, 130
Todd, Samuel B.; see Samuel N. Todd
Todd, Samuel N., 193
Todd, Thomas, 23
Todd, William L., 131
Toledo, Ohio, 34
Toles, Henry, 230
Tolin, Morgan, 205
Tombs, Anderson, 228
Tombs, Benjamin, 216
Toms, Anderson, 228
Tomson, Charles, 111
Tomson, Sally Payne, 111
Tooks, William, 179
Toom, Benjamin, 181
Toronto, Canada, 167
Toulon, Illinois, 121, 123
Tour, John, 190
Townley, John, 193
Townsend, George, 212
Townsend, William, 179
Trammell, James, 179
Transylvania University, 84, 109-10, 128, 130, 136
Trigg, Susan Hickman, 152
Trigg, Major William, 102
Trigg, William K., 152
Trimble, Robert, 183
Trotter, Colonel George, 153
True, William, 225
Truman, John, 214
Tucker, Joseph, 219
Tucker, Robert, 201
Tucker, William W., 214
Tuggle, John, 205
Turner, James, 209
Turner, Julius, 84, 181
Turner, Tarlton, 209
Turtles Town, 30
Tutt, Lewis Y., 223
22nd Regiment, Kentucky Militia, 151
Tyler, John, 216
Tylor, William, 214
Typhus fever, 38
Tyree, Tarlton, 185

Underwood, Benjamin, 221
Underwood, Bennett, 219
Underwood, Edward, 195
Underwood, Nathan, 189
Uniform of volunteers, 19, 148, 231

United Daughters of 1812, Kentucky, 150
United States Bank, 11
Updike, William, 221
Upper Sandusky, 42-43
Upton, Benjamin, 228
Utah, 124

Valandingham, Corporal Merit, 217
Valandingham, Richard, 197
Vallandingham, Hugh, 205
Vance, John W., 193
Vance, Joseph, 193
Vancleave, Benjamin, 216
Vancleave, Thomas, 216
Vanding, Stephen, 212
Vanhook, Aaron, 228
Vanhook, Lawrence, 228
Vanpelt, Derick, 193
Varble, Jacob, 225
Varvel, Andrew, 183
Vasvil, Daniel, 223
Veale, James, 225
Venable, Hamden S., 207
Venard, Absalom, 201
Venard, Thomas, 201
Verdon, William, 193
Vickers, William, 190
Viley, Warren, 181
Vinage, John, 197
Vincennes, Ind., 118
Vinsant, John, 190
Virginia Levies, 116
Virgus, Jordan, 209
Voorhies, Peter G., 152, 207, 219

Wabash Expedition, 139
Wabash River, 45
Wabash Valley, 23
Wager, Absalom, 207
Waindawgay, 63n
Walk-in-the-Water, 169; biography, 170
Walker, Alexander, 188
Walker, James, 195
Walker, Jeremiah, 174, 176
Walker, John, 187, 216
Wallace, Abraham, 207
Wallace, James, 207
Wallace, William, 201
Waller, Edward, 218, 230
Walls, Gabriel, 228
Walls, Isaac S., 228
Walls, Jacob, 228
Walton, Corporal William, 229
War Hawks, 8

Bibliography and Index 279

Warburton, Lieutenant Colonel ------, 97n, 99
Ward, Armistead, 183
Ward, George S., 195
Ward, John, 185
Ward, Thomas, 181
Ward, William, 181, 195
Ware, Catherine, 119
Ware, Catherine Todd, 119
Ware, Dr. James, Jr., 119
Ware, John, 228
Warfield, Lieutenant Benjamin, 197
Warren, Anne Wilcox, 129
Warren, Gabriel, 228
Warren, Joel, 216, 228
Warren, Letitia Sorrell, 129
Warren, William, 129
Washington, General George, 30, 85
Washington, Ky., 121
Waterford, Pa., 95
Waters, Lewis, 207
Watkins, Pleasant, 208
Watkins, Thomas, 203
Watson, Lieutenant ------, 97n
Watson, Bartholomew, 214
Watson, Julius, 183
Watson, Laban, 190
Watts, Jeremiah, 216
Watts, Corporal Johnston, 189
Wayne, General Anthony, 6, 35, 117, 125, 139, 151, 163; campaign of 1794, 24-25
Wayne, William, 209
Weaks, Mabel, C., xii
Weaver, Abram, 187
Webb, Adam, 176
Webb, James, 230
Webb, James C., 197
Webb, Richard, 216
Webber, Benjamin, 195
Webster, Thomas, 230
Webster House, Winchester, Ky., 158
Welch, Arabella Scott Davis, 119
Welch, Corporal John, 224
Welch, Sylvester, 119
Weldon, Corporal William, 196
Wells, ------ Carty, 112
Wells, Basil, 212
Wells, Benjamin, 212
Wells, Charles, 112
Wells, Derit, 185
Wells, Haydon, 112
Wells, James Q., 199
Wells, John, 212
Wells, Ensign Levi, 173; death, 113

Wells, Mary Kearney, 113
Wells, Mary Spears, 113
Wells, Rebecca, 113
Wells, Rebecca Pope, 113
Wells, Colonel Samuel, 23, 36, 122, 173; appointed to command, 17; arrives at Frenchtown, 57; at Fort Defiance, 32-34; at Potawatomi towns, 30; biography, 112-13; leaves camp at Frenchtown, 59-60; marches toward Detroit, 44; reports defeat to Shelby, 89-90
Wells, Samuel, Jr., 113
Wells, Thomas K., 173
Wells' Station, 112
Welsh, Alexander, 207
West, Edward, 164
West, Captain Lewis, 164
West, Captain Lynn, appointed to command, 16; biography, 164-65; company of, 184-85
West, Roger P., 230
West, Sarah Mahoney, 165
West, Susan, 164
West, Susan Jackson, 164
West, Van, 221
West, William, 221
West Point Military Academy, 119, 130
Westbrook, Thomas, 197, 199
Western Cemetery (Old), Louisville, Ky., 156
Western Citizen, Paris, Ky., 156
Wetherford, Elijah, 216
Wetherford, Martin, 216
Wharton, Joseph, 207
Wheat, Ann Logan, 135
Wheat, Judge Zachariah, 135
Wheeler, George N., 201
Wheeler, Joshua, 187
Wheeler, Samuel, 199
Wheeler, William, 187
Whiles, Sergeant John, 226
Whiskey, Indians find at Frenchtown, 80-81, 89; served to militiamen, 19
Whitaker, Aquilla, 216
Whitaker, John, 216
White, Brockman, 181
White, Charles, 176
White, James, 183
White, John D., 183
White, William, 183
White, Willis, 190
Whitehead, Dr. ------, 155
Whitehead, Jane Kelly, 155
Whitehurst, James W., 196

Whitledge, Lyne, 219
Whitledge, Thomas, 219
Whitley, Mrs. Wade Hampton, xiii
Whitney, Sergeant John, 191
Whitsett, Samuel, 199
Whittington, John, 225
Whittlesey, E., 56n
Wickersham, James, 185
Wiggins, Thomas, 185
Wilcox, Anne, 129
Wiles, Sergeant John, 226
Wiley, Nathaniel, 181
Wilhite, John, 201
Wilkinson, General James, 139
Wilks, Corporal Mills, 189
William, Lieutenant _____, 51
Williams, Ann Harrison, 165
Williams, Barnett, 178, 180
Williams, Benjamin Warfield, 166
Williams, Bennett, 181
Williams, Caroline Frances, 166
Williams, General Dick; see General Richard Luttrell Williams
Williams, Elias, 216
Williams, Corporal Elisha, 194
Williams, Eliza Ann, 165
Williams, Fanny Cluke, 165
Williams, Frances Amanda, 165
Williams, George, 208
Williams, Harriet Amanda, 166
Williams, Henrietta Hamilton, 165
Williams, Henry Clay, 165
Williams, James, 166
Williams, John, 158, 216
Williams, John B., 223
Williams, General John Stuart "Cerro Gordo," 165
Williams, Lue Rogers, 166
Williams, Maria, 111
Williams, Maria Louisa, 165
Williams, Martha McCracken, 158
Williams, Mary, 165
Williams, Mary Kerfoot, 138
Williams, Minerva, 165
Williams, Nancy L., 165
Williams, Olly, 197
Williams, Peter, 125
Williams, Rebecca, 165
Williams, General Richard Luttrell, 165
Williams, General Roger, 138
Williams, Rolla, 165
Williams, Captain Samuel Luttrell, 46-47, 51, 61, 69n; appointed to command, 16; biography, 165-66; company of, 197-99

Williams, Silas, 176, 185
Williams, Squire, 209
Williams, Sergeant Thaddeus, 198
Williams, Thomas Jefferson, 165
Williams, Walter Raleigh; see Rolla Williams
Williams, Wesley, 183
Williams, William, 223
Williams, Zephaniah, 193
Williamson, Anderson, 225
Williamson, Elizabeth, 141
Williamson, Jesse, 199
Williamson, Lieutenant John, 181, 187, 214
Williamson, Lucas, 201
Williby, Ashby, 214
Willis, John, 207
Willis, William, 207
Willmin, James, 223
Wills, David, 179
Wilmott, Charles P., 219
Wilson, Abraham, 199
Wilson, Alexander, 205
Wilson, Cumberland, 217
Wilson, David A., 205
Wilson, Ephraim, 229
Wilson, Henry, 231
Wilson, James, 197, 199, 221
Wilson, John, 179, 199, 231
Wilson, Mathias, 197
Wilson, Samuel, 189
Wilson, Thomas, 195
Wilson, Thornton, 217
Wilson, William, 225, 231
Winchell, Peter, 176
Winchester, Caroline E., 108
Winchester, Elizabeth Farrar, 109
Winchester, George, 107
Winchester, George W., 109
Winchester, Brigadier General James, 17, 21, 34-35, 80n, 93, 102, 120; advises Harrison of arrival at the Rapids, 46; advises Harrison of march to Frenchtown, 47-48; advises Harrison of occupation of Frenchtown, 57; Aide-de-camp, 109-10; appointed to command, 15; arrives at Frenchtown 57; assumes command at Fort Wayne, 30; assumes command of Kentucky troops, 31; assumes command of left wing of Northwestern Army, 36-37; at Battle of River Raisin, 64ff; authorized to advance to Rapids, 41; biography, 107-09; captured by Indians 68, 71-72; de-

clines Harrison's recommendations to abandon march to Rapids, 44-45; defeat at River Raisin, 62ff; defense, 108; founder of Memphis, Tenn., 108; in Frenchtown, 58; in retreat at Frenchtown, 67, 123; relinquishes command, 36; reasons for surrendering, 72n; secretary of, 135-36; tricks played on, 31; unpopularity, 29-31
Winchester, Lucillus, 108-09
Winchester, Lydia Richards, 107
Winchester, Malvina Gaines, 109
Winchester, Marcus, 38, 108; captured by Indians, 68
Winchester, Peter, 176
Winchester, Susan Black, 108
Winchester, William, 107
Winchester, Ky., 16
Winlock, Eliza L., 135
Winlock, General Joseph, 135
Winn, Adam, 226
Winn, John, 231
Winn, Thomas, Jr., 226
Wise, William, 205
Withers, Betsy, 133
Wolf, Henry, 185
Wolf, John, 212
Wolftown, 44
Wood, Benjamin B., 201
Wood, John, 176
Wood, Corporal Thomas, 196
Woodford County, Ky., militia company from, 222-23
Woodruff, Benjamin, 209
Woodruff, William B., 209
Woods, Andrew W., 210
Woods, Archibald, 208, 210
Woodson, Obediah, 195
Woodyard, Alexander, 189
Woodyard, Walter, 231
Wooldridge, Robert, 223
Woolfolk, Captain John H., 38, 61, 91, 135; biography, 135-36; burial, 102; death, 83, 135-36

Woolfolk, Joseph Harris, 135
Woolfolk, Mary Harris, 135
Woolfolk, Sowel, 135
Woolfolk, Sowel, Jr., 135-36
World, Robert, 212
Worles, Robert, 212
Worley, Ann McClenahan, 124
Worley, Stephen, 124
Worrel, Jonathan, 185
Worsley, W. W., 29, 38n, 55n
Wright, Jacob, 197
Wright, James, 181
Wright, Mary, 111
Wright, Morgan, 197
Wright, Reuben, 214
Wyandot Indians, 72, 170
Wymore, Lieutenant Martin, 202

Yancy, George, 221
Yankton, S. D., 131
Yates, Enoch, 198
Yates, George, 226
Yates, William, 181
Yellowstone Expedition, 162
Yelton, Jesse, 218
Yokum, Solomon, 219
York, Bartlett, 203
Young, Sergeant Edward, 195
Young, Eli, 183
Young, Joel, 195
Young, John, 197
Young, John M., 210
Young, Corporal Joseph, 196
Young, Merritt, 223
Young, Richard, 195
Young, Richard M., 223
Young, Robert C., 197
Young, William, 185, 197

Zimmerman, Philip, 189

NOTES ON KENTUCKY VETERANS

OF THE

WAR OF 1812

G. GLENN CLIFT

Borderland Books
Anchorage, Kentucky

1964

These random notes were gathered in the course of research and reading for a planned volume concerning *The Battles and Massacre on River Raisin, January 18-23, 1813.* The absence of even partial rosters of troops who served at Raisin prompted a search for participants in the two battles and at the massacre.

Sources generally were newspaper files owned by the Society, county pension lists, county histories and contributed cemetery and other local records. Newspaper accounts of the annual reunions held by the veterans at Paris, Kentucky, were read for names of veterans attending. These reunions were inaugurated in 1866 and held annually until 1883 or 1884. At the 1883 meeting, the 8 old soldiers attending voted one more reunion, to be held June 18, 1884. No account of this reunion was found and it is possible that the last was held in 1883. Oddly, at the 1877 reunion 39 of the veterans attended and 39 deaths were reported; at the 1878 meeting, 25 met and 25 were reported dead; the 1880 reunion saw 15 answer roll call, and the historian announced 15 dead; 12 met for the 1881 meeting, and again 12 were reported dead since the last gathering.

No concerted attempt was made to authenticate the soldier's organizational unit and time of service. A listing from the Adjutant General's report of Kentuckians in the War of 1812 was given, however, when it was apparent that reasonable accuracy could be maintained.

G. GLENN CLIFT

An explanation of the abbreviations used follows the last entry.

ADAMS, ELISHA. One of the last three veterans; living in Lincoln County. in Sept., 1879. *Yeoman*, 16 Sept. 1879. AG: Pvt., Capt. James S. Wade's Co., 7th Regt., U. S. Inf.

ADAMS, WILLIAM. Fayette and Harrison counties. Enlisted at Georgetown in Aug., 1812; also served in the Revolution; received pension No. S-6464. *Harrison County Pension List*.

ADAMS, WILLIAM. Mt. Vernon, Ky. Pvt., Capt. Ellis' (later Richard Matson's) Co., Aug. 15-Oct. 15, 1812; married Rebecca Lawrence, b. 1784-d. 1844. *NSUSD 1812, Ohio*, No. 9917.

ADAMSON, GEORGE. Mason County. Attended 11th annual reunion, 1876, aged 85. *Yeoman*, 24 June 1876; *TK*, 21 June 1876. AG: Pvt., Capt. John Dowden's Co., Pogue's Regt., KM.

AKERS, LARKIN (N. or H.) Jessamine County. Ensign, Capt. Thomas Lewis' Co., KM, commanded by Col. William Dudley; WIA at Dudley's Defeat, 5 May 1813; resident of Muhlenberg County in 1854. *Christian County Pension List*.

ALLEN, GEN. JAMES. Greensburg, Ky. Born Apr., 1770, Albermarle Co., Va.; officer War of 1812; killed by a fall from his horse 25 Nov. 1836. *OR*, 14 Dec. 1836; *C*, 7 Dec. 1836.

ALLEN, JOHN. Mason County. Born 9 Oct. 1771, on the ship *Partless*, while his parents were coming from England; remembered the Revolution and was a soldier in 1812; also recollected having seen General Washington and hearing him converse. *TK*, 22 Mar. 1876.

ALLEN, CAPT. JOSEPH. Hardinsburg, Ky. Born 20 Sept. 1774; his father emigrated to Kentucky about 1780, remaining a short time in the fort at Danville. "That place becoming too straight for him, he, together with Mr. Daviess (father of the celebrated Jo. H. Daviess) put up a couple of log cabins three or four miles from the fort, where they lived for some years." Capt. Allen went to Breckinridge County when it was almost a wilderness, was elected Clerk of the County Court in 1800 and held the office for 56 years. In the war of 1812 "he was active in raising volunteers, and in keeping with his character, put his own person in the fore front of the peril." He died at Hardinsburg, 23 April 1862. *C*, 7 May 1862.

ALLEN, M. W. Scott County. Attended 6th annual reunion, 1871, aged 81. C, 7 July 1871. Not in AG under these initials.

ALLEN, WILLIAM W. Franklin County. Attended 8th annual reunion, 1873, aged 82; 11th reunion, 1876, aged 85. WC, 24 June 1873; Yoeman, 24 June 1876; TK, 21 June 1876. AG: Pvt., Capt. Joseph Clark's Co., 3rd Regt., KMV.

AMMERMEN, ALBERT. Pendleton County. Pvt., Capt. Michael Glaves' Co., 1st Regt., KVM; WIA Jan. 18, 1813, at Frenchtown; moved from Kentucky to Adams County, Illinois, in Sept., 1835; placed on Kentucky pension rolls, 30 Nov. 1820. *Pendleton County Pensions; Sen. Doc. 514.*

ANDERSON, JOHN. Christian County. One of 150 picked Kentucky volunteers who fought with Perry on Lake Erie; assigned to the *Niagara.* Not listed in U. S. War Dept. list of these "Horse Marines." Perrin, W. H., *History of Christian County* . . . 1884, p. 171.

ANDERSON, OLIVER. Jessamine County. Born in Jessamine County [sic] 18 Feb. 1794; "he enlisted in the army which marched from Kentucky in 1813 to the relief of the Northwestern frontier and was present at several battles . . . and was wounded and taken prisoner at River Raisin." He died in Lexington in Jan., 1873. *Yoeman,* 6 Feb. 1873. AG: Pvt., Capt. Patrick Gray's Co., Lewis' Regt., KVM.

ANDREWS, ABRAM M. Fayette County. "An old soldier of 1812; died in Fayette County, 10 Aug. 1875, aged 81 years; he was father-in-law of A. H. Sidener. He was buried at Old Union." *TK,* 11 Aug. 1875; *C,* 7 July 1871; *WC,* 24 June 1873.

ARCHER, MOSES. Pvt., Capt. Doherty's Co., 7th Regt., U. S. Inf.; enlisted from Adams Co., Miss., 1 Dec. 1811; injured; discharged 25 Dec. 1812 at New Orleans; married Mary Clark, 21 Apr. 1841. He died 18 Mar. 1846 in Polk Co., Mo. *Caldwell County* (Ky.) *Pension List.*

ARMSTRONG, BENJAMIN. Hopkins County. "He was a soldier of 1812, and was with 'Old Hickory' at the battle of New Orleans on the 8th of January, 1815, and from that time until the period of his death he never failed to observe, in his quiet and unobtrusive way, the 8th day of January; and at the close of the 8th day of January, 1873, he calmly breathed his last." *Yeoman,* 15 Feb. 1873. AG: Pvt., Capt. Robert Thruston's Co., KDM, 10 Nov. 1814-10 May 1815.

ARMSTRONG, JAMES R. Boyle County. Born in Penna., 1787; attended the 1870 and 1871 annual reunions. *TK,* 22 June 1870; *C,* 7 July 1871. AG: Pvt., Capt. George Trotter's Co., 1st Regt., Ky. Light Dragoons.

ARMSTRONG, THOMAS. Franklin County. Pvt., Capt. Peter Dudley's Co.; POW at the Rapids, 1813. *Argus,* 12 Feb. 1814.

ARMSTRONG, WILLIAM. Bourbon County. Pvt., Capt. Maurice Langhorne's Co.; married Mary Wilson, in Harrison Co., 31 Jan. 1816; living in Scott County when placed on pension roll, 10 Oct. 1821. He died 16 Oct. 1831. *Scott County Pension List; Sen. Doc. 514.*

ARTUS, JAMES. Another who fought with Perry on Lake Erie. *Yeoman,* 11 Jan. 1879. AG: 4th Sgt., Capt. John Payne's Co., Ky. Light Dragoons.

ASBURY, HENRY. Jefferson County. Pvt., Capt. William Walker's Co.; enlisted 1 Sept. 1812; discharged 25 Dec. 1812; he lived later in Highland Co., Ohio, and in Madison Co., Ohio. *Jefferson County Pensions.*

BAILEY, ABRAM. Daviess County. Attended 10th annual reunion, 1875, aged 80. *Yeoman,* 26 June 1875. Not in AG.

BAKER, JOHN. Fayette County. Enlisted 1813 as a regular, for 5 years, in Capt. Caleb Holder's Co., 17th Regt.; married Cynthia Hutchinson, in Madison County, 30 Apr. 1817. He died at Lexington, 22 Oct. 1856. Issue: Surilda Baker; Palina Baker, b. 9 May 1842; Ellen Baker. *Fayette County Pension List.*

BAKER, JONATHAN. Clark County. Born in Clark, 1794; attended reunion of 1870. *TK,* 22 June 1870. AG; Pvt., Capt. John H. Morris' Co., KMVM.

BAKER, COL. JOSHUA. Mason County. Born 11 Mar. 1763, Frederick Co., Va.; married Mason Co., Ky., 9 June 1790, Susannah Lewis (9-13-1768 - 11-24-1813). He was at Strode's Station at the time of the siege, 1 Mar. 1781. "This distinguished patriot commanded a regiment in 1815 at New Orleans. He died at Nashville, Tenn., in April, 1816. *Lexington Reporter,* 10 Apr. 1816. Col. Baker was actively identified with the early military history of Mason County.

BAKER, OBEDIAH. Cumberland County. "He was a volunteer in the last war in Gen. King's Brigade, though past the age for military duty. He died 19 May 1839, at an advanced age." *C,* 28 May 1839. AG: Pvt., Capt. Samuel Wilson's Co., KMVM.

BALL, LEWIS H. Nicholas County. Attended 8th annual reunion, 1873, aged 80; also reunions of 1875 and 1876. *Yeoman,* 26 June 1875; *WC,* 24 June 1873; *TK,* 21 June 1876.

BANTA, PETER. Bourbon County. Attended annual reunions of 1871, age 80; 1873, 1874; died 22 Mar. 1875, aged 83. *C,* 7 July 1871; *WC,* 24 June 1873; *Yeoman,* 27 June 1874, 26 June 1876. AG: Pvt., William M. Rice's Co., KMV.

BARKER, JUDGE THOMAS. Bourbon County. Born there 10 Jan. 1795; married, 1818, Frances Dawson, "who yet lingers at death's door;" removed to Missouri, 15 Oct. 1838, resided in Monroe County until his death, 20 Feb. 1875. He was a Whig and Union man, but Democrat after the war. He was a noted short horn trader; member of the Christian church for 30 years, and buried by the

3

Masons. His home was near Paris, Mo. *TK*, 3 Mar. 1875, which states that "he was a soldier in 1812, and served faithfully."

BAY, JOSEPH. Montgomery County. Born in Pendleton Co. [sic]; Pvt., Capt. Thomas Morris' Co.; applied for pension while living in Montgomery County, 3 Apr. 1833, aged 66 years. *Montgomery County Pension List.* He was placed on the pension roll before, 29 Dec. 1820. *Sen. Doc. 514.*

BEALL, LEONARD. Winchester, Ky. Attended annual reunions of 1871, aged 75; 1873-1875 and 1876. *C*, 7 July 1871; *WC*, 24 June 1873; *Yeoman*, 27 June 1874; *TK*, 21 June 1876. Not in AG. Two Leonard Ball entries.

BEALMEAR, DANIEL V. Crittenden County. Cpl., Capt. Robinson's Co., 7th U. S. Inf.; enlisted 15 Apr. 1814; WIA. *Union County Pensions.*

BEAN, JOHN AUGUSTUS. Mason County. Born in Charles Co., Md., 5 Mar. 1792, son of Leonard Bean, a revolutionary soldier; they came to Mason County in 1806. "John A. Bean enlisted in Capt. Moses Dimmett's Co." He died in Aug., 1879. *Yeoman*, 12 Aug. 1879. Not in AG, Demmitt's Co.

BEARD, HENRY. Fayette County. "Served in the 42nd Regt.; died 17 Mar. 1838, at an advanced age." *KG*, 22 Mar. 1838. AG: Pvt., Capt. N. G. S. Hart's Co., Lewis' Regt.

BEATTY, JAMES. Fayette County. Attended 8th annual reunion, 1873, aged 79. *WC*, 24 June 1873.

BELL, THOMAS. Franklin County. A volunteer in Capt. Thomas Morris' Co.; injured about 1 Jan. 1813 (right arm dislocated). He also served three years in the American Revolution. *Franklin County Pension List.*

BELL, WILLIAM. Bourbon County. Served in Capt. Maurice Langhorne's Co.; was living in Henry Co., Ind., 1821 or 1822. *Scott County Pension List.*

BELT, DENNIS. Pvt., Capt. George Stockton's Co.; served in Capt. Holme's Co., 28th Regt., U. S. Inf., when wounded in action 4 Mar. 1814. *Fleming County Pension List.*

BENNETT, DR. JOHN. Covington, Ky. A successful practitioner at different times in Cynthiana, Falmouth, Newport and Covington. In 1813 he entered the army under the appointment of Assistant Surgeon; 1841, elected to Kentucky Senate; died at the Covington residence of Mr. H. B. Clemons, 31 Jan. 1847, aged 53. *C*, 10 Feb. 1847. AG: Surgeon's Mate, Williams' Regt., KVM, commanded by Col. William Williams.

BERRY, COL. ROBERT. Nicholas County. "He was a native of Virginia and one of the early pioneers of Kentucky; engaged in almost all of the campaigns against the Indians and was out three times as captain of a company in 1812. A braver man, or a better soldier never faced an enemy. On one occasion he, alone, took 17 British soldiers prisoners." He died 10 Feb. 1850, aged 82. *C*, 26 Feb. 1850. AG: Capt., Lt. Col. James Allen's Regt., 18 Sept.-30 Oct. 1812; Capt., Col. Richard M. Johnson's Regt., 20 May-19 Nov. 1813.

 BERRY, S. M. Scott County. Attended annual reunions of 1876, aged 80; 1881 and 1883. *Yeoman*, 24 June 1876, 20 June 1881, 21 June 1883.

 BERRY, WILLIAM. Living in Owen County when he applied for pension, 5 Oct. 1866, aged 80 years; married Sally Dawson, Owen County, 4 June 1848. He was charged with disloyalty and his pension suspended because he was said to be in favor of the seceded states. *Scott County Pension List.*

 BERRY, WILLIAM C. Clark County. Veteran of 1812 who died between June, 1870, and June, 1871, annual reunions. *C*, 7 July 1871.

 BICKNALL, LINSFIELD. Estill County. Pvt., Capt. Leslie Comb's Spies, 2 June-29 Sept. 1813; Pvt., in same, 17 Apr.-3 June, 1813; pensioned 28 July 1820. *Sen. Doc. 514.*

 BINGHAM, ISAAC. Madison County. Pvt., Capt. Christopher Irvine's (James Dyametto's) Co. POW at the Rapids, 1813. *Argus*, 12 Feb. 1814.

 BLAKE, GEORGE. Carlisle, Ky. Attended annual reunions of 1873, aged 79; 1874-1876. *WC*, 24 June 1873; *Yeoman*, 27 June 1874, 26 June 1875; *TK*, 21 June 1876.

 BOSTON, CAPT. JOHNNY. Woodford County. "A soldier of 1812. Died 13 Jan. 1875, aged 93 years." *TK*, 20 Jan. 1875; *Yeoman*, 26 June 1875.

 BOURNE, WALKER. Montgomery County. Born 5 May 1790, Culpepper Co., Va.; emigrated to Kentucky when 7 years old with father, James Bourne, a Revolutionary soldier; magistrate of Montgomery County for many years and at one time sheriff; served at the battle of the Thames; he was a teacher of note and one of his pupils was Richard Menifee, under whom Bourne served in 1812. He died 6 Feb. 1873. Reid, Richard, *Historical sketches of Montgomery County*, 1926, p. 64-5.

 BOWMAN, WILLIAM. Woodford County. Died in October, 1875. His death was reported at the 1876 annual reunion in "Deaths of soldiers of the War of 1812 since June 18th, 1875." *TK*, 21 June 1876.

 BOWMAR, JAMES H. Served in Capt. McCracken's Co., KVM . Died about 1 Dec. 1812 at Fort Defiance. *Palladium*, 10 Feb. 1813, with poem by friend.

 BOYD, A. Harrison County. Attended 8th annual reunion, 1873, aged 81. *WC*, 24 June 1873.

 BOYD, MAJOR WILLIAM. Bath County. Born 1796; died 30 Mar. 1881. "He was a drummer in Col. Owen's Regt., War of 1812." *Yeoman*, 5 Apr. 1881.

BRADFORD, CHARLES. Fayette County. Cpl., Capt. Nathaniel Hart's Co., at River Raisin; WIA, Jan. 18, 1813; POW, Jan. 22, 1813; pensioned 29 Dec. 1820; died 1 Sept. 1822. *Fayette County Pension List; Sen. Doc. 514.*

BRANHAM, CAPT. BENJAMIN. Scott County. Died at New Castle, of cholera, July, 1833. *OR,* 7 Aug. 1833. One of this name was Captain of a company, KMI, commanded by Col. Richard M. Johnson, 20 May-15 Aug. 1813.

BRANHAM, STANDFORD. Scott County. One of the veterans reported as having died between June, 1870, and June, 1871, annual reunions. *C,* 7 July 1871. Sanford Branham listed in AG as serving in Capt. John Duvall's Co., KDM.

BRENAUGH, THOMAS. Lincoln County, Pvt., Capt. Armstrong Keir's Co.; POW at the Rapids [Dudley's Defeat]. *Argus,* 12 Feb. 1814.

BREST, JOHN, JR. Garrard County. Entered service as Pvt., 1 Feb. 1813, Capt. William Garrard's Co., Vol. Light Dragoons; WIA 30 Apr. 1813 at Fort Meigs. He applied for a new pension certificate, to replace one lost, 17 Feb. 1865, at Xenia, Ohio. *Bourbon County Pension List.*

BRIEN, JAMES. Marshall County. "A resident of the Purchase for 55 years, a soldier of the War of 1812, one of the oldest and most consistent Democrats in Kentucky. Died Apr. or May, 1875, aged 83 years." *TK* 19 May 1875. Probably the James Brian listed in AG.

BRITTAIN, GEN. GEORGE. Harlan County. An early settler of Kentucky; served with the 54th Regt. (Knox County) during the war; died in Nov., 1850, aged 83. *C,* 22 Nov. 1850.

BRITTAIN, WILLIAM. Mason County. Pvt., Capt. John Baker's Co.; served with distinction at the two sieges of Fort Meigs. Died 2 Mar. 1876, aged about 84. *TK,* 15 Mar. 1876.

BROWN, HENRY. Pvt., Capt. Adair's Co., 17th Regt., U. S. Inf.; enlisted 25 Apr. 1814 and died in service 11 Jan. 1815. *Wayne County Pension List.*

BROWN, IRWIN. Pvt., Cpt. William Ellis's (Richard Matson's) Company of Kentucky Rifles; placed on pension rolls 8 Dec. 1825; died 8 March 1826. *Sen. Doc. 514.*

BROWN, JOHN. Born in Ireland; enlisted 23 July 1813 in 23rd Regt., U.S. Army; a shoemaker. *Woodford County Pension List.*

BROWN, SAMUEL. Floyd County. Enlisted May or June, 1813, in Capt. Charles Quary's (?) Co.; WIA; discharged in 1815. *Floyd County Pension List.*

BROWN, SCOTT. Franklin County. Emigrated from Virginia, 1790; for many years a magistrate of the county and for two years sheriff; "volunteered in the late war when nearly 50 years old, marched to the frontier and ventured his life to protect his country;" died at his home four miles above Frankfort, near the Kentucky River, 3 June 1842, in his 77th year. *C*, 14 June 1842.

BROWN, WILLIAM. Pvt., Capt. Gray's Co., 3rd Regt., U. S. Inf.; injured 27 Oct. 1817. *Christian County Pensions.*

BRUCE, ELI. Winchester, Ky. Attended 9th annual reunion, 1874, aged 79; died in Feb., 1876, aged 81. *Yeoman*, 27 June 1874; *TK*, 21 June 1876. AG: Pvt., Capt. James Sympson's Co., 5th Mounted Vol. Inf., 20 Sept.-20 Nov., 1814.

BRUCE, JOHN. Harrison County. Pvt., Capt. Thompson Ward's Co., Pogue's Regt.; pensioned 21 May 1833. *Sen. Doc. 514.*

BUCKNER, GEORGE. "An old citizen of Lexington and soldier of 1812; died at Lexington, Missouri, 17 Jan. 1871; father of William Buckner who resides with his brother-in-law, Asa Bean." *TK*, 1 Feb. 1871. AG: Pvt., Capt. John Edmiston's Co., 1st Rifle Regt., 15 Aug.-14 Oct. 1812.

BULLOCK, JAMES P. Clark County. For many years Clerk of the County Court. "In early manhood he volunteered in Capt. Clark's Co., from Clark County, in the War of 1812, and was terribly wounded in the engagement of Dudley's Defeat, from the effects of which he never fully recovered and which finally caused his death." Died in Sumner Co., Tenn., 2 Feb. 1858. *C*, 5 Mar. 1858. AG: Pvt., Capt. Joseph Clark's Co., KM., 4 Mar.-4 Sept., 1813.

BUSEY, ARTHUR. Shelby County. Attended 10th annual reunion, 1875, age 79. *Yeoman*, 26 June 1875. AG: Pvt., Capt. James Ford's Co., KDM., 10 Nov. 1814-10 May 1815.

BUSH, NELSON. Clark County. Attended 6th annual reunion, 1871; 8th, 1873; died 3 Oct. 1874, aged 84. *C*, 7 July 1871; *WC*, 24 June 1873; *Yeoman*, 26 June 1875. AG: 1st Cpl., Capt. Joseph Clark's Co., KDM., Mar.-4 Sept. 1813.

BUSH, COL. PLESANT. Clark County. Died Sept. 9, 1853. (Lexington, Ky.) *Statesman*, 13 Sept. 1853. AG: Ensign, Capt. James Sympson's Co., KMVM., 26 Aug.-5 Nov. 1813.

BUTLER, COL. ANTHONY. Logan County. "Born in South Carolina about 1774; as a lawyer and statesman he stood high in the confidence of Gen. Sumpter and patriots of the Revolutionary era; in 1807 he removed to Logan County, where he served as President of the Branch Bank at Russellville;" appointed Lt. Col., 28th Inf., U. S., 11 Mar. 1813; Col., 2nd Rifle, 21 Feb. 1814; discharged 15 June 1815; when victory was won in the Northwest he was placed in command at Detroit, Malden and Sandwich; after returning to private life he represented Logan County in the Legislature, 1818-19; in 1820 he was defeated by John Adair for the governorship; he had moved to Monticello, Miss., by the end of 1824. *Argus,* 20 April 1820; Heitman, v. 2, p. 268; Draper MMS.

CALMES, GEN. MARQUIS. Woodford County. "Served in the Revolution and in the War of 1812; died 27 Feb. 1834." *OR,* 6 Mar. 1834. Not in AG.

CALVERT, WILLIS. Boone County. Entered service 15 Aug. 1812, Pvt., Capt. John Hamilton's Co., Lewis' Regt.; WIA, 18 Jan. 1813; POW, 22 Jan. 1813; married 14 Feb. 1828, Rebecca A. He died 15 June 1849 at Nashville, Tenn. *Boone County Pension List.*

CAMPBELL, JOHN. Mason County. Born there; enlisted there, 1812, as rifleman; 1st Sgt., Capt. Henry R. Graham's Co., 1st U. S. Rifles; discharged at Newark, 6 Nov. 1813, because of wounds. Later lived in Madison and Lincoln Counties. *Mason County Pension List; Madison County Pension List.*

CAMPBELL, LT. COL. JOHN B. Of 11th Regt., U. S. Army; died at Williamsville, 28 Aug. 1814, of wounds received at the battle of Chippewa (5 July 1814). *KG,* 19 Sept. 1814.

CAMPBELL, ROBERT M. Clark County. Born Mercer County, 1793; attended annual reunions of 1871, 1873, 1875 (from Fayette Co.) 1876, 1883 (from Winchester, Ky.) aged 90 years. *C,* 7 July 1871; *TK,* 22 June 1870, 21 June 1876; *Yeoman,* 26 June 1875, 21 June 1883; *WC,* 24 June 1873. AG; Pvt., Capt. Abraham S. Drake's Co., KVM, 8 Feb. 1814-8 Aug., 1815.

CARLISLE, ROBERT. Fayette County. Attended 8th annual reunion, 1873, aged 78. *WC,* 24 June 1873.

CARRICK, ROBERT. Scott County. Born Penna., 1795; attended reunions of 1871, aged 77; 1875-6 (from Fayette County). *TK,* 22 June 1870, 21 June 1876; *C,* 7 July 1871; *Yeoman,* 26 June 1875.

CARTER, WILLIAM. Pvt., Capt. Lynn West's Co.; placed on pension rolls, 1816, 1824, 1833. *Sen. Doc. 514.*

CARVER, BILLY. Gallatin County. "Uncle Billy Carver, a pensioner of 1812, is 83 years old, yet as full of fun as a dog is of fleas." *TK,* 22 Mar. 1876.

CASE, JOSEPH. Bourbon County. Born there, 30 Aug. 1791 (same year and month in which his wife was born); soldier War of 1812, served as a spy; died 25 Mar. 1870. aged 79 years. *TK,* 30 Mar. 1870.

CASEY, THOMAS. Falmouth and Pendleton County. Attended annual reunions of 1873, aged 76; 1874-76. *WC,* 24 June 1873, *Yeoman,* 27 June 1874, 26 June 1875, 24 June 1876.

CAWTHON, (CORTHRAM), ELEAZER. Madison County. Pvt., Capt. Dudley Farris' Co.; POW at the Rapids, 1813. *Argus,* 12 Feb. 1814.

CHAMBERLIN, THOMAS. Fayette County. Cpl., Sgt., in Capt. Nathaniel

Hart's Co., 14 Aug. 1812-10 Mar. 1813; in battles of Jan. 18 and 22, 1813; WIA, Jan. 22, POW Jan. 22 or 23, 1813; returned from captivity in Mar., 1813; pensioned 4 June 1833. *Fayette County Pension List; Sen. Doc. 514.*

CHAMBERS, MAJ. BENJAMIN S. Scott County. Lived at Georgetown; removed to Little Rock, Ark., where he died 14 Oct. 1833, leaving his wife and six small children, all daughters. Benjamin Stuart Chambers was an officer in 1812, member of Col. William Whitley's "Forlorn Hope," member of the Legislature and clerk of the Scott Circuit Court. *OR*, 31 Oct. 1833; *C*, 12 Nov. 1833. AG: Quartermaster, Col. Richard M. Johnson's Regt., KMI, 20 May-19 Nov. 1813.

CHAMBERS, GEN. GEORGE. Louisville, Ky. Born 1793; his death was announced at the annual reunion of June, 1875, as one of 19 old soldiers who had died since the 1874 reunion. He was a son of Dr. James Chambers, who was killed in a duel with John Rowan, at Bardstown, 3 Feb. 1801. His mother was Jude, a daughter of Judge Benjamin Sebastian. His father, Dr. James, was a colonel in the American Revolution, the son a volunteer in 1812. "Judge for twenty years without intermission, of the thousands of cases litigated before him not one was ever reversed by the Court of Appeals. When only 15 years of age he could split rails at the rate of 100 per day. He first learned the hat business, then studied law. He was married three times. He had a beautiful female child born unto him in his 74th year, which was made occasion for an assembly of the Bar and the presentation of a silver cup to his little daughter, Maggie White." He died near Louisville 8 Jan. 1875, aged 81. One of his daughters, Martha M., died 1 Aug. 1836, aged 19 years. One George and one George M. Chambers listed in AG: *Louisville Daily Journal,* 4 Aug. 1836; *Yeoman,* 26 June 1875; *TK,* 20 Jan. 1875. CORRECTION —

His mother was Amelia Sebastian, daughter of Judge Benjamin Sebastian, not Jude as stated therein. James Chambers and Amelia Sebastian were married in Jefferson County, probably in 1789, the bond being dated 30 Oct. 1789. *Jefferson County Book I, p. 9.*

CHAMBERS, JOHN. Mason County. Born New Jersey, 6 Oct. 1780; brought to Washington, Mason County, 1794; served on staff of Gen. William H. Harrison, War of 1812; Governor, Territorial Iowa; died at Paris, Ky., 21 Sept. 1852. *C,* 27 Sept. 1852.

CHAMBERS, JOHN. Coles County, Illinois. Attended 6th annual reunion, 1871, aged 80. *C,* 7 July 1871.

CHANDLER, W. L. Robertson County. A pensioner of War of 1812; died 22 May 1875, aged 82 years, 1 month, 10 days. His father was Circuit Clerk Chandler, of Robertson. *TK,* 21 June 1875; *Yeoman,* 5 June 1875.

CHINN, DR. JOSEPH G. Bourbon County. Born there 1 Apr. 1797;

volunteered at age of 15 and was severely wounded in the foot; attended annual reunions of 1870-71, 1873-76, 1881, 1883, from Lexington. *TK*, 22 June 1870; *C*, 7 July 1871; *Yeoman*, 27 June 1874, 21 June 1883, 20 June 1881; *WC*, 24 June 1875. AG: 1st Cpl., Capt. William Hutchison's Co., KMVM, 31 Aug.-8 Nov. 1813.

CHINN, WILLIAM. Bourbon County. Moved to Bourbon about 1847; was in the battles of River Raisin; died in Scott County, 22 Jan. 1872, aged 82. *TK*, 31 Jan. 1872.

CHISM, JAMES. Clark County. Attended annual reunions of 1870, aged 83; 1873, 1876. *TK*, 22 June 1870; *WC*, 24 June 1873, 24 June 1876.

CHORN, SAMUEL. Clark County. Born Mercer Co., 6 Apr. 1787; moved to Clark Co., 1793; attended annual reunions of 1870-71. *TK*, 22 June 1871; *C*, 7 July 1871.

CHRISTIAN, THOMAS. Fayette County. He was at Dudley's Defeat and one of the men who ran the gauntlet there; died 9 Jan. 1876, in Fayette Co., aged 85. *TK*, 26 Jan. 1876, 21 June 1876. AG: Pvt., Capt. Archibald Morrison's Co., KDM, Mar. 2-Sept. 2, 1813.

CHURCH, WILLIAM S. Franklin County. "He was a soldier of the War of 1812, and one, and almost the last, of the family of Churches so well known in an early day as spies, Indian fighters and true and faithful soldiers." He died at his residence on Main Elkhorn, near Stedmanville, 20 Apr. 1876, in his 85th year, and was buried near his home by his neighbors. *Yeoman*, 25 Apr. 1876; *TK*, 26 Apr. 1876.

CLARK, JOSEPH. Franklin County. Born Frederick Co., Va., 28 July 1793, son of Matthew and cousin of Gen. George Rogers Clark; removed with his parents to Nelson Co., Ky., 1798, later to Franklin; enlisted at 18 in Capt. Paschal Hickman's Co., captured at Frenchtown and held until war's end, being one of the 12 or 13 of this company of 86 who escaped to return home; sheriff of Franklin Co., 1831, and farmer until his death, 10 Nov. 1875. Portrait in Kentucky Historical Society. *C*, 9 June 1871.

CLAY, GREEN. Madison County. Born Powhatan Co., Va., 14 Aug. 1757; became Major-General on outbreak of War of 1812; headed 3,000 Kentuckians at the relief of Fort Meigs; died 31 Oct. 1828, and was buried on his estate within a few hundred yards of the present White Hall. Lexington *Reporter*, 19 Nov. 1828.

COMBS, GEN. LESLIE. Fayette County. Born near Boonesboro, 27 Nov. 1793; his wife Mary was born at Little Compton, R. I., 16 June 1823 and died 10 Aug. 1857. He joined the Kentucky volunteers in 1812 at Fort Wayne. Here he was attached by General Orders, Ensign, 1st Regt., KV, under Colonel Scott. He carried General Winchester's intelligence of advance toward Frenchtown t) General Harrison and so was absent from both battles and the massacre there, Jan. 18-23, 1813. He died 22 Aug. 1881. *Notes by Chas. R. Staples; Narrative of Gen. Leslie Combs, p. 5.*

COMBS, CAPT. WILLIAM R. Frankfort, Ky. "The eldest living brother of Gen. Leslie Combs. He was a gallant officer in the War of 1812-15; in peace, as fearless as any man on earth, and very powerful in single combat." He died on Easter Monday (April, 1866) in his 80th year. *Yeoman,* 5 Apr. 1866.

CONNELLY, ALEXANDER. Frankfort, Ky. Died 16 Apr. 1868, aged 75, at the residence of his nephews, A. and T. Carrick. An old soldier of 1812. C, 8 May 1868. AG: Alexander Conley, Pvt., Capt. James Hall's Co., 3rd Regt., KDM, 1 Sept.-25 Dec. 1812; Pvt., Capt. Andrew Coombs' Co., KM, 8 Feb.-7 Mar. 1815.

COOK, WILLIAM. Scott County. Pvt., Capt. Joseph Redding's Co.; enlisted 15 Aug. 1812, discharged 4 Mar. 1813; residence in 1814, 1824, 1850-56, Grant County, Ky.; 1864, Bartholomew Co., Ohio; 1871, Soldiers' Home, Montgomery Co., Ohio; WIA, POW, Jan. 22, 1813; married Sarah S. Reed. He died 16 March 1884. *Fayette County Pension List.*

COONS, BENJAMIN. Oldham County. Enlisted at Newcastle, Ky., 29 Aug. 1813; Ensign, Capt. Edward George's Co., KMV. He was 75 in 1850 and still residing in Oldham. *Oldham County Pension List.*

CORD, ZACHEUS. Fleming County. 1st Lieut., Capt. Phillips's Co., 10th Regt., KM.; discharged 29 Sept. 1813; lost his eyesight due to illness in service. *Fleming County Pension List.*

CRADDOCK, JESSE. Hart County. Born Pendleton County, S. C., 25 Dec. 1794; removed to Kentucky when 4 or 5 years of age; "he participated in the struggles, and endured the hardships and fatigues of two campaigns in the War of 1812, the last campaign being under the command of Gen. McArthur." He died at his residence in Munfordville, Hart Co., 28 Feb. 1847, in his 53rd year. C, 16 Mar. 1847.

CRAIG, GEORGE W. Harlan County. "His services were rendered to his country in the last war, as an officer. He was at his death surveyor of the county of Harlan, which office he had held in that, and the county of Knox, together, for upwards of 30 years. By his judicious arrangement of difficulties, he acquired the name of Yellow Creek Pacificator, in the portion of Harlan in which he resided. He died in Nov., 1833, leaving a large family." C, 26 Nov. 1833. AG: 1st Lieut., Capt. Thomas Laughlin's Co., KMVM.

CRAWFORD, A. B. Bourbon County. "Born in Montgomery Co., Md.; removed to Kentucky 1811; served in war of 1812 in Capt. Morris' Co.; reared

8 children; died 27 Apr. 1876, at the home of his son-in-law, B. F. Soper, aged 87 years lacking 15 days." *TK*, 3 May 1876. He is not in the AG list of Capt. John H. Morris' Co., from Bourbon County. He lived at North Middletown, Bourbon Co. *Yeoman*, 27 June 1874.

CRAWFORD, J. B. Clark County. Attended 8th annual reunion, 1873, aged 77 years. *WC*, 24 June 1873.

CRAWFORD, THOMAS. Boyle County. He was 84 in 1877; was in the battle of the Thames, in Capt. McAfee's Co. *Yeoman*, 16 Oct. 1877. AG: Pvt., Capt. Robert B. McAfee's Co., KMI, 20 May-19 Nov. 1813.

CRAWFORD, WILLIAM. Boyle County. Attended annual reunions of 1871, aged 76, and 1875. *C*, 7 July 1871; *Yeoman*, 26 June 1875. AG: Pvt., Capt. Joseph Allen's Co., KMVM, 16 Sept.-30 Oct. 1812

CREWS, JOHN, Enlisted at Newcastle, Henry County, Ky., 1812, in 7th U. S. Inf.; married Lucy Hardwick, in Bedford Co., Va., in 1794 or 1795, when she was 16 or thereabouts. *Trimble County Pension List*.

CRIGLER, NICHOLAS. Boone County. Born Madison Co., Va., 2 Feb. 1772; removed to Boone Co., Ky., 1829; married 23 Jan. 1816; father of Robert L. Crigler. A soldier in 1812 from Virginia? He died in Boone County 13 Jan. 1871. *TK*, 1 Feb. 1871.

CUNNINGHAM, CAPT. JOHN. Bourbon County. "He had been a prominent citizen of Bourbon for years, and had represented that county in both houses of the Legislature, and held the office of Justice of the Peace for a number of years. He was a soldier of the War of 1812." Died 17 Aug. 1864, in his 70th year. *C*, 22 Aug. 1864.

CURL, JOHN. Bourbon County. Attended annual reunions of 1871, 1874-75; voted in the Clintonville precinct, 1874, aged 86 years. *C*, 7 July 1871; *Yeoman*, 27 June, 8 Aug. 1874, 26 June 1875.

CURRY, MAJOR J. R. Harrison County. Attended 6th annual reunion, 1871, aged 82; 1875-76. *C*, 7 July 1871; *Yeoman*, 26 June 1875.

CURRY, JAMES. Mercer County. Attended 8th annual reunion, 1873, aged 76; 1875. *WC*, 24 June 1873; *Yeoman*, 26 June 1875.

CURTIS, ELIJAH. Lincoln County. "The oldest man at present living in the county; 101 years of age. He was a teamster in the War of 1812, and recollects the incidents of that war as readily as we do those of our late civil contest." *Yeoman*, 18 Sept. 1877.

CURTIS, JAMES. Pvt., 7th Regt., U. S. Inf., under Capt. Jeofry Robinson; WIA at age of 40, on 23 Dec. 1814 at New Orleans. *Hopkins County Pension*

List.

DANIEL, ABNER G. Boyle County. Attended 10th annual reunion, 1875, aged 83. *Yeoman*, 26 June 1875. "His wife, Mary, died 24 Aug. 1876, aged 65, to make the handsome old veteran of 1812 a widower for the fourth time." *TK*, 21 June 1876.

DANIEL, HENRY. Montgomery County. Born in Virginia; removed to the southeastern part of Clark Co., Ky., when quite small; read law with Henry Clay, obtained license in 1809 and settled in Mt. Sterling until the outbreak of War of 1812; volunteered and rose to Captain. "A brave man never drew a sword or bore a commission." He died 5 Oct. 1873, nearly 91 years of age. Reid, Richard, *Historical Sketches of Montgomery Co., Ky.*, 1926, p. 46-7; *Yeoman*, 14 Oct. 1873.

DANIEL, JESSE. Fayette County? Died of erysipelas, 13 Mar. 1853, in his 88th year. *C*, 12 Apr. 1853. AG: Lieut., Capt. William Farrow's Co., 3rd. Regt., KMV, 1 Sept.-Oct. 1, 1812.

DARNELL, SPENCER. Served in KM, under Lt. Col. William Dudley; WIA, 5 May 1813 at Fort Meigs; POW, paroled 10 May 1813. *Fayette County Pension List.*

DAVENPORT, COL. RICHARD. Danville, Ky. Major, 17th Inf., U. S., 12 Apr. 1812; resigned 1 Feb. 1813; Lt. Col., Ky. Volunteers, 31 Aug.-8 Nov., 1813; died in August, 1818. Lexington, Ky., *Reporter*, 26 Aug. 1818.

DAVIDSON, COL. JAMES. Lincoln County. Served in 63rd Regt. (Lincoln Co.) He was at the battle of Tippecanoe and stated later that John King, *q.v.*, killed Tecumseh. He was Treasurer of Kentucky, 1825-1840; died 31 May 1861, aged 83 years, 6 months and 18 days. *C*, 14 June 1861; *Yeoman*, 14 June 1881.

DAVIDSON, CAPT. MICHAEL. Lincoln County. Served as Ensign, Capt. George Murrell's Co., KMV, 18 Sept.-30 Oct. 1812; Captain of his own company, KMV, Davenport's Regt., 25 Aug.-8 Nov. 1813. He died 9 Mar. 1847, aged 69 years. *OR*, 20 Mar. 1847.

DAVIS, GEORGE. Mercer County. He was in the battle of New Orleans; attended 8th annual reunion, 1873, aged 77; 1875-76. *WC*, 24 June 1873; *Yeoman*, 24 June 1875; *TK*, 21 June 1876.

DAVIS, JAMES S. Pvt., Capt. B. W. Saunders Co., 17th Regt., U. S. Inf.; WIA about 14 Aug. 1814 at Mackinaw, Mich.; married Jane Elam, in Wayne Co., Ky., 24 Dec. 1831. He died in Wayne County 29 Nov. 1844. *Wayne County Pension List.*

DAVIS, SOLOMON. Pulaski County. "He was a soldier of '12, never drew a pension; an inmate of the Asylum for the Poor, he fell dead from his chair in December, 1876, aged 80 years." *TK*, 9 Feb. 1876, 21 June 1876.

DAVIS, MAJOR WILLIAM MILTON. Shelby County. "During the late war with Great Britain, he held a captain's commission in the volunteer army of the U. S., and was at the battles of the Thames and New Orleans, and for several years past has been one of the confidential commissioners of the Federal Government in the Indian negotiations." He died 24 Dec. 1836 in his 40th year. *C*, 18 Jan. 1837.

DAWSON, JOHN. Sgt., Capt. Michael Glaves Co.; born 24 Nov. 1791, Bracken Co., Ky.; at battles of River Raisin; died 12 Nov. 1850; buried Clear Lake District, Sangamon Co., Ill. *Honor Roll of Soldiers buried in Illinois*, Vol. 1. (MS)

DERBIN, NAPOLEON M. Harrison County. Served in War of 1812; died in March, 1871, aged 55 years. *TK*, 22 Mar. 1871.

DILLARD, REV. R. T. Attended 9th annual reunion, 1874, aged 77. *Yeoman*, 27 June 1874.

DOHONEY, WILLIAM (Dehoney). Pvt., Capt. John Duvall's Co., KVM; WIA, 5 May 1813; received a pension commencing 4 June 1821. *Owen County Pension List*.

DOLLARHIDE, COL. THOMAS. Pulaski County. Senator from Pulaski, 1819-1821; member House of Representatives (Kentucky), 1814-1818; died at Frankfort, 18 Nov. 1821. Lexington, Ky., *Reporter*, 17 Dec. 1821. AG: Capt., Kentucky Mounted Volunteers, 18 Sept.-27 Oct. 1812.

DOUGHERTY, HENRY. Harrison County, 1st Cpl., Capt. John D. Thomas' Co., Boswell's Regt.; pensioned 21 Mar. 1817. *Sen. Doc. 514*.

DRAKE, CAPT. ABRAHAM S. Lexington, Ky. Born 1781; died 6 Sept. 1831. Lexington, Ky., *Reporter*, 14 Sept. 1831. He was Capt., Col. Francisco's Regt., 4 Feb.-8 Aug. 1815.

DUCKER, ENOCH. Fayette County. Enlisted 29 Mar. 1812 (or 9 Mar. 1813 ?) in Capt. John C. Morrison's Co.; married Mary Craig, in Woodford Co., 4 June 1846 or 1848; (her first husband, William M. Craig, died 14 Sept. 1832); he died 27 or 29 March 1871. *Woodford County Pension List*.

DUDLEY, AMBROSE, JR. One of eleven sons of Rev. Ambrose Dudley, famed Baptist minister of Fayette and Captain in the American Revolution;

Ambrose the son saw much service in 1812 including action at Thames. *Yeoman*, 18 Sept. 1884.

DUDLEY THOMAS. Brother of Ambrose, Jr., above. He saw extensive service in 1812 and in 1815 was Captain of a company in Lt. Col. John Francisco's Regt. *Yeoman*, 18 Sept. 1884.

DUDLEY, JEPTHA. Brother of Ambrose, Jr., and James, above. He resided in Franklin County and died there 20 Mar. 1863, aged 85 years. *C*, 23 Mar. 1863. He resigned 13 May 1813 as magistrate of Franklin and was commissioned an officer in the 28th Regt., U. S. Inf., under Col. Thomas Deye Owings. (Capt., 28th Inf., 29 May 1813; resigned 1 June 1813. Heitman, v.1,p. 386.; *Yeoman*, 18 Sept. 1884.

DUDLEY, COL. PARKER. Fayette County. Served in battle of New Orleans and was Receiver of the U. S. Land Office at Palmyra, Mo., where he died in Sept., 1853. Lexington, Ky., *Statesman*, 27 Sept. 1853.

DUDLEY, PETER. Franklin County. Another of Rev. Ambrose Dudley's sons; born 21 Mar. 1787; the family moved to Frankfort in Dec., 1804; engaged in trading expeditions between Frankfort and New Orleans, and was in the mercantile business until war broke out; served as Lieut. in Capt. Paschal Hickman's Co., 1812-13; after the massacre of Hickman's men, Lieut. Dudley returned to Frankfort and raised his own company, which he headed and led into action; as major of Kentucky Mounted Volunteer Infantry, he led his troops in action now referred to as "McArthur's Raid;" in private life he headed many public enterprises, including service as commissioner to contract for two Kentucky state houses; he was president of the Old Bank of Kentucky and Adjutant General for more than 20 years; Treasurer of Kentucky, 1840, and member of the Military Board of 1861. He died 17 June 1869. *C*, 18 June 1869; 25 June 1869; *Yeoman*, 18 Sept. 1884.

DUDLEY, THOMAS PARKER. Fayette County. Another of Rev. Ambrose Dudley's sons, (see above for others); born in Fayette County, 31 May 1792; moved to Frankfort when 16 and remained there until the war of 1812 broke out; enlisted and was wounded at River Raisin; was Quartermaster General at battle of New Orleans; later he was Quartermaster General of Kentucky for two years, and for eight years cashier of a bank in Frankfort. He became pastor of his father's church at Bryan Station and held that office 62 years. He died 10 July 1886. *KG*, June 1, 1870; Western Reserve Historical Society, *Historical and Archaeological Tracts, No. 1.*

DUDLEY, WILLIAM. Fayette County. Colonel under Gen. Green Clay at Fort Meigs where he was severely wounded, then slain, in action known as "Dudley's Defeat." *Yeoman*, 18 Sept. 1884.

DUNCAN, CAPT. JAMES, JR. Bourbon County. Born 8 July 1782, son of Capt. James and Elizabeth Strode Duncan; served in War of 1812; married 2 Apr. 1807, Nancy Musick. He died in Clay Co., Mo., 25 March 1841. Mrs. W. B. Ardery, *The Duncans of Bourbon County*, c 1943, p. 5-6.

DUNCAN, MAJOR JERE (JEREMIAH). Paris, Ky. Born there 12 May 1792; attended annual reunions of 1870-71, 1873-76; died 5 Oct. 1876. *TK*, 22 June 1870, 21 June 1876; *C*, 7 July 1871; *WC*, 24 June 1873; *Yeoman*, 27 June 1874, 26 June 1875. AG: Pvt., Capt. Richard Matson's Co., KMI, 15 Aug.-19 Nov. 1813.

DUNKERSON, WASHINGTON. Christian County. "One of the 150 picked Kentucky volunteers who fought with Perry on Lake Erie; assigned to the *Niagara*. Not listed in the War Department list of these first "Horse Marines." Perrin, W. H. *County of Christian* . . . 1884, p. 171.

DUNLAP, MAJOR ALEXANDER. "He was a Kentuckian by birth; volunteered in the War of 1812, was taken prisoner at 'Dudley's Defeat,' and would have been sacrificed if he had not been recognized as a Mason by a British officer. He was afterwards in the battle of the Thames, and for his gallantry on that occasion he was made a Captain, U. S. Army. He died 10 Nov. 1853 at Jacksonville, in his 68th year." *C*, 29 Nov. 1853. AG: Pvt., Capt. James Dyametto's Co., KDM, 12 Mar.-12 Sept. 1813; paroled by the enemy 5 May 1813.

DUVALL, COL. JOHN. Scott County. "Died at his residence in Scott, 7 Sept. 1859, in his 77th year. He was a citizen of Scott for 67 years and had represented that county in the Legislature, besides filling various other · civil offices in it. He commanded a company in the last war with Britain and served a campaign under General Harrison." *C*, 23 Sept. 1859.

EASLEY, WOODSON G. Shelby County. Born in North Carolina; removed to Kentucky 1811; volunteered in 1812 and served a tour of duty with the Northwestern army; died at his residence in Shelby County, 8 Dec. 1854, aged 64 years, 3 months and 22 days. *C*, 18 Dec. 1854. AG: 2nd Cpl., Capt. James S. Whitaker's Co., KMV, 25 Aug.-8 Nov. 1813.

EASTIN, MAJOR CHARLES. Fayette County. "The first white child born in Lexington, Ky.; died at the residence of his son, Capt. J. M. Eastin, 16 Sept. 1865, aged almost 90 years. He married in Shelbyville, in 1803, and from there emigrated to Indiana, settling in Madison. He served in the War of 1812, during the years of 1812 and 1814. He moved to Kentucky from Indiana in the spring of 1830, settling in Fayette county about 8 miles from Lexington. He was entirely blind for six or seven years preceding his death. He was survived by his wife and five of 13 children, three daughters and two sons." *OR*, 27 Sept. 1865.

EASTIN, THOMAS. Bourbon and Clark counties. Pvt., Capt. William Garrard's Co.; WIA at battle of Mississinewa, Ind., about 18 Dec. 1812; married 18 Dec. 1823, Meriam Colmers, in Woodford County; he was 5′ 10″ tall, had auburn hair and blue eyes. He died 20 May 1859. *Clark County Pension List.*

ECKLAR, JOHN. Harrison County. Attended 6th annual reunion, 1871; his death was reported at the 1876 reunion as occurring between the meeting of 18 June 1875 and that of 17 June 1876, aged 82 years. *C,* 7 July 1871; *TK,* 21 June 1876.

EDDLEMAN (EDELMAN), AARON. Harrison County. Attended the 6th annual reunion, 1871, aged 80; 1873-74, 1876. *C,* 7 July 1871; *WC,* 24 June 1873; *Yeoman,* 27 June 1874; *TK,* 21 June 1876.

EDDLESON, I. Harrison County. Attended the 11th annual reunion, 1876, aged 80. *Yeoman,* 24 June 1876.

ELDEN, JOHN. Harrison County. Attended 8th annual reunion, 1873, aged 78. *WC,* 24 June 1873.

EMERSON, CAPT. JOHN. Burkesville, Cumberland County. Born near Chambersburg, Pa., in which state he lived until the close of the Revolution; served in that war, and was at the fall of York, where he witnessed the surrender of Lord Cornwallis; removed to Kentucky at a very early date. "He wielded the axe that struck the first blow where now stands the proud city of Lexington, Kentucky . . . at the advanced age of 62 years he volunteered his services under Hopkins to be led once more, as a *private soldier.* Entering the army, as mentioned above, at the commencement of the revolution, he was appointed Lieutenant of his company, and was engaged at Brandywine, Germantown and Monmouth, among other battles . . . As a member of the lower branch of our State Legislature, he was a firm friend of the head-right settlers south of Green River, and the first mover of that series of laws which have received the appellation of the Relief System . . . At the age of 54 he studied law as a profession . . . and arrived at the highest honor of his profession." He died at his home in Burkesville, 17 Feb. 1836, aged 86 years, and was given a military funeral on 18 Feb. 1836. *C,* 2 Mar. 1836.

ESTES, ABRAHAM. Clark County. Pvt., Capt. Edmonson's (afterwards Capt. Richard Bledsoe's) Co.; WIA at River Raisin 18 Jan. 1813; POW, 22 Jan. 1813; married in Fayette County, 24 Dec. 1813, Beulah Schooler; he died in Clark County, about 11 Sept. 1825. *Clark County Pension List; Bourbon County Pension List; Senate Doc., 514.*

ESTES, CLEMENT. Bourbon County. Cpl., Capt. Richard Bledsoe's Co.,

Col. Allen's Regt.; WIA, 18 Jan. 1813, at River Raisin. *Bourbon County Pension List.*

EUBANKS, JOSEPH. Lincoln County. One of the last three veterans of the War of 1812 living in Lincoln in Sept., 1879. *Yeoman,* 16 Sept. 1879.

EVANS, GILEAD. Headquarters, Nicholas County. Born in Delaware, 4 July 1794, only child of John and Rachel (Taylor) Evans; married first Anna Trigg (1794-1864); second, Mrs. Rose Ann Sanders. *History of Bourbon, Scott, Harrison and Nicholas Counties,* 1882, p. 777-8. He attended the annual reunions of 1871, 1873-76, 1881, 1883. *C,* 7 July 1871; *Yeoman,* 27 June 1874, 26 June 1875, 20 June 1881, 21 June 1883; *TK,* 21 June 1876. AG: Pvt., Capt. Robert Henley's Co., KVM, 10 Sept.-9 Oct. 1814.

EWALT, SAMUEL. Bourbon County. Attended 6th annual reunion, 1871, aged 79 years. *C,* 7 July 1871.

EWING, COL. YOUNG. "One of the earliest settlers in this part of Kentucky. He was in several of the most important battles to the north during the last war between the United States and Great Britain, and he served in the Legislature of Kentucky [from Christian County for more than 30 years]. He died in La Grange, Tenn., 5 Oct. 1833, aged about 60 years. *C,* 19 Nov. 1833, from *Green River Advocate.*

FAIR, JAMES. Lexington, Ky. A native of Bedford Co., Va. He was a soldier in the late war with Great Britain and a spy attached to Gen. Wayne's Army. He died 10 Feb. 1847, aged 80 years. *OR,* 24 Feb. 1847. AG: Pvt., Stewart W. Megowan's Co., KV, 15 Aug.-14 Oct. 1812.

FARROW, JUDGE KENAZ. Montgomery County. Born Culpepper Co., Va., 23 Dec. 1794; emigrated to Kentucky 1810 and was studying law when war broke out. After the war he married Susan French, his cousin, and sister of Richard French, and practiced law in Mt. Sterling. He died 31 Aug. 1864 at the Mt. Sterling home of his son-in-law, Judge Peters, aged about 75. He was an able jurist and for many years on the Circuit Court Bench. *C,* 5 Sept. 1864. AG: Kennox Farrow, Pvt., Capt. James Sympson's Co., KMVI, 20 Sept.-20 Nov. 1814.

FENWICK, LEWIS B. Franklin County. One of the 13 survivors of Capt. Paschal Hickman's Co., battles of River Raisin. He was living in the county in 1862. Probably a son of William (1758-18 June 1833) a private, Maryland Militia, Revolutionary War, and Catherine Fenwick who died 25 June 1835. This Lewis B. Fenwick married, 1829, Monarcha Holton, sister of John A. Holton, *q.v. Fenwick Family notes,* Kentucky Historical Society.

FIFE, R. B. Born Fredericksburg, Va., 15 Apr. 1792; attended 1870 annual reunion from Louisville; 1874 from his home in Lexington. *TK*, 22 June 1870; *Yeoman*, 27 June 1874.

FISHEL, MICAEL. Fayette County. Lieut., Capt. George Trotter's Co. A cooper by trade. WIA during attack on the Mississinewa Towns. *Fayette County Pension List*.

FLEET, WILLIAM. Nicholas County. Sgt., Capt. Coleman A. Colliers' Co.; enlisted 15 Aug. 1812; placed on pension rolls 26 Jan. 1822. *Nicholas County Pension List; Sen. Doc. 514*.

FLOYD, CAPT. WILLIAM. Woodford County. Died 15 Jan. 1875, aged 82 years. A soldier in the War of 1812. *TK*, 20 Jan. 1875.

FLYNN, COL. MICHAEL. Clark County. Died 17 Aug. 1847, aged 66 years. *OR*, 24 Aug. 1847.

FOLEY, DANIEL. Mason County. Died in May, 1876, aged 85. *TK*, 21 June 1876.

FORD, REUBEN. Franklin County. "One of the gallants who so freely shed their blood in the War of 1812; died 7 Apr. 1856, aged about 65 years." *C*, 11 Apr. 1856. AG: Pvt., Capt. Virgil McCracken's Co., 15 Aug.-14 Oct. 1812; Pvt., Capt. James Anderson's Co., 1 Sept.-1 Oct. 1812.

FOSTER, WILLIAM T. Grant County. Attended 6th annual reunion, 1871, aged 74 years. *C*, 7 July 1871. AG: Pvt., Capt. James Dudley's Co., KM, 8 Feb.-7 Mar. 1815.

FOWLE, ISAAC. Nicholas County. A native of Vermont, born 24 Mar. 1791; hatter by trade; settled in Bourbon County, 1816; having served in the war of 1812; attended annual reunion of 1871, 1873. *C*, 7 July 1871; *WC*, 24 June 1873. He died 30 Dec. 1879. *History of Bourbon, Scott, Harrison and Nicholas Counties*, p. 772.

FOXWORTHY, SAMUEL. Fleming County. Died 9 June 1875, in his 87th year. *TK*, 23 June 1875. AG: Pvt., Capt. George Matthews Co., KMVM, 27 Aug.-3 Nov. 1813.

FUGATE, JOHN H. Pendleton County. Pvt., Capt. William Sebree's Co., Boswell's Regt. Pensioned 7 Aug. 1820. *Sen. Doc. 514*.

FUNK, ADAM. Fayette County. Pvt., Capt. Archibald Morrison's Co., 29 Mar.-31 July 1813; WIA, 5 May 1813, at "Dudley's Defeat." He married 13 Dec. 1841, Susannah Shackles. He died 24 Dec. 1849 in Barren County. *Green County Pension List*.

FURY, JOHN. Pvt., 1st Regt., U. S. Inf.; WIA in campaign against the Indians at Chicago, 16 Aug. 1812; a native of Ireland. *Jefferson County Pension List*.

GAITHER, HENRY. Cincinnati, Ohio. Attended 5th annual reunion, 1870, aged 80 years. *TK*, 22 June 1870.

GAYLE, WILLIAM E. Attended 8th annual reunion, 1873, aged 98 years. *WC*, 24 June 1873.

GILFILLIN, JOHN. "He was a lieutenant in the U. S. Army during the late war with Great Britain, and held that office till the disbandment at the cantonment in Mississippi." He died at Frankfort, 10 Apr. 1846, aged 63. *C*, 14 Apr. 1846.

GOANS, JAMES. Pvt., 28th Regt., U. S. Inf.; enlisted 22 Apr. 1814, for the period of the war; died at Detroit, 24 Nov. 1814. His land allotment papers were signed by George Stockton, late Capt., 3rd Regt., U. S. Inf., Flemingsburg, Ky., 7 June 1814. "Lavicia Goans, guardian, 3 children." *Bath County Pension List.* Date of Stockton's statement probably 7 June 1815.

GOLDEN, WILLIAM. Madison County. Died 11 Sept. 1866, in his 106th year. He was born in Albermarle Co., Va., 1760. He was a rough carpenter and sawed timbers used in the first court house at Richmond. He served in the War of 1812 and was at Fort Meigs. *C*, 2 Oct. 1866. AG: Pvt., Capt. James Dyametto's Co., Dudley's Regt.

GOODNIGHT, GEORGE. Harrison County. Attended 6th annual reunion, 1871, aged 82; died between June, 1874, and June, 1875, reunions, aged 85. *C*, 7 July 1871; *Yeoman*, 26 June 1875.

GOODNIGHT, MICHAEL. Harrison County. Born Fayette County, 5 Nov. 1793; living in Connersville, Harrison County, 1874; attended annual reunions of 1870, 1873, aged 78; 1874-76. *TK*, 22 June 1870, 21 June 1876; *Yeoman*, 27 June 1874; 26 June 1875; *WC*, 24 June 1873.

GORIN, JOHN. Barren County. Born 15 May 1763, Fairfax Co., Va.; pvt., cpl. and sgt., Virginia Militia; Capt. and Major in Kentucky Mounted Vols., Lt. Col. Philip Barbour's Regt., War of 1812; moved to Barren County, 1782; married there 26 May 1825, Elizabeth Duvall, b. 1793; received pension; died 5 Aug. 1837. *Barren County Pension List.*

GRAHAM, DR. CHRISTOPHER COLUMBUS. Louisville, Kentucky. Born near Danville, 10 Oct. 1784; died at Louisville, 3 Feb. 1885. Attended 1875, 1881 and 1883 reunions of the veterans at Paris. After the 1883 meeting, when he was 99 years of age, Dr. Graham stated that he had been mustered into service 71 years before, that he was the last remaining man who had seen Daniel Boone and that he had slept with him. *Yeoman*, 26 June 1875, 20 June 1881, 21 June 1883. For an extended sketch of the life and writings of Dr. Graham see Altsheler,

Brent, "C. C. Graham, M.D., 1784-1885, Historian, Antiquarian, Rifle Expert, Centenarian," in *Filson Club History Quarterly*, v. 7 (April, 1933), p. 67-87. AG: Sgt., Capt. Martin L. Hawkin's Co., 1 Jan.-31 Oct. 1814.

GRANT, DANIEL. Bourbon County. Born in Virginia; removed to Kentucky and settled in Bourbon when a boy; married there Miss Alice Elgin; served in War of 1812 as member of Capt. Maurice Langhorne's Co.; POW at Frenchtown; was drawing pension at time of his death; died 16 April 1876, near Columbia, Mo., in his 88th year. He left six children, two sons and four daughters, all married and settled in Boone County, Mo. *TK*, 26 Apr. 1876.

GRANT, JOHN. Boone County. Pvt., Capt. Jacob Stucker's Co.; enlisted 20 May 1813; WIA; discharged 19 Nov. 1813. He married 16 Feb. 1820, in Boone County, Polly Willis. He died 30 May 1849 in Boone. *Boone County Pension List*.

GRAVES, COL. JOHN. Fayette County. Served in 10th Regt., Fayette County; died 5 Aug. 1848, aged 76 years. *OR* 23 Aug. 1848.

GRAVES, THOMAS H. Scott County. Pvt., Capt. Lynn West's Co., enlisted 15 Aug. 1812; captured by Indians at Raisin River 22 Jan. 1813; he was born about 1793; married first Gabrilla Dollman, who died 1834; married second Elisa W. Graves, in Scott County 22 Oct. 1832; soldier moved to Hamilton County, Ohio, 1850, and five years later to Cincinnati. He died 6 Jan. 1855. His youngest child was then five years of age. *Scott County Pension List; Fayette County Pension List*.

GRAVITT, GEORGE S. Resident of Owen but a native of Franklin County. Served in 1812 under Col. Peter Dudley; was one who escaped at Fort Meigs 5 Mar. 1813; he died 1 Mar. 1864, aged 84. *Commonwealth*, 13 Apr. 1864. AG: Pvt., Capt. Peter Dudley's Co., KDM.

GRAY, ISAAC. Bath County. Capt., 10th Regt., KM; WIA 25 July 1813 at Fort Winchester. He moved from Bath to Trimble County, 1839. *Bath County Pension List*.

GRAY, PRESLEY. Gallatin County. Appointed by Governor Shelby to command 13th Regt., KM, destined for New Orleans; mustered in with the regiment at Louisville 10 Nov. 1815; resigned because of ill health; also served in Indian wars and in the Revolution, enlisting in latter at age of 17. *Hardin County Pension List*.

GRAYSON, JOHN. Fleming County. "A soldier of 1812, nearly 90 years old, is stout and active and says he is going to the Centennial with a pocket knife over 30 years old." *TK*, 10 May 1876. AG: Pvt., Capt. Samuel Gooden's Co., KVM.

GREENE, JESSE P. Pendleton and Clark counties. Pvt., Capt. Michael Glaves Co., 1st Regt., KM; WIA at Raisin River 22 Jan. 1813; received pension. *Pendleton County Pension List; Sen. Doc. 514, p. 5*.

GRIDER, HENRY. Warren County. Native of Lancaster County, Pa.;

born 9 May 1755; removed with his father and father's family about 1770 to Virginia, where he lived until 1781; came to Kentucky this year, settling in Fishers' Station, near the present Danville; removed to Warren County in 1799; married Aug., 1782, a sister of Jesse Smith, of Danville, who survived him; he was in his first engagement when 19 years old, at the mouth of Big Kanawha (Battle of Point Pleasant) and in the battle at Blue Licks, where he received an injury from which he never fully recovered; served in various campaigns under Wayne, Harrison, McIntosh, Scott and Clark; in War of 1812 served in Hopkins's campaign. He died in Warren County 5 Feb. 1843, in his 88th year, at the residence of his son, John Grider. *Commonwealth,* 17 Feb. 1843.

GRIDER, JOHN. Warren County. Lieutenant in Capt. Alexander Stuart's Co., 3rd Regt., KDM. Pensioned 17 July 1820. *Sen. Doc. 514.*

GRIFFIN, GEN. JOHN. Pulaski County. Served with the 44th Regt. for many years and was Representative and Senator from Pulaski. He died 17 Oct. 1854, aged 81, one of the oldest residents of his county. *Commonwealth,* 23 Oct. 1854. AG: Pvt., Capt. Thomas Dollarhide's Co., 12 Sept.-27 Oct. 1812; Pvt., Capt. John Evans's Co., KDT, Nov. 1814 for six months. Both he and his wife Mary (died 31 Aug. 1831, aged 60) are buried in James Family Graveyard, east of Somerset, Kentucky.

GRIGGS, WILLIAM P. Bath County. Attended 6th annual reunion, 1871, and 8th of 1873, aged 82 years. *Commonwealth,* 7 July 1871; *WC,* 24 June 1873.

GROVER, WILLIAM. Sardis, Kentucky. Died Mar., 1879, in his 83rd year. He had been married 56 years to his wife who survived him. A soldier of 1812. *Yeoman,* 18 Mar. 1879. Not in AG.

GUNTER, WILLIAM. Enlisted 11 Feb. 1815, for five years, in Capt. Richardson's Co., 1st Regt., U. S. Inf.; injured in service. *Franklin County Pension List.*

HADEN, BARTHOLOMEW. Volunteered in Wayne County in 1813 in Micah Taul's Co.; elected ensign; 2nd Lieut., Capt. Thomas Miller's Co., 7th Regt., KMV, 1813. *Wayne County Pension List.*

HALL, T. Danville, Kentucky. "A soldier of the War of 1812, and served as an orderly for General Cass." He died 23 Oct. 1869, in his 78th year. *C,* 12 Nov. 1869.

HALLEY (HOLLEY, HAILEY), DANIEL. Served in Capt. Richard Matson's Co.; WIA at Raisin 22 Jan. 1813. *Harrison County Pension List.*

HAMBLEN, WILLIAM A. Shelby County. A soldier of 1812; a Union man and hostile to the rebellion. He died 29 Aug. 1864, in his 73rd year. At the time of his death he was in Trimble County, on his annual fishing excursion. He was buried near his Shelby County residence. *C,* 7 Sept. 1864. AG: Pvt., Capt. Bland W. Ballard's Co.

HAMILTON, COL. WILLIAM. Carlisle, Nicholas County. Attended annual reunions 1871, 1873-1876, aged 83 or 84 at last reunion. *C*, 7 July 1871; *WC*, 24 June 1873; *Yoeman*, 27 June 1874, 26 June 1875; *TK*, 21 June 1876.

HANDLEY [HENDLEY], ELKANA. Pvt., Capt. Richard Bledsoe's Co.; WIA about 25 Sept. 1812; discharged 30 Oct. 1812 . *Fayette County Pension List.*

HARBOUR, JEREMIAH. Born near Lexington, Kentucky, 1797; enlisted June, 1812, at Glasgow, Barren county, in Capt. William Bradford's Co., 17th U. S. Regt., for 5 years; WIA at Fort Erie in Canada, 1815; also Pvt., Capt. Edward Wadsworth's Co., 1st Rifle Regt., Regular Troops. He married 19 March 1837, at Scottsville, Tenn., Louisa F. Estes, born 1814; he had married first, Nancy Bohon (Behan). Soldier's pension began 13 June 1815. He died 28 Jan. 1860 in Hart County, Ky. Louisa F. Harbour, widow, resided in Marion Co., Kansas, after 1874. *Barren and Hart County Pension Lists.*

HARDESTY, FRANK. Lowe's Station, Bourbon County, Attended 1873 annual reunion, aged 83; 1874, 1876. *WC*, 24 June 1873; *Yeoman*, 27 June 1874, 24 June 1876.

HARDING, THOMAS. Robertson County. Born Fairfax Co., Virginia, Nov., 1787; Sgt., Capt. Robert Henley's Co., KVM; attended annual reunion 1870-1871, aged 84 years. TK, 22 June 1870.

HARRIS, WILLIAM. Harrison County. Attended annual reunions of 1871, aged 78; 1873-1876. *C*, 7 July 1871; *WC*, 24 June 1873; *Yeoman*, 27 June 1874, 26 June 1875; *TK*, 21 June 1876.

HARRISON, DR. BURR. Nelson County [near Bardstown]. Moved to that place 1785; served at age of 18 as Surgeon's Mate, Wayne's last campaign; in 1815 he was at battle of New Orleans as Inspector General; died 3 Aug. 1845, in his 70th year. *C*, 30 Sept. 1845.

HARRISON, MAJOR MICAJAH "MIKE". Mt. Sterling, Ky. A son of Joseph Harrison, of Louisa Co., Va.; married Polly G. Payne. "A soldier of the last war, he died 23 Apr. 1842, in his 66th year." *C*, 10 May 1842; data contributed 11 Nov. 1952 by Mr. George H. S. King, Fredericksburg, Va.

HARRISON, MICHAEL. Born 16 July 1796 in Virginia; Pvt., Capt. Nimrod Moore's Co., 28th Regt. of Regulars; enlisted at Burkville, Ky., July, 1813; discharged in July, 1814, at Detroit; War Dept. records indicate he enlisted 21 June 1813; granted military bounty land warrant, 160 acres, 27 Nov. 1852, located in Whiteside Co., Illinois. He married 27 Aug. 1822, in Fayette Co., Ky., Rachel Rupert (born in Kentucky, 1792, and died in Whiteside Co., Illinois, 31 Jan. 1879.) He died in Whiteside Co., Ill., 2 Dec. 1863. He and his wife are buried in Grove Hill Cemetery, Morrison, Illinois. *Information contributed by George Harrison Sanford King, Fredericksburg, Virginia.*

HAVENS, WILLIAM. Enlisted in Flemingsburg, Ky., and served as Pvt., Capt. Daniel Goodwin's Co., KM, 10 Sept. 1814-19 Mar. 1815; married 13 Apr. 1814, at Floyd Court House (Prestonsburg) Elizabeth Shriver, who died prior to 1871; he was allowed pension on application executed 7 Apr. 1871, while living in Winchester, Adams Co., Ohio, aged 77. *Survivor Certificate No. 4594, Bureau of Pensions.*

HAWKINS, HENRY. Jefferson County. Pvt., Capt. Frederick Geiger's Co.; WIA at battle of Tippecanoe; pensioned 2 Jan. 1816. *Jefferson County Pension List; Sen. Doc. 514.*

HAWKINS, COL. STROPHER JONES. Henderson County. Born 1790, Fayette County, District of Kentucky; served at battle of the Thames, receiving honorable mention in dispatches; died "recently" at his residence near Henderson, aged 77 years. *C*, 11 Oct. 1867.

HAZELRIGG, CHARLES. Served two campaigns in 1812; died at his residence in Montgomery County 7 Mar. 1863. *C*, 16 Mar. 1863.

HEARD, MAJOR MORGAN A. Russellville, Ky. He died 5 Sept. 1833. AG: One Morgan H. Heard, Ensign in Capt. Thomas L. Butler's Co., U. S. Inf., 1814. *OR*, 15 Sept. 1833.

HEDGES, PETER B. Clark County. Attended 8th annual reunion of veterans, 1873. Not in AG. *WC*, 24 June 1873.

HENDLEY, ELKANAH. See Elkana Handley.

HENDRICK, GEORGE. Harrison County. Pvt., Capt. Thomas's Co., Col. Dudley's Regt.; WIA at the Rapids of the Maumee, 15 May 1813; his pension was transferred to Corydon, Indiana. *Harrison County Pension Lists.*

HENDRICKS, THEOPHILUS. Bath County. Attended 10th annual reunion, 1875, aged 84 years. *Yeoman*, 26 June 1875.

HENRY, JOHN F. Born Scott County, Ky., 17 Jan. 1793; educated at Georgetown Academy; studied medicine and in 1813 was appointed Surgeon's Mate in Boswell's Regt. at Fort Meigs; afterwards graduated from New York University; settled in Hopkinsville, Ky., 1822; subsequently moved to Burlington, Iowa, where he died in November, 1873. *Yeoman*, 18 Nov. 1873.

HENRY, GEN. WILLIAM H. Born 1761; died at Hopkinsville, Ky., 23 Nov. 1824. AG: 4th Cpl., Capt. George Trotter's Co., 27 Aug.-31 Oct. 1812; 2nd Lt., Capt. Johnston Megowan's Co., 2 Apr. 1813; Major General at Battle of the Thames. *No. 4931 Texas Society, USD of 1812.*

HERAN, CAPT. JAMES L. Lexington, Ky. Ensign Capt. Nathaniel G. S. Hart's Co., Lewis's Regt., 15 Aug.- 14 Oct. 1812. He died at Lexington 21 Aug. 1821, aged 32 years. *R*, Aug., 1821.

HEWLETT, LEMUEL. Hopkins County. Pvt., Capt. William R. McGary's Co.; Pvt., Capt. Alney McLean's Co., KDM. Pensioned 16 Apr. 1823. *Sen. Doc. 514.*

HEWLIT, SAMUEL. Pvt., Capt. Alney McLean's Co.; WIA near New Orleans; married Rebecca Browder, in Muhlenberg Co., 4 Sept. 1817; served in War of 1812 from 20 Nov. 1814-20 May 1815. *Hopkins County Pension List.*

HICKMAN, JAMES L. Todd County. "He served his country in the tented field in the War of 1812, and for many years was a Magistrate of Todd County." He died 24 Aug. 1855, in his 67 year. Formerly a resident of Fayette County. *C,* 3 Sept. 1855. AG: Pvt., Capt. Nathaniel Hart's Co.

HICKS, REV. JOHN G. Fleming County. A veteran of 1812 and for a long time a local preacher of the M.E. Church, South He died 14 Sept. 1876, aged about 85. *TK,* 21 June 1876.

HIGHFIELD, LEONARD. Pvt., Capt. William Sebree's Co.; WIA 5 May 1813, at Fort Meigs. *Pendleton County Pension List.*

HIGHTOWER, JOSHUA. "Emigrated with his father, who was a Revolutionary hero, from Virginia to Jessamine County, Ky., in 1791; married there twice; first Miss Childs, second, Miss Spencer. He made thirteen trips to New Orleans on flat boats and walked back to Kentucky eleven times. Was a soldier in 1812, serving two terms, and participated in the siege of Fort Harrison and the Thames, Tippecanoe, and other bloody battles, and saw the dead chief, Tecumseh, on the battle field. He died [in Logan County?] April 27, 1876, in his 97th year." *TK,* 10 May 1876.

HOLEMAN, HARROD. Served through the War of 1812, with his brother William B. Holeman, *q. v.* He was at the battle of Tippecanoe and always claimed to have killed Tecumseh. See also William B. Holeman, below. *Yeoman,* 9 Nov. 1880.

HOLEMAN, WILLIAM B. Born in Shenandoah County, Va., 11 Jan. 1797; died at his home in Orange County, Florida, 21 Oct. 1880. He came to Kentucky at the age of 8 with his father, J. Harrod Holeman, and his brother, Harrod Holeman, above, and settled at Georgetown. The two sons served through the War of 1812 and after that conflict settled in Frankfort where they commenced publication of the *Commonwealth.* They were several times elected to the office of Public Printer. William B. Holeman married 11 Jan. 1823 Margaret P. Major, daughter of George Major. About 1875 William B. Holeman moved to Orange County, Fla., where he engaged in orange growing. He left his wife and four children: W. B. Holeman, of Evansville, Ind., Rev. F. R. Holeman, of Florida, Mrs. James M. Jones, of Whitley County, and an unmarried daughter living with her mother in Frankfort. *Yeoman,* 9 Nov. 1880.

HOLLIDAY, THOMAS. Fayette County. Attended 9th and 10th annual reunions, aged 80 at the last gathering, in 1875. *Yeoman,* 27 June 1874, 26 June 1875. AG: Pvt., Capt. Robert Hambleton's Co.

HOLTZCLAW, BENJAMIN. Lincoln County. Served in battle of New

Orleans. He died in Lincoln, in September., 1879, aged 92. (He was burried on September 8.) *Yeoman,* 16 Sept. 1879.

HOMES, SAMUEL. Falmouth, Ky. Attended 9th annual reunion, 1874, aged 92 years. *Yeoman,* 27 June 1874.

HOWELL, DAVIS. Montgomery County. Born Delaware, 12 Sept. 1797; died 16 April 1874; attended annual reunions of 1870 and 1873. *TK,* 22 June 1870; *WC,* 24 June 1873. AG: 3rd Sgt., Capt. William E. Young's Co., 27 Aug.-31 Oct. 1812; Pvt., Capt. John Crawford's Co., 26 Aug.-5 Nov. 1813.

HOWELL, MASON. Daviess County. A native of Daviess; a soldier of 1812. He died in (October), 1875 in Indiana where he was long a prominent legislator. He was 81 at the time of death. *TK,* 27 Oct. 1875.

HUDNUT, ELIAS P. Mason County. Attended annual reunions of 1873, aged 79; 1874-1876. *WC,* 24 June 1873; *Yoeman,* 27 June 1874, 26 June 1875; *TK,* 21 June 1876. AG: Pvt., Capt. John Baker's Co., KDM.

HUFFMAN, GEORGE. Served in Capt. Forrest's Co., KM; was living in Grant County when he applied for pension, 4 Feb. 1834, and was then 59 years of age. *Montgomery County Pension List; Sen. Doc. 514.*

HUNTER, JAMES. Franklin County. Capt., 17th Regt., U. S. Inf. He was living in Bracken County 14 Oct. 1829. He was Adjutant, Kentucky Mounted Rifles, 1811; Captain, 17th Infantry, 12 March 1812; honorably discharged 1 June 1814; received by resolution of Congress 13 Feb. 1835 the testimonial of a sword for being engaged in defense of Fort Stephenson. Heitman, v. i., p. 557.

HUTCHISON, WILLIAM. Harrison County. Attended 8th annual reunion, 1873; died before next reunion, June 18, 1874. *Yeoman,* 27 June 1874.

IRVINE, CAPT. CHRISTOPHER. A son of Col. William Irvine, who died at Richmond, Ky., 20 Jan. 1819. Captain Irvine was killed at Fort Meigs, 5 May 1813. *Argus,* 5 Feb. 1819.

ISGRIGG, DANIEL. Bourbon County. Born Baltimore, Md.; a soldier of the War of 1812; died at the residence of his son-in-law, John W. VanHook, 11 Feb. 1871, aged 84. *TK,* 15 Feb. 1871; *C,* 7 July 1871. AG: Sgt., Capt. Memorial Forrest's Co., KVM.

ISRAEL, WILLIAM. Campbell County. Mustered in at Cincinnati, April, 1812, as Pvt., Capt. John Ferris's Co., Ohio Militia, for 6 months; attached to Regt. of Col. James Findley; injured 12 Sept. 1812. He was 89 years of age 19 Apr. 1864. *Bourbon County Pension List.*

JACK, HENRY. Fayette County. Pvt., Capt. Thomas Lewis's Co.; POW at the Rapids, 1813. *Argus,* 12 Feb. 1814.

JACKSON, GEN. JARVIS. Laurel County. He was 98 years of age in 1879. One of this name listed in AG as Lieut., Capt. James McNeil's Co., 2nd Regt., KM. *Yeoman,* 22 Mar. 1879.

JACKSON, JOHN. Franklin County. One of the old soldiers listed as having died, 8 Oct. 1875, aged 87; announcement made at annual reunion of veterans in June, 1876. *TK*, 21 June 1876.

JAMESON, JOHN. Ohio County. Attended 8th annual reunion, 1873, aged 80. *WC*, 24 June 1873.

JAMISON, BENONI. Harrison County. Served in Indian wars, 1791-94; enlisted in war of 1812 on 5 May 1813, as Pvt., Capt. John D. Thomas's Co.; WIA at Marietta, Ohio, May, 1813; pensioned 27 Apr. 1832. *Harrison County Pension List; Sen. Doc. 514.*

JANES, THOMAS. Pvt., Capt. Warfield Shirley's Co., KM, 23 Aug.-8 Oct. 1812; married Ann P. Golloher, in Adair County, 16 Nov. 1849; married first, Elizabeth Biggs. He was WIA at St. Mary's in Sept. or Oct., 1812. He died 12 June 1873 in Adair County. *Henry County Pension List.*

JEWELL, JOSEPH. Attended 8th annual reunion, veterans of the War of 1812, 1873, aged 80 years. *WC*, 24 June 1873.

JOHNSON, BENJAMIN B. Franklin County. "In early life he served his country honorably in the north-western army. He was appointed Postmaster of Frankfort, Ky., by General Jackson in 1829 and held this office until removed in 1840. He was a member of the Kentucky Legislature, 1841-44. He died at his Frankfort residence 10 Mar. 1848, aged 56 years." *Yeoman*, 17 Mar. 1848. AG: 1st Sgt., Capt. Robinson Graham's Co., KMVM.

JOHNSON, COL. JAMES. Scott County. Born Orange Co., Va., 1 Jan. 1774; moved to Kentucky, 1779; served as Lieut. Col., war of 1812, and commanded the right wing at the battle of the Thames. Elected to the U. S. Congress he died in office 13 Aug. 1826. *R*, Aug. 14, 21, 1826.

JOHNSON, MOORE. Mt. Sterling, Ky. Attended annual reunions of 1871, 1873-76, 1881 and 1883, being 88 years of age at the last meeting. *C*, 7 July 1871; *WC*, 24 June 1873; *Yeoman*, 27 June 1874, 26 June 1875, 20 June 1881, 21 June 1883; *TK*, 21 June 1876.

JOHNSON, THOMAS. Greenup County. Pvt., Capt. Coleman's Co.; POW at the Rapids, 1813. *Argus*, 12 Feb. 1814.

JOHNSON, GEN. WILLIAM. Scott County. Died 8 Feb. 1875, aged 77 years. Nine listings of this name in AG. *Yeoman*, 26 June 1875. (Probably not a soldier of the war of 1812 inasmuch as he would have been only 14 or 15 years of age at this time.)

JOHNSON, COL. WILLIAM. Scott County. He was the second son of Col. Robert Johnson. "He was one of those patriots . . . who fought in 1812; he commanded a battalion of the Kentucky militia and helped protect Fort Meigs from British and savage assaults, and was the first (with his battalion) of the troops under General Clay who reached that place, 5 May 1813. He continued in the service six months." He died at his Scott county home Monday evening, 25 April 1814. *Argus,* 30 Apr. 1814.

JOLLY, JOHN. Born in Penna., 18 Apr. 1788; removed with his parents to Bourbon County, Ky., when two years of age; 1835 removed to Callaway County, Mo., where he died 14 July 1873, aged 85 years, 3 months. In the war of 1812 he served under Capt. Ellis, of Bourbon County, and fought until the close of the war. He drew a pension from 1871. *TK,* 6 Aug. 1873. AG: Sgt., Capt. Henry Ellis's Co., KVM, 10 Sept.-9 Oct. 1814. Other listings in AG.

JONES, LEROY. Boone County. Pvt., Capt. William Sebree's Co., Boswell's Regt.; enlisted 29 Mar. 1813; discharged I July 1813; wounded at storming of York, 1813; captured by Indians on his way home and taken to Malden; exchanged Aug., 1814; married, 23 Aug. 1813, at Burlington, Ky., Melinda Rosell. They had nine children. He died 9 June 1836 at Pleasant Run, Ky. *Argus,* 12 Feb. 1814; *Boone County Pension List.*

JONES, SAMUEL B. F. Fleming County. "A veteran of the war of 1812; died in Fleming County Tuesday evening, 6 Nov. 1883. He was at the battle of the River Basin and at Fort Meigs, and his age was 95." *Yeoman,* 10 Nov. 1883.

JONES, THOMAS. Paris, Kentucky. Born Fayette County, 19 Jan. 1792; his father was James Jones, a revolutionary soldier who was born about 1758 in Spottsylvania Co., Va.; his mother was Sallie Schooler, also of Virginia; Thomas Jones was a volunteer in 1812, a member of Col. Johnson's Regt. of cavalry; he was at the battle of the Thames. He married 22 Jan. 1814, in North Middletown, Patsey Ashurst, born 1787, a daughter of Josiah and Rebecca (Kennedy) Ashurst. Thomas Jones was 88 years of age in 1880. At that time he had four living sisters whose ages were: Mrs. Nancy Ashurst, of Scott County, 91; Mrs. Sallie D. Talbott, of Bourbon County, 78; Mrs. E. A. Scott, of Clark County, 76, and her sister, Miss Mary W. Jones, 85. *Clark County Democrat,* 20 Oct. 1880: Perrin. William H., *History of Bourbon, Scott, Harrison and Nicholas Counties* . . . Chicago, O. L. Baskin & Co., 1882, p. 474.

JONES, THOMAS. Fleming County. Pvt., Capt. Benedict Bacon's Co., 16th Kentucky Regiment; WIA 21 Jan. 1815. *Fleming County Pension List.*

JORDAN, MAJ. GEN. PETER R. Mercer County. He was a Captain in the war of 1812 and commanded a company of volunteers; after that service he held office in the Kentucky militia, and rose by regular grades from Captain to Major General; he was one of the Justices of Mercer for many years and sheriff of the county just prior to his death; elected to Kentucky Legislature in Aug., 1846. He died at his Mercer County home 10 Feb. 1848, "aged upwards of 70 years." *Yeoman,* 17 Mar. 1848. AG: Capt., Barbee's Regt., KM.

KARSNER, JOHN. Owen County. He was a volunteer in 1812 and was wounded in the battle "in which the lamented Col. Dudley fell." He was living in Fayette County when he applied for increase in pension, for service as Pvt., Capt. John C. Morrison's Co., 9 Mar.-9 Sept. 1813. He died 29 Oct. 1853, in his 65th year. *C*, 22 Nov. 1853; *Woodford County Pension List.*

KEENE, GREENUP. "Doorkeeper to the lower house of the legislature. He served his country in the War of 1812." *C*, 15 Oct. 1850. One Greenup Keene, Scott County, was born there, 1791. His ancestors were from England and settled originally in Maryland. He was a son of S. Y. Keene and died in 1875. Perrin, *op.cit.*, p. 600.

KELLY, SAMUEL. Clark County. Enlisted in Aug., 1812, as Musician, Capt. Wiley R. Brassfield's Co.; applied for pension 20 May 1834, aged 47. *Sen. Doc.* 514; *Trimble County Pension List.*

KENADY (KENEDY), DAVID. Enlisted at Newport, fall of 1814, in Capt. Edward Whaley's Co.; pension transferred to Clark County, Indiana. *Harrison County Pension List.*

KENDALL, REASON. Henry County. Pvt., Capt. William M. Rice's Co.; POW at the Rapids, 1813. *Argus*, 12 Feb. 1814.

KENEDY, DAVID. (See David Kenady above). Harrison County. Pvt., Capt. Michael Wolf's Co., 1st Regt., KMM; pensioned 10 May 1834. *Sen. Doc.* 514.

KENDRICK, MITCHELL. Scott County. Enlisted 29 Mar. 1813 as Pvt., Capt. John D. Thomas's Co., Boswell's Regt. In 1853 he was living in Brown County, Illinois, aged 63. *Scott County Pension List.*

KENNEDY, JESSE. Bourbon County. Born 11 Aug. 1787 on Kennedy's Creek, Bourbon County, on the farm settled in 1785 by his father Thomas Kennedy "who redeemed it from a wilderness and transmitted his name to the stream which ripples through it, after he had lived several years in the fort at Boonesboro—had assisted Capt. Strode in building Strode's Station and had with Michael Stoner cleared and planted 'Stoner's field' noted in the early annals of Kentucky." Jesse Kennedy in 1812 commanded a brigade of Pack horses in the service of his country. In 1813 he was appointed a constable of Bourbon, holding that office for six years; as early as 1819 and for several years thereafter he was a contributor of learned articles to *The Western Citizen;* later he was a Justice for Bourbon and in 1829, 1831-32, 1841, elected to the Kentucky Legislature. He died 3 April 1863, in his 76th year. *C*, 15 Apr. 1863.

KENTON, THOMAS. Robertson County. Only survivor (in 1879) of Capt. Moses Dimmet's Co., war of 1812. *Yeoman*, 12 Aug. 1879.

Capt. Moses Dimmet's Co., war of 1812. *Yeoman,* 12 Aug. 1879.

KILGORE, WILLIAM. Caldwell County. Named at annual reunion, 1875, as having died in April of that year, aged 82. *Yeoman,* 26 June 1875.

KING, DAVID. A sharpshooter in the war of 1812 credited by William Poe, *q.v.,* with the killing of Tecumseh. *Yeoman,* 11 Feb. 1875. There was a David King in Capt. James Davidson's Co., Col. Richard M. Johnson's command. (See John King, below, also credited with slaying Tecumseh).

KING, JOHN. Credited with the slaying of Tecumseh. When the Indian's body was examined it was found to contain two rifle bullets of the same size, and matching by weight the gun used by Col. William Whitley, killed in the battle. It was said by survivors that John King picked up Whitley's rifle as the latter fell from his horse, and added a second charge, not knowing that the gun was loaded. This accounted for the two balls in the Indian's body. John King's claim was borne out by Col. James Davidson, *q.v.* King was buried "on the farm of Squire J. S. Murphy, three miles south of Frankfort." *Yeoman,* 14 June 1881.

KING, GENERAL JOHN EDWARDS. Cumberland County. Enlisted 13 Aug. 1813; served as Brigadier General at the battle of the Thames. He died at Burkesville, Kentucky, in June, 1828. *R,* 25 June 1828.

KING, PHILIP. Bracken County. 1st Lieut, 17 U. S. Inf. His pension application rejected 19 Jan. 1830 due to his good health. He married 4 Dec. 1841, in Bracken County, Margaret Kendall, who was living at Dover, Kentucky, in 1866, aged 65. Her husband died 28 July 1862. *Bracken County Pension List.*

KINGERY, JOSEPH. Monroe County. Pvt., Capt. Henry Yakey's Co., 3rd Regt., KDM. He was pensioned 27 July 1824. *Sen. Doc. 514.*

KNOWLES, THOMAS. Served eighteen months, from 12 July 1812 in 2nd Regt., U. S. Light Dragoons; he was then 24 years of age; also Pvt., Capt. Samuel G. Hopkins's Co.; WIA 30 July 1813; moved to Polk County, Mo., 1847, and was living there 16 Dec. 1854. *Shelby County Pension List.*

LACEY, MAJOR WALTER. Mason County. Ensign, 29th Regt. (Mason County) 17 May 1814; Adjutant same unit, 4 June 1814. He died Aug. (?) 1833, "an old and highly respectable citiben." *C,* 6 Aug. 1833; *Commissioned Officers of the War of 1812-1816,* MS, Kentucky Historical Society.

LAMB, JOHN. Mason County. Attended annual reunions of 1873-1876, being 85 at the time of the last meeting. *WC,* 24 June 1873; *Yeoman,* 27 June 1874, 26 June 1875; *TK,* 21 June 1876.

LANKHART, JOSEPH. Fayette County. Attended 6th annual reunion, 1871, aged 80 years. *C,* 7 July 1871.

LASHBROOK, PETER. Mason County. Attended annual reunions of 1873-1876, was 83 years of age at last meeting. *WC,* 24 June 1873; *Yeoman,* 27 June 1874, 26 June 1875; *TK,* 21 June 1876.

LEE, ZACHARIAH. "A soldier in the last war and served faithfully on the Canadian frontier." He died 17 July 1862, aged 76 years and 7 months. *C*, 1 Aug. 1862.

LEER, M. Attended 8th annual reunion, 1873, aged 84 years. *WC*, 24 June 1873.

LEFARGE, AYRES. Popular Plains, Ky. Listed in AG as Airs Leforgy, Pvt., Capt. George Matthews's Co., KMV ,commanded by Col. John Donaldson. Lefarge stated that a soldier by the name of Gealding killed Tecumseh. Ayers Lefarge died at Popular Plains in May or June, 1881. *Yeoman*, 14 June 1881.

LEWIS, MAJOR J. A. Boyle County. One Jaqualine A. Lewis listed in AG as Pvt., Capt. George Murrell's Co., KMM. He died 18 June 1874, aged 88. *Yeoman*, 26 June 1875.

LEWIS, JOHN, of Llangollen. Born 25 Feb. 1784, son of Col. Zachary Lewis, of Belair, Spottsylvania Co., Va. In 1812 he was in command of a troop of horses and entrusted with watching the movements of the British Fleet in the Potomac. He removed to Kentucky in 1832, settling in Georgetown, where he estabilished a female academy. He died in Frankfort, 15 Aug. 1858. Biographical account in *C*, 18 Aug. 1858.

LEWIS, LEROY. Harrison County. A soldier of the war of 1812; died in March (?), 1871. *TK*, 22 March 1871.

LINDSAY, THOMAS. Fayette County. Born Culpepper County, Va., 10 May 1789; attended annual reunions of 1870-71, and the 8th meeting, 1873; died before the reunion of 1874. *TK*, 22 June 1870; *C*, 7 July 1871; *WC*, 24 June 1873; *Yeoman*, 27 June 1874.

LUCKETT, MAJOR BENJAMIN. Frankfort, Ky. He held several offices in Franklin County and was a soldier in the war of 1812. He died at his Frankfort residence, 17 June 1866, at a very advanced age. *Yeoman*, 18 June 1866. AG: 2nd Sgt., Capt. Isaac Cunningham's Co., KMM.

McAFEE, COLONEL GEORGE. Mercer County. "During the late war he was with the army on the frontiers of Indiana and Illinois; in 1813 he volunteered as a private in Col. Johnson's regiment of mounted riflemen; was shortly after promoted and was in the front of the Battle of the Thames, October 5 of that year; again in the fall of 1814 he commanded a company in Col. Slaughter's regiment, descended to New Orleans and was in the ever memorable battle of 8 January 1815." He died at his residence on Salt River, in Mercer County, 28 May 1819, in his 42nd year. *Argus*, 11 June 1819.

McAFEE, GENERAL ROBERT B. "He was among the first born of Kentucky's citizens, and lived and died near the spot of his birth . . . He served a campaign in the North Western Army in the war of 1812, and afterwards wrote the history of that war. He served many years in the Legislature of this State, being repeatedly elected to both branches. He was elected Lt. Governor of the

State [1824-1828]." *Yeoman,* 22 Mar. 1849. His account of the war of 1812 was *History of the Late War in the Western Country.* . . Worsley & Smith, Lexington, Ky., 1816. In volume 25 (1927) of *The Register* of the Kentucky Historical Society was published his *The Life and Times of Robert B. McAfee and his family and connections. Written by himself.* Commenced April 23rd, 1845, and in volume 29 (1931) his *The History of the rise and progress of the first settlement on Salt River and the establishment of the New Providence Church.*

McBRAYER, ANDREW. Anderson County. An early emigrant to Kentucky; was at McAfee's Station when it was beseiged; served "his country in the field and its councils and was elected to the Legislature" [1829, 1838]. He is listed in AG as 1st Cpl., Capt. Edmond Bacon's Co., KMV. He died 16 May 1839, in his 62nd year. *C,* 21 May 1839.

McCARTHY, Squire JOHN. Mason County. Attended annual reunions of 1873-74, 1876, aged 85 years at his last meeting. He died at Maysville 23 May 1880. *Yeoman,* 1 June 1880, 24 June 1876, 27 June 1874; *WC,* 24 June 1873.

McCLAIN, JOHN. Butler Station, Pendleton County. Attended 9th annual reunion, 1874, aged 79 years. *Yeoman,* 27 June 1874.

McCONNELL, EDWARD. Bourbon County. Enlisted 15 Aug. 1812 at Georgetown, as Pvt., Capt. Maurice Langhorne's Co.; later promoted to 1st Sgt.; WIA at Raisin 18 Jan. 1813. *Bourbon County Pension List.*

McCONNELL, JOSEPH. Bourbon County. Farrier in Capt. William Garrard's Co.; WIA 18 Dec. 1812, at the Missionary Towns. *Caldwell County Pension List.*

McDOWELL, COLONEL JAMES. Fayette County. An officer in the Revolution and served throughout the war of 1812 with his son, Capt. John Lyle McDowell, below. "The father of Col. James McDowell fought at Braddock's Defeat and was an officer in the Revolution; his father fell in Indian warfare [Foote, in his *Annals,* says he was the first white man killed in the valley of Virginia.]" Col. James McDowell married Mary Lyle. *Yeoman,* 2 Jan. 1879.

McDOWELL, CAPTAIN JOHN LYLE. Born Aug., 1794, in Fayette County; served throughout the war of 1812 with his father, Col. James McDowell, above. Captain John Lyle McDowell was an elder for many years in the First Presbyterian Church, Lexington. He died 23 Dec. 1878, at the Franklin County home of his son-in-law, Capt. Samuel Steele, in his 85th year. *Yeoman,* 2 Jan. 1879.

McELROY, JAMES. Lincoln County. Served in Capt. Kerr's Co.; POW at the Rapids, 1813. *Argus,* 12 Feb. 1814.

McFARLAND, ROBERT. Bethel, Bath County. Attended annual reunions of 1874-76, aged 82 years at his last meeting. *Yeoman,* 27 June 1874, 26 June 1875; *TK,* 21 June 1876. AG: Pvt., Capt. Samuel Gooden's Co., KVM.

McGOODWIN, MAJOR J. K. Boyle County. Attended annual reunion of

1871, aged 80 years; died 26 Jan. 1875. *C,* 7 July 1871; *Yeoman,* 26 June 1875. AG: James McGoodwin listed as Pvt., Capt. William Whitsett's Co., KMM.

McHATTON, JAMES. Owen County. Enlisted in Scott County, March, 1813, as Cpl., Capt. John Duvall's Co., KDM. He moved from Scott to Owen County in 1829. *Owen County Pension List.*

McHATTON, GENERAL ROBERT. Major, 77th Regt., Kentucky Militia, 1816. He was born in Fayette County 17 Nov. 1788 and died in Marion County, Indiana, 20 May 1835. *C,* 30 May 1835. No record of service in war of 1812.

McKEE, JOHN. Franklin County. Born Rockbridge County, Va., 21 Oct. 1787; brought to Kentucky in 1790, settling in Woodford and removing to Franklin County in 1808; married, 1812, Elizabeth Crockett, daughter of Col. Anthony Crockett; "at the beginning of the war of 1812 he was one of the volunteers who marched to the relief of Vincennes and the Wabash River country." He died 24 Feb. 1875, aged 87 years, four months and 4 days. *Yeoman,* March 2, 4, 1875.

McLEER (McLEAR), FRANCIS. Fayette County. Born in Ireland 16 May 1789; came to Lexington, Kentucky, from Philadelphia in 1814. Attended annual reunions of Kentucky veterans, war of 1812, in 1870, 1874 and 1875. *TK,* 22 June 1870; *Yeoman,* 27 June 1874, 26 June 1875. Service probably in Pennsylvania.

McMANAWAY, GEORGE. Enlisted 1813 in Capt. Mosby's Co., 28th Regt., U. S. Inf. to serve on board Commodore Perry's squadron on Lake Erie; WIA 20 Sept. 1813; reenlisted 1815; discharged 1815. *Garrard County and Fayette County Pension Lists.*

McMICKLE, ROBERT. Lincoln County. Served in Capt. Coleman Collier's Co., enlisting 15 Aug. 1812; WIA 15 Jan. 1812, "at Camp No. 3 below Fort Defiance on the Miami of the Lakes." Discharged 21 Feb. 1813. He moved to Missouri. *Gallatin County Pension List; Sen. Doc. 514.*

McMILLIN, JOHN. One of the last three veterans of 1812 living in Lincoln County in Sept., 1879. *Yeoman,* 16 Sept. 1879. AG: 1st Lt., Capt. James Coleman's Co., KMI.

McMILLIN, WILLIAM. Fayette County. Pvt., Capt. Thomas Lewis's Co.; POW at the Rapids, 1813. *Argus,* 12 Feb. 1814.

McROBB, WILLIAM. Mason County. "Satisfactory evidence was adduced to the Mason County Court to show that Joseph Robb is father to and legitimate heir at law of William Mac or McRobb, late a soldier in the Army of the U. S., who enlisted with Capt. Henry R. Graham in Washington, Mason County, Ky., on 13 May 1812 for five years and died whilst in the service of the U. S., which is ordered to be certified to the Secretary of War." *Mason County Court Order Book I* (Feb. Court, 1818) p. 175.

MADDOX, CAPT. WILSON. Shelby County. Listed in *Commissioned Officers of the War of 1812-16,* MS, as promoted from Ensign in 85th Regt., commanded by Lt. Col. George Wilcox, 18 May 1813. He died 12 June 1853, in his 73rd year. *C*, 21 June 1853.

MAHAN, FRANCIS. Campbell County. Pvt., Capt. William Sebree's Company; POW at the Rapids, 1813. *Argus*, 12 Feb. 1814.

MAHANAH, JOHN J. Enlisted 5 July 1808 in New London, Conn., 4th Regt., U. S. Inf.; after the war he lived in Vermont, Ohio and had his pension transferred to Bath County, Ky., 4 March 1818. He also lived in Scott and Owen counties. *Scott County Pension List.*

MAJOR, CAPTAIN THOMAS P. Came to Kentucky in early youth, residing here about 50 years. "In 1811 . . . he equipped himself and started off to the scene of action, met some others at Louisville and with these tendered his services to Governor Harrison; was present at the battle of Tippecanoe; again volunteered for twelve months service and joined Col. Johnson's regiment of mounted men and witnessed the termination of the war in the Northwest by the brilliant victory at the Thames." He died at his residence near Frankfort 18 July 1850, in his 68th year. *C*, 6 Aug. 1850.

MANGUM, LEWIS. Campbell County. Pvt., Capt. Posey's Co., U. S. Inf.; injured 7 Nov. 1811 at Tippecanoe. *Campbell County Pension List.*

MANWARING, GEORGE. Scott County. Served in the U. S. Artillery; his pension began in New York, 17 Feb. 1815; transferred to Scott County, Ky., 23 July 1817. *Scott County Pension List.*

MARKS, CAPTAIN HASTINGS. Clark County. "Joined the North-Western Army under General Wayne at the same time with the lamented Harrison. Their commissions were of the same date and they drew for rank; acted with bravery at Fort Recovery and in the battle of the Rapids, which terminated the war; served under Harrison in the last war." He died 27 Feb. 1843, in his 73rd year. *C*, 7 Mar. 1843. AG: Pvt., Capt. John Martin's Co., Lewis's Regt.

MARTIN, ARMISTEAD. Montgomery County. Attended 6th annual reunion, 1871, aged 85 years. *C*, 7 July 1871.

MARTIN, NIMROD. Woodford County. A soldier of 1812; attended 10th annual reunion, 1875; died at his residence near Midway, 26 Nov. 1876, aged 83; buried Versailles on Monday, 27 Nov. 1876. *Yeoman*, 7 Dec. 1876; 26 June 1875.

MARTIN, ROBERT E. Clark County. Born there 1 Feb. 1794; attended annual reunion of 1870. *TK*, 22 June 1870. AG: Pvt., Capt. James Sympson's Co., KMVM.

MASON, CAPTAIN JOHN. Montgomery County. Born Virginia, 29 Feb. 1776; Lieut. in Henry Daniel's Co., war of 1812; died in Oct., 1855. Reid, Richard, *Historical sketches of Montgomery County* (1926) p. 63.

MASTERSON, JOHN. Mason County. Died between annual reunion of 18 June 1875 and that of 19 June 1876. *TK*, 21 June 1876.

MAYFIELD, SOUTHERLAND. Pvt., Capt. Robert Edwards's Co.; transferred to Capt. Richard Hightower's Co., 17th Regt., U. S. Inf.; in battles of River Raisin; POW 22 Jan. 1813. He married Amelia Story, 30 Nov. 1824. He died 31 Aug. 1852. *Shelby County Pension List.*

MAYHALL, JOHN. Franklin County. Born 23 Apr. 1792; died 20 June 1862 and buried in Jackson Burying Ground, on the Louisville road near Frankfort. He was one of 13 of Capt. Paschal Hickman's Co. who survived the battle and massacre at Raisin.

MAYHALL, TIMOTHY. Franklin County. "He was a volunteer under Gen. Wayne in the early days of the West, and was again a volunteer under Gen. Harrison in the last war." He died 29 Feb. 1840 in his 66th year. *C*, 3 Mar 1840.

MAYHALL, WILLIAM. "One of the oldest residents of Frankfort; a native of Kentucky when our country became involved in the war of 1812, he was one of the first to march." He died 14 Nov. 1860, aged 84 years. *C*, 19 Nov. 1860.

MEEK, ADAM R. Decatur County, Ill. Attended 6th annual reunion, Kentucky veterans of 1812, aged 82 years. *C*, 7 July 1871. AG: Pvt., Capt. Thomas Metcalfe's Co., KDM.

MEENACH, ALEXANDER. Mason County. Born Cumberland County, Pa., 1781; emigrated to Mason County, 1784, with his father James Meenach. "Served in the war of 1812 with his five brothers, and is supposed to have been a member of Capt. Joshua Baker's company." He died in Aug., 1879. *Yeoman*, 12 Aug. 1879.

MEENACH, JAMES. Mason County. Born in Pennsylvania; came to Bourbon County, Ky., with his parents, 1794; learned the hatter's trade in Millersburg, 1800. A soldier of the war of 1812. He died in March, 1876, aged 99 years. *TK*, 10 May 1876.

MEFFORD, JOSEPH. Pvt., Capt. Bacon's Co., Col. Francisco's Regt., KVM. His wife, Margaret Mefford, received a land warrant of 40 acres. *Franklin County Pension List.*

MELVIN (MILLION), RODNEY. Madison County. Pvt., Capt. Christopher Irvine's (James Dyametto's) Co.; POW 5 May 1813. *Argus*, 12 Feb. 1814.

MENIFEE, R. P. Kenton County. Attended 6th annual reunion, 1871, aged 82. *C*, 7 July 1871. AG: Capt., Donaldson's Regt., KVM.

MILLER, COLONEL JOHN. Scott County. "A veteran of two wars." He died 3 Feb. 1853, aged 86 years, 7 months and 28 days. *C*, 15 Feb. 1853.

MILLION, RODNEY. See Rodney Melvin.

MITCHELL, JOHN. Woodford County. A soldier of the war of 1812. His parents emigrated to Kentucky in the fall of 1779. In his youth he was a soldier and noted huntsman. He died 5 Aug. 1841, aged 75 years, 7 months and 14 days. *C*, 24 Aug. 1841.

MONTZ, WILLIAM, SR. Born in Pennsylvania, June 14/July 4, 1787; an old soldier of the war of 1812; died at Louisville 1 Nov. 1869. *C*, 5 Nov. 1869; *National Society U. S. Daughters of 1812, No. 98.*

MOORE, BENJAMIN. Harrison County. Attended annual reunions of 1873-1876, aged 85 at his last meeting. He lived at Cynthiana. *WC*, 24 June 1873; *Yeoman*, 27 June 1874, 26 June 1875; *TK*, 21 June 1876.

MOORE, DANIEL (or DAVID?). Edmonson County. "A native of the Old Dominion; a soldier of the war of 1812; he lived in celibacy until he had considerably passed his 80th year, when he married an aged lady by the name of Roundtree; died in March, 1876, aged 94 years." *TK*, 10 May 1876.

MOORE, R. L. Greensburg, Ky. Attended 5th annual reunion, 1870, aged 74 years. He was born "west of Boyle County." *TK*, 22 June 1870.

MOORE, COLONEL THOMAS P. "Born Mercer County, 1796. As early as 1812 while yet a minor he volunteered in the service of his country, and conducted himself gallantly during the war. In 1814 he was in command of a company on the northern frontier; he was thrice married; died 21 Sept. 1853." *C*, 2 Aug. 1853.

MORRIS, CALEB. Harrison County. Native of Virginia; emigrated to Kentucky when a young man; died 1870, his wife in 1826. (She was Eliza Northcutt.) *Bourbon, Scott, Harrison, etc.,* p. 480.

MOSBY, MICAJAH. Mercer County. Born 3 Sept. 1773; an old soldier of the war of 1812. "He knew Governor Shelby well and told of 'posum hunts which they took together." He died in Oct., 1875, aged 102 years, 1 month and 6 days. *TK*, 20 Oct. 1875; *Yeoman*, 22 Feb. 1873. AG: Pvt., Capt. Robert Paxton's Co., KDM.

MOSELEY, COLONEL JOHN. Jessamine County. A native of Virginia, he emigrated to Kentucky in 1776; served with 9th Regt., of Jessamine County. He died 9 Jan. 1847, aged 81 years and a few days. *OR* 27 Jan. 1847.

MOTHERSHEAD, NATHANIEL. Served in the war of 1812 and enlisted at Independence, Mo., 12 June 1847, for service in the Mexican War. He was then about 68 years of age. He volunteered for service in 1812 in Dec., 1812, in Westmoreland County, Va., where he then resided. He was living in Oldham County, Ky., in 1836. *Scott County Pension List.*

MULDROW, COLONEL A(NDREW). Woodford County. One of this name was Lieut., Capt. William Crouch's Co., KMVM, 12 Sept.-Oct. 20, 1812. He died 24 Aug. 1829. *R*, 26 Aug. 1829.

MURPHY, PETER. Pvt., 17th U. S. Inf.; lost his right eye at "Dudley's Defeat." *Fayette County Pension List.*

MYERS, GEORGE. Served in Capt. Robert McAfee's Co., war of 1812. *Yeoman*, 16 Oct. 1877.

NEWELL, HUGH. Harrison County. "A soldier of 1812 and was at the battles at Frenchtown on the River Raisin; served repeatedly in the Legislature, was four years a State Senator and was a member of the Convention which formed the present Constitution of Kentucky; he was a native of Bourbon but was for 80 years a resident of Harrison County." He died 13 Sept. 1875, in his 85th year. *Yeoman,* 18 Sept. 1875.

NEWLAND, BENJAMIN S. Shelby County. Attended 6th annual convention, 1871, aged 84 years. *C,* 7 July 1871. AG: "Benoni S. Newland" was Pvt., Capt. William E. Young's Co., 1st Regt., Ky. Light Dragoons.

NEWTON, JAMES. Adjutant, Porter's Regt., KM, war of 1812. *Yeoman,* 9 Nov. 1878.

NICHOLAS, MAJOR CAREY. One of this name Capt. of a company in 7th Regt., U. S. Inf., commanded by Elijah Montgomery, Jan., 1814. Major Nicholas died in Tallahassee, Fla., May 1829. *R,* 3 June 1829.

NICHOLS, ERASMUS. Lexington, Kentucky. Born Pennsylvania, 1790; attended 5th annual reunion of Kentucky veterans, war of 1812, in 1870, aged 86 years. *TK,* 22 June 1870. AG: Pvt., Capt. William Hutchinson's Co., KMVM.

NOEL, LITTLEBERRY. Boone County. "A soldier of the last war and one of the few survivors of Dudley's Defeat, and was in the campaign of Gen. Jackson." He died 23 Mar. 1846, in his 70th year. *C,* 28 Apr. 1846.

NORRIS, CAPTAIN JOHN. Petersburg, Boone County, Kentucky. "He was a soldier of the war of 1812, and participant in Commodore Perry's victory, Sept. 10, 1813. He was a native of Maryland, born 13 April 1791. He removed to Mason County, Ky., with his parents when eight years old. At the age of 20 (in 1813) he enlisted from Mason County in Captain Payne's Co., and was assigned to Colonel Johnson's regiment. He was one of 20 who volunteered to take part in the celebrated naval battle on Lake Erie, Sept. 10, 1813, and was ordered to duty on the ship *Caledonia.* He was selected for superior marksmanship and bravery to take post in the maintop of his ship as sharpshooter; but before being ordered to his post, that enviable place was shot away, and fell to the decks. He assisted in the management of the guns, and actually fired the last shot, which caused the enemy, His Majesty's ship *Hunter,* to strike her flag. Young Norris was one of 20 men selected as a picked crew to take charge of the captured vessel. They found her in a sinking condition, but by hard work at the pumps, brought her to port, and later received $300. as prize money. The engagement lasted three and one-half hours, and the *Hunter* was literally riddled. This battle decided the contest with Great Britain on the Lakes, and Mr. Norris returned home and married. Six children were born to him, three of whom were living at the time of his death. Several years ago there was an effort made to gather together all the survivors of Perry's victory, at Put-in-Bay, and only four could be found. Since that time all have died, Mr. Norris being the last to pass away. The Legislature of Kentucky, on 17 Feb. 1860, directed the Governor to procure four gold medals—one each for James Artus, Dr. William T. Talliaferro, John Tucker, and John Norris, "as survivors of the Kentucky volunteers, who, with such ready alacrity and heroism" assisted Perry in achieving his glorious victory." He died in January (?), 1879 in his 88th year. *Yeoman*, 11 Jan. 1879.

NORTHCUTT, BENJAMIN. Bourbon County. Born in Frederick Co., Va., 1790 and at the age of 8 removed with his father, Jeremiah Northcutt, Revolutionary soldier, to Bourbon County, Ky. He lived here until his removal in 1852 to Missouri. He was a soldier of 1812, in Col. R. M. Johnson's regiment, and was at the battle of the Thames. He died at Columbia, Mo., residence of his daughter Mrs. Julia Jones, 21 Dec. 1874, aged 85 years. He left four children, three daughters and one son, T. M. Northcutt, of Columbia, Mo. *TK*, 20 Jan. 1875.

NORTON, ARNEY. Attended 6th annual reunion, 1871. *C*, 7 July 1871.

NORTON, JAMES. Served in the Revolution and "in the war with the Indians in the Northwest." He died in Nicholas County, 21 Oct. 1857, aged 96 yeares. *C*, 6 Nov. 1857, AG: Sgt., Capt. William Farrow's Co., 3rd Rgt., Kentucky Mounted Riflemen.

NORVELL, JOHN. Born Garrard County; fought in 1812; was editor of the *Kentucky Gazette*. He died 24 Apr. 1850, aged 58. *S*, 1-5, 8 May 1850.

NUNLEY, ROBERT. Fayette County. Enlisted at Lexington 15 Aug. 1812, in Capt. John Edmiston's Co.; married 14 June 1814, Sarah Davis, daughter of John Davis. He was placed on pension rolls 13 Dec. 1823. He died 24 Jan. 1852. *Scott County Pension List; Sen. Doc. 514*.

NUNNALLY, ROBERT. See Robert Nunley.

OAKLEY, THOMAS. Bath County. Pvt., Capt. George Pugh's Co. Captain Pugh and William Manley, of the same company, heard Thomas Oakley's will 9 Feb. 1813, at Camp at the foot of the Rapids; will probated 12 Apr. 1813, in Bath County Court. *Bath County Court, Will Book A, p. 33*.

OVERTON, THOMAS J. 1st Lieut., 17th U. S. Inf.; KIA January 22, 1813, at Frenchtown. *Heitman*, v. 1, p. 763.

OWENS, JOHN. Pulaski County. His death announced at annual reunion of veterans, 1875; died 18 Apr. 1875, aged 84. *TK*, 28 Apr. 1875; *Yeoman*, 26 June 1875.

OWINGS, COLONEL THOMAS DEYE. Colonel, 28th Inf., 11 Mar. 1813; honorable discharge, 15 June 1815. He died at his residence in Brenham, Texas, 6 Oct. 1853, aged 77 years. *C*, 22 Nov. 1853; *Heitman*, v. 1, p. 764.

PARKER, JOHN E. Athens, Fayette County. Attended annual reunions of 1871, 1873-1875, aged 80 at his last meeting. *C*, 7 July 1871; *WC*, 24 June 1873; *Yeoman*, 27 June 1874, 26 June 1875.

PATTEN, WILLIAM. Harrison County. Attended 6th annual reunion, 1871, aged 76 years, *C*, 7 July 1871.

PARKER, MAJOR THOMAS. Lewis County. Died 9 Feb. 1853, in his 83rd year. Two listings in AG but 1812 service not proved. *C*, 22 Feb. 1853.

PARKS, MOSES. Mercer County. He was born and reared within a few miles of where he died. "Parksville" was named in his honor. He died in Oct., 1866, aged 77 years. *Yeoman*, 23 Oct. 1866. Two lisings of this name in AG.

PATTERSON, JOHN. Jessamine County. "An old citizen soldier of 1812." He died 10 Apr. 1870. *TK*, 20 Apr. 1870.

PAUL, HOSEA. Attended annual reunion of Kentucky veterans of 1812, from Aberdeen, Ohio, in 1876. He was then 85. *TK*, 21 June 1876.

PAXTON, JOSEPH. Pvt., Capt. Leslie Comb's Co.; WIA at Fort Meigs 1 May 1813; served until 28 Sept. 1813; married Minty Paxton, in Greene County, Mo., 16 June 1844. He died in Dade Co., Mo., 15 May 1850. *Campbell County Pension List*.

PAYNE, ASA. Payne's Depot, Scott County. Born there 1788; was aide to his father, Gen. John Payne, war of 1812; attended annual reunions of 1870-1871, 1874, aged 86 at his last meeting. *TK*, 22 June 1870; *C*, 7 July 1871; *Yeoman*, 27 June 1874.

PAYNE, INNIS B. Campbell County. Attended annual reunions of 1871, 1874-1876, aged 83 at his last meeting. *C*, 7 July 1871; *Yeoman*, 26 June 1875, 27 June 1874; *TK*, 21 June 1876.

PAYNE, JUNIUS. Newport, Kentucky. Born Mason County, 21 Oct. 1793; attended annual reunions of 1870, 1881. (Also listed as Enos Payne.) *TK*, 22 June 1870; *Yeoman*, 20 June 1881.

PAYNE, CAPTAIN WILLIAM. Franklin County. Served in war of 1812; died in Jan., 1871, aged 84. *TK*, 25 Jan. 1871.

PENDLETON, GENERAL EDMUND. Clintonville, Bourbon County. Attended annual reunions of 1873-1876, aged 87 at the last meeting. *WC*, 24 June 1873; *Yeoman*, 8 Aug. 1874, 26 June 1875; *TK*, 21 June 1876.

PENN, JOHN. His death announced at annual reunion of veterans, 1875; died 18 Mar. 1875, aged 79. *Yeoman*, 26 June 1875.

PENNY, CAPTAIN JOHN, JR. Anderson County. "During the progress of the late war with Great Britain, he gave ample proofs of his devotion to his county by entering personally into her most active service." He died in Rockcastle County, 20 Feb. 1827, in his 29 year. He was a son of the Reverend John Penny. He left a widow and several small children. *Argus*, 7 Mar. 1827.

PERKINS, JOHN. Garrard County. Pvt., Capt. John Yantis's Co.,; POW at the Rapids, 1813. *Argus*, 12 Feb. 1814.

PERRIN, DR. GEORGE H. Cynthiana, Kentucky. Served in 1814 in 16th Regt., commanded by General McArthur; attended annual reunions of Kentucky veterans, 1871, 1873-76, 1881, 1883, aged 89 at his last meeting. *C*, 7 July

1871; *WC*, 24 June 1873; *Yeoman*, 27 June 1874, 20 June 1881, 21 June 1883; *TK*, 21 June 1876.

PIATT, JOHN H. Furnished commissary stores to the Northwestern Army; a long standing claim for moneys involved during his services to the army was decided in favor of the heirs in 1875. The sum recovered was $131,508. *TK*, 26 May 1875.

PIATT, SALEM. Lexington, Ky. Died in January, 1813, from a wound received at Mississinewa, 17 Dec. 1812. A public demonstration was held for him, and Henry Riddle, in Lexington on 22 Feb. 1813. *Kentucky Gazette*, 26 Feb. 1813.

POE, WILLIAM. "An octogenarian of Holt Co., Mo., who stated that a sharpshooter named David King killed Tecumseh. Poe was in the fight when the 'big Injun' was killed, in the battalion commanded by Col. Richard M. Johnson." *Yeoman*, 11 Feb. 1875

POINDEXTER, MAJOR JOHN. Christian County. A soldier of 1812; died 21 Jan. 1877, aged 85 years. His wife died four days later, aged 79. *Yeoman*, 30 Jan. 1877.

PORTER, COLONEL JOHN. Butler County. "A soldier of the Revolution; member elect of the Legislature; served with the 66th Regt., war of 1812; died 24 Sept. 1833, aged 74 years." *OR*, 17 Oct. 1833.

PORTWOOD, JOHN. Nicholasville, Kentucky. Born Madison County in Nov., 1787; attended annual reunions of 1870-71, 1874-76, aged 88 years at the time of the last meeting. *TK*, 22 June 1870, 21 June 1876; *C*, 7 July 1871; *Yeoman*, 27 June 1874, 26 June 1875.

POWELL, CHARLES. Washington County. A soldier of 1812; died in June (?), 1876, aged 84 years. *TK*, 5 June 1876. AG: Pvt., Capt. Robert Burnet's Co., Barbee's Regt.

POWERS, ANDERSON. Bridgeport, Franklin County. "A soldier of the war of 1812, and fought at New Orleans; died 1 Jan. 1878, one day shy of 84 years." (Frankfort, Ky.) *Weekly Roundabout*, 5 Jan. 1878: see also *Yeoman*, 15 Jan. 1878 for obituary of Powers and sketch of the battle of New Orleans. AG: 1st. Cpl., Capt. George McAfee's Co., KDM.

PRESTON, WILLIAM. Campbell County. "A soldier of the war of 1812 and his wife who have lived together for 60 years do all their work and are as sprightly as new beginners." *TK*, 3 Mar. 1875.

PREWITT, ROBERT HURT. Enlisted Jessamine County, as Pvt., Capt. Richard Hightower's Co., 17th Regt., U. S. Inf. He was born in 1791 and died in 1845. *National Society Daughters of 1812, Kansas, No. 12739.*

PREWITT, CAPTAIN VANALLEN. Scott County. Ensign, Capt. John

Edmiston's Co., 1st Rifle Regt., 15 Aug.-14 Oct. 1812. He died in Feb., 1826. *R,* 20 Feb. 1826.

PREWITT, GENERAL WILLIAM C. Fayette County. Appointed Lieut., 8th Regt., Lt. Col. Dudley commanding, 2 Sept. 1812; he died 21 Sept. 1854. *C,* 25 Sept. 1854.

PRICE, CAPTAIN RICHARD. 2nd Lt., 28th Inf. U. S., 30 June 1813; Adjutant, Aug. to Nov., 1813. He died 11 Nov. 1813, in service, a few days after returning to Cincinnati from the Northwest Army. He married in 1801 Hannah Upshaw, daughter of Col. John Upshaw, of Essex Co., Va., in whose house she was married. She died in March, 1853, in her 79th year. *C,* 29 Mar. 1853; *Argus,* 20 Nov. 1813; *Heitman,* v. 1, p. 806.

PRIEST, DANIEL. Sideview, Montgomery County. Attended annual reunions of 1873-1876, aged 81 years at his last meeting. *WC,* 24 June 1873; *Yeoman,* 27 June 1874, 26 June 1875; *TK,* 21 June 1876. AG: Pvt., Capt. Benjamin Warfield's Co., 20 May-19 Nov. 1813.

PRICHARD, BENJAMIN B. Montgomery County. Pvt., Capt. Samuel Williams's Co., Lewis's Regt.; died at the home of Horace Benton, 30 June 1835, aged 45 years. He weighed 525 or 550 pounds. *OR,* 5 Aug. 1835.

PUCKETT, JOHN. Woodbury, Butler County. He served in 4th Virginia guarding Washington, D. C. He was 88 years of age in 1876. *TK,* 21 June 1876.

PUGH, JOSEPH. A soldier of 1812; died in the vicinity of Covington, 28 Mar. 1842. *C,* 5 Apr. 1842.

QUARLES, TUNSTALL. "He filled various public stations, and served his country in the capacity of captain in the war of 1812." Later he was elected to Congress. He died near Somerset, 7 Jan. 1855, aged about 75 years. *C,* 15 Jan. 1855. AG: Capt., 2nd Regt., KM.

QUISENBERRY, ROGER. Clark County. Born there 23 Sept. 1792; attended annual reunion, Kentucky veterans of the war of 1812, in 1870. *TK,* 22 June 1870.

RAMEY, WILLIAM. Pvt., Capt. Wiley Brasfield's Co.; POW at Frenchtown, Jan. 22, 1813, later paroled. Born in Kentucky, 1790; died 1823. Lived in Caldwell County. Texas N.S.D. 1812, No. 4807.

RANDALLS, NATHANIEL. Fleming County. Died August, 1876, aged 86 years. *TK,* 30 Aug. 1876. AG: Pvt., Capt. Johnston Megowans's Co., U.S. Inf.

RAYBURN, HENRY. Harrison County. Attended 6th annual reunion, veterans of the war of 1812, 1871, aged 76 years. *C,* 7 July 1871. AG: Pvt., Simon Galaspie's (Gillespie's) Company, Francisco's Regt.

REAM, JOHN. Fleming County. A member of Capt. George Stockton's company of 100 volunteer marines who served on Perry's ships on Lake Erie; WIA in battle there 10 Sept. 1813. He was Pvt., Capt. Joseph C. Belt's Co., 28th Regt., U.S. Inf. *Fayette County Pension List.*

REDDING, WILLIAM. Scott County. Enlisted 15 May 1812, 17th U.S. Inf.; MIA 22 Jan. 1813. Left widow, Sally Brown Redding, whom he had married 3 Feb. 1810, and one daughter, Ann, six years of age in 1817. *Scott County Pension List.*

REDMAN, JOSEPH. Mason County. Pvt., 1st U.S. Rifle Regt.; enlisted 25 May 1813; WIA in battle of Lake Erie, 10 Sept. 1813; served in Capt. H. R. Graham's Mason County company. *Campbell County Pension List.*

REES (REESE), JONATHAN. Mason County. 2nd Lieut., 19th U.S. Inf.; enlisted 15 May 1813 from Brown County, Ohio; living in Maysville, Kentucky, when he applied for pension 12 Jan. 1831. *Madison County Pension List.*

REEVES, JOSEPH. Owen County. Pvt., Capt. Joseph Funk's Co., 38th Regt., Jan. 1813-3 May 1813; injured 28 Apr. 1813 near Hackett's Tavern in Kentucky; living in Henry County when he enlisted. *Shelby County Pension List.*

REGAN, SAMUEL. Pvt., 24th Regt., U.S. Inf.; WIA at Mackinaw, Michigan; discharged 4 Aug. 1814. *Floyd County Pension List.*

RENICK, JAMES. Winchester, Kentucky. Attended 5th annual reunion, 1870, aged 76 years; attended reunions of 1871, 1873-76; voted in Clintonville precinct, Bourbon County, 1874, then 80 years of age. *TK,* 22 June 1870; *C,* 7 July 1871; *WC,* 24 June 1873; *Yeoman,* 27 June 1874, 26 June 1875, 24 June 1876, 8 Aug. 1874. AG: Pvt., Capt. Isaac Cunningham's Co., KMVM.

RENNICK, COL. A. H. Frankfort, Kentucky. Son of John and Mary (Huston) Rennick, of Pennsylvania; emigrated to Kentucky about 1790, settling near Lexington; Colonel Rennick was born 25 Aug. 1791; volunteered in Capt. Paschal

ROBINSON, MICHAEL (MITCHELL). Pvt., Capt. Patrick Gray's Co. who escaped the battles and massacre at River Raisin; was deputy clerk or clerk of several of the courts at Frankfort "for most of the time since 1807"; died 18 Dec. 1871. Biography in *C,* 26 May 1871, 22 Dec. 1871.

RHODES, SAMUEL. Harrison County. Attended 8th annual reunion, 1873, aged 80; died Fleming County, March, 1876. *WC,* 24 June 1873; *TK,* 21 June 1876. AG: Pvt., Capt. George Matthews's Co., KMVM.

RICHARDSON, DAVID. Mercer County. Entered the Revolutionary army from Baltimore, Md.; was with General Wayne against the Indians; "marched with Shelby to Canada." He was 77 years of age 2 Sept. 1833 when he made these statements. *Mercer County Pension List.*

RICHARDSON, JOHN. Franklin County. Born 9 June 1792; died 18 Dec. 1875. Served in Capt. Paschal Hickman's Co., 1st Rifle Regiment, and was one of 13 of this company to escape the battles and massacre at River Raisin. N.S.D. 1812, Ky., No. 111.

RICHARDSON, JOHN. Estill County. A soldier of 1812; died Feb., 1876, aged 84. *TK*, 9 Feb, 21 June 1876.

RIDDLE, HENRY. Lexington, Kentucky. Died Jan., 1813, from wounds received at the battle of Mississinewa, 17 Dec. 1812. *KG* 26 Jan. 1813. AG: 2nd Cpl., Cpt., Capt. George Trotter's Co., Ky. Light Dragoons.

RITCHEY (RICHEY), ESAU. Nicholas County. Enlisted 29 Mar. 1812 as Pvt., Capt. Thomas Metcalfe's Co., Boswell's Regt., KDM; married in Bourbon County, Sept., 1805, "Nancey Webster, alias Combs or Coombs," daughter of Joseph Combs. Soldier died in Harrison County, 4 Dec. 1870. *Nicholas County Pension List.*

RITCHEY, JOHN. Harrison County. Pvt., Capt. John Duvall's Co.; pensioned 14 July 1830. *Sen. Doc. 514.*

ROBERTS, DR. JOSEPH G. Frankfort, Kentucky. Born 19 Feb. 1789; "during the War of 1812 he was assistant Surgeon on board the vessel commanded by Commodore Porter." Also served under Gen. Taylor in the Mexican War, and again in the Civil War as Surgeon of the 40th Ky. Mounted Inf., and as Brigade Surgeon, 1st Brigade, 5th Div., 23rd Corps. He died 3 July 1868, aged 79 years. *C*, July 10, 17, 1868; *Yeoman*, 4 July 1868.

ROBERTS, RICHARD. Simpson County. Attended 10th annual reunion, Kentucky veterans of the War of 1812, in 1875, aged 87 years. *Yeoman*, 26 June 1875.

ROBERTSON, THOMAS. Pvt., Capt. Hoskins's Co., 2nd U.S. Dragoons; WIA at the battle of Mississinewa, Dec., 1812. *Henry County Pension List.*

ROBINSON, MICHAEL (MITCHELL). Pvt., Capt. Patrick Gray's Co. Soldier was born 1796, died after 1850 in Cass County, Michigan. U.S.D. 1812, Michigan, No. 3589.

ROBSON, CAPTAIN JOHN SPRY. Franklin County. Born in Maryland, 27 Sept. 1789; resided in Franklin County, Kentucky, since 4 July 1814; "oldest Mason in the county, having been made a Mason in 1818"; served in war of 1812 in Capt. Meyer's Co., Maryland Militia, stationed at Fort McHenry; died in Franklin County, 27 June 1880. More in *Yeoman*, 3 Aug. 1880.

ROGERS, SAMUEL. Nicholas County. Attended 10th annual reunion, 1875 and 1876, aged 87 at last meeting. *Yeoman*, 26 June 1875; *TK*, 21 June 1876.

RONYAN, FRANCIS. Fayette County. Pvt., Capt. Thomas Lewis's Co.; POW at the Rapids, 1813. *Argus*, 12 Feb. 1814.

ROSSON, JOHN. Franklin County. "Served two campaigns in the War of

1812. He was a member of the Company of which Gen. Peter Dudley was then First Lieutenant, when he first volunteered [Capt. Paschal Hickman's Company]. In his second tour, Gen. Dudley was then his captain. Col. A. H. Rennick and Capt. John A. Holton were two of his mess-mates." He died at Madison, Indiana, 7 March 1868, aged 90 or 91 years. *C,* 27 Mar. 1868.

RUDD, JOHN H. Bracken County. Served in 28th Regt.; died in Yazoo County, Miss., 12 May 1835. *C,* 4 July 1835; *OR* 1 July 1835.

RUNYAN. See RONYAN.

RUSSELL, MAJOR HENRY. Nelson County. A soldier of the war of 1812; died at Warrensburg, Missouri, in Oct., 1876, aged about 88 years. *TK,* 21 June 1876.

RUSSELL, CAPTAIN JOHN W. Franklin County. Born 11 Oct. 1794 on the farm where he died; "in 1813 he joined Peter Dudley's company and bore part in the siege of Fort Meigs and other engagements on our northern frontier." He died 1 Aug. 1869. *C,* 6 Aug. 1869.

RUSSELL, COLONEL WILLIAM. Lexington, Kentucky. Colonel, 7th Regiment, war of 1812; died 3 July 1825, aged 66 years. *R,* July 4, 11, 1825.

RUTLEDGE, ISAAC. Grant County. Attended 6th annual reunion, 1871, aged 83 years. *C,* 7 July 1871.

SALISBURY, ANDREW. Enlisted 16 Nov. 1812, as Pvt., Capt. Samuel G. Hopkins's Co.; WIA 18 Dec. 1813; born Rowan County, N.C., removed to Ohio. *Shelby County Pension List.*

SANDERS, ISAAC D. Boone County. Entered service in 1813 as Sgt., Capt. Henry R. Graham's Co.; WIA in 1814 at Fort Erie. *Boone County Pension List.*

SCOBEE, ROBERT. Clark County. Served in Colonel Francisco's Regt., war of 1812; died 31 Oct. 1835. *OR,* 11 Nov. 1835.

SCONCE, ROBERT. Scott County. Lieut., Capt. Robert E. Yates's Co., war of 1812; died at the residence of his son, William Sconce, 26 Sept. 1875, aged 83 years. Taken to Bourbon County for burial. *Yeoman,* 2 Oct. 1875.

SCOTT, JOEL. Woodford County. Born 15 Nov. 1781 near Abingdon, Va.; came with father, John Scott, to Woodford County, 1785; member conventions to form the Constitution of Kentucky; represented Bourbon County many years in General Assembly; took charge of Kentucky Penitentiary, 1824-1834; was on the first Board of Trustees, Georgetown College; removed to Franklin County, 1834; died at his residence in Woodford County, 28 June 1860, in his 79th year. *C,* 2 July 1860. AG: One Joel Scott was Lieut., 12th Regt., war of 1812.

SCOTT, MATTHEW T. Lexington, Kentucky. A native of Pennsylvania; emigrated to Kentucky in 1810; died Aug., 1858, in his 74th year. He was President, Northern Bank of Kentucky. *C*, Aug. 25, 27, 1858. AG: One Matthew T. Scott listed in Capt. Thomas Lewis's Co., KM, commanded by Col. William Dudley "absent."

SCOTT, CAPTAIN WILLIAM. Paris, Kentucky. "A soldier in the late war." He died 13 Aug. 1847, aged 74 years. *OR*, 21 Aug. 1847.

SCOTT, WILLIAM. Bourbon County. Volunteered at Paris about 20 Aug. 1812, in Capt. William Garrard's Light Dragoons; discharged at Franklinton, Ohio, about 20 Aug. 1813; WIA 18 Dec. 1812 at Mississinewa. He removed to Illinois to live. *Bourbon County Pension List*.

SCRUGHAM, COLONEL JOSEPH. Lexington, Kentucky. Served in 8th Regt., war of 1812; died in Lexington 17 Jan. 1856, aged 76 years. *C*, 22 Jan. 1856.

SEWELL, JOSEPH. Henry County. Attended 10th annual reunion, 1875, aged 82 years. *Yeoman*, 26 June 1875. AG: Pvt., Capt. Archibald Morrison's Co., KDM.

SHACKELFORD. JAMES. Casey County. "This veteran of the War of 1812 died recently at his Casey county home, at the advanced age of 99 years. He was the maker of the celebrated Shackelford rifle, a rifle that for years has been the pride of this portion of the country. The last rifle that he made was when he was 96 years old, and it is said to be a marvel both of beauty and excellency." *KG*, 13 Dec. 1879. (Contributed by C. Frank Dunn.) AG: Two of this name listed: Pvt., Capt. Thomas Kennedy's Co., and Pvt., Capt. John Falkner's Co.

SHANNON, JAMES. Franklin County. "He was a companion of John A. Holton and Peter Dudley in the war of 1812." He died 2 July 1869, aged 80. *C*, 9 July 1869. AG: Pvt., Capt. Peter Dudley's Co., 1812; Pvt., Capt. Peter Dudley's Co., KDM, 9 Mar.-9 Sept. 1813.

SHARON, SAMUEL. Fayette and Scott counties. Pvt., Capt. Lynn West's Co.; living in Scott County when his pension commenced in 1814; wounded in action. *Scott County Pension List*.

SHARP, JOHN. Fayette County. Served in the U.S. Inf.; was living in Fayette County in 1830, aged 55 years; died 28 Apr. 1839. *Jessamine County Pension List*.

SHAWHAN, JOSEPH. Harrison County. Attended 6th annual reunion, 1871, aged 90 years. *C*, 7 July 1871.

SHEPHERD, PRESLEY. Fayette County. Pvt., Capt. Butler's Co., 44th Regt., U.S. Inf.; enlisted 1814; WIA 23 Dec. 1814; discharged 1815. He moved from Tennessee to about 14 miles from Lexington, Kentucky. *Clark County Pension List*.

SHIVERY, G. W. Fayette County. Served in Capt. Stewart W. Megowan's Co., Lewis's Regt. (name spelled Shirevry); attended 1870, 1871 annual reunions; died 25 July 1875, aged 83 years. He had been married 50 years in Dec., 1870. *TK*, 22 June 1870, 21 June 1876; *C*, 7 July 1871.

SHOEMAKER, SPENCER. Pvt., Capt. William Ellis's (later Capt. Richard Matson's) Co.; WIA 18 Jan. 1813; placed on pension rolls 5 Jan. 1818; died 11 Nov. 1819. *Harrison County Pension List; Sen. Doc. 514.*

SIMRALL, JOSEPH. Shelbyville, Kentucky. Col., 1st Regt., Kentucky Light Dragoons, 22 Aug.-31 Oct. 1812; Lt. Col., Kentucky Volunteers, 25 Aug.-9 Nov. 1813; died 7 Sept. 1837. *KG*, 28 Sept. 1837.

SKINNER, PETER. Bourbon County. Attended 6th annual reunion, 1871, aged 73 years. *C*, 7 July 1871.

SMITH, BIRD. Woodford County. Born Prince Edward County, Va., 1787; enlisted at Lexington, Kentucky, at age of 21; Pvt., Capt. George Trotter's Co.; 2nd Sgt., Capt. Tunstall Quarles's Co.; married Elvira Price, 1 Feb. 1825; died in Woodford County, 9 Apr. 1860. *C*, 23 Apr. 1860; *Woodford County Pension List.*

SMITH, JOHN SPEED. Madison County. Born Jessamine County, 1 July 1792; studied law but gave up his practice to march with General Harrison's army on the Wabash; fought in battle of Tippecanoe; admitted to the bar in Kentucky in 1812; 1813 again fought against the British, this time as Brig.-Major. He authored the inscription on the marble block contributed by Kentucky to the Washington Monument. He died in Madison County, 6 June 1854, aged 62. *S*, June 6, 13, 20, 1854.

SMITH, JOSEPH. "He was a volunteer from Nelson County, Kentucky, and served a six month's campaign in 1812 under Bob Wilcox." He died at his residence (the Salt Lick Farm) in Ohio County, Ky., 11 Oct. 1853, aged 68 years, 6 months and 20 days. *C*, 8 Nov. 1853.

SMITH, THOMAS S. Jessamine County. Served in the 9th Regt., war of 1812; died 17 Sept. 1837, aged 58 years. *KG*, 21 Sept. 1837.

SMITH, WILLIAM. Rockcastle County. "Born Russell County, Va., 1773; after the close of the Revolution he served as an Indian spy on the Clinch and Kentucky waters; emigrated to Kentucky, 1795, settling in the present Rockcastle County; shortly after married the daughter of Col. Richard Singleton (a Major at King's Mountain) and had two children, Col. E. Smith and the wife of Col. James Terrill; his wife dying he subsequently married the daughter of Thomas Fish; in the war of 1812 he commanded a company; he served in the Legislature some twenty-odd years, in both branches." *Yeoman*, 1 Mar. 1849.

SOUTHERLAND, WILLIAM. Casey County. Born Scotland; emigrated to America at the age of 14, before the Declaration of Independence; entered

Revolutionary service very early in that struggle; served from Virginia on seven tours in succession; after the war he rejoined his family and moved to Kentucky; at the age of 55 he volunteered for service in the war of 1812 and was with Governor Shelby at the battle of the Thames; died 19 July 1843, in his 88th year. *Kentucky Tribune* (Danville) 8 Sept. 1843.

SPEGAL, ———. Born North Carolina, 1788; attended annual reunion, 1870. *TK*, 22 June 1870. AG: Martin Spiegle was Pvt., Capt. James Ellis's Co., KVM, 10 Sept.-9 Oct. 1814.

SPOON, HENRY. Scott County. Served in U.S. Inf., enlisting in July, 1812; living in Jefferson County 6 Oct. 1851, aged 63 years. *Scott County Pension List.*

SPROUL, ALEXANDER. Cumberland County. Served in Capt. William Wood's Company of volunteers from Cumberland; was thought to have served in the Revolution. He died in service in 1814. *Clinton County Pension List.*

SPURR, RICHARD, SR. "He was a soldier in the war of 1812 and was in action at the battle of the Thames." He died 21 April 1853, in his 76th year. *C,* 3 May 1853.

STANFORD, JOHN. Shelby County. Attended 10th annual reunion, 1875, aged 80 years. *Yeoman,* 26 June 1875.

STANFORD, LUCAS. Simpson County. A soldier of 1812; died 27 Jan. 1876, aged 81 years. *TK,* 9 Feb. 1876; 21 June 1876.

STAPLES, MRS. ELIZABETH. Montgomery County. "The widow of a soldier in the war of 1812, she prepared papers for pension in April, 1878, at the age of 83. Mrs. Staples can walk one half mile without resting, milks two cows night and morning, can churn, knit, sew, in fact is never idle. During the war she made clothing for the soldiers preparing to leave for the service." *Yeoman,* 25 Apr. 1878. Only one of this name, Joshua Staples, listed in AG roster of Kentucky volunteers. He was Pvt., Capt. John V. Bush's Co., Lt. Col. John Francisco's Regt.

STEPHENSON, THOMAS. Mercer County. Attended 8th annual reunion, 1873, aged 79 years. *WC,* 24 June 1873. AG: Pvt., Capt. Armstrong Kerr's Co.

STEVENS, THOMAS. Campbell County. Served in KM in Col. William E. Boswell's Regt.; WIA 5 May 1813; honorably discharged in Sept., 1813; also served in the Revolution. *Campbell County Pension List.*

STEWART, JAMES. Served in Capt. Joyce's Co., KM; WIA at New Orleans; married 3 Mar. 1816, Polly Phillips. He died 22 Sept. 1842 at Cincinnati, Ohio. *Jefferson County Pension List.*

STEWART, JAMES. Clark County. "Attended 6th annual reunion, 1871, aged 80 years. *C,* 7 July 1871. He died in Feb., 1876, aged 84 years." *TK,* 21 June 1876.

STEWART, ROBERT. Born Nicholas County, 1792; attended annual reunions of 1870-71. *TK*, 22 June 1870; *C*, 7 July 1871.

STIVERS, EDWARD. Montgomery County. Musician, 3rd U.S. Inf.; born in present Montgomery County, 1770; enlisted 15 June 1814. Children: Eleanor Stivers Harrington, aged 40 years in 1833; Catherine Stivers Brown, 38; William Stivers, 37; Susan Stivers Ogden, 27; Martin Stivers, 25. *Montgomery County Pension List.*

STOCKTON, GEORGE. Fleming County. Commanded a company of Marines who went on board Perry's ship on Lake Erie; had 100 men who volunteered for this duty. He returned to Fort Seneca for clothes for his men and did not return to the ship until the action was over. *Fayette County Pension List.*

STONE, JOSEPH. Berry's Station, Harrison County. Attended annual reunions of 1874-1876, aged 85 at the last meeting. *Yeoman*, 27 June 1874, 26 June 1875; *TK*, 21 June 1876.

STREET, JOHN PARKE. Newport, Kentucky. Attended 9th annual reunion, 1874, aged 79 years. *Yeoman*, 27 June 1874.

STUCKER, JACOB. Scott County. "One of the most celebrated Indian fighters who protected Kentucky through her infancy. He was also a captain in Johnson's mounted regiment and fought on the Thames in the late war." He died in Scott County "lately." *Argus*, 29 June 1820.

STURGEON, ELISHA (ELIJAH). Grant County. Attended annual reunions of 1870-1871, aged 84 at the last meeting. "He was in Crittenden 1 Mar. 1876, pension day, with several other old veterans of 1812. He was then 97 years old." *TK*, 22 June 1870, 15 Mar. 1876; *C*, 7 July 1871.

SUBLETT, JOHN S. Green County. Served in Capt. Armstrong Kerr's Co. from March, 1813; fought at Meigs, was wounded and captured. *Green County Pension List.*

SUDDUTH, COLONEL WILLIAM. Owingsville, Kentucky. One William M. Sudduth served in 65th Regt. (Bath County) in the war of 1812. Col. Sudduth died 28 Aug. 1845, aged 80 years. *OR* 3 Sept. 1845.

SUMMERFIELD, EPHRAIM. Cpl., 17th Regt., U.S. Inf. under Captains Holder and Whistler; born 1795; died about 1876 in Michigan. U.S.D. 1812, Michigan, No. 9929.

SUTHERLAND, FRED. Clark County. His death, on 18 Nov. 1874, at the age of 85, was announced at the annual reunion of veterans, June, 1875. *Yeoman*, 26 June 1875.

SUTHERLAND, WILLIAM. Enlisted in Capt. James Hunter's Co., 17th U.S. Inf.; disabled and discharged 19 Nov. 1814. *Wayne County Pension List.*

SWEARINGEN, HENRY THOMAS. Shepherdstown, Va. "A Captain in the line and fought in several battles on the St. Lawrence; WIA and captured; after the war he was sent as Colonel of the line to effect exchange of prisoners of war for the U.S.; died at Glasgow, Kentucky, 18 Jan. 1820. He had come here to attend to a valuable estate inherited from his father. He was married not long before his death. A young man." *Argus*, 26 Jan. 1820.

SYLVA, SAMUEL. Anderson County. Pvt., Capt. Robert B. McAfee's Co., KMI; placed on pension roll 14 Jan. 1832. *Sen. Doc. 514.*

TALLIAFERRO, DR. WILLIAM T. Born 1795; practiced medicine in Mason County, later lived in Cincinnati; volunteered in Bracken County and was one of the volunteers who served on Perry's ships on Lake Erie; attended annual reunion of veterans, 1870; died between June, 1870, and June, 1871, reunions. *TK*, 22 June 1870; *C*, 7 July 1871; *Yeoman*, 11 Jan. 1879.

TANDY, WILLIS. Fayette County. Pvt., Capt. John Hamilton's Co.; received a bomb fragment in his left eye during the action at Frenchtown, Jan. 22, 1813; captured and paroled 26 Feb. 1813 at Newark, Upper Canada; married, 31 Oct. 1823, Martha Reed (his first wife was Mary or Polly Cloud who died in Fayette County); he died in Morgan County, Illinois, 5 Sept. 1849, aged 60 years, 9 months and 17 days; buried East Cemetery, Jacksonville, Ill. *Fayette County Pension List; Honor Roll . . . Soldiers of 1812 Buried in Illinois*, v. 1 (MS); *Sen. Doc. 514.*

TAPP, NELSON. Born in Virginia, 1790; removed to Kentucky, 1794; attended annual reunions of 1870-71, 1873; died 19 July 1874, aged 84 years. *TK*, 22 June 1870; *C*, 7 July 1871; *WC*, 24 June 1873; *Yeoman*, 26 June 1875.

TATE, THOMAS L. Franklin County. "Was distinguished as a participant in the war of 1812 and for many years a citizen of Franklin County; married the oldest daughter of Rev. John Taylor." Thomas L. Tate, according to his tombstone record, was born 14 Aug. 1787 and died 7 Nov. 1852. He was buried in the Taylor burying ground on the Macklin farm at Forks of Elkhorn. (One Thomas L. Tate married in Franklin County, 15 June 1829, Mrs. Nancy T. Gray.) Thomas Tate's name is on the original roster of Capt. Paschal Hickman's Co. He was one of twelve or thirteen of this unit to escape the battles and massacre at Frenchtown, Jan., 1813. *Yeoman*, 15 July 1873.

TAYLOR, COLBY H., Colbyville, Clark County. Served in 36th Regt., War of 1812; died 10 Sept. 1853, aged 73 years. *S*, 1 Oct. 1853.

TAYLOR, CAPTAIN HUBBARD. Clark County. "Served in the war of 1812 under Dick Johnson (Pvt., Capt. James Johnson's Co., 3rd Regt.) and also under Gen. James Taylor; he was educated for a lawyer and followed this profession for about 20 years; was twice sent to the Legislature of Kentucky, once from Clark and once from Bourbon County; at the time of his marriage, in 1814, at the age of 26, he had a law office in Winchester; he moved to Paris in 1823, living there until 1832 when he moved back to Clark and became a farmer; he married 13 Oct. 1814, Mary, daughter of Thomas Arnold, for many years Clerk of the Bourbon Circuit Court; (her father, Thomas Arnold, was an apprentice for five years in the office of Levi Todd, Circuit Court Clerk of Fayette and grandfather of Mrs. Abraham Lincoln); on 14 Oct. 1874 Capt. Taylor and his wife celebrated their 60th wedding anniversary; she was then 76 years of age and he was 86." Captain Hubbard Taylor died 9 June 1876, aged 88. He had been a member of the Masonic fraternity for 61 years and was buried by them. *Yeoman,* 24 Oct. 1874; *TK,* 21 June 1876.

TAYLOR, ISAAC. Campbell County. Pvt., Capt. William Sebree's Co.; POW at the Rapids, 1813. *Argus,* 12 Feb. 1814.

TEVIS, SAMUEL. Shelby County. "During the last war he served two campaigns, one as First Lieut. of a company and the other as Adjutant of a Regiment." He died 7 Apr. 1841 near Shelbyville, aged 53 years. *C,* 27 Apr. 1841.

THEOBALD, THOMAS S. Frankfort, Kentucky. Born Bourbon County, 1791; came to Frankfort in 1806, at the age of 15; at the outbreak of the war he assisted in raising a company of which he was elected lieutenant (1st Lieut., Morrill's Co., Kentucky Mounted Rifles); at the conclusion of this tour his company had assembled at Vincennes for mustering out when it was found there was no money to pay the men—the nearest source being Louisville. Rather than allow his men to disperse without pay, he led a squad to Louisville and back without losing a dollar of the pay roll. After the war he held many public offices including that of Keeper of the Penitentiary, 1834-44. He married 22 July 1813 Sarah Watkins Keene, born Scott County 3 May 1793, died in Frankfort 10 Jan. 1876. Thomas S. Theobald died there 30 Dec. 1873. Five years before, on 21 June 1871, he had received the first pension certificate as a veteran of the war of 1812 issued to a Kentuckian. It entitled him to eight dollars per month. *Collins,* v. 1, p. 215; *Yeoman,* 3 Jan. 1874, 11 Jan. 1876; *C,* 15 Mar. 1872.

THOMAS, ISAAC. Mason County. "Born Mefford's Station, 8 Nov. 1789 or 1788 and was consequently in his 86th year when he died in July, 1875. He was a noncommissioned officer in the war of 1812 and served with distinction at the battle of the Thames." *Yeoman,* 29 July 1875.

THOMASSON, RICHARD. Scott County. Served in 12th Regt.; died 10 Mar. 1855, one of the oldest citizens of the county. *C,* 26 Mar. 1855. AG: One of this name was Pvt., Capt. Jacob Stucker's Co., KMI.

THORNTON, GENERAL W. F. A former citizen of Bourbon County, Kentucky, and resident of Shelbyville, Illinois. "He was a native of Virginia, where he figured as editor of the *Alexandria Gazette* and General in the War of

1812. His wife, Miss McClannahan, was an aunt of Mrs. Brutus J. Clay. He was a cousin of ex-State Senator John Roots Thornton, Paris, Ky. He died 21 Oct. 1873, aged 84 years." *Yeoman,* 1 Nov. 1873.

TILFORD, ALEXANDER. Scott County. Pvt., Capt. Lynn West's Co.; died Sept., 1831, aged about 50 years. *C,* 27 Sept. 1831.

TILFORD, ROBERT. Boyle County. Attended 6th annual reunion, 1871, aged 83 years. *C,* 7 July 1871. AG: 5th Cpl., Capt. Archibald Bilbo's Co.

TODD, SAMUEL B. Fayette County. Enlisted in Fayette Co., 14 Aug. 1812, in Capt. Nathaniel G.S. Hart's Co.; married 27 Nov. 1827 Caroline Barr; applied for pension while living in Boone Co., Mo., 6 June 1871,. aged 78 years; was living in Howard County, Mo., in Nov., 1850. *Jessamine County Pension List.*

TONGATE [TUNGATE], MEREDITH. Garrard County. Pvt., Capt. Whistler's Co., 3rd U.S. Inf. He was born in Amherst Co., Va.; married in May, 1824, Elizabeth Baker, in Garrard Co., Ky. He died in Orange Co., Ind., 7 Aug. 1842. *Garrard County Pension List.*

TOWLES, HENRY. Bourbon County. Pvt., Capt. William Garrard's Troop of Light Dragoons; WIA at siege of Fort Meigs, May, 1813; discharged at Franklinton, Ohio, 13 Aug. 1813. *Bourbon County Pension List.*

TRIMBLE, DAVID. Greenup County. Born Frederick Co., Va., June, 1792; served as brigade quarter master, First Brigade, KMM, later as Pvt., Major Peter Dudley's Bn., KMVI; elected to Fifteenth and four succeeding Congresses, 1817-1827; died at Trimble's Furnace, Greenup County, 20 Oct. 1842. *C,* 25 Oct. 1842; *Biographical Directory of the American Congress, 1774-1927.*

TRIMBLE, JAMES. Fayette County. Attended 5th annual reunion, 1870, aged 74 years, and the meeting of 1871. *TK,* 22 June 1870; *C,* 7 July 1871. AG: Pvt., Capt. James Coleman's Co., KMI.

TUCKER, JOHN. One of the Kentucky volunteers with Perry on Lake Erie. *Yeoman.* 11 Jan. 1879.

TURNER, EDWARD. Mason County. Pensioned 18 Mar. 1813. This name listed in AG as Pvt., Capt. Joseph C. Belt's Co., Pvt., Capt. William R. Payne's Co., and Pvt., Capt. Zechonias Singleton's Co. *Sen. Doc. 514.*

TURNER, JOHN. Madison County. Served in Capt. Christopher Irvine's Co.; POW at the Rapids, 1813. *Argus,* 12 Feb. 1814.

TURNER, JULIUS. Pvt., Capt. Joseph Redding's Co.; in action at River Raisin Jan. 22, 1813. *Fayette County Pension List.*

UNDERWOOD, JOSEPH R. Warren County. Born Goochland Co., Va., 24 Oct. 1791; removed to Kentucky at the age of 12 and was adopted by a maternal uncle; graduated from Kentucky University, 1811, after which he read law with Robert Wickliffe; in 1812 he served as Lieut., Capt. John C. Morrison's Co., Dudley's Regt., and was wounded and captured at Dudley's Defeat; after the war he practiced law, held many public offices in Kentucky, including that of Judge of the Court of Appeals, 1828-35, and was elected to the Twenty-fourth and three succeeding Congresses, 1835-43; elected to U.S. Senate and served 1847-53. He died near Bowling Green, Kentucky, 23 Aug. 1876. *Yeoman*, 26 Aug. 1876; *Biographical Directory of the American Congress, 1774-1927*. His son, John Cox Underwood (Sept. 12, 1840-Oct. 26, 1913) was Lieutenant-Governor of Kentucky, 1875-79.

VAN PELT, WILLIAM, SR. Fayette County. Born 18 Oct. 1784, died 5 Oct. 1872. "From the time of his eligibility he never lost a presidential vote from James Madison in 1808 to Gen. Grant in 1868." He served with the 42nd Regt. in the war of 1812. *Yeoman*, 21 Dec. 1872.

VOORHIES, MAJOR PETER GORDON. A soldier of the war of 1812. He was born in Trenton, N.J., and in 1790 emigrated to Frankfort, Ky.; he moved to Red River where he died in July or August, 1851, aged 79 years. *S*, 8 Aug. 1851. AG: Ensign, Capt. Paschal Hickman's Co.

WALKER, COLEMAN. Madison County. Pvt., Christopher Irvine's (James Dyametto's) Co.; POW 5 May 1813 at the Rapids. *Argus*, 12 Feb. 1814.

WALKER, WILLIAM. Franklin County. Attended 8th annual reunion, 1873, aged 85 years. *WC*, 24 June 1873. AG: twelve listings this name.

WALL, LEWIS H. Carlisle, Kentucky. Attended 9th annual reunion, 1874, aged 80 years. *Yeoman*, 27 June 1874.

WALLACE, JOSEPH (or JOHN). Bourbon County. Attended 6th annual reunion, 1871, aged 78 years; 1873 reunion. *C*, 7 July 1871; *WC*, 24 June 1873.

WARD, ANDREW. Harrison County. Enlisted 20 May 1812 as Pvt., Capt. Bradford's Co., 17th U.S. Inf.; also served in Capt. Larrabee's Co., 3rd U.S. Inf.; WIA at Fort Meigs, 5 May 1813. *Harrison County Pension List*.

WARD, JOHN. Garrard County. Pvt., Capt. John Yantis's Co.; captured 5 May 1813 at the Rapids. *Argus*, 12 Feb. 1814.

WARD, THOMAS. Pvt., Capt. Redding's Co.; placed on pension rolls 2 Dec. 1814. *Sen. Doc. 514*.

WARD, COLONEL WILLIAM. Served with the 12th Regt., war of 1812; lived in Scott County, Ky.; died in Mississippi, 15 July 1836. *KG*, 4 Aug. 1836.

WARDEN, WILLIAM B. Served in Capt. Alexander Kerr's Co., Mar. 26-Sept. 28, 1813; Capt. Armstrong's Co., 10 Nov. 1814-10 May 1815; WIA at Dudley's Defeat; married Catherine Jordan. He died 5 Apr. 1865. He was also in the Battle of New Orleans. His first wife was Elizabeth Meirlin. *Hickman County Pension List*.

WARE, COLONEL THOMPSON. Bourbon County. Served with 71st died 9 Sept. 1852, in his 84th year. *C*, 21 Sept. 1852.

WARFIELD, BENJAMIN. Fayette County. Lieut., Capt. Samuel L. Williams's Co.; Captain of his own company, Col. Richard M. Johnson's Regt.; died home in Fayette 20 Oct. 1856, in his 67th year. He was twice married, his second wife surviving him. He left a family of three sons and one daughter, en of his first wife. He was educated at the University of Kentucky and trained for the bar. *C*, 19 Nov. 1856.

WARREN, CHARLES. Attended annual reunion, 1876, aged 83 years, com- om Kearney, Mo., for the meeting. *TK*, 21 June 1876. AG: Cpl., Capt. William Davis's Co., KM.

/ARRING, EDWARD. Scott County. Attended 6th annual reunion, 1871, aged 77 years. *C*, 7 July 1871.

WATSON, AARON. Mason County. "A soldier of 1812 [in Capt. Moses ......iitt's Co.]; married 10 Aug. 1794, in Mason, Leah Furr [the marriage record lists him as *Moses* Watson]." *Mason County Genealogical Notes*, Kentucky His- Society.

WEBB, JAMES G. Winchester, Kentucky. Born 3 Feb. 1792; captured during action on River Raisin, Jan., 1813; died 12 Mar. 1844, Loami Township, San- i Co., Ill. *Honor Roll Soldiers of 1812 buried in Illinois*, v. 1. (MS).

WEBB, JOHN. Madison County. Attended annual reunions of 1873, 1876, 4 years at last meeting. *WC*, 24 June 1873; *Yeoman*, 24 June 1876.

WEBB, COLONEL JOHN V. Scott County. Served in 77th Regt.; died 7 '839. *C*, 18 June 1839.

WEBB, JOSHUA. Madison and Fayette counties. Attended annual reunions of 1873, 1876, 1881, aged 89 years at last meeting. *WC*, 24 June 1873; *TK*, 21 876; *Yeoman*, 20 June 1881.

WEBSTER, LARKIN. Grant County. Attended annual reunions of 1870- 73, 1875, aged 83 years at the last meeting. *TK*, 22 June 1870; *C*, 7 July 1871; *WC*, 24 June 1873; *Yeoman*, 26 June 1875. He appeared in Crittenden, Grant County, 1 Mar. 1876, with several old veterans of 1812 to get his pension He was then 84. *TK*, 15 Mar. 1876.

WELLS, LEVI. Ensign, 7th Inf., U.S., 13 Nov. 1812. He was killed Jan. 22, during the action at River Raisin—on detached service with the 17th U.S. Inf., commanded by his father, Col. Samuel Wells. *Heitman*, v. 1.

WELSH, DAVID. Pvt., 1st U.S. Inf., Capt. Packland's Co., 20 June 1814- b. 1816; wounded in action 23 Dec. 1814 during fighting below New Orleans. (Mississippi pension). *Henry County Pension List*.

WEST, BENJAMIN (or BENONI). Boyle County. Attended annual reunions of 1871 and 1875, aged 86 at the last meeting. *C*, 7 July 1871; *Yeoman*, 26 June 1875. AG: Cpl., Capt. James Anderson's Co.

WHITE, COLONEL ANDREW S. Shelby County. Member Constitutional Convention of 1849-50; senior partner of A. S. White & Co., pork packers, Louisville; died 12 June 1855. *C*, 18 June 1855. AG: One of this name was Pvt., Capt. John Hall's Co., KMVM.

WHITE, COLONEL PHILIP. Franklin County. One of this name was Major in Col. John Calloway's Regt., KV; died 22 Aug. 1822, aged 58 years. *R*, 26 Aug. 1822.

WHITE, SAMUEL W. Shelby County. Pvt., Capt. Frederick Geiger's Co., 23 Oct.-18 Nov. 1811; WIA at battle of Tippecanoe; pensioned; died in Shelby County, 17 Nov. 1862, lacking four days of 86 years. *Shelby County Pension List; C,* 21 Nov. 1862; *Sen. Doc. 514*.

WHITE, THOMAS. Bourbon County. Attended 10th annual reunion, 1875, aged 81 years. *Yeoman*, 26 June 1875.

WHITEHEAD, ARMISTEAD. Served as 3rd Lieut., 5th U.S. Inf.; WIA at Lyon's Creek, Upper Canada. *Harrison County Pension List*.

WILKS, MILLS. Boone County. Enlisted 15 Aug. 1812, for six months, in Capt. Uriel Sebree's Co.; WIA 18 Jan. 1813 at Frenchtown; POW 22 Jan. 1813; received his discharge from Major Richard Gano, acting colonel of the Regt., 4 Mar. 1813; placed on pension rolls 21 Feb. 1834. He was Cpl., Capt. Sebree's Co. *Boone County Pension List; Sen. Doc. 514*.

WILLIAMS, ELISHA. Mercer County. Attended 8th annual reunion, 1873, aged 87. *WC*, 24 June 1873. AG: Cpl., Capt. James C. Price's Co., Lewis's Regt.

WILLIAMS, GEORGE. Lincoln County. A veteran of the war of 1812, receiving a pension in 1878. *Yeoman*, 21 May 1878.

WILLIAMS, JAMES. Cumberland County. Born Sullivan Co., Va., 1763; enlisted for Revolutionary service from Sullivan in 1778; removed to Cumberland Co., Ky., about 1802; enlisted for 1812 service in Capt. William Wood's company of Cumberland volunteers; 8 Aug. 1838, had his pension transferred to Hempstead Co., Arkansas. *Clinton County Pension List*.

WILLIAMS, MAJOR JOHN. Simpson County. Enlisted in Revolutionary service at the age of 16 and was in the battles of Brandywine, Germantown, Monmouth and other battles and skirmishes. "He was one of the earliest settlers of the west and an Indian fighter in the neighborhoods of Nashville and Gallatin. When the fort at Greenville was attacked by 300 Indians, there being only a few men, women and children in the fort, he was one of a little band that went to the rescue. In the war of 1812 he again volunteered his services and was chosen to command a company of horse under General Hopkins. He was ten years in the Senate of Kentucky, from Warren County. He died in September (?), 1833, in his 74th year. *C,* 24 Sept. 1833.

WILLIAMS, COLONEL WILLIAM. Madison County. Commanded a Regt., mustered 31 Aug. 1812; died in Aug., 1824, aged 45 years. *R,* 23 Aug. 1824.

WILLIAMS, ZEPHENIAH. Fayette and Franklin counties. Pvt., Capt. N.G.S. Hart's Co.; POW at Frenchtown, 22 Jan. 1813. For many years he was a Ruling Elder of the McChord church, Lexington, and on his removal to Frankfort, an Elder in the Presbyterian church there. About 1857 he removed to Dubuque, Iowa, where he died 21 July 1858. *C,* 9 Aug. 1858.

WILLSON, PETER G. Boyle County. Attended 10th annual reunion, 1875, aged 82 years. *Yeoman,* 26 June 1875.

WILSON, HAMILTON. Bourbon County. Attended 11th annual reunion, 1876, aged 84 years. *TK,* 21 June 1876; *Yeoman,* 24 June 1876.

WILSON, JAMES L. Fleming County. Attended 8th annual reunion, 1873, aged 78. *WC,* 24 June 1873. A Colonel J. Wilson, Oldham County, died 10 Jan. 1875, aged 79 years. The same? *Yeoman,* 26 June 1875.

WILSON, WILLIAM. Fayette County. Pvt., Capt. William Sebree's Co., KM; WIA at Fort Meigs, 5 May 1813. *Fayette County Pension List; Argus,* 12 Feb. 1814.

WILSON, WILLIAM. Scott County. Pvt., Lewis's Co.; captured at the Rapids, 1813. *Argus,* 12 Feb. 1814. Same as above?

WINLOCK, FIELDING. Born Jefferson County, 4 May 1789; served in Simrall's Regt.; died in Shelbyville, 24 Feb. 1874. He was a son of Gen. Winlock, of Shelby. *Yeoman,* 28 Feb. 1874.

WINLOCK, GENERAL JOSEPH. Shelby County. Officer, 1st Regt., KMM; died March, 1831, aged 73 years. *R,* 6 Apr. 1831.

WINLOCK, DR. JOSEPH. Shelby County. One of this name was Surgeon's Mate, 1 Sept. 1812-25 Dec. 1813; died 11 Feb. 1814, aged 22 years. He was a son of Gen. Winlock, of Shelby. *Argus,* 5 Mar. 1814.

WITHINGTON, THOMAS. Fayette County. Pvt., Capt. Archibald Morrison's Co.; POW at the Rapids, 1813. *Argus,* 12 Feb. 1814.

WITT, ELISHA. Estill County. A soldier of 1812; died 2 Sept. 1858, in his 65th year. *C,* 13 Sept. 1858.

WOLF, JESSE. Enlisted in Scott County, in Capt. Jacob Stucker's Co.; married in Scott County, Mary Polk; applied for pension from Union County, Ind., 30 Oct. 1873 when he was 78. *Harrison County Pension List; Sen. Doc. 514.*

WOOD, BENJAMIN. Harrison County. Attended 6th annual reunion,

1871, aged 77 years. *C*, 7 July 1871. AG: Pvt., Capt. John W. Redding's Co., KMI.

WOOD, JOHN. Enlisted at Lexington, Kentucky; WIA Jan. 18 or 22, 1813, during action on River Raisin (sworn to by George Morris and James Munday who knew him there). He married Rebecca Ballard, in Charleston, Indiana, 21 Oct. 1821. Children: Sidney S., aged 39 in 1879 and Frances Crawley, aged 56 in 1879. *Madison County Pension List*.

WOOD, THOMAS. Pvt., Capt. Wiley R. Brasfield's Co.; mustered in at Georgetown, 15 Aug. 1812; in 1855 he was living in Fayette County; on 6 Jan. 1872, when he applied for pension, he was living in Owen County. He was then 84. *Owen County Pension List*.

WOOD, WILLIAM. Cumberland County. Raised a company of volunteers there in the spring of 1813. *Clinton County Pension List*.

WORNALL, THOMAS. Clark County. One of this name captain of a company, KMVM, commanded by Samuel South. Thomas Wornall died in Nov., 1838, at an advanced age. *OR* 17 Nov. 1838.

WRIGHT, COLONEL WILLIAM. Paris, Kentucky. Attended annual reunions of 1871, 1873-76, 1878, aged 94 years at the last meeting. *C*, 7 July 1871; *WC*, 24 June 1873; *Yeoman*, 27 June 1874, 26 June 1875, 29 June 1878; *TK*, 21 June 1876.

YOUNGLOVE, EZRA. Christian County. One of the 150 picked volunteers who fought on Lake Erie with Perry; assigned to the *Niagara;* listed as Pvt., Capt. Thomas L. Butler's Co., 28th U.S. Inf.; living in 1859. *Quisenberry*, p. 78.

ZINN, JOSEPH. Grant County. Attended annual reunion, veterans of the war of 1812, in 1871, 1873 and died between the meeting of June, 1874, and that of June, 1875. He was 78 at the time of his death. *C*, 7 July 1871; *WC*, 24 June 1873; *Yeoman*, 26 June 1875. AG: Pvt., Capt. James Ellis's Co., Ky. Vol. Militia.

ARTHUR, CAPTAIN AMBROSE. Knox County. Born Bedford Co., Va., 5 June 1776; raised a company in Knox and led it at the battle at Fort Meigs; married 22 Jan. 1811, in the same county, Jane Gilbert Fletcher (5 Oct. 1787-4 Dec. 1880). Captain Arthur died 20 July 1859. Contributed by Mrs. George C. Lewis, Bryn Mawr, Pa.

BOND, WILLIAM. Franklin County. Pvt., Capt. Peter Dudley's Co., raised to avenge the loss of Capt. Paschal Hickman and most of his company at River Raisin, Jan., 1813. There are three other listings of this name in the AG. William Bond later lived in Anderson County. He married, 5 Nov. 1813, Mrs. Rebecca Johnson Marshall. Contributed by Mrs. George C. Lewis, Bryn Mawr, Pa.

BRANDENBURGH, ABSALOM. Settled in Virginia on coming to America; later removed to Paducah, Kentucky, where he was a plantation inspector and meat inspector; founded and lived in Brandenburgh, Ky.; served in 1812 with the 3rd Regt., KDM, and fought at New Orleans; removed to Mauchport, Ind., where he engaged in making brandy and distillery products and where he died and was buried. He was married four times. Wayne Guthrie in *Indianapolis* (Ind.) *News*, 7 Oct. 1952. Contributed by Miss Thelma Murphy, Indianapolis, Ind.

BUTLER, MAJOR THOMAS L. Louisville, Kentucky. "The oldest member of the Butler family in Kentucky. He served as an army officer for a number of years and was aid to General Jackson at New Orleans; filled various offices under several administrations and was member of the Kentucky Legislature for many terms. He was a brother of Gen. William O. Butler. He died at the Louisville home of his son-in-law, P. O. Turpin, 'last week,' aged 99 years." *Clark County* (Ky.) *Democrat*, 10 Nov. 1880.

CAYSE, THOMAS. Garrard County. Served in the 17th U.S. Inf., under Philip King. He died in Jan., 1813. Forrest Calico, "Veterans of the War of 1812 from Garrard County," *Register*, v. 48 (1950).

EDWARDS, JAMES H. Born Montgomery County, Va., and reared in Jefferson County, Ky.; Pvt., Capt. Peter Funk's Co.; WIA at battle of Tippecanoe, 7 Nov. 1811. Moved to Denton County, Texas, 1858. *Henderson County Pension List*.

FERIS, DR. M. A. Georgetown, Kentucky. Surgeon, 17th U.S. Inf., under Col. Samuel Wells. He was living in 1830. *Bracken County Pension List*.

FISHER, JOHN BOLEYN. Born Pennsylvania, 1 Mar. 1768; moved to Virginia and served as Indian fighter, 1791-94 from Boutetourt County; served later under General Anthony Wayne and was wounded and tomahawked; married in Virginia, 14 Oct. 1801, Mary L. Brown; removed to Kentucky between 1801-05, settling in Mt. Sterling where he lived until 1843; enlisted in the war of 1812, in Capt. Warner Elmore's Co., KMM; later was Cpl., Capt. Simon Gillespie's Co., Francisco's Regt.; removed to Hodgenville, Larue County, where he died 27 Aug. 1870, aged 102. Contributed by Mrs. Leonard T. Harris, Chicago, Ill.

MERCER, DAVID. Born Greene County, N.C., Dec., 1791; enlisted a Pvt., Capt. Silvanus Massie's Co., KM, 1 Sept. 1812; died Marion Co., Ill., 14 June 1834. He married 21 Dec. 1814, Elizabeth Searcy (1797-17 Oct. 1843). Soldier listed incorrectly in AG as David *Messer*. Contributed by Kenneth Mercer, Webster Groves, Mo.

MORGAN, JOHN. Born Shelby County, 1790, son of William and Rachel (Pheamister) Morgan; enlisted in 1812 struggle on 31 Aug. 1813, from Franklin County, serving under Matthew Flournoy; removed, 1840, from Fayette County to Hannibal, Marion County, Mo., where he died 6 Aug. 1872. He was married three times: 26 Oct. 1813, to Mary Orr; 14 May 1822, to Jane Wason (d. 1825) and 13 Feb. 1827, to Rebecca Orr. *John Morgan Government Registry No. WO 44 494*, Kentucky Historical Society.

KEY TO ABBREVIATIONS

AG. *Report of the Adjutant General of the State of Kentucky. Soldiers of the War of 1812.* Frankfort, Ky., Capital Office . . ., 1891.
Argus. (Frankfort, Ky.) *Argus of Western America.*
C. (Frankfort, Ky.) *Commonwealth.*
Collins. Collins, Lewis, *Collins' Historical Sketches of Kentucky. History of Kentucky. . . . Revised, enlarged four-fold, and brought down to the year 1874, by his son Richard H. Collins* . . . Louisville, J. P. Morton, 1924. 2 v.
Heitman. *Historical Register and Dictionary of the United States Army* . . . By Francis B. Heitman. 2 v. Washington, Government Printing Office, 1903. [57th Congress, 2 sess. House of Representatives, Document No. 446.]
KDM. Kentucky Detached Militia.
KG. (Lexington, Ky.) *Kentucky Gazette.*
KIA. Killed in action.
KM. Kentucky Militia.
KMI. Kentucky Mounted Infantry.
KMV. Kentucky Mounted Volunteers.
KMVM. Kentucky Mounted Volunteer Militia.
MIA. Missing in action.
OR. (Lexington, Ky.) *Observer and Reporter.*
Pension Lists. Typescripts, War Department pension records for Kentucky.
Quisenberry. Quisenberry, Anderson Chenault. *Kentucky in the War of 1812.* Frankfort, Ky., The Kentucky Historical Society, 1915.
R. (Lexington, Ky.) *Reporter.*
S. (Lexington) *Kentucky Statesman.*
Sen. Doc. 514. *Report from the Secretary of War, in obedience to Resolutions of the Senate of the 5th and 30th of June, 1834, and the 3rd of March, 1835, in relation to the pension establishment of the United States.* Washington, Printed by Duff Green, 1835. Vol. III.
TK. (Paris, Ky.) *True Kentuckian.*
WC. (Paris, Ky.) *Western Citizen.*
WIA. Wounded in action.
Yeoman. (Frankfort, Ky.) *Kentucky Yeoman.*

www.ingramcontent.com/pod-product-compliance
Lightning Source LLC
Chambersburg PA
CBHW050614300426
44112CB00012B/1497